# Lecture Notes in Economics and Mathematical Systems

Managing Editors: M. Beckmann and W. Krelle

248

# Plural Rationality and Interactive Decision Processes

Proceedings of an IIASA (International Institute for Applied Systems Analysis) Summer Study on Plural Rationality and Interactive Decision Processes
Held at Sopron, Hungary, August 16–26, 1984

Edited by
M. Grauer, M. Thompson and A.P. Wierzbicki

Springer-Verlag
Berlin Heidelberg New York Tokyo

ISBN 3-540-15675-5 Springer-Verlag Berlin Heidelberg New York Tokyo
ISBN 0-387-15675-5 Springer-Verlag New York Heidelberg Berlin Tokyo

Printing and binding: Beltz Offsetdruck, Hemsbach/Bergstr.
2142/3140-543210

# PREFACE

These Proceedings report the scientific results of the Summer
Study on Plural Rationality and Interactive Decision Processes organized jointly by the System and Decision Sciences Program of the International Institute for Applied Systems Analysis (located in Laxenburg,
Austria) and the Hungarian Committee for Applied Systems Analysis. The
Study, which was held in Sopron over the period 16-26 August 1984, had
a very special character. Sixty-eight researchers from sixteen countries participated, most of them contributing papers or experiments.
In addition many members of IIASA's Young Scientists Summer Program
were present. All of these participants were heavily involved in discussions; discussions that were not limited to the allotted time but
extended well into the evenings and nights. By design, the Study
gathered specialists from many disciplines, from philosophy and cultural anthropology, through decision theory, game theory and economics,
to engineering and applied mathematics. A further element of diversity
was the representation of several varieties of culture, from typically
Western countries, through Middle and Eastern Europe, to the Far East.

The unifying factor was a common interest in the topic of plural
rationality and its implication: the need for an interactive, learning approach to any decision situation in which diverse rationalities
might occur. This does not mean that the very concept of plural rationality was clearly understood by all of the participants at the beginning of the meeting. However, as the discussions progressed, the
concept of plural rationality became more clearly defined, involving
not only differences in tastes, interests and values, but much more
fundamentally, different frameworks for perceiving what type of behavior
can be regarded as rational. Such differences have deeply rooted disciplinary or cultural origins, relate to basic cultural or ideological
values, and develop (either intuitively and holistically, or formally
and analytically) into frameworks for rational behavior.

Examples of the holistically developed frameworks mentioned in the
discussions include: an intuitively formed, "naive", individualistic
rationality of the "zero-sum game" type ('if I make any concessions,
the other player will win'); an equally "naive" worst-case rationality
('prepare for the worst'); and complex cultural rationalities from the
Far East, such as those implied by the various forms of Buddhism.
Formal and abstractive frameworks are also diverse: the maximum utility
theory that accompanies an individualistic cultural background; the
schools of bounded rationality and satisficing behavior that have

emerged in response to the culture of big organizations; and the goal-
and program-oriented management school that has grown up against a
background of planning.  The issue of individualistic versus cooperative approaches to rationality was an important element in the discussions and was much stimulated by Rapoport's paper on the use of experimental games in increasing the understanding of social traps and
the evolutionary need to develop more cooperatively and socially informed attitudes to rationality.  Other issues discussed in detail
include the "soft" versus "hard" approaches to systems and decision
analysis; holistic versus analytic types of decision making; maximizing
versus satisficing; decision making versus decision support; and the
content versus the context of decisions.

An unusual characteristic of the meeting was the relatively large
number of experimental sessions (not all involving computers) in which
decision support systems and the behavioral strategies and rationality
frameworks of the participants were tested.  Thus, those present were
able to take part in the various stages of the cognitive cycle - from
description, through abstraction, to prescription and implementation.

Of the forty-two papers presented during the meeting, only twenty-
eight are included in this volume.  Some excellent contributions were
not available for publication; some very good papers of survey character also had to be excluded for reasons of space.

The congenial atmosphere of the meeting was in large part due to
the efficiency of the organizers, in particular Ms. Nora Avedisians
from IIASA and Dr. Tibor Ashboth from the Hungarian Committee for Applied
Systems Analysis.  Helen Gasking put in much work editing the papers
and preparing the final version of these Proceedings for publication.

Manfred Grauer
Michael Thompson
Andrzej Wierzbicki

# CONTENTS

# I. CULTURAL ASPECTS OF RATIONAL PERCEPTION

# INTRODUCTION

This section presents a collection of papers reviewing the classical concepts of rationality and presenting various critiques and redefinitions of these concepts, mostly, but not exclusively, from a cultural perspective. At the meeting, these papers were followed by discussions that helped participants to gain a better understanding of the concept of plural rationality as a culturally conditioned framework for perceiving what constitutes rational action. One of the papers presented in this group, *Technologies as cultural products* by Brian Wynne, is unfortunately not available for the Proceedings.

In his paper *The approach to plural rationality through soft systems methodology*, Checkland gives a succinct review of two perceptions of the concept of a system. The result is two distinct methodological approaches: "hard systems thinking" and "soft systems thinking". The first is based on the perception of a system as a part of reality, as an organized composition of elements; it stresses the reductionist (and Cartesian) analytical approach to systems investigation. The second is based on the perception of a system as a mental (culturally dependent) model of reality, or as a means of perceiving and trying to understand reality; it stresses the holistic and dialectical approach to systems investigation. In the latter case systems analysis is seen as a study of organized human actions ("human activity systems") and as a learning process that does not necessarily lead to precise scientific models of reality.

Further discussions, while accepting Checkland's arguments, stressed that their logical conclusion would be to recognize the need for some synthesis of "hard" and "soft" systems approaches. Several attempts at such a synthesis have been made during the last decade.

The paper *Beyond the politics of interest* by Schwarz and Thompson gives a fundamental critique of the classical, interest-oriented theory of decision making. The authors distinguish between "rational", "incrementalist", and "mixed" approaches in the classical theory; these approaches take different views of the problems of social aggregation of interests, bounds on rationality, mutual adjustment and social negotiations, and different ways to resolve these controversial and often paradoxical issues. However, all these strands within the classical theory take for granted goal-seeking behavior with given interests. The fundamental deficiency of this theory is the exclusion of questions concerning the origins of interest, of purpose, of culturally-motivated moral determinants, of goal-setting processes.  The authors propose an approach based on the perception of social organizations as cultural entities bound by common moral commitments (shared basic cultural values).  From this position of constrained relativism, they arrive at the conclusion that the goal-setting process must be viable in terms of justifying the goals by asserting basic cultural values.  Further discussions showed that the views of Schwartz and Thompson can be accepted only with considerable difficulty by classical theorists; however, it may be that this tension between the various schools of thought is more pronounced in the western European and North American cultural settings.  The middle and eastern European cultures have already produced scientific approaches close to those suggested by Schwartz and Thompson.  The concepts of constrained relativism and dependence on cultural and ideological premises, the role of purpose in research, modeling and decisions, and the impact of all these factors on learning in goal- or aspiration-setting, are issues widely discussed and accepted in the eastern European scientific literature.

The paper *The plural rationality and interest of national planners: experiences in Hungary* by Báger supports the thesis that goal-setting is widely recognized as culturally dependent; this view seems to be held by a number of Hungarian economists (even if economists are always more prone than other social scientists to concentrate on the interests rather than on their cultural determinants).  The paper presents an in-depth analysis of the planning culture in Hungary, and its changing determinants and basic values, including the shift away from an emphasis on products and means towards the idea that social and human values are important in planning.  This, in turn, leads to the explicit recognition of the need to take diverse rationalities into account in the planning process itself.

Further discussions at the meeting stressed the need for a clear conceptual distinction between plural rationality and plural interests. A rationality is a conceptual framework for perceiving what constitutes rational action:  for example, an individualistic market-oriented culture will tend to identify rationality with the maximization of individual interests and will tend to neglect the question of how these interests actually arise.  After all, if the hidden hand is to do its miraculous work it must remain hidden.  Interests may be as diverse as the individuals who hold them but all that diversity is ultimately unified by the single rationality of the market.

But, in a social system that has elected to operate not through the market but through the imperfections of the market – the institutionally organized reduction of diversity in individual interests – the opposite will apply. Attention will then focus on the *patterns* of interest that institutions give rise to. Here rationality will tend to be understood as a highly visible link between certain basic cultural values and the survival – the viability – of certain social institutions. Such an emphasis focuses attention on the question of legitimacy and on the consistency of interests and institutional goals; it takes for granted the proposition that diverse individual interests cannot be socially aggregated unless they are supported by common basic cultural, ideological or moral values. But, of course, different institutions can give rise to different patterns of interests and these patterns may well be in conflict. In this case, the market solution (to destroy the patterns) simply is not available since the choice to work through the patterns has already been taken. Each pattern has to be understood in terms of the particular rationality that informs and sustains it.

There are many possible frameworks for advancing this sort of understanding. We can try, explicitly or implicitly, to judge the patterns – to pronounce upon the quality of the rationality embedded in each of them – or we can try simply to describe, abstract and predict their development and their mutual interactions.

In his paper *Beyond rationality*, Dreyfus presents another deep and fundamental critique of the classical concepts of rationality. His argument is that most decision analysis is based on what he calls "calculative rationality", that is, a system of answers to "what-if" questions. Against this he sets up the concept of "intuitive and deliberative rationality" and illustrates this new concept by describing the ways in which decision makers at various levels of experience approach a problem. A novice or advanced beginner (or even a competent decision maker) requires calculative analysis which becomes more sophisticated as he becomes more experienced. A more proficient decision maker learns to see the situation as a whole, while an expert typically does not need any conscious analysis at all to choose the right course of action. He might deliberate, if he feels uneasy about certain aspects of a given situation, but this deliberation serves only to convince himself that he is approaching the problem from the right perspective. When this perspective has been found, he knows what to do without breaking the problem down into its components and calculating the best strategy.

Dreyfus' contribution is challenging and points to important new directions for research in decision theory. However, further discussions served to point out that, while holistic expert decision making is truly the most effective approach in standard situations, decision analysis is usually applied in situations that are perceived to be novel. If this is indeed the case then a "calculative" analytical approach might be necessary even if experts on more traditional aspects of the situation are available. The real challenge then would lie in a deeper understanding of the holistic decision-making process in order to combine it with elements of more analytical decision making for application to new problems. Some of the approaches to interactive decision analysis presented in Section IV try to take into account the holistic perceptions of the decision maker. However, much still remains to be done in this area.

Krieger's paper, *The culture of decision making*, has some disconcerting things to say about big and little decisions. Little decisions are bound by existing practices, technologies and ideologies; big decisions often violate those bounds - they radically alter the settings in which they occur. Since this means that the same decision can be little in one setting and big in another, the whole focus of our attention is shifted away from the decisions themselves and towards the sorts of settings in which they can occur. The result is a typology of cultures of decision making.

Krieger's paper, perhaps more than any of the others at this meeting, highlights a major stylistic divide between the participants. The classical decision theorists are *contentualists*; their cultural critics are *contextualists*. Each is busy rejecting what the other holds to be the essence of decision. Thesis and anti-thesis were boldly contrasted as the meeting progressed. Whether there has also been real progress towards synthesis will become apparent only when the dust has finally settled. Decisions over what decision theory is are themselves big or little according to their cultural setting. It may well be, as we have already suggested, that this one will be big in the West and little in the East.

The paper *Different dissolutions of the man-and-world problem* by Zsolnai and Kiss considers possible perceptions of the real world in relation to possible systems of belief. The issue is illustrated by a comparison of the Western and the Buddhist systems of economic thought. These two systems differ considerably in their attitudes towards nature and towards consumption, in their perceptions of the role of the individual versus the group, and in their acceptance of self-interest as a legitimate value. In view of these contradictions, it is difficult to imagine a framework for rational action that would encompass both belief systems.

The final paper in this section, *Rationality and equivalent redescriptions* by MacLean, returns to a more detailed critique of the premises of the most widely known Western perception of individualistic maximizing rationality. In a sense, it provides a bridge to the next section. It analyzes the axioms of expected utility theory and concentrates on one of these: the axiom of independence. By considering the Allais paradox, MacLean examines in detail the various ways of justifying classical expected utility theory and concludes that the assumption of independence cannot be justified in real-life situations. Cultural and moral values, he concludes, make it impossible for problems to be liberated from their contexts.


Michael Thompson
Andrzej Wierzbicki

# THE APPROACH TO PLURAL RATIONALITY THROUGH SOFT SYSTEMS METHODOLOGY

Peter Checkland

*Department of Systems, University of Lancaster, Bailrigg, UK*

PREFACE

We can get no nearer to 'reality' than the mental representations we make of it. And those mental representations will derive to a large extent from our cultural endowment, from the Weltanschauungen we learn to adopt - and do not question - through our membership of specific social groups and of a specific society.

At the University of Lancaster Department of Systems in the early 1970s this problem faced us dramatically. We were attempting, through tackling real-world problems, to find out what happened to the well-established methodologies for "systems engineering" when they were applied to very messy and ill-defined problem situations. The methodology of 'hard' systems approaches can be reduced to: (1) define the objectives to be achieved; (2) working from the objectives, engineer the system necessary to achieve them. We were working in situations in which the fact that clear objectives could not be defined was a significant part of the problem. Different actors in a situation, with their culturally-determined plural rationalities, perceived different objectives as desirable. In such situations 'hard' systems methodology could never complete its first phase.

Out of our experiences a new systems methodology emerged, one so different from the systems engineering with which we started that it required a new name. We call it "Soft Systems Methodology".

This paper[†] describes what is normally meant by "applying a systems approach", and relates our experience of developing soft systems method-

---

A version of this paper was given at the Annual Meeting of the European Association of Programmes in Health Services Studies, Rennes, France, June 1984.

ology to that received view. It argues that plural rationalities, deriving from cultural differences, cannot be ironed out but must be accepted. Accepting them entails accepting a systems paradigm of learning rather than optimizing.


INTRODUCTION

The word "system" has become one of the most common abstractions in everyday language. Although the concept may have a precise definition within professional discourse in many different fields, its most common usage is in everyday language. We casually refer to any complex set of purposeful arrangements or procedures as "a system". We refer all to easily to transportation systems, education systems, political systems, health care systems. It is no surprise at all to read in the Declaration of the 1978 International Conference on Primary Health Care (1) that:

> Primary health care . . . forms an integral part both of the
> country's health system, of which it is the central function
> and main focus, and of the overall social and economic develop-
> ment of the community. (Author's emphasis)

Note the assumption, taken as given, that any country will have an entity called "a health system". From that assumption, and hundreds like it in other fields, follows the next unquestioned assumption, namely that to adopt "a systems approach" is to focus on "systems" in the real world, usually with a view to designing them or improving their efficiency.

The experiences described here will tend to shake that assumption. It will argue that this idea that the world contains systems which can be "engineered" (in the broad sense of that term) is the systems thinking of the 1950s and 1960s. In the 1970s a new version of systems thinking has emerged in which it is the process of inquiry which is "the system", rather than, necessarily, the thing upon which inquiry focusses. This new systems thinking is relevant to any messy real-world problem situations in which views differ, resources are limited and objectives are problematical; hence it is ripe for application to the problems of providing health care, this provision being subject to resource scarcity at a time of rising expectations.

APPLYING A SYSTEMS APPROACH: THE RECEIVED VIEW

A working conference held under the auspices of NATO's civilian Science Programme in 1982 provides an excellent illustration of the normal assumptions surrounding the application of a systems approach in a particular field, that of health care. The conference was called "Re-orienting Health Services: Application of a Systems Approach", and its deliberations have been recently published (2).

The organisers of the conference had an excellent idea for ensuring the coherence of the discussions. An initial paper (3) presented a systems model of any 'health service system', and sessions of the conference then focussed on particular sub-systems of the model. The scene-setting paper begins:

> In every country there is a system of health services, just
> as there are systems of education, of agriculture, transport-
> ation and many other social activities.

This is a very clear expression of the normal view of "a systems approach", namely that it involves taking the world to consist of or contain systems of various kinds. The paper presented a view of a health service system as consisting of a central sequence of operational sub-systems: acquire resources; organise programmes; deliver services. These are then all supported by two other sub-systems, concerned with provision of economic support and provision of management. This instrumental view of what is meant by a "health service system" certainly served to provide a co-herent intellectual shape for the meeting.

Other papers at the meeting reinforced this received view of "a systems approach". Ten papers described the "health service system" in ten different countries, and several other papers made explicit the assumption that the world is systemic; for example:

> In the systems approach reality is considered as a system (4)

> The health services are a system with many elements and a
> myriad of relationships (5)

It was interesting to note at the meeting that the one pre-prepared paper to cast doubt upon the value of a systems approach was the one concerned

with research and development.  Affeld's paper (6) introduced the cultural
dimension.  He queried whether the systems view of health services could

> . . . cope with the concrete peculiarities and given problems
> in historically specific situations of health care in different
> countries.

This was significant in the conference discussions, in which the general
satisfaction with the systems model <u>as a means of structuring discussion</u>
did not extend to satisfaction with it as a means of grappling with
cultural issues and problems in health care.  A sense of frustration with
the systems model developed, and an account of the 'alternative' systems
approach was prepared and presented <u>in situ</u> (7).  It is that alternative
systems approach, <u>not</u> based on the ontological assumption that "reality"
is a system", which is the subject of this paper.  It will be presented
by discussing the origins of systems thinking and the two main manifestations of a systems approach - the 'hard' tradition of the 1950s and 1960s,
and the 'soft' tradition developed in the 1970s.  (This account draws
upon other recently published accounts (8, 9, 10)).

THE ORIGIN AND NATURE OF SYSTEMS THINKING

All civilisations have possessed their own art, religion and technology.
What makes our own civilisation, Western civilisation, unique is its
development of the most powerful way of finding things out which man has
discovered: the method of natural science.  This method, a combination
of (repeatable) observation and rational thinking, became explicit in
the so-called Scientific Revolution in the 17th Century and developed
with the rise of rationalist philosophy.  Given this perspective, one of
the most important books in Western civilisation is Rene Descartes'
<u>Discourse on Method</u> of 1637.  In that great book Descartes offers four
rules for using the mind.  It is the second which urges that, faced with
complexity, the best approach is to split it up into several parts and
tackle the parts one by one.  This principle of <u>reduction</u> is very successful in the natural sciences (that is why we know them, arbitrarily,
as separate subjects of study) but it is obvious that the reductionist
principle has a profound limitation.  Descartes made the unquestioned
assumption that the part is the same when separate from its parent whole
as when it is within the whole.

My medical student daughter tells me that she learnt much about 'the hand' by dissecting a hand previously cut from a cadaver; but it is obvious that a hand which is part of a living body is rather different from a hand severed from the organism.

From this illustration we can see that it is not surprising that the questioning of reductionism - the attempt to develop explicit forms of holistic thinking - was initiated by biologists.  It seemed to the so-called Organismic biologists in the early years of this century that the reductionist method of natural science was probably not the best way to try to answer the question: What is a living organism?  They developed thinking in terms of wholes; they are the pioneers of the development of self-conscious systems thinking (11) - even though the history of thought reveals many intuitive systems thinkers, figures such as Plato, Aquinas, Locke, Marx.

The most important idea in systems thinking is the notion that whole entities have properties which have no meaning in terms of the parts which make up the whole.  The wetness of water, for example, is a property of that substance which has no meaning in terms of the hydrogen and oxygen which are water's components.  Such properties are described as emergent, and systems thinking is thinking in terms of wholes having emergent properties.

The idea of emergence is the most important idea in systems thinking. To that we must add three more to assemble the core concepts upon which systems thinking is based: hierarchy, communication and control.  Taking the four ideas together we get the basic systems image or metaphor: of a whole (showing emergent properties) which may itself contain smaller wholes and be part of a larger whole in a hierarchical structure; and which, possessing processes of communication and control (in the control engineer's sense) may adapt and so survive in an environment which changes.  Taking a "systems approach" simply consists of consciously using this concept of a surviving entity in a changing environment to understand the world or to tackle problems within it.

A SYSTEMS APPROACH: THE 'HARD' TRADITION - 'SYSTEMS ENGINEERING' AND 'SYSTEMS ANALYSIS'

The best-known version of the organised use of a systems approach is that which developed in the 1950s under such names as "Systems Engineering" and "Systems Analysis".

In Bell Telephone laboratories the scientists and technologists sought procedures for ensuring that they could generate "organised creative technology" (12). Simultaneously but independently the RAND Corporation analysts were formalising a process by which they could help real-world decision takers faced with a problem of choice to decide which of the possible alternative systems would best meet their needs. The Bell Telephone engineers generalised their methodology from project experiences; the RAND analysts put together ideas from engineering and economics to define the process called "systems analysis" (13).

Both "systems engineers" and "systems analysts" in these methodologies are professionals operating within the value systems of their clients. A systems engineer making a study of transportation systems will look at alternative means of transportation, comparing their technology and costs and thinking carefully about the criteria for selecting between alterna-tives. A RAND analyst, asked by the Department of Defence to make a study of radar systems, will propose the realisable system nearest to optimum requirements, balancing benefits against costs. It is inconceiv-able within the methodology of systems analysis that his recommendations might be to re-think foreign policy!

The reason for this, revealed by analysis of many accounts of this kind of systems thinking (11), is that they all reduce to a procedure having these characteristics: the real-world client (person, group or society as a whole) is taken to be the owner of the problem; his needs are taken as given and expressed as the objectives to be achieved by a system; there follows a systematic search for an efficient system to achieve the known-to-be-desirable end. In other words, this "hard" systems method-ology tackles the question: how? By definition, if objectives are them-selves problematical, if the questions to be answered are 'what' as well as 'how' questions, then "the system" cannot be taken as given, and the approach must be modified. This modification has occurred in the 1970s.

A SYSTEMS APPROACH: THE 'SOFT' TRADITION - 'SOFT SYSTEMS METHODOLOGY'

The first systems approach assumed that there is a need to be filled and that real-world arrangements to do so can be taken to be systems; these "systems" can be "engineered". This perspective has several good results. It requires the analyst to take a broad view and directs his attention to connections and interactions.

Inevitably, though, it concentrates on the logic of arrangements to meet the defined need, and will be most helpful in situations in which the logic of the real-world manifestations is faulty, a not uncommon occurrence. For example, the model of a health service system upon which the conference described above was based expressed an implicit logical argument of the following form:

- There is a need for the delivery of health care.

- This need can be met by providing appropriate resources, defining programmes, and delivering services via those programmes.

- These three operations (provide; define; deliver) must themselves be supported by the provision of (a) management, (b) finance.

Now, in the real world of health service provision this may well be useful: resources may be fundamentally inadequate or inappropriate, programmes may be inadequately defined, or spoilt by inadequate delivery; management may be neglecting the balance needed between programme definition and delivery capability; finance and feasible programmes must be matched, etc. On the other hand, real world problems are not usually signalled in so logical a manner. In a real-world problem in a hospital, for example, the observed "problem" might seem to be a history of bad relationships between administrators conscious of the need to spread resource use over the period of a budget and clinicians acting upon the principle of taking medical decisions on purely medical grounds. Here is an example of Affeld's "concrete peculiarities" in "historically specific situations". The general model of a logical health care delivery system may not seem very relevant to these particular peculiarities!

It was findings of this kind - in a general management, rather than a health service context - which led to the re-thinking of "a systems approach" during the 1970s.

In the research programme of the Department of Systems at Lancaster we wished to research the relevance of systems ideas to problem solving in these ill-structured situations in human affairs which are far more common than the rather well-structured situations for which systems engineering and RAND systems analysis were developed.

The approach adopted was one of 'action research', working in real situations with real problem owners. With the benefit of hindsight it

is possible to see the decade of work which followed in terms of the
systems model of Figure 1. Here, definition of systems methodology
leads to its use; its use yields learning; and that learning is a source
of the original definition. Of course, such a system can never begin
operations, since the definition requires the learning, which requires
the use, which requires the definition! Like all self-creating ("auto-
poietic") systems it is organisationally closed.

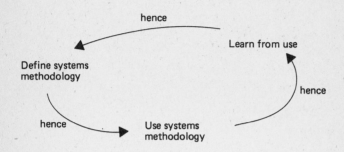

FIGURE 1: The Methodology-Creating System

In the action research programme we broke into the closed system by
taking systems engineering methodology as given, applied it in unsuitably
"soft" problem situations (in which whats as well as hows were problematical), did what seemed best in the circumstances of the individual
projects, and then generalised the lessons learned in the re-definition
of the methodology. Soft Systems Methodology is the redefined Systems
Engineering which emerged from this process.

The most difficult learning to acquire during the action research programme was a deep appreciation of the kind of system concept most relevant
to our interventions in soft real-world problem situations. Much is
known about the concept natural system, which can be mapped onto such
things as river basins, forests and frogs, and much too about the concept
designed system, which can map either physical manifestations such as
fire engines, bicycles and computers, or abstract ones such as mathematics
or philosophy. Our notion was that a set of human activities linked
together so that the whole constitutes purposeful action constituted a
system concept relevant to real-world problems in which, in the midst of
differing perceptions and interpretations, purposeful action is sought.
We were developing the concept human activity system. (The reader will
have noticed that I am going to some lengths to avoid describing the
world as consisting of systems.)

The difficult learning was to appreciate the nature of this particular
system concept.  The point is this: where accounts of real-world manifestations of natural or designed systems will be publicly testable (if
I say "this bicycle has two wheels and a saddle", you can check whether
this is correct) accounts of human purposeful activity will not be testable in the same way.  Linked activities in the real world which one
observer may describe as "terrorism" will for another observer constitute
"freedom fighting".  Such descriptions are not publicly testable.
Consider another example: if you ask people to answer the question "What
is a prison?", many different answers will emerge.  It is to be described
in terms of a punishment system, a rehabilitation system, a system for
revenge, a system to protect society, a system which constitutes a
'university of crime'?  Many such answers might emerge, and it would be
unhelpful to try to decide which one was "correct".  All the answers
given - and many other possible answers - could produce valid accounts
of a prison as a human activity system, valid that is according to a
particular image of the world, a Weltanschauung which the observer is
taking as given.

Use of the concept of human activity system has always to consider:
(human activity system + Weltanschauung) and to explore a wide range of
possible world views which concerned observers might regard as meaningful.
For this type of system the idea of an account being meaningful has to
replace the idea of any one account being correct.  (Of course, actual
real-world activity is always simultaneously meaningful to different
observers according to different and changing images of the world; this
reminds us that technically, as I have tried to insist, any account of
a human activity system is an intellectual construct, an account which
one-sidedly emphasises a particular Weltanschauung, rather than a proposed description of part of the real world.  This careful separation
between the real world and systemic accounts which relate to it is
important in understanding human activity.  It does not matter if a
systems model of an industrial plant (describable as a designed physical
system) is casually treated as a surrogate for the plant itself.  It
does matter if this kind of mapping is assumed casually in the case of
systems models of human activity systems.  Such models are "ideal types"
in Max  Weber's sense; they are models relevant to inquiring into real-
world human activity, not models of that activity (14).

As an example of the use of these ideas, consider the U.K. charity 'Oxfam'.
We carried out a systems study aimed at improving the management informa-

tion available to Oxfam's managers.  Here the organisation as a whole is
to be regarded as a relevant system but there is no single answer to the
question: What kind of human activity system is Oxfam?  It can be taken
to be a relief-providing system.  That is what is implied in its name,
which derives from its origins as the Oxford Committee for Famine Relief.
But Oxfam in the field can be observed carrying out such projects as
providing water pumps for African villages: it is legitimately viewed as
an aid-provision system.  At a higher level of abstraction it may be
regarded as a political education system, one concerned to persuade the
rich countries of the world to devote more of their resources to helping
the developing countries.  None of these accounts of Oxfam are "correct";
the thing to do is to treat  each of them as relevant, make models of
the systems named, use those activity models as a means of defining
information flows, and compare those information flows with the ones
reaching Oxfam's managers, in order to bring about improvements.


SOFT SYSTEMS METHODOLOGY AS A PROCESS

I am now in a position to describe the formal structure of the systems
methodology which uses the human-activity-systems concept: "soft systems
methodology" (11).  Being concerned with helping to achieve improvements
in real-world situations regarded as problematical, it can most simply
be expressed as a way of getting from "finding out" about a problem
situation to "taking action" in that situation.  It does that not by
relying on previous experience (which is the most common way of moving
from finding out to taking action) but by introducing an organised use
of systems thinking.

After finding out about the problem situation (for which formal guidelines have been developed) some human activity systems which the analyst
hopes will be relevant to the problem situation are selected and named.
The naming needs to be done carefully and explicitly, since the names
will be used as a basis for making models of the systems selected.  This
is so important that we use the technical term "Root Definitions" to
describe the names of these (hopefully) relevant systems.  Ways of making
sure the Root Definitions are well-formulated have been developed (11,
15).  In the example of Oxfam, above, the three concepts of famine-relief,
aid provision and political education could each be the basis of a Root
Definition.

For each Root Definition a model of the system named is now built.  The
components of human activity systems are words defining activity, namely
verbs, so the building of "Conceptual Models" from the Root Definitions
consists of assembling and structuring the minimum necessary verbs needed
to describe the activities which would have to go on in the system named
in the Root Definition.  The Definition is what the system is; the conceptual Model is what it does; but remember that the model is derived
from pure Weltanschauung, it does not describe parts of the world.
Hence it is important to build the model from the words in the Root
Definition, not from real-world knowledge of any activity which may
superficially appear to be close to that in the Root Definition.  The
Conceptual Models themselves, of course, are a manifestation of the
systemic metaphor: emergence, hierarchy, communication and control.

Once the models are built (the techniques for building and testing them
are ignored here - see (11) and (16)) then we are in a position to bring
the models to the problem situation in order to make a comparison between
the models and what is in the situation.  The comparison itself may
entail doing more finding out about the situation, or may quickly suggest
new "relevant systems" not thought of initially.  Both of these things
happen on the way to achieving the ultimate aim of the comparison, which
is that it should comprise a debate, discussion or argument out of which
come possible changes which could be made in the problem situation.  These
changes must meet two criteria simultaneously, that they are systemically
desirable, given the systems analysis via Root Definitions and Conceptual
Models, and culturally feasible for these particular problem owners in
their historical situation.  Meeting both criteria at once is not easy!

Once the debate stages have revealed possible changes, then the new
problem situation becomes that of implementing these changes in the real-
world.  Learning has been achieved in arriving at these particular changes
and the cyclic learning process can begin again as the new situation is
confronted.  The methodology never "solves" "problems" out of existence
(that language is a poverty-stricken representation of what goes on in
purposeful activity); it is a learning rather than an optimising system,
and the competent analyst will always iterate many times round its various
stages.  Figure 2 illustrates the shape of the methodology as a whole.

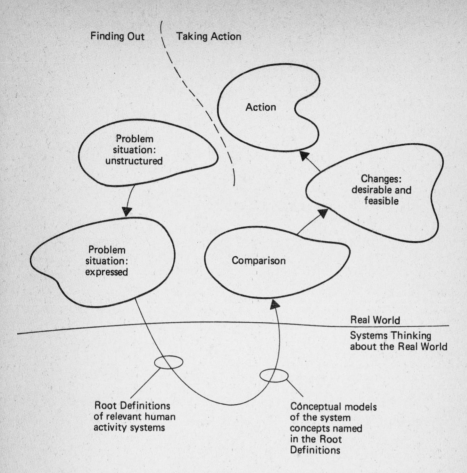

Finding Out    Taking Action

FIGURE 2:   The Structure of Soft Systems Methodology

CONCLUSION

More than a hundred applications of Soft Systems Methodology have convinced its users that it marks a significant move away from the hard
methodology which was its parent.   That is concerned with questions of
how, given that what is required can be sharply defined at a broad level.
The soft methodology assumes that both what and how questions are unanswered: it helps people learn which (and whose) objectives are (or are
not) relevant, as well as explores possible hows.

Soft Systems Methodology is itself an inquiring system, a learning system.
It does not assume that the world contains systems to be optimised;

rather it uses systems models built specifically because of their perceived relevance to the "concrete peculiarities" of "historically
specific" situations, to orchestrate a debate about change.  It finds
its way to accommodations of the permanently conflicting perceptions
which always characterise human cultures.

When Affeld (6) refers to

> the inadequacy of system approaches to cope with concrete
> peculiarities and given problems in historically specific
> situations of health care in different countries

he has in mind the 'hard' approach with its concentration on the logic
of need-provision systems.  The soft approach, accepting the degree to
which a splendid and rich illogicality informs the activity of mere
humans, offers - at the cost of giving up the idea of optimising in
favour of learning - the prospect of the "new dimension" in the ongoing
discussion which Affeld suggests is needed if system approaches are to
transcend their present marginal role in real-world decision making.


REFERENCES

(1)  Primary Health Care: Report of the International Conference on
     Primary Health Care, Alma-Ata, USSR, September 1978, Page 3.

(2)  Pannenborg, C.O., van der Werff, A., Hirsch, G. and Barnard, K.,
     (Eds.), Reorienting Health Services: Application of a Systems
     Systems Approach, Plenum Press, New York, 1984.

(3)  Roemer, M.I., Analysis of Health Service Systems - A General
     Approach, in Reference (2), Pages 47-59.

(4)  Meijer, A.W.M., Some Aspects of Alternative Approaches to Planning,
     in Reference (2), Pages 69-89.

(5)  Delesie, L., Financing and Health Service Systems, in Reference
     (2), Pages 99-114.

(6)  Affeld, D., Research and Development and the Health Systems
     Approach, in Reference (2), Pages 153-163.

(7)  Checkland, P.B., 'A Systems Approach' and 'Health Service Systems':
     Time to Rethink?  in Reference (2), Pages 61-66.

(8)  Checkland, P.B., Systems Concepts Relevant to the Problem of
     Integrated Production Systems, In Wilson, B., Berg, C.C. French,
     D. (Eds.), Efficiency of Manufacturing Systems, Plenum Press,
     New York, 1982, Pages 35-49.

(9)   Checkland, P.B., The Application of Systems Thinking in Real World
      Problems: The Emergence of Soft Systems Methodology. First Inter-
      national Symposium on Industrial and Systems Engineering, Mexico
      City, March 1983.

(10)  Checkland, P.B., Systems Theory and Information Systems, in
      Bemelmans, Th. M.A. (Ed.), Beyond Productivity: Information
      Systems Development for Organisational Effectiveness, North-
      Holland, Amsterdam, 1984, Pages 9-21.

(11)  Checkland, P.B., Systems Thinking, Systems Practice, John Wiley,
      Chichester, 1981 (Chapter 3, Science and the Systems Movement).

(12)  Hall, A.D., A Methodology for Systems Engineering, Van Nostrand,
      Princeton, 1962.

(13)  Hitch, C.J., An Appreciation of Systems Analysis (1955), in
      Optner, S.L. (Ed.), Systems Analysis, Penguin Books,
      Harmondsworth, 1973.

(14)  Weber, M., Objectivity in Social Science and Social Policy (1904),
      in Shils, E.A. and Finch, H.A., (Ed.), Max Weber's Methodology
      of the Social Sciences, Free Press, New York, 1949.

(15)  Smyth, D.S. and Checkland, P.B., Using a Systems Approach: The
      Structure of Root Definitions, Journal of Applied Systems
      Analysis, 5 (1), 1976.

(16)  Checkland, P.B., Techniques in  Soft  Systems Practice Part 2:
      Building Conceptual Models, Journal of Applied Systems Analysis,
      6, 1979.

# BEYOND THE POLITICS OF INTEREST

Michiel Schwarz[1] and Michael Thompson[2]
[1] *Department of Social and Economic Studies, Imperial College of Science and Technology, London, UK*
[2] *International Institute for Applied Systems Analysis, Laxenburg, Austria*

## INTRODUCTION

Most political theorists share the basic assumption that the pursuit of self-interest lies at the heart of political behaviour. In consequence, theoretical approaches in political analysis, diverse though they may be, can all be assembled under one rubric — *the politics of interest*. In this perspective, the political realm is seen as an arena into which individual or group interests enter in some fashion, to be dealt with by certain processes and to be transformed into outcomes, policies or outputs.[1] This notion of political processes treats political society, not as a single entity—a community—but as fragmented into groups that are distinguished by their respective interests. On this view, groups and their interests constitute the essence of politics, providing the conceptual terms in which political behaviour is to be explained.

This idea of politics as the conflict of interests has been widely reflected in the work of political theorists during the past decades. Indeed, the characterization of political behaviour in terms of competing preferences for actions, demands or wants—in short, interests— is sufficiently prevalent in modern political science for us to be able to argue that the pursuit of interest is the dominant assumption in the analysis of political events. We will question this assumption, arguing that it is unsatisfying as a conceptual premise for understanding political action, that it sets up a circular explanation of distressingly small circumference, and that, since an alternative formulation is available, we are not forced to remain trapped within it.

## THE POLITICS OF INTEREST

Policy analysts and decision theorists alike have largely concerned themselves with examining the 'logic' of political decision-making in terms of competing interests. Analyses of the determinants for political behaviour have reflected this conceptual focus and the dominance of the *politics of interest* is inherent in much of the political science literature. Various kinds of interest definitions can be found among political theorists concerned with the 'essence of politics'. Their number and prevalence supports the claim that they share a basic common premise about the nature of political events.

## The essence of politics

Van Dyke, for example, defines politics as a struggle among actors pursuing conflicting desires on public issues, public issues being defined as concerned with groups in some way[2]. Harold Lasswell in his classic book on *Politics* sees the political arena as being occupied by political actors who, having certain "base values", "demands" and "political strategies", attempt to achieve specified outcomes which are seen to maximize their "value indulgences".[3] For Lasswell individuals and groups of individuals are moved by fundamental goals and objectives that they seek to achieve. Their desired value patterns provide the motivating force for action and choice. Value preferences are also considered the key to the formation of coalitions, arising out of aggregation of *interests*, whenever there is a substantial degree of overlap.[4] The interest premise in political theory is also reflected in David Easton's highly influential definition of political events as those concerned with "the authoritative allocations of values for a society."[5] It is fundamentally dependent on an understanding of values as preferences or demands held by those involved in political society.

The politics of interest readily includes the "interest group" theories of Bentley, Truman, Latham and others who have made group interests the main characteristic and *raison d'etre* of organisations. In the words of Arthur Bentley, the founder of "group theory" in political science, "there is no group without its interests".[6] The notion of goals and goal-attainment are likewise fundamental to the group approach to society. Group actors involved in political processes are seen as being impelled by their respective interests and claims upon the other actors in the system to participate in the 'group struggle' that constitutes society. In this perspective the drive for *goal-attainment* or *goal-seeking* is accepted as the single most important motivating force of the political process.

Common to all theoretical statements involving interest politics is the idea that each political actor has a set of preferences and associated goals that determine his behaviour. The interest bias in political science is particularly striking in the analysis of policy-making and political choice.

Public policy has been defined as a set of inter-related decisions taken by political actors concerning the selection of goals and the means of achieving them.[7] Within the politics of interest, policy analysis is reduced to explaining actors' behaviour *in relation to the interests* displayed by each policy actor. Interest theories of political behaviour are purposive, with the policy goals taken as givens. They assume that attention to particular aspects of issues and the selection of policy options follow *preferences* (as identified by each policy actor). Policy actors' respective interests are somehow accepted as being self-evident; they are the *premise* of most political analysis.[8]

## The good lie

Political scientists are a disputatious lot yet they have been remarkably reticent over the limitations of their various analytical models based on the politics of interest.[9] The concept of interest itself has not been properly scrutinized for the theoretical assumptions that underpin its use in politics and decision-making. There has been no real attempt, for example, to clarify the relationships between economic and non-economic interests, between egoistic and non-egoistic interests, or between individual and group interests on the one hand and the more general social interests that transcend them on the other. But, even though political scientists may have tacitly agreed not to poke about in the foundations of the edifice they all inhabit, cracks have started to appear. The politics of interest model is more and more under stress in relation to the empirical reality of political phenomena.

Politics of interest models consider interests as psychological facts; simply as behaviour without any references to the social contexts impinging upon the state of mind of the actors. Cochran, for example, has said of this reductionist approach:

> The politics of interest, following the lead of modern natural science, ignores the reality of purpose and thus is incapable of understanding the total experience of political life. Indeed, one of the manifestations of the politics of interest is its definition of politics without reference to purpose.[10]

In the broader context of policy analysis, but in similar vein, Majone has criticized 'causal' theories of policy-making of which the politics of interest may be seen as a prime example. He has argued that causal accounts of political behaviour seriously restrict the range of questions that can and should be asked about the policy process.[11] Majone has specifically identified the shortcomings of traditional policy analysis by pointing at the processes of legitimation and consensus building which are considered so essential for "policy viability". He argues that policy analysis should move beyond the limited utilitarian perspective where success and failure in policy choice is considered to be dependent solely on whether it correctly determines the actions required to achieve a given goal.

The failure of the politics of interest to deal with the issue of policy viability must be sought in the fact that it considers the determinants of goal maximization in a social and cultural vacuum. The major limitation of this theoretical conceptualization is the assumption of the *pre-existence* of the preferences held by policy actors. The pursuit of self-interest as premise for policy choice assigns to "the decision-maker" a position devoid of social relations: each policy-maker will act singularly on the basis of the merits of alternatives in relation to his self-proclaimed objectives. Majone rightly points out that the practice of public policy-making is seriously at odds with this theoretical perspective:

In public life to decide, even to decide rationally, is not enough: decisions must always be justified. However whimsically policy actors come to their conclusions, good reasons have to be given for their preferences if they are to be taken seriously in the forums of public deliberations.[12]

Policy analysis within the confines of the politics of interest has over-stated its singular concern with policy action as the selection of the best means to achieve a *given* end. In this limited perspective, rationality in decision means maximizing something; it means selecting the best alternative, subject to a pre-existing set of constraints.[13]

To understand the limitations of such a goal-*seeking* model of social choice, we will have to examine the notion of rationality that sustains it. Can rationality exist in a social and cultural vacuum? Can a model of social choice that is predicated on isolated decision-makers—automata that arrive miraculously upon the political scene completely equipped with pre-programmed goals—tell us *anything* about political life in society? Are not 'rational' models of decision-making coming to the end of their explanatory life, if they prove unable to handle the inescapable social environment on which politics depends?

## DECISION RATIONALITY AND THE PURSUIT OF INTEREST

Theoretical models of decision-making and rationality have been numerous. Rather than re-iterating the well-established decision-making literature—which would, in any case, go beyond the scope of this paper—the discussion below will be cast in terms of the two headings under which much of the decision theoretical literature has conventionally been organized. The conceptual models concerned with *'rational'* decision-making and those dealing with *'incrementalism'* are conventionally presented as extremes on some theoretical continuum. A third group of "mixed" theoretical approaches have been positioned in between as partial criticisms, as well as refinements of, the two 'extreme' models. This range of three clusters of theoretical models of policy-making will serve as the framework for reviewing the theoretical literature on decision-making and rationality, with the specific aim of exposing the extent to which the various models are dependent on some notion of the pursuit of goal attainment as premise for policy actions.

### The first extreme

*Rational* decision-making models consider policy as effective goal achievement or goal maximization: a "rational" decision is one that most effectively achieves a given end. Simon has phrased the classic notion of synoptic rationality in public decision-making as follows:

The task of rational decision is to select that one of the strategies which is followed by the preferred set of consequences.[14]

More precisely, as to the steps or activities involved in making a decision in the rational-synoptic model, March and Simon have provided the following description:

> (The decision-maker) has laid out before him the whole set of alternatives from which he will choose action ... to each alternative is attached a set of consequences ... At the outset the decision-maker has a "utility function" or a preference ordering that ranks all sets of alternatives from the most preferred to the least preferred ... The decision-maker selects the alternative leading to the preferred set of consequences.[15]

In their most extreme form, models of synoptic rational decision-making are based on comprehensive knowledge of all possible policy options and their consequences, as well as of the desired goals and values which make up the "utility function". It is the choice of the best means to desirable ends.

The criticism levelled at the rational synoptic model has been most pronounced in relation to public policy-making, and centres around the assumptions that have to be prerequisite for the process of rational choice in policy-making, namely:

(i) carrying out a comprehensive comparison of all alternative policy options and all their consequences; and

(ii) finding agreement on a single set of collective ends or values which are to be maximized.

Lindblom has been the most prominent policy theorist among critics of the ideal of synoptic rationality, arguing that

> Too many interacting values are at stake, too many possible alternatives, too many consequences to be traced through an uncertain future — the best we can do is partial analysis.[16]

These practical objections to the synoptic rational model as a description of policy-making behaviour, have not remained unanswered in the rationality literature. The 'modifications' which have been made to the notion of rationality in decision-making have exposed the behavioural assumptions underlying the rationalist models. Simon himself has introduced the notion of *bounded rationality* conceding that "it is obviously impossible for the individual to know all his alternatives and all his consequences".[21] Bounded rationality allows for ways of *limiting* the number of policy options which are being compared and evaluated.

At the heart of the process of decision-making is thus some form of "closure"—some restriction on the number of variables and options which are included in policy-making. The essential issue in relation to the analysis of policy behaviour thereby shifts towards finding explanations for the *imposition of boundaries* on the scope of decisions under consideration. The choice of "rules of closure" will inevitably have a direct impact upon the outcome of any policy-making exercise.[22]

Indeed, proponents of the rational school of policy-making have come to accept that they are using a model of "limited" or "partial" rationality that takes into account only *some* alternatives, and *some* consequences, related to *some* objectives.[19] Simon himself has advanced three procedures for "closure": (i) decision-makers ignoring those consequences which are not of interest, (ii) "satisficing" by choosing a satisfactory rather than a single optimum policy, and (iii) adjusting scopes of concern in the light of experience from earlier decisions.[20]

Whatever strategy is followed to limit the scope of analysis, the crux of the matter is that it is assumed that agreement can be reached on the set of goals and objectives (of an organisation or community) which are being pursued. The fact that attempts at a comprehensive comparison of alternatives is meaningless *unless* there is prior agreement on the criteria for evaluation, leads us to the second objection of the rationalist model of policy-making: the need for consensus on *ends*.

This objection stems from Arrow's demonstration of the impossibility of a "social welfare function" in public decision-making, that is, a preference ranking by society on some set of alternative options.[21] Lindblom, again, can be cited as representing the major political theory attack on the rationalist contention that agreement on a social welfare function is possible. In his words,

> In synoptic analysis the common requirement that values be clarified and systemised in advance of analysis is impossible to meet in many circumstances ... disagreement on values guarantees that no stated principles or welfare function can command agreement ...[22]

This theoretical objection to rational decisions, on the grounds that it is impossible to find agreement within society over the set of values to be embodied in policy-making, has shifted the whole emphasis of policy analysis away from a single welfare function for society.

It has been argued, for example, that a form of rationality can still be aimed for in the *absence* of a social welfare function, as long as the decisions are "vindicated", so that consensus is reached on the process by which decisions are arrived at, when disagreements persist on the desired outcome of policies.[23] In this perspective, the notion of rational decision-making is modified in such a way as to remove the requirement for a social welfare function, for it is substituted the policy-maker's own preferences.

Reluctant to concede outright that a social welfare function should not be aimed for, proponents of rational decision-making have asserted that only a "working social welfare function" is required to provide a set of objectives. In this view the optimization of such a function is the aim of rational decision-making. When it is asserted, however, that "alternative functions are the stuff of political opposition",[24] it becomes obvious that here too prior agreement on a set of values to be pursued is no longer guaranteed, or expected.

Following such 'modifications' of the rational model of decision-making to their logical conclusion, has important implications for policy analysis: the set of goals which are being pursued become, in principle, open for negotiation. Competition between alternative goals is allowed to become a central feature of political decision-making, and in the process the notion of rationality is reduced to its narrowest form. Simon has emphasised that the "substantive rationality" by which policy actors make choices can only relate to the adoption of appropriate means to achieve preferred ends. In his words,

> "... the rationality of behaviour depends on the actor in only one respect — his goals".[25]

With every policy actor in the decision-making process (in this definition) attempting to behave 'rationally' with respect to *his own goals*, the outcome of political decision-making comes to be viewed as a struggle over which of the competing objectives are to be pursued. The central question from such a pluralist view of rationality in decision-making becomes: *"Whose* welfare function?". With the rationalist model of political decision-making no longer dependent on the adoption of a single agreed utility function for society, the arena of public policy-making is seen to be made up of different actors attempting to pursue their respective goals. Consequently, it is only one step removed from Lindblom's incrementalist conception of "partisan mutual adjustment" in policy making. The "rules of closure" in the context of Simon's "bounded rationality" are thus made dependent on the particular set of preferences which is being adopted in decision-making. The comparison of policy alternatives (in whatever form) and their evaluation will be based on the rankings of objectives of policy actors. The process of public decision-making thus becomes the product of interacting policy actors *pursuing different interests*—in short, the politics of interest.

### The second extreme

The incrementalist model of policy-making, whilst rejecting the rationalist idea that decisions are based on a sequential means-ends distinction (of first isolating ends, followed by a selection of means), is similarly committed to a notion of the pursuit of self-interest by each policy actor. So incrementalist theorists are in fundamental agreement with the idea of bounded rationality in so far as they acknowledge that, in choosing which policy option to adopt, it is necessary to make reference to a limited set of alternatives, namely those which are seen to be in the actor's *interest*.

Lindblom has introduced the idea of "partisan mutual adjustment" to emphasize that decisions are the product of "give and take" among numerous participants in the policy process.[26] Competing interests and policy preferences are at the heart of his model. A major idea underpinning this incrementalist model of "successive limited comparison" of policy options is that decision-making is concerned with finding agreement between groups. Lindblom's recipes for "incremental" policy changes, and "muddling through" are explicitly designed to minimise the expected disagreement among policy actors, each behaving in his own self-interest.[27] In relation to our concern for policy analysis, the degree of convergence between the underlying assumptions of the two 'extremes' of the theoretical continuum is considerable. Whilst the rationalist school stresses the possibility of reaching agreement among policy actors on ends (which can subsequently be pursued through the selection of appropriate means), the incrementalist model of decision-making depends on achieving mutual consensus (through bargaining and incremental adjustments) between groups of policy actors on outcomes. Both models, however, are squarely based on political decision-making as consisting of some sort of balancing of *interests* (or preferences) represented by policy actors.

## The third cluster

The difference between the two theoretical models is to be sought more in terms of differing conceptions of the *feasibility* of different policy-making strategies for limiting the choice of options so as to make decision manageable and to achieve acceptable decisions.[28] But this is not relevant for our concern or to the determinants of policy behaviour. What we are interested in is identifying the underlying behavioural assumptions about the policy actors' motivations. In this respect, both the rationalist and incrementalist models embody assumptions that policy actors will try to act in their self-interest. Their arguments are dependent on a shared conception of goal-seeking in decision-making. This common ground between the motivational underpinnings of the rationalist and incrementalist models of decision-making is also reflected in a third cluster of conceptualizations of policy-making that seeks to combine the two. Whilst this part of the theoretical literature has a more normative rather than empirical bias, the central concern with preferences and goal-seeking by policy actors remains significant. The models advanced by Etzioni ("mixed scanning")[29] and Dror ("optimal rational decision-making"),[30] as well as the elaborations advanced by Gershuny ("iterative mixed scanning")[31] share a common focus. They are all concerned essentially with avoiding the exclusion of *desirable* policy options from consideration as a result of restrictive closure in decision-making (such as those inherent in incrementalist adjustment), whilst acknowledging that some notion of "bounded rationality" (i.e. the adoption of certain "rules of closure") is inevitable in policy-making.

The key to these approaches is to combine rationalist and incrementalist techniques in order to select "rules of closure" so as to include those policy options which are *in the interest* of the policy-makers.[32] The interests which are pursued in decision-making are at the heart of the conceptualizations of Etzioni and Dror. Disagreement on values, i.e. conflicting interests, are thereby seen to lead to alternative choices of the "rules of closure" in the inevitable process of limiting the scope and nature of analysing policy alternatives.

In summary, it must be concluded that *the pursuit of interest* as the key to understanding political behaviour constitutes the central underlying assumption common to the main body of theoretical models of the process of public decision-making. This is also reflected in the way policy analysis has (empirically) focused on explaining policy outcomes in terms of the interactions between policy actors pursuing their respective interests. Central to these approaches has been the idea that actors' interests provide a self-evident starting point from which purposive behaviour can be studied scientifically. The analysis of public decision-making is thereby reduced to a single level—the politics of interest—with the pre-existence of goals as its essential *premise*. The next section examines the deficiency of this conceptualization for the determinants of social choice in political decision-making. It suggests the direction in which alternative analytical approaches may be sought, in an attempt to overcome some of these theoretical limitations of the politics of interest.

## BEYOND INTEREST MODELS OF SOCIAL CHOICE

The theories of decision-making reviewed in the previous section assume the pre-existence of preferences as providing a motivation for policy actors to select particular courses of action. They accept that the process of decision-making can be understood by looking at actors' interests as prior attributes to behaviour. Individuals and organisations are expected to explain their own actions, as well as those of others, in terms of interest premises that are presumed to be antecedent to behaviour.

The major fundamental deficiency of this model lies in the fact that it fails to concern itself with the *origins* of interest. It treats the interests adopted by policy actors as self-evident, ignoring the question as to how the alignment of particular interests and actors is actually determined. Politics of interest models of decision-making cannot handle the question "How do policy actors who behave in their own best interest come to know where that interest lies?".

Policy actors trying to determine what their interests are can only do so with reference to certain 'rules of closure'. But the setting of these boundaries on analysis and choice has itself been considered (within the politics of interest model) an action requiring reference to a policy actors' goals. In other words, any attempt at determining one's own best interest is itself dependent on prior knowledge of the set of objectives which are being pursued. In short, to know one's own interest one must know one's own interest.[34] It is at this point that the historical models premised on predetermined interests break down as an analytical basis for explaining political events and the particular positions that policy actors take up in decision-making.

The cause of this total breakdown (for that is what it is) is political science's rejection of *purpose*. It has failed at four crucial points. First, it has focused on goal-seeking and disregarded goal-setting. Second, it has ignored the need for decisions to be morally justifiable. Third, it has treated rationality as extensional—as having an existence independent of organisational context. Fourth, it has viewed social institutions as aggregations of individuals and not as cultural entities.

## Goal-seeking and goal-setting

Interest-premise theories of decision-making are too tidy and ignore the dynamics and ambiguity involved in policy processes. Goals can change over time. Hence conceptual models for the analysis of decision-making will have to move beyond theories of goal-seeking, in order to be able to account for the processes of goal-setting. To move beyond the limitations of the politics of interest model, it is necessary to place the process of goal-maximization in a broader context which looks for determinants of policy objectives outside the utilitarian means-end scheme of traditional decision theories. In other words, if we want to avoid the pitfalls of such a circular goal-seeking notion of rational decision-making, we will have to acknowledge the social and cultural context as the determining factor in setting boundaries to the 'rules of closure' which are adopted by policy actors.

Of course, one way of trying to overcome the problem of pre-determined goals in models of political decision-making—which presuppose that outcomes reflect purely the pursuit of interest—is to take a totally relativistic approach. One could simply move away from the assumption that decision outcomes are necessarily intentional. In this view, policy actions are no longer dominated by the intentions of goal-seeking actors. Such an approach leads to a conceptualization of decision-making in a context of anarchy, based on a fluidity and an ambiguity of goals. March and Olsen have formulated such a "garbage can model" of decision-making, built on the belief that the "processes and outcomes are likely to appear to have no close relation with the explicit intention of actors".[35]

Such a model views the process of decision-making as a mixture of problems, solutions, policy actors and choice opportunities. It provides a conceptualization of how organisations operate in processes of decision-making, but cannot be convincingly translated to an *inter-organisational* context of public decision-making. It requires a view of society where coalitions between policy actors are constantly in arbitrary flux. Indeed, the whole question of which interest is linked to which particular group of policy actors becomes not only irrelevant (in the sense that objectives are fluid and ambiguous anyway and actions unintentional) but excluded from the frame of reference. The definition of a policy actor would itself become ambiguous once the arena of decision-making was seen to be made up of a complicated intermeshing of ever-changing organisational policy choices, problems and solutions.

In the "garbage can" concept all configurations are in principle possible. It is based on a high degree of *unconstrained relativism* of policy actors and the way they view and evaluate policy problems. The infinite number of possible juxtapositions of policy actors with their respective goals and policy perceptions (be they fluid and ambiguous) would make any attempt at analysing public policy choices in terms of goal dissensus among policy actors impracticable, if not meaningless. The question of inquiring into the origins of interest would be empirically unmanageable, but, above all, theoretically irrelevant.

## Justification and cultural accountancy

What such an approach in terms of complete anarchy ignores, however, is that in observing actual cases of public decision-making it is obvious that there is a certain degree of social 'stability' in the system. A limited number of policy actors can be seen to be operating for significant periods of time; social organisations involved in decision-making do seem to align themselves with particular policy objectives. It is this viability criterion of *justifiability* that gives rise to a certain measure of repetition in the observed phenomena. If there were no recurrent regularities in those phenomena then there would be nothing to talk about, yet the paradox is that the relativists have insisted in talking about it all without acknowledging the existence of these moral claims that are precisely what makes it possible for them to talk about it all. In other words, a position of complete relativism fails to acknowledge that the policy actors are social organisations whose maintenance and viability depends on their accounting for their actions.

Much of the literature on decision-making and rationality is based on this *individualist fallacy*. It has implicitly developed in the mistaken belief that its inquiry as applied to individuals can simply be extended to the level of social organisations. Individual choice processes, as the basic unit of analysis, may draw us initially to the belief that the pattern of 'rules of closure' in decision-making is unlimited in variation. Given that different individuals may have markedly different definitions of the situation they encounter, there could be as many goal-setting directions in their behaviour as there are individuals in the polity. At the level of policy actors as social organisations, however, rules of closure in decision-making have to be made credible, and shareable, by mustering social support for the way they 'home in' on particular objectives.

The idea that some policy problems and some policy solutions can form relatively stable alliances with some policy actors in the arena of decision-making, and that these are the ones that "survive", leads us to abandon the idea of complete relativism. We can reject the 'garbage can' models of random streams of policy actors, problems, solutions and choice opportunities, and return to the question of the origins of interest in terms of a purposive conceptual model. Acknowledging that the dynamic nature of processes of decision-making indicates that a static, deterministic framework of policy behaviour is inappropriate, (but that, at the same time, policy actors are subject to the stringent viability criteria of accountability, credibility and shareability) we arrive at a position of *constrained relativism*.

We are now in a position to formulate what may be called an 'accountancy model' of interests, based on the notion that only a limited number of groups of policy actors with their particular interests can convincingly account for their actions in such a way as to be socially viable. From this perspective, we can address the question of the origins of interest, and take aboard the significant issues of credibility and policy justification as an essential element of political decision-making and social choice. In effect, we are returning here to the question of the boundaries of analysis and rules of closure in social decision-making. In terms of the language of decision-making theory, we are re-introducing the question of what kinds of boundaries can occur in relation to the rationalities of policy actors operating *in a social environment*.

### Rationality and its contexts

Although social constraints on choice situations have received only limited attention in the literature, the idea of bounded rationality does allow scope for social factors to be systematically included in the decision-making analysis. It is clear that the social environment imposes constraints upon choice and sets boundaries on the range of feasible alternatives, and Simon himself has suggested that these constraints and boundaries are in some way built into the perspectives of rational decision-makers.[36]

> The givens in the situation of choice (that is the environment) and the behaviour variables (that is the organism itself) are usually kept strictly apart, but we should be prepared to accept the possibility that what we call "the environment" may lie, in part, within the skin of the biological organism.[37]

Once we concede that the "organism" may to some extent create its own "environment", we are led directly to a framework of cultural pluralism within which the self-interest of each policy actor is embedded in the environment he creates for himself. This notion of social institutions as different cultural entities, which provide both the social constraints and incentives for policy choices, is the key to a goal-setting model of decision-making. The essential feature is that cultural differentiation among organisational policy actors will result in alternative socially constructed boundaries to the 'rules of closure' governing the framing of policy problems and the selection of goals. Each organisational culture will justify its policy choices in relation to the internal and external social constraints under which it operates. The boundaries to rationality thus depend on the cultural orientation of each policy actor.

### Social institutions as cultural entities

At the centre of such a cultural approach to the politics of interest is the insistence that the social viability of organisations be seen primarily in terms of the construction and maintenance of shared meanings and justificatory mechanisms whereby its members collectively sustain their distinctive pattern of relationships. Organisations can thus be treated as cultures, which are only viable in the social environment if they are able to ensure the commitment of their members to a particular way of making sense of the situations they encounter. Organisational cultures are viable only if people are willing and able to support them; the sustained survival of policy actors will depend on the credibility that individuals grant to them.[38] This idea of cultural pluralism among organisational policy actors is able to account for the process of goal selection by making reference to those incentives offered and actions taken which ensure the stability of organisational boundaries.

However, the internal world of the organisation cannot be isolated from the world external to it. The moral commitment that organisational members make to a particular institutional (i.e. cultural) perspective is inextricably linked to the social context in which they operate. Any cultural orientation of an organisation will be closely tied to the social context that renders it meaningful. The social environment can be viewed as the breeding ground for a particular cultural orientation, whilst at the same time the resultant socially-constructed perspective provides the basis for the justification and legitimation of its position in the social world. This notion of *essential* cultural pluralism implies that each distinctive organisational culture, whilst denying alternative institutionally induced perceptions of social reality, is in fact dependent on those divergent cultural contexts for its own survival and social viability.[39]

## REFERENCES

1. Clarke E. Cohran, "The Politics of Interest: Philosophy and the Limitations of the Science of Politics", *American Journal of Political Science*, Vol. 17, No.4 (November 1973), pp. 745-766.

2. Vernon van Dyke, "The optimum scope for political science". In James C. Charlesworth (ed.), *A Design for Political Science*, Philadelphia: American Academy of Political and Social Sciences, 1966.

3. Harold Lasswell, *Politics: Who Gets What, When and How?*, Cleveland: Meridian Books, 1958, pp. 208.

4. Oran R. Young, *Systems of Political Science*, Englewood Cliffs: Prentice Hall, 1968, pp. 68.

5. David Easton, *A Framework for Political Analysis*, Englewood Cliffs: Prentice Hall, 1965.

6. Arthur Bentley, *The Process of Government*, Evanston, Ill.: Principia Press, 1949, p. 211.

7. Based on W.I. Jenkins, *Policy Analysis: A Political and Organisational Perspective*, London: Martin Robertson, 1978, p. 15.

8. Cf. David G. Garson, *Group Theories in Politics*, Beverly Hills, California: Sage 1978.

9. Clarke E. Cochran, "The Politics of Interest: The Eclipse of Community in Contemporary Political Theory", Ph.D. Thesis, Durham, North Carolina: Duke University, 1971.

10. ibid.

11. G. Majone, *Uses of Policy Analysis*, mimeo, International Institute of Applied Systems Analysis, 1983.

12. ibid., Chapter 4.

13. G. Majone, "The Uncertain Logic of Standard-Setting", *Zeitschrift fuer Umweltpolitik*, 1982 (4), pp. 321.

14. H.E. Simon, *Administrative Behavior*, New York: MacMillan 1947, first edition.

15. J.G. March and H.E. Simon, *Organizations*, New York: Wiley, 1958.

16. C.E. Lindblom, "Still Muddling, Not Yet Through", *Public Administration Review*, Vol. 39, 1979, pp. 517-626.

17. Simon, 1947. Op.cit., second edition, 1957, pp. 198.

18. J.I. Gershuny, "Policymaking Rationality: A Reformulation", *Policy Sciences*, Vol. 9 (1978), pp. 295-316.

19. M. Carley, *Rational Techniques in Policy Analysis*, London: Heinemann Educational, 1981.

20. H.E. Simon (1957), op.cit.

21. K.J. Arrow, *Social Choice and Individual Values*, second edition, New York: Wiley 1954.

22. C.E. Lindblom, *the Intelligence of Democracy*, New York: The Free Press, 1965, pp. 130-140.

23. Gershuny, 1978, op.cit.; see also Gershuny, "What should forecasters do - a pessimistic view", in P. Baehr and B. Wittroc (eds.), *Policy Analysis and Policy Innovation - Particular Problems and Potentials*, London: Sage, 1981.

24. J. Cutt, "Policy Analysis: A Conceptual Base for a Theory of Improvement", Policy Sciences, Vol. 6, 1975, p. 226.

25. H.A. Simon, "From substantive to procedural rationality", in S.J. Latsis (ed.), *Method and Appraisal in Economics*, Cambridge: Cambridge University Press, 1976.

26. C.E. Lindblom, "The Science of Muddling Through", *Public Administration Review*, Vol. 19 (1959), pp. 79-99.

27. Cf. D. Braybrooke and C.E. Lindblom, *A Strategy of Decision*, Free Press, 1963.

28. In this context it has also been argued that the rationalists and incrementalists are not arguing about the same things: their respective concerns are with what *ought* to be attempted in decision-making, and what *is* feasible in real-life instances of policy making. Cf. G. Smith and D. May, "The Artificial Debate", *Policy and Politics*, Vol. 8 (1980), pp. 147-161.

29. A. Etzioni, *The Active Society*, New York: Free Press, 1968.

30. Y. Dror, *Public Policy Reexamined*, Scranton, N.J.: Chandler, 19xx.

31. Gershuny (1978), op.cit.

32. ibid., p. 302.

33. R.A. Dahl and C.E. Lindblom, *Politics, Economics and Welfare*, New York: Harper, 1963, p. 63.

34. It is exactly because of this circularity that some *normative* models of public decision-making, such as the strategy advanced by Gershuny (op.cit.) have insisted on the need for an (never-ending) iterative component to attempts at rational decision-making.

35. J.G. March and J.P. Olsen, *Ambiguity and Choice in Organisations*, Bergen: Universitetsforlaget, 1976, p. 37.

36. M. Douglas and A. Wildavsky, *Risk and Culture*, Berkeley: University of California Press, 1982.

37. H.A. Simon, "A Behavioral Model of Rational Choice", *Quarterly Journal of Economics*, Vol. 99 (1955), 99-118.

38. Cf. Michael Thompson, "A Three-Dimensional Model". In: Mary Douglas (ed.), *Essays in the Sociology of Perception*, London: Routledge and Kegan Paul, 1982; see also other contributions to this volume.

39. The strength of this notion of cultural pluralism is that it is essentially a way of coming to terms with the dilemma of the relationship between cultural values and behaviour. It provides a conceptual basis for avoiding the apparent contradiction between those social theorists who consider cultural categories as reflections or by-products of social action and those who see culture as the rule book that specifies what action is possible and what is seen as credible. Cf. Michael Thompson, *Rubbish Theory*, Oxford: Oxford University Press, 1979.

# THE PLURAL RATIONALITY AND INTEREST OF NATIONAL PLANNERS: EXPERIENCES IN HUNGARY

Gustav H. Báger

*National Planning Office, Budapest, Hungary*

Plural rationality and interest as cultural factors in national planning are almost untackled subjects of scientific enquiry. This has been a challenge for the present paper, although only the first steps could be made in it towards a comprehensive study. The course of consideration will be as follows: Strongly linking human beings and communities to the basic nature of planning, it was possible to find frames which have helped to analyze and synthetize some relevant features of plural rationality and interest in national planning work. Using these frames, important insights were derived which might facilitate further and more detailed examinations.

## 1.  NEED FOR PLANS AND PLANNING

Planned actions and their results are requisite characteristics of human species. Still the socializable traditions and experiences - for cyclical repetitions in every new generations of a society - have such characteristics. But in unexpected circumstances and in the case of new activities, goals, products and economic situations, the cultivated ability to design actions and results, etc. is specially indispensable. This ability might be the source of innumerable advantages, e.g.:

   (i) The proportion of trial-and-error actions can be reduced to a minimum
        thereby increasing the chance of desired success.
  (ii) The efficiency of activities is increased by comparing the cost-benefit
        alternatives and selecting the best or acceptable one.
 (iii) The results of activities and their consequences might be predictable with
        greater probability, thereby decreasing the risks, as well.

Planned actions and goals are characteristic not only of individual human beings but also of large organizations, and increasingly so in a historical perspective. Institutions, governments and socio-economic organizations bear testimony to the fact that the significance of planned actions and goals is going to become more and more important for mankind. It is striking to see how many fields transform intuitive and diffuse planned work into well organized and formalized planned work.

## 2. NATIONAL PLANNERS AND THEIR WORKS: A SUBCULTURE WITHIN A NATION

Why may it be said that there are cultural aspects in the plural rationality and interest of national planners? Some arguments may be raised to support this proposition, suggesting some possibilites for generalization.

In a socialist country, such as Hungary, the national planners represent a special expert-subculture within a nation. This subculture is multifaceted: its members or groups of members are special experts in different disciplines and competencies. These members have attitudes of their own and have special faculties to perceive and assess relevancies, or problems. They belong to special institutions which have clearly outlined responsibilites, activity spheres, interests, external relationships and a special power within the state administration. We might as well say that this subculture of planners has a special systemic character. Put together, these features may be regarded as important sources of special nonhomogenouos rationality and interest.

Such and similar facts have not been recognized consciously up till now. But our socialist planning culture has reached such a progressive stage where enough evidence has accumulated to prompt an awareness of these facts. My paper may be taken as an expression of this recognition which at the same time suggests some possibilities of how to enterpret intuitively the accepted paradigm "plural rationality and interest" in the sphere, or subculture, of national planners and their work.

## 3. RATIONALITY AND INTEREST IN NATIONAL PLANNING WORK

### 3.1. Rationality and interest belong together

Our considerations discussed later suggest a conclusion which requires to be expressed explicitly: national planners' plural rationality may not be studied and discussed without planners' plural interest, or else misleading interpretations will result. Rationality and interest are strongly linked together. Rational considerations on a subject matter may release special interests and value-laden judgements, and, conversely, values and interests set off a special train of reasoning and inferences. So rationality and interest are mutually intertwined, although separate examination of them may also be justified. But when one thinks about national planning work in light of the paradigm of "plural rationality", plural rationality must be strongly connected with plural interest. Hungarian national planning praxis uses them in such a context where both are complementary.

## 3.2    Frames for studying plural rationality and interest

In our preliminary enquiry three ordering frames helped us to identify a few
manifestations of plural rationality and interest within national planning of
Hungary. Although these frames do not encompass the whole area, our observations
seem to be relevant, and each frame has worked as a tool in analysing and synt-
hetizing our evidence: (i) specialization in an unusual interpretation turned
out to be one of the frames, (ii) planned human work with specific phases became another ordering frame, (iii) finally, the natural stages of planning work
also helped us to perceive and reveal important facts.

The three frames are not at all independent of each other. Behind specialization the most decisive constraints are the limited abilities of human beings an
important source of plurality in rationalities and interests. The seqential
character of planned human work and its successive phases seems to be a specific differentiating agent within the phenomenon of specialization. Similarly,
successive stages of planning (problem-solving) work may provide a deeper
insight into the nature of the first phase of planned work.

## 3.3    One source of pluralities: specialization

Present and future trends in specialization are probably  determining factors
in a continually emerging planning culture. The diversified division of labour
with a growing complexity of cooperation can hardly be considered successful
and efficient without planning the activities, the results and the resources
used. In this sense specialization may occur according to (a) types of products,
(b) types of activities, (c) abilities required to produce products and perform activities. These kinds of specialization are treated in a quite general
sense. Product-types may be tools, means (mass-and individually  produced),
wealth, human beings (educated, socialized, cured, trained, etc), community,
organization, institution, or harmonized symbiosis between man, artefacts and
nature. Activity-types are of course determined by types of product, and abilities must be adjusted to the nature of product  , and activities. Any one of
the three analytic aspects may be used  separately, but only their  combined
usage is meaningful. These kinds of specialization necessarily require varied
competence in knowledge, in manufacturing, selecting and distributing the resources, etc. And all these are necessarily incidental  to varied rationalities
and interests.

Specializations stemming from product diversity are revealed by and large in
professional differences embodied in various state-administrative, local

council, corporate and other organs. The divergent rationalities and interests
of these organs are exposed particularly in cases when the product structure
and market position of an industrial sector is being streamlined, or the proportions of fund allocations between sectoral and infrastructural branches
determined.

Activities are most diverse in case of even a single product, a fact most aptly
demostrated by an often rather long process (from "raw-state" to "end-state")
of creating a product. For example, if one takes a glance at the aluminium
industry, the process starts with the bauxite yet to be extracted, continues
with the bauxite being extracted, then processed by using chemical and metall-
urgical technologies (activities), and rolled to transform it into an input
material for various industries. There are innumerable examples for such long
production processes. Whilst representatives of certain production stages in
the activities are amalgamated in various industrial sectors (e.g., mining,
chemical industry, metallurgy, machine engineering, etc.), these branches
reveal conflicting  rationality and interest-patterns even if they take part
in the production process with the same poles of "raw-materials" and "end-pro-
ducts". The interdependence caused by this participation notwithstanding, a
coordinated collaboration with a common interest would seem essential. If,
however, the bureaucratic isolation of the branches were successfully overcome,
such chain activities would naturally produce compatible views and interests.

Specialization according to abilities is less determined than according to
products and activities. Abilities are brought into light in the possible future manifestation, on the one hand, and restricted in their action spheres, on
the other. These features of human abilities influence very strongly the organizational life of every society. The functions in a society are performed by
members with different abilities and  qualifications who are increasingly interdependent and require such structural, organizational, enterprisal, interor-
ganizational and even inter-state forms of division of labour as to ensure the
collaboration of individuals with specialized skills. Differentiation of knowledge, expertise and erudition results in a divergency of views on the self-
same subject even though each view happens to be a true, if fractional, reflection of reality. Divergent views lead to diverging estimations and inferences
as far as problem-solving is concerned. As collaboration in the division of
labour basically presupposes the creation of compatibility between the views
guiding actions, planning as a means of rational co-ordination in the decision-
making process is a fundamental cultural necessity.

## 3.4   Ordering phases of planned work

As empirical evidence implies, one needs to distinguish two different phases: "P" for the planning, and "I" for the implementing phase. Both may be further differentiated depending on the nature of the work object, product, abilities,etc. In the framework of a national economy, practical ordering strength may be gained from the following four phases: "P" planning, "A" accepting, "I" implementing  and "E" evaluating phase. It will also be useful for our consideration of rationalities and interests in national planning  to differentiate in each phase the planning practice further with very great variety. We must note that over a longer period of planned economy we may perceive a series of P-A-I-E cycles in shorter or longer forms, relating hierarchically to each other in time. It is a conceded necessity that national planners must think in terms of the whole P-A-I-E cycle, and of a series of such cycles. The chief characteristics of this cycle are as follows:

PLANNING PHASE:  (a)  An analytical-synthetical fact-finding phase exploring the society, the economy and the multiple surroundings

(b)  The phase elaborating the possible future alternatives

(c)  The phase for elaborating the plan guidelines or conceptual plan

(d)  The phase for elaborating the detailed plan

ACCEPTANCE PHASE:  This phase of the cycle is hard to be refined as there does not· exist as clear-out a segmentation as in the planning phase in reality either.

PHASE OF IMPLEMENTATION:  The phase of direct implementation. The phase of adjusting, modifying and reshaping the plans (this admittedly depending on whether or not the accepted plans should be adaptively modified for whatever reason and at whatever stage of implementation. If need be, this phase generally blends with the immediate phase of implementation).

PHASE OF EVALUATION:  This phase is not differentiated either.

The institutions and social forces related to the P-A-I-E cycle may be conceived as being responsible for the survival and the planned operation and development of the society. Their responsibility is determined through their interest related to the cycle. Moreover, the nature of this interest may be differentiated according to the stages of the cycle. At the same time, the practical  assertion of responsibility is strongly influenced by interests. Interests related to the responsibility and the spheres of competence may be modified by other contexts of interests stemming from habits, scales of values and characteristics of life styles. In the final analysis, they may be considered to either contribute to, or block, the survival and planned development, i.e. the functioning and progress of the society and the economy accor- ding to certain criteria. In order to prevent the latter possibility from happening, the society is in need of an as open a coordination of interests as possible so as to aleviate by way of competition or cooperation the unjustified inequalities prevailing in the distribution. Planned work to coordinate the interests in this second sense may be considered as a cultural necessity if culture is understood to mean not only "high culture" but, to cite Colette Guillaumin, "the totality of the knowledge and practi- ces, both intellectual and material" (of the society).

Now the first question emerges: is it possible on the basis of criteria of the des- cribed frame of reference to meet simultaneously the rational and interest-charged requirements during the operation of a planner organization? In certain conservative and ideologically biased views, there is no such possibility, nor necessity. There are also conflicting approaches maintaining that this task can be unambiguously and easily solved by an omniscient and omnipotent planner organ. It is more expedient to contrast these extreme approaches giving preference to heterogenistic, independent and random elements, on the one hand, and to homogenistic, hierarchical elements, on the other, to an apprehension of the society and the planned institutionalized creative work as an ensemble of heterogeneous elements being in multi-directional interaction aimed at attaining common benefits (positive-sum game assumption). A similar reply in the affirmative is given in the CAVALLO REPORT (1979) and by HAJNAL (1981). Their findings testify in a very important interpretation that specialization and hetero- genity of interests are not necessarily disintegrating factors. If we succeed to re- solve the counteracting tendencies of isolation and interdependence, then they may turn into one of the preconditions of evolution.

## 3.5 Ordering stages of planning work

After answering the question in principle, it is proper that we should review against the background of the Hungarian national planning work what the practical experience reveals at individual stages of institutionalized planned work. To begin with, it warrants attention that (a) the criterion of rationality is the measure of scientific cognition, of appropriate supply of information and of practical proficiency, and (b) only the planning phase is dealt with.

For a qualitative change in Hungary there is a precedent in the reform of economic management of 1968 when the earlier methods of planning with detailed breakdowns of the plan were abandoned and a system of economic regulators, i.e. prices, wages,

fiscal, trade and credit policies, was established in order to influence the course
of economic activity. Hence, the planners of corporations and local governments have
gained great independence since 1968, economic management has embarked on a virtual
course of decentralization, and the system of planner organizations has generated
three constituents: national, corporate and local government planning. National
planning embraces planning of reproduction as an overall process, particularly the
economic activity of the state. Corporations plan the shaping and organizing of the
companies' own goals and activities. Local governments plan the accomplishment of
the Councils' tasks, largely related to the infrastructure and the area concerned.
Once freed from the enormous burden of making detailed decisions, national planners
have been able to delve deeper into the analysis of economic conditions and marco-
economic processes. Between national planning and corporate planning a new two-way
relationship has developed. On the one hand, the state draws the companies into the
process of national planning, and on the other, the state helps the companies in their
planning work. There is also an integral conformity between local government and national planning organizations, and between corporate and local government planners
a manifold exchange of information has evolved.

From the standpoint of advancement in the sophistication of the Hungarian planning
expertise a decisive change has come to pass in the fundamental conception: the
economic planning is gradually transformed into socio-economic planning (BÁGER-
HAJNAL 1975). The change is marked by a change in the planners' approach, the object
of the plans, the patterns of planners' thinking, the interests and scales of interests employed for the assessment of prevailing facts and for selecting future alternatives. The most remarkable, however, is the change observed with what the thinking
of planners starts and ends along the planning process.

Many years ago the planner organization started and ended its thinking in material
wealths, tools, means and their economic implications; but this planning practice
existed previously can be found today as well. On the contrary of this, the socio-
economic planning requires from the planners that their thinking has to be started
in the societal facts of human beings and in the antecendents of these fact, and further their thinking has to be ended in the societal possibilities and their consequences. The first case can be named as "thinking started-ended in means", and the second as "thinking started-ended in human being". To quote just a few examples of
thinking primarily in "means vs. man": (1) Schools and means of education vs educated,
highly cultivated and skilled individuals. (2) Servicing institutions vs individuals
whose needs in services have been satisfied. (3) Hospitals and their equipments vs
individuals whose health has been preserved or restored. (4) Old-age pensions vs el-
derly persons living in healthy conditions. (5) Cultural institutions (theatres,

concert halls etc.) vs. people with enriched personality and with sophisticated ability to further progress. These five examples reveal that the domain of the planners'
thinking focused on human beings instead on means is necessarily broader and more
intricate, a fact having far-reaching consequences in planning work (HAJNAL 1979,
MORVA 1982).

### 3.5.1 Revealing and assessing the present facts

The question "Where are we now?" must be answered analytically and synthetically in
the first phase of planning work by identifying relevant facts and unsolved problems.
The result of this activity is the picture (image) of present facts. This image is
Janus-faced: a rational picture on the one hand, and an interest-charged picture on
the other. The delineation of future possibilities is only placed on an appropriate
foundation if identical inferences are deduced from both as regards the solution of
the problem. Looking at the participants and the contributors in the national planning
work, one might easily infer to what kinds of views and interests guide their activities. A list of these planners or contributors might only suggest such orientations:

1. Policy decision makers

2. National planners: National Planning Office, ministries, etc.

3. Council /local, municipal/ planners

4. Company planners

5. Bodies representing interest groups

6. Public organizations of a political nature

7. Scientists and scientific institutions, universities, the Hungarian Federa-
   tion of Technical and Scientific Societies

8. Population.

In most of the cases conflicts arise because congruity between comprehensive and fractional examinations can be attained not all or through extremely long procedures only.
This conflict generally emerges between the National Planning Office, the Central Statistical Office and the functional ministries on the one hand, and the sectoral ministries, company planners and council planners on the other. The conflict finds expression in a number of forms.

Typical case:    The fractional branch rationalities and interests - the sectoral
                 ministries and the company and council planners make the production
                 bottlenecks standing in the way of their advancement appear graver
                 than they really are. Allegations are often made nowadays to the
                 shortage in certain areas of imported items, above all those

purchased for hard currency, investment funds and labour. In these pronouncements the underlying motivation is evident: edging towards a position of advantage over other planners of national economy in arguing for a larger slice of central allocations and subsidies. The rational motivation exacerbating the harmonizing process is also conspicious: the fractional analyses are elaborated on the basis of in-depth socio-economic and technological data on the specific area concerned and information bases arranged in dissimilar system.

Typical case:   <u>The cosmetic rationalities and interests</u> - the sectoral ministries and the company and council planners make their achievements appear larger than they really are for the same consideration of interest or prestige. Examples can easily be found in the fields of energy and materials conservation related to central programmes of economic development. The rational motivation impeding harmony is conspicuous here, too: it is yet to be revealed how the comprehensive performance indices affect the conservation of energy and materials in the microsphere.

It is often difficult <u>to achieve a balanced view when analyzing the considerations of the autonom means-aspects and the autonom man-aspects.</u> Representational bodies, scientists and others maintain that the present picture continues to reflect the factor of means too much. This judgement of national economy planners, however, is only partially justified: in this respect they obviously do not display interest-charged counter-motivation! The relatively slow progress made is besically explained by the prevailing shortage of information on the social standing (income, consumption, etc.) of specific strata and groups of population. In order to take the autonom man-aspects into consideration more consistently, it is necessary to create the conditions required for rational motivations to take hold.

National economy planners and scientists often clash over <u>the implementation of new methods of analysis and indices.</u> In these situations the scientists' "implement-everything-henceforth" attitude conflicts with the reluctance, if only initial at best, of the planners.

Typical case:   <u>Rationalities and interests in using special methods</u> - the planners' need in new indices can be satisfied with even more intricate indices which casts doubt on the improved analytical proficiency as compared with increased costs. For example, the controversy over the method of computing growth rates adjusted to worsened terms of trade is far from over even at present.

Typical case:   <u>Rationalities and interests in using oversimplified formalized schemes</u> - it often happens that the new methods recommended for implementation are typically simple (linear) in their functional approach even if the interdependences between the phenomena examined are more intricate or different.

### 3.5.2 Generation of preconceptions

These pictures of the future combine of necessity the following:

(i)    prognosis-type pictures of the spheres that can  not be influenced,

(ii)   plan-type pictures of spheres that can be influenced,

(iii)  considerations stemming from the readiness for unforecastable,
       unexpected or spontaneous phenomena.

It can be seen that in the course of generating these pictures of the future intuition plays an understandably greater role than logic as compared to the phase of revealing, perceiving  and judgeing facts.

The generation of prognosis-type pictures is of special importance for forecasts of
changes in world economy ( Hungary has an open economy and high debt service payments
in convertible currency). In this field, however, it is a recurrent contingency un-
dermining the rationalizations that forecasts of external conditions (e.g., price
forecasts on external markets) are not reliable enough. Hence, it is expedient to
enhance their reliability by virtue of new scientific methods, prompt supply of information and continuous adjustment of forecasts. It can and should be achieved by
way of a coordinated use of formalized tools ( models) and various expert methods.
Breakthroughs are also expected from having the planners, including the economics
research institutes of the Hungarian Academy of Sciences, increasingly elaborate
parallel forecasts which will be clashed at open forum of experts. The openness of
the forum places heightened responsibilities for the forecasts on the planners. In
these cases we might speak about the different rationalities and prestige-interests
of specialists.

With respect to forecasts relating to international markets, a peculiar interest-
charged debate has evolved between the representational bodies and public organs of
a political nature, on the one hand, and the national economy planners, on the other.
It so happened that due to insufficient command of information the former group considered the forecasts of world economy as too pessimistic and, hence, the curtail-
ment of domestic consumption, above all, the decline in investments effected in order to improve the external equilibrium and solvency as too drastic. These cases
might be interpreted as examples for "attitudinal" rationalities and interests.

### 3.5.3  Elaboration of plan conceptions

The task at the "plan conceptions" stage is to elaborate in greater detail the conceptions of possible future alternatives which are compatible with the goals and strategies of social, economic and other domains of policy and which contribute to the implementation of these policy measures. ( In the course of elaborating the five-year
plan, these goals and strategies are summed up in a policy paper wich is approved by
the government at the inception of the "plan conception" stage. This paper aims at

providing central policy guidelines for planners.) Here, the number of alternatives is smaller, but they are elaborated in greater detail than at the stage of preconceptions.

In the first half of the "plan conception " stage the emphasis in planning shifts from the National Planning Office to the other planning organizations, above all, to sectoral and functional ministries, companies involved in national economic planning and county councils. They are responsible for substantiating the plan conception with detailed information and for elaborating component conceptions and component forecasts.

It follows from the manner of working out such intellectual products within the stage of plan conception that the constituent conceptions and constituent forecasts are elaborated through screening fractional rationalities and interests. There are moderators builts into the methods and programs of planning work through which these screening effects might be counterbalanced:

(i)     the afore-mentioned policy paper which outlines the economic policy conceptions;

(ii)    bulletins edited by the National Planning Office which help to fulfil the requirements of comprehensive  rationality and general (social) interests, as well as to the necessity of close working ties between planners;

(iii)   a way of organizing the planning entrusting specific constituent task to a number of planning and representational bodies thereby inducing them to harmonize their views and interests;

(iv)   professional discussions of the constituent conceptions and constituent prognosises involving every planner, short of the population;

(v)    discussion and advancing official positions regarding the specific constituent conceptions elaborated at the sessions of the State Planning Commission.

Typical case:    Priority-seeking rationalities and interests - the State Planning Commission puts on its agenda such constituent concepcitons that require identifying new priorities. Such is, for exapmle, the constituent conception of investment policy.

Typical case:    Preferences indirectly mediated - discussion and elaboration of an official position regarding the conceptions and recommendation for streamlining the system of economic management. This is at present as high-priority subject because as from January 1, 1985 a significant multi-stage streamlining process is planned to be embarked upon.

At the second part of this phase, planning work is chiefly done at the National Planning Office. It is at this stage that the previously elaborated data and contributions are synthesized and coordinated both quantitatively and qualitatively, and then a draft of the plan conception is elaborated in several alternatives, and its discussion is prepared. If all goes well, a plan conception draft recommended for approval contains an acceptable compromise between the comprehensive and fractional rationalities, on the one hand, and the general (societal) and fractional interests, on the other. At times its precondition is, that on the recommendation of the State Planning Commission and the National Planning Office planners should revise their earlier conceptions and recommendations. In this syntetizing second part of this phase two interesting phanomena may be observed:

(a) Among others we might mention the process of how the rationalities and interests of the whole state and society - wich are socialist ones - confront with the rationalities and interests of ministries, counties, trade unions, etc. We may not speak about pre-decided and pre-sanctioned state/societal rationalities and interests in general, although the policy paper might as well suggest such standpoints too. Instead it is more correct to characterize this planning phase as the planners' and contributors' etc. continuous effort to be open to each other and to seek acceptable solutions to the problems with acceptable compromises.

(b) Another observation may be interesting too. Two kinds of rationality and interest may be identified according to their way of manifestation: overt and covert. The overt ones are declared and brought into debate forum openly, whereas the covert ones not. In politics it is generally observed that the covert efforts are often stronger and more effective than the overt ones, although we may discover fractional rationalities and interests beyond the surface of covert activities.

## 3.5.4 Elaboration of the plan

Plans are appropriately detailed pictures with a specified number and inter-relation of indices relating to future alternatives qualified as feasible at the plan conception stage. These indicators and their relationships can be illustrated in a more detailed way by a chart ( see Fig. 1). Here, beginning with the population (labour force), resource base and known technology, the national economy is built on four basic elements: production, final use, value-added and disposable income. Among these four basic elements, final use and disposable income are shown as forming five markets.

49

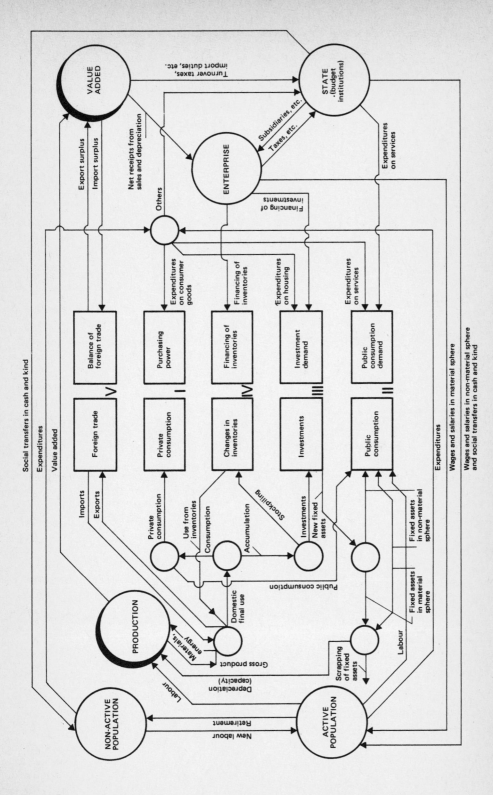

FIGURE 1: Indicators and their relationships

In planning practices this plan-model is, of course, decomposed so as to separate the individual branches into spectrum components, e.g. age groups, strata, branches, industries, product groups and regions, thus resulting in a much more complex model (or models) of the relationships considered (BÁGER-HAJNAL 1972, BALASSA 1979).

In this last stage of planning work the problems of plural rationality and interest are going to become more difficult than before. Rational and interest-charged considerations become more differentiated, require more integrating efforts. The details need more specialized competencies and the greater the specialization the more divergent the rational and value-laden intentions of those competent. Hardly could these problem situations be looked over and influenced directly by any central agencies. Only indirect influence may be more or less effective, and in the Hungarian economy economic regulators mediate the central rationalities and societal interest towards the representatives and agencies of fractional rationalities and interests. A draft of these indirect mechanisms may also be edifying. A short description of the types of plans seems to be the most informative in our framework.

Thus the plan does not merely contain indices and levels concerning the main indicators ($p^g$ goal plan) but also the instruments to reach its objectives. These instruments, direct government decisions and decisions on economic regulators form the other group of planning tasks ($p^a$-action plan).

Direct government decisions ($P_d^a$ plan) are made for the   goals reachable in the form of a product. In the plan, these direct decisions affect the following issues:

- state investments (individual "large" investments, "aim-grouped" investments e.g., housing, development of telephone network, ant "other" state investments), which have a considerable bearing on the structure of the national economy; these are Government approved;

- central development programmes and their means of execution aiming to solve basic structural tasks; these programmes are also Government approved;

- actions (including the provision of subsidies) to ensure fulfillment of international  commitments.

Beside the direct decisions the incentive system consists of economic regulators - prices, wages, fiscal, trade and credit policies - which indirectly influence the course of economic activity ($P_i^a$ plan). Economic regulators within the plan-model control certain flows of the income sub-system. These are not connected directly to the real economic sphere (a product flow sub-system in this model),[1] but on one hand through the direct flow linking up value added and production and, on the other hand, through the market. (Here, it is desired to realize the $P_i^g$ plan too, e.g. the indirect goals through the operation of economic units.)

As the recommendations regarding the direct state decisions and,to a large extent, the economic regulations are worked out by the sectoral and functional ministries, the National Planning Office is often confronted with their fractional rationalities and interests.

Typical case: Competing interest and reasoning to get from limited sources—the needs for state investments are more larger than the distributable investment resources.

Typical case: Competing interests and reasoning to get from limited supports—corporate requests submitted for state grants are larger than the available central funds.

Typical case: Regulated agencies' efforts for loosening regulators - the sectoral ministries, the Hungarian Chamber of Commerce and above all the companies themselves deem the economic regulators (or their extent) too stringent and apply for their alleviation or for an exemption from the general (normative) rules, viz. for a favoured treatment.

From what has been said so far it is clear that there are complex mutual relationships tying together the goals and means in the planning model and the organizational-institutional system. Although the goals together are the decisive factor, the other two strongly influence it. If these mutual relationships are not applied to a sufficient degree, the effectiveness of planning and plans is decreased, so that the goals, the activities (i.e, actions programe, incentives, motivations, strategies) and organization must be coordinated. When meeting this requirement the National Planning Office usually faces some typical problem areas. Each problem implies many specially intertwined and interwoven relationships between agencies with different rationalities and interests.

4.    WIDER SOCIAL PARTICIPATION IN PLANNING

Planning demands a high degree of professional competence that must constantly be de-

---

(1) An exception is that of price regulation, which enters the whole system of economic flows. This effect is not made explicit in the plan-model however.

veloped by expanding scientific and professional knowledge. For instance ever more complex and true-to-life plan-models can and indeed must be worked out using the results of modern science. Sociology, psychology and other social sciences might be employed in understanding and developing both the nature of social phenomena and the planners' own capabilities and work. But alongside the ever developing strandards of the planning profession in this sense and the competence required of planners, there is also a need for a broader involvement of society in planning. Although this is the most natural development in our society, one often meets, for instance, the "technocratic" view that laymen are needless and meaningless in planning or economic decision-making. The participation is not primarily essential as a strengthener of the professional elements in planning, of course, but of the policy element. There is a need to elaborate plans and plan variants over which a more widely debated and acceptable social consensus has emerged, starting out from the differences of views and interest that exist. These implicate competent vs. laymen views and interests.

However participation by society cannot be a spontaneous, disorganized "contribution". Planning is a specific work process which has defined stages, and to these stages the mechanism and forms of participation by society must be adjusted. The participation by society must be so perfected as to make it clear who can help in perceiving and exploring unsolved problems, choosing the acceptable future variants in connection with what plan documents and on what basis of interests. It is particularly important that there should be a broad debate in society not only on the ready plan proposal but on the thinking that emerges in the early stages of preparing the plan, and indeed on the analytical and evaluating picture of the present situation and the initial conceptions of future as well. And the debate should not be confined to the leading bodies of the various political and social institutions, but embrace under public opinion as well. Participation by society in this sense can greatly help in revealing any contradictions to be found in adopting variants that follow from society's system of values.

However the views and interests of the individual strata and groups in society not only reach the planners through warnings from outside by elected bodies and bodies representing specific views and interests (as "negative feedback"). This representation of interests is also embodied in the fact that the planner organizations also represent various views and interests and can thus effectively promote the selection of the socially most acceptable of the variant plans worked out. In this connection, e.g, particular importance will attach to the role of the councils, because their scope will be increased by their growing economic independence. The funtion of reconciling views and interests must also be assessed when the programmes of planning work are drawn up. There is a need for work programmes that bring the planning partners together to prepare specific decisions at certain planning phases in a more purposeful fashion than before.

5.    A CHALLENGE TO STUDY: THE PLURAL RATIONALITY AND INTEREST IN NATIONAL PLANNING

The relevance of plural rationality is generally recognized in certain scientific communities. The importance of values and interests is also well-known, although less accepted. Nevertheless in spite of these recognitions hardly can one find researchers who tried to interprete and study the national planners' work in terms of plural rationality and interest. Our former considerations  suggest that the overt and covert plural rationality and interest in national planners' work might be recognized as challenging area for scientific examinations.

6.    NATIONAL PLANNING WORK IN THE LIGHT OF PLURAL RATIONALITY AND INTEREST

Is it possible to gain new impression about national planners and their work if we study their nature in terms of plural rationality and interest? Our answer is "yes". And in a sketchy way I have tried to illustrate the results of the experiment to apply and interpret these two related concepts to the Hungarian planning practice. In what follow I shall summerize concisely the most relevant conclusions which may imply further possibilities for less intuitive and more ordered considerations or studies. My summary in not more than a list of proposals.

1.  Applying the plural rationality and interest to a planned economy, the right frame of reference is the whole process of planned work which may be analized in terms of "planning - accepting - implementing - evaluating" stages.

2.  Specialization along the course of planned work is a very determining source of plural rationality and interest, and the coordination of views and values involves special planning tasks.

3.  It was possible to identify some special variations of what kinds of diverging views and interests emerge:

    . rationality and interest according to a thinking which starts and ends with "means vs. human being",
    . fractional rationalities and sectoral interests,
    . cosmetic rationality and interest,
    . rationalities and interests in using special methods in planning work,
    . rationalities and interests in using oversimplified schemes for plans and planning procedures,

. prestige rationalities and interests of experts,
. attitudinal rationalities and interests (e.g. pessimistic, radical,etc.),
. priority seeking rationalities and interests of top decision-makers
along the planning procedures,
. indirectly mediated rationalities and interests for corporations (economic units) through declared preferences,
. comprehensive (state, society) vs. fractional (branch, county) rationalities and interests,
. competent vs. layman rationality and interest,
. competing reasonings and interests to have a share in limited resources,
. competing reasonings and interests to get from limited state support,
. diverging efforts of corporations for loosening one or another economic
regulator,
. rationalities and interests of those who represent the different parts,
strata, communities, etc. of population in the different stages of
planning work.

4. One may also observe overt and covert rationalities and interest. It is
desirable   to make the covert standpoints and values  overt,too, in order
to discuss them openly and to make them compatible to each other.

## REFERENCES

BALASSA, Á.: The Bases of the Planning of the Hungarian People's Economy (in Hungarian). Publishing House Economics and Law. 1979. Budapest

BÁGER, G. - HAJNAL, A.: The growing complexity of plans and planning (in Hungarian).
Közgazdasági Szemle I-II. 1972. No.4. and 5.

BÁGER, G. - HAJNAL, A.: Organizational aspects of social planning. (In TRAPPL-HANIKA,
eds.: Progress in cybernatics and systems research 1974. Vienna Symposium. Hemisphere
Publ. Co. 1975. Washington.)

CAVALLO, R.E.(ed.): Systems research movement: characteristics, accomplishments
and current development. - General Systems Bulletin. Special Issues-Summer.
1979.Vol IX. No.3.

HAJNAL, A.: Means-finality and man-finality in the thinking of planners.(In Hungarian).
Institute of Economic Planning. 1979. Budapest.

HAJNAL, A.: Knowledge, method and culture in the systems research movement -
Notes on Cavallo Report. Institute of Economic Planning 1981. Budapest.

MORVA, T.: Report on the work of Section "Planning of social processes, life standards
and living conditions", in Planning of the future - The future of Planning. Proceedings
of Conference Held at the Thirty-Fifth Anniversary National Planning. Institute of
Economic Planning 1982. Budapest.

# BEYOND RATIONALITY

Stuart E. Dreyfus
*Department of Industrial Engineering and Operations Research,
University of California, Berkeley, California, USA*

Most mathematical models in management science and symbol-manipulating programs in artificial intelligence attempt to describe the relevant problematic world in terms of facts, decisions or actions taken in the present and often also in the future, and relationships specifying how facts and decisions combine to generate new facts. Alternative decisions or policies are compared and one is chosen according to some specified rule. This description is general enough to include not only the more traditional approaches but also decision analysis (where the present is frequently taken as an undecomposed single fact and possible futures are decomposed into sequences of choices and events with associated subjective probabilities) and expert systems (where the rules by which facts combine to ultimately produce a decision usually take the form of "if...then..." inferences). Decision support systems generally dispense with the rules for choosing a decision, leaving that up to the human user, but still depend on facts, and relationships for modeling the future so as to answer various "what if" questions. When, in any sense, the problematic world is decomposed into facts, rules, and relationships in the course of addressing a problem, we shall say that the decision is based on calculative rationality.

It is my contention that only beginners, experienced decision makers when facing entirely novel problems, and modelers of structured problems where what constitutes the relevant facts, rules, and relationships is objectively determinable, should employ calculative rationality. Experienced decision makers facing unstructured problems do not, and should not, adopt this calculative methods of problem describing and solving. To show that an alternative exists, and that it uses a kind of holistic pattern recognizing capacity not modelable in terms of calculative rationality, I shall briefly describe what I see as the five stages of the human skill acquisition process.

To develop this model I studied the skill-acquisition process of airplane pilots, chess players, automobile drivers and adult learners

of a second language and observed a common pattern in all cases. The
reader need not merely accept my word, but should check to see if a
similar pattern can be detected in the process by which he or she acquired various skills. After I developed this description, a group
of research nurses who had acquired considerable data about the acquisition of nursing skill found that my model fit very well with their
data. The results of this study may be found in the book From Novice
to Expert: Excellence and Power in Clinical Nursing Practice, by
Patricia Benner (Addison-Wesley, 1984).

When I am finished, I hope that you will understand that there is
a mode of understanding and acting that goes beyond calculative rationality in that it employs no conscious, and I believe no unconscious,
decomposition of the problem situation into facts, rules, and relationships. The skilled and experienced human, immersed in his or her world,
responds fluidly and almost instantaneously to his environment based on
perceived similarities with concrete prior experiences. This intuitive
behavior involves neither the solving of problems by comparison of alternatives nor explicit thought about the future of the sort called
planning. Yet, observation of intuitive behavior discloses better performance than produced by calculative rationality.

To set your minds at rest, let me acknowledge here that, when time
permits, the involved intuitive skilled performer deliberates about his
behavior in a detached manner that can be called rational because it
involves decomposition. But it is his or her intuitive understanding
that is examined and decomposed, not the problem itself. I call this
detached meditation about one's intuitive understanding deliberative
rationality, and offer this form of rationality, which I shall describe
at the end of my talk, as the sort of rationality that should be studied,
taught, and encouraged as preferable to calculative rationality. I have
thus far failed to find a role for computational procedures such as
mathematical modeling or decision support systems in buttressing deliberative rationality, but I hope one exists. It is not calculation, but
scientific problem solving, that I fear degrades decision making by experienced experts in unstructured situations and has hindered the growth
to full intuitive maturity of our bright young analytical managers.

I shall now describe the typical skill acquisition process of an
adult learning a new skill by instruction rather than by trial and
error.

Stage 1: Novice. Normally, the instruction process begins with
the instructor decomposing the task environment into context-free features which the beginner can recognize without benefit of experience.

The beginner is then given rules for determining actions on the basis of these features, like a computer following a program. This is pure calculative rationality. The beginning student wants to do a good job, but lacking any coherent sense of the overall task, he judges his performance mainly by how well he follows his learned rules. After he has acquired more than just a few rules, so much concentration is required during the exercise of his skill that his capacity to talk or listen to advice is severely limited.

For purposes of illustration, I shall consider two variations: a bodily or motor skill and an intellectual skill. The student automobile driver learns to recognize such interpretation-free features as speed (indicated by his speedometer) and distance (as estimated by a previously acquired skill). Safe following distances are defined in terms of speed; conditions that allow safe entry into traffic are defined in terms of speed and distance of oncoming traffic; timing of shifts of gear is specified in terms of speed, etc. These rules ignore context. They do not refer to traffic density or anticipated stops.

The novice chess player learns a numerical value for each type of piece regardless of its position, and the rule: "always exchange if the total value of pieces captured exceeds the value of pieces lost." He also learns, among other rules, that when no advantageous exchanges can be found center control should be sought, and he is given a rule defining center squares and one for calculating extent of control. Most beginners are notoriously slow players, as they attempt to remember all of their rules and their priorities.

Stage 2: Advanced beginner. As the novice gains experience actually coping with real situations, he begins to note, or an instructor points out, perspicuous examples of meaningful additional components of the situation. After seeing a sufficient number of examples, the student learns to recognize them. Instructional maxims now can refer to these new situational aspects recognized on the basis of experience, as well as to the objectively defined non-situational features recognizable by the novice. Cultural background plays an important role in perceiving and naming aspects. The advanced beginner confronts his environment, seeks out features and aspects, and determines his actions by applying rules. This is still calculative rationality, except that some inputs are intuited. The subjective probabilities of decision analysis are examples of situational aspects. The advanced beginner shares the novice's minimal concern with quality of performance, instead focusing on quality of rule following. His performance, while improved, remains slow, uncoordinated, and laborious.

The advanced beginner driver uses (situational) engine sounds as well as (non-situational) speed in his gear-shifting rules, and observes demeanor as well as position and velocity to anticipate behavior of pedestrians or other drivers. He learns to distinguish the behavior of the distracted or drunken driver from that of the impatient but alert one. No number of words can serve the function of a few choice examples in learning this distinction. Engine sounds cannot be adequately captured by words, and no list of objective facts about a particular pedestrian enables one to predict his behavior in a crosswalk as well as can the driver who has observed many pedestrians crossing streets under a variety of conditions. Holistic recognition based on experience goes beyond rationality, which depends on decomposition and recombination. But it is certainly not irrational, that is, contrary to calculative thinking. Intuition accomplishes what formal description cannot.

With experience, the chess beginner learns to recognize over-extended positions and how to avoid them. Similarly, he begins to recognize such situational aspects of positions as a weakened king's side or a strong pawn structure despite the lack of precise and universally valid definitional rules.

Stage 3: Competence. With increasing experience, the number of features and aspects to be taken into account becomes overwhelming. To cope with this information explosion, the performer learns, or is taught, to adopt a hierarchical view of decision-making. By first choosing a plan, goal or perspective which organizes the situation and by then examining only the small set of features and aspects that he has learned are the most important given that plan, the performer can simplify and improve his performance. This is a more sophisticated form of calculative rationality.

Choosing a plan, a goal or perspective, is no simple matter for the competent performer. It is not an objective procedure, like the feature recognition of the novice. Nor is the choice avoidable. While the advanced beginner can get along without recognizing and using a particular situational aspect until a sufficient number of examples makes identification easy and sure, to perform competently requires choosing an organizing goal or perspective. Furthermore, the choice of perspective crucially affects behavior in a way that one particular aspect rarely does.

This combination of necessity and uncertainty introduces an important new type of relationship between the performer and his environment. The novice and the advanced beginner applying rules and maxims feel little or no responsibility for the outcome of their acts. If they have made no mistakes, an unfortunate outcome is viewed as the result of in-adequately specified elements or rules.  The competent performer, on the other hand, after wrestling with the question of a choice of perspective or goal, feels responsible for, and thus emotionally involved in, the result of his choice.  An outcome that is clearly successful is deeply satisfying and leaves a vivid memory of the situation encountered as seen from the perspective finally chosen.  Disasters, likewise, are not easily forgotten.

Remembered whole situations differ in one important respect from remembered aspects.  The mental image of an aspect is flat in the sense that no parts stand out as salient.  A whole situation, on the other hand, since it is the result of a chosen plan or perspective, has a "three-dimensional" quality.  Certain elements stand out as more or less important with respect to the plan, while other irrelevant elements are forgotten.  Moreover, the competent performer, gripped by the situation that his decision has produced, experiences and therefore remembers the situation not only in terms of foreground and background elements but also in terms of senses of opportunity, risk, expectation, threat, etc. These gripping, holistic memories cannot guide the behavior of the com-petent performer since he fails to make contact with them when he re-flects on problematic situations as a detached observer, and holds to a view of himself as a computer following better and more sophisticated rules.  As we shall soon see, however, if he does let them take over, these memories become the basis of the competent performer's next ad-vance in skill.

A competent driver beginning a trip decides, perhaps, that he is in a hurry.  He then selects a route with attention to distance and time, ignores scenic beauty, and as he drives, he chooses his maneuvers with little concern for passenger comfort or for courtesy.  He follows more closely than normal, enters traffic more daringly, occasionally violates a law.  He feels elated when decisions work out and no police car ap-pears, and shaken by near accidents and traffic tickets.  (Beginners, on the other hand, can perpetrate chaos around them with total uncon-cern.)

The class A chess player, here classed as competent, may decide after studying a position that his opponent has weakened his king's defenses so that an attack against the king is a viable goal.  If the attack is chosen, features involving weaknesses in his own position created by his attack are ignored as are losses of pieces inessential to the attack.  Removal of pieces defending the enemy king becomes sa-lient.  Successful plans induce euphoria and mistakes are felt in the pit of the stomach.

In both of these cases, we find a common pattern: detached planning, conscious assessment of elements that are salient with respect to the plan, and analytical rule-guided choice of action, followed by an emotionally involved experience of the outcome.

Stage 4: Proficiency. Considerable experience at the level of competency sets the stage for yet further skill enhancement. Having experienced many situations, chosen plans in each, and having obtained vivid, involved demonstrations of the adequacy or inadequacy of the plan, the performer sees his current situation as similar to a previous one and so spontaneously sees an appropriate plan. Involved in the world of the skill, the performer "notices," or "is struck by" a certain plan, goal or perspective. No longer is the spell of involvement broken by detached conscious planning. Intuitive understanding replaces calculative description.

What is remembered as prototypical situations and as appropriate plans is strongly influenced by the instructional process, by the experiences of the learner, and by the trained-in cultural background of the individual.

There will, of course, be breakdowns of this "seeing," when, due perhaps to insufficient experience in a certain type of situation or to more than one possible plan presenting itself, the performer will need to take a detached look at his situation. But between these breakdowns, the proficient performer will experience longer and longer intervals of continuous, intuitive understanding.

Since there are generally far fewer "ways of seeing" than "ways of acting," after understanding without conscious effort what is going on, the proficient performer will still have to think about what to do. During this thinking, elements that present themselves as salient are assessed and combined by rule to produce decisions about how best to manipulate the environment. The spell of involvement in the world of the activity will thus temporarily be broken, and calculative rationality will be employed.

On the basis of prior experience, a proficient driver approaching a curve on a rainy day may sense that he is traveling too fast. He then consciously determines an appropriate lower speed based on such salient elements as visibility, angle of road bank, criticality of time, etc. (These factors would be used by the competent driver consciously to decide that he is speeding.)

The proficient chess player, who is classed a master, can recognize a large repertoire of types of positions. Recognizing almost immediately

and without conscious effort the sense of a position, he sets about calculating the move that best achieves his goal. He may, for example,
know that he should attack, but he must deliberate about how best to do
so.

Stage 5: Expertise. The proficient performer, immersed in the world
of his skillful activity, sees what needs to be done, but decides how to
do it. For the expert, not only situational understandings spring to
mind, but also associated appropriate actions. The expert performer,
except of course during moments of breakdown, understands, acts, and
learns from results without any conscious awareness of the process.
What transparently must be done is done. We usually do not make conscious deliberative decisions when we walk, talk, ride a bicycle, drive,
or carry on most social activities. An expert's skill has become so
much a part of him that he need be no more aware of it than he is of
his own body. Calculative rationality is no longer needed or present.

We have seen that experience-based similarity recognition produces
the deep situational understanding of the proficient performer. No new
insight is needed to explain the mental processes of the expert. With
enough experience with a variety of situations, all seen from the same
perspective or with the same goal in mind, but requiring different tactical decisions, the mind of the proficient performer seems gradually
to decompose this class of situations into subclasses, each member of
which shares not only the same goal or perspective, but also the same
decision, action, or tactic. At this point, a situation, when seen as
similar to members of this class, is not only thereby understood but
simultaneously the associated decision, action, or tactic presents itself. As with intuitive proficient understanding, training, experience
and culture determine each individuals prototypical memories.

The number of classes of recognizable situations, built up on the
basis of experience, must be immense. It has been estimated that a
master chess player can distinguish roughly 50,000 types of positions.
Automobile driving probably involves a similar number of typical situations. We doubtless store far more typical situations in our memories
than words in our vocabularies. Consequently these reference situations,
unlike most situational elements learned by the advanced beginner, bear
no names and, in fact, defy complete verbal description.

The expert driver, generally without any awareness, simply slows
when his speed feels too fast until it feels right, which certainly
depends on his culture. He shifts gears when appropriate with no conscious awareness of his acts. Most drivers have experienced the disconcerting breakdown that occurs when suddenly one reflects on the gear

shifting process and tries to decide what to do.  The smooth, almost automatic, sequence of actions that results from the performer's involved immersion in the world of his skill is disrupted, and the performer sees himself, just as does the competent performer using calculative rationality, as the manipulator of a complex mechanism.  He detachedly calculates his actions even more poorly than does the competent performer since he has forgotten many of the guiding rules that he knew and used when competent, and his performance suddenly becomes halting, uncertain, and even inappropriate.

The expert chess player, classed as an international master or a grandmaster, in most situations experiences a compelling sense of the issue and the best move.  Deliberation of a sort that we shall describe below then follows.  While the quality of this deliberation may separate one grandmaster from another, we have performed an experiment that shows how little it contributes to overall skill level compared to intuitive understanding.  International master Julio Kaplan was required rapidly to add numbers presented to him audibly at the rate of about one number per second while at the same time playing 5-second-a-move chess against a weaker, but master level, player.  Even with his analytical mind completely occupied by adding numbers, Kaplan more than held his own against the master in a series of games.  Deprived of the time necessary to see problems, construct plans, or deliberate about his intuitions, Kaplan still produced fluid and coordinated play.

Having seen how involved, holistic, intuitive behavior gradually replaces and outperforms calculative rationality, in the space remaining I shall describe the sort of detached, decomposed, deliberation that can improve still further the performance of the intuitive expert.  I shall illustrate the process with respect to chess, but of course it is equally applicable to managerial decision making and policy setting.

Few if any situations in chess or life are seen as being of exactly the kind for which prior experience intuitively dictates what move or decision must be made.  Certain aspects of the situation are generally slightly, yet disturbingly, different from what would make one completely comfortable with acting based on prior experience.  The master chess player deliberates about these differences, searching for a move that keeps all intuitively desirable options open while decreasing this uneasyness.  Failing this, he seeks to modify slightly the intuitively suggested move so as to take account of these differences.

A second focus of deliberation is the overall strategy being pursued.  While a master player never calculates a best strategy by a formula applied to decontextualized features of the position as might a merely competent player or a very sophisticated computer program, he always <u>experiences</u> his position as having certain salient strengths and weaknesses due to positional issues that prior experience causes him to see as important.  These issues gradually evolve and change as moves are made, however, so this organizing perspective, while an indispensable asset to intuitive understanding, holds as well the potential for disaster.  Maintaining a perspective in the face of persisting disquieting evidence is called tunnel vision and can sometimes be avoided by a type of detached deliberation.  By focusing on aspects of a situation that seem relatively unimportant when seen in terms of a certain perspective, it is possible that another perspective, perhaps that of one's opponent, will spring to mind.  Should this happen, blunders caused by completely failing to anticipate an opponent's move can be avoided.

To experience this ability to change a perspective by focusing on a non-salient element until it becomes salient, consider the figure below.

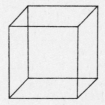

You probably see it as a three-dimensional cube with a certain face projecting out of the page toward you.  Now focus your attention on the corner of the cube behind that particular face.  Most likely, a face of the cube containing that corner suddenly became the face closest to you, and you saw the cube from a new perspective, with the face that originally stood out now being in the background.  (If you saw the figure only as a pattern of rather unrelated lines on a flat page, you saw it as a beginner perceives his skill domain, before he attains competency and imposes a perspective.)  Most real situations don't switch as easily as this cube since they frequently have only one interpretation consistent with past experiences.  Tunnel vision is refusing to see a switch when it is potentially there and when the new perspective better explains recent past events and better dictates future actions.

Deliberation about the relevance and adequacy of those past experiences that are presumably producing current intuitive understanding can prove helpful.  One can ask: Is what would normally appear to be the best move or strategy still the best in view of the time pressures of this particular game or one's standing at present in this particular tournament?

And even if typical past experience passes this test and is deemed still relevant, might there be a better move or decision than what experience brings to mind? Chess masters sometimes sense opportunities beyond what they can spontaneously see in a position, presumably because much better results would be anticipated in several similar positions which, while not enough like the present one to trigger an intuitive move, are still similar enough to produce a sense of opportunity.

So calculative rationality evolves, with concrete experience, into holistic intuitive understanding, which, in turn, is tested, shaped, and fine-tuned by deliberative rationality. Except for completely novel or structured problems, reduction of understanding to calculation and reason based on facts and relationships describing the problem represents a regression that substitues an illusion of detached scientific clarity for involved wisdom and good judgment. If decisions must be negotiated or justified then the proper vocabulary is that of deliberative rationality, e.g., perceived historical precedence, salient issues, similarities and differences, unfulfilled expectations etc. Vague, impressionistic, groping toward communicating the wisdom embodied in a lifetime of concrete experiences is far more productive than precise explanations using abstract and outgrown facts, rules, and relationships. Wise practitioners have always known this, but scientific managers and management scientists seem to overlook this human reality.

# THE CULTURE OF DECISION MAKING

Martin H. Krieger
*Program in Science, Technology and Society, Massachusetts Institute of
Technology, Cambridge, Massachusetts, USA*

Life goes on. Every once in a while we seem to be able to
isolate particular events, isolable not only in principle but in
practice too. For example, there are situations in which we say that
we are making a decision or that a decision has been made. Such
decision events are nexuses, and they may also be turning points. I
want to describe two kinds of isolable events--little and big
decisions--and then describe a variety of situations--economy, law,
rites of passage, heroic action, judgment, and entrepreneurship--
which make use of them. My motivation is to enlarge our notion of
decisionmaking: to include both religious conversion and consumer
choice, both transcendent struggle and deliberate planning.

One kind of discrete isolable event are acts or steps which are
independent of each other yet which are commensurable. The events are
meant to be combined into larger sequences of action. Those larger
sequences are then taken to be the addition of smaller events, with
byways that reverse each other canceling out (just as in arithmetic +X
and -X cancel). Markets and the marginalist analysis of decision
theory are the best known realizations of this model.

Mathematically, there are a variety of devices for doing the
arithmetic (besides the arithmetic of real numbers), including the
calculus, probability theory, and equilibrium analysis. The calculus
provides for a way of thinking of continuous addable changes, changes
that add up as long as there is continuity. The fundamental theorem
relates the changes to the sum, the derivative to the integral; and it
is the property of Riemann sums that how you do the addition does not
matter. Probability theory might be described as the study of
independence (of events) and its perturbations (as in Markov chains).
And so it provides ways for adding up events. And equilibrium analysis
is again about the addition of small changes (say in the excitation of
normal modes, or in marginal changes off equilibrium), their net effect
sometimes being independent of the order in which they are made. In

each case, each little decision is unto itself, dumb, nicely combinable with others (although the modes of addition, as in stochastic integrals, may be curious at first). If there is little overlap among each of the decisions and each decision is ahistorical, the little decisions have many of the features of the billiard balls or the particles of the physicist. If there is hierarchy and lots of interaction of the decisions, then we may have something that is more like organization and systems analysis. And in between there are models of satisficing and negotiation.

My characterization of little decisions is of course quite rough. But I think it captures the general tone of the programme we engage in when we are trying to find a set of little decisions that will explain what people do. Now, for example, one might also have little decisions in a legal framework, so I think that the picture of discrete isolable acts or steps is not restricted to voting, economy, or physics. (Rather, it is about liberalism.) The great problem for this programme is how do you find good separable individuals and a reasonable mode of addition or combination so that it all adds up. Put differently, how do you create a suitable level of "alienation" so that the events are isolated, and a suitable mode of interaction so that they work together so as to get a harmonious whole.

The other kind of decision might be termed "big," for they involve relatively large-scale transformations marked by a single crucial event. There cannot be subparts or sub-events that analyze and so smooth out the big decision, for then it would no longer be simply big--but rather something big that is made up of little decisions. Moments of religious conversion, of turning in transcendent or revolutionary struggle, and of reversal or commitment in war, narrative, or myth are supposed to be big decisions--at least as they are related in canonical accounts.[See Krieger, 1981, Part II] Think of Augustine's conversion, national revolutions, or major corporate commitments (as in IBM's development of the 360 line, or Boeing's of the 747--where one is "betting the company"[Newhouse]). Big decisions are presented as discontinuous, irreversible, and as preemptive moves. They are commitments to a way of life. They mark history, and so they are stigmatizing.

There are physical models that might simulate some big decisions: for example, phase transitions (freezing), cracking, buckling, and random walks. In each case a small change in a parameter (say temperature, pressure, load, or initial choice) will result in large changes in the state of the system. These models suggest two facts that haunt all big decisions. First, from another point of view they may be seen as "continuous," and also analyzable, as composed of molecular small decisions. One might have to invent ingenious new modes of smoothing (as in averaging over ground state symmetries in physics, or in bifurcation theory, or say by looking at a different scale of time, space, or in a larger dimension), or new ways of adding things up (as is done in the block spin story of renormalization group accounts of freezing). But still big decisions, those isolated crucial events, can be articulated. A secular biography of Augustine or a more dispassionate account of revolution points out earlier failed attempts, Thermidors, regressions, historical rewriting, and so forth. None of this denies the truth of big decisions, for in their own terms they are big and discontinuous. But there are other terms, other modes of explanation they are subject to. Conversely, the discrete little events that make up little decisions are almost always constructed to add up "right." They are set up to do big work. Rational economic men are given just those properties needed for the general equilibrium market. Electrons in crystal lattices are individuals in the special sense needed to account for macroscopic crystal behavior. None of this denies the truth of little decisions. But they are subject to an account of how their alienation from each other (and their dumbness and additivity) is a social creation.

I have been employing a version of the story of parts and wholes. Individual notes in a piece of music make sense in terms of how they appear in the corpus of musical works, yet still they are individual. And whole pieces of music are composed of notes, yet those pieces surely have an integrity of their own. I have also been rehearsing an argument in historiography, about the necessity of "events" in history-writing, and that necessity being related to the fact that history is written narratively. Just as there is an attempt in physics to "smooth out" big changes by showing how they are composed of many little ones or are typical of a general form, so too in history there is a dialectical play between a history composed of great decisions and one of ordinary events taking place alongside a larger trend.

Now in actuality there really are big and little decisions. Building a rapid transit system nowadays is a big decision, but buying a thirteenth pencil is a small or little one. "Shall I eat a peach?" is a big decision, but the thirty-seventh dam might well be conceived of as a little one. It all depends on the situation, and it is to

TABLE I:  A Culture of Decisionmaking

| Practice | Technology | Phenomenology | Ideology | Main Theme |
|---|---|---|---|---|
| [WORLD] | | | | |
| Marginalism | calculus, probability | modular, smooth, objective | local, steering, rearrangeable | SMOOTH |
| Gap | rite of passage, marge, instability, phase transition | fluctuations, gaps, zeroes, beginnings | big changes, initiation | fluctuations anxiety |
| Untouchable | structures of tabu, redemption | wholeness, resistance, sacrifice | plain world, connectedness | DIVISION |
| [ROLE] | | | | |
| Action | will, hero | struggle, epic | getting things done, initiation | ACTOR |
| Entrepre-neur | virtue, skill, risk | unknown: chance, fortune | deserts, ownership | will, O's anxiety |
| Judgment | rational appeal | argument, resistance, impartiality | rational community | SPECTATOR |

those situations that I now want to turn.

As we shall see, decisionmaking may well be a matter of steering and information management, but it also may be a matter of legal interpretation, of a rite of passage, of heroic action, of reflective judgment, or of entrepreneurship. We set up situations in which each of these decisionmaking practices will make sense. So, for example, steering is more possible in a reasonably smooth and homogeneous world; legal interpretation is sensible in one filled with tabus; rites of passage suit transformations among opposed states; heroic action is needed when sacrifice must be justified; reflective judgment suits times when we want to demand agreement from others; and, entrepreneurship is needed when we must attribute a decision to a single individual even if he is acting in a much larger supporting social framework.


## A Culture of Decisionmaking

The play of big and little decisions takes place in an encompassing culture of decisionmaking. The culture consists of a set of decisionmaking practices, such as markets and sacred tabus. The practices must work together if each is to make sense, yet each is enacted as if it is the only one that is going on, and so in effect denying any other practice. Markets ignore but do not violate the tabus on what is to be traded; tabus ignore how markets may indirectly trade what is taken as sacred. [NOTE: This section is excerpted from a larger paper on the culture of decisionmaking.]

Schematically (see Table I), the culture of decisionmaking consists of a set of practices, which use technologies to organize and "automate" their operation, which have ideologies that justify them, and which feature particular phenomenological details of the world. For example, marginalism uses the calculus as its technology; it takes the local nearby here-and-now features of the world as crucial; it is preoccupied with steering as the major problem; and, it sees the world as modular, smooth, and objectively distant.

I now want to briefly review each of the practices.

The prevalent model of decisionmaking is that of marginalism, a practice of small and smooth changes, of partial derivatives from equilibrium states, of mostly uncorrelated and relatively independent events, and of probabilities in a universe of reasonable possibilities.

In marginalism the world changes smoothly, and you can backtrack as well.  At each point you figure out what to do next by looking locally around you.  And there are rules, those of the calculus and of probability theory, for doing that looking around in such a way that the sum of your choices is best.  Things add up.  And if the world is composite, a marginal change in a component will make sense in terms of and be consistent with the whole.

A very different practice is needed if the world is not taken as smooth but as "balkanized," broken up and divided, and marked by tabus and difficult-to-bridge separations.  Such is the case in a dogmatic orthodoxy, or in family relationships, or in a large project thought to be quite risky.  There is falsity and truth, incest and allowed relationships, waste and prudence.  It is a world of untouchable (or tabued) and touchable parts.  One has to master the law:  the structure of forbiddenness and allowedness; and, also, the means of sacrifice and redemption, the ways of restoring order when there is transgression.  Yet despite its division, this world has a wholeness and connectedness. It is not rearrangeable and arbitrary, as the world seems to be in marginalism. It is resistant to plasticity.  This world is orderly and traditional.  One knowledgeably figures out how to live according to the law, and how to deal with the inevitable violations.

Marginalism makes sense just because there are some things that are untouchable, that are not to be traded or exchanged although they may be sacrificed or canonized.  Mama or Papa are ontologically and morally different from guns or butter.

The untouchable world is stable, albeit multiply bifurcated by tabu and the like.  We can imagine the untouchable world violated but not reconciled, a world in the middle, on the marge:  a world of the gap between relatively stable polar situations.  For example, say we are in the middle, rather than before or after a big decision, or we have a mixture of properties, rather than polar black or white.  The gap is a world of mixture and crisis and tumolt and flux, and here decisions appear as not so fully encompassed by the law as they are in the practice of untouchability.  Chance and fluctuations seem to play a very large role in how things turn out.  Still, such a world has patterned modes of transition, such as in bank rescues, which always take place on weekends, in comedy and tragedy, which have an archetypal moment of revelation, and in phase transitions, which are of a universal form--all transitions leading to reconciliation and stability.  The practice of decisionmaking is a play between such

patterns of ritual and transformation and otherwise untempered chance
and fluctuations.


The culture of decisionmaking, as I have described it so far,
incorporates crucial features of big decisions.  Big decisions do have
marginal aspects and may even be the "sum" of little ones; they violate
what is untouchable and lead to sacrifice and redemption; and, they
transit a mediating gap between a before and an after.

Marginalism, untouchability, and gaps are decisionmaking
practices that address themselves to the world in which you find
yourself.  But you have a "transcendent" role in such a world, and that
decisionmaking role may also be described in terms of practices.

One may be an actor, perhaps heroic, who expresses his will in an
epical struggle with the world, subject perhaps to tragedy, even blind
to the consequences of what he does.  For example, that is how New York
City's park-builder Robert Moses is presented in Caro's biography.
Such an actor initiates by inseminating the world with his power.
Through his will he violates what has been otherwise taken as
impossible, so the actor "gets things done."  Such an actor is often
presented in contrast to a manager or housekeeper or
maintainer--although the actor's effectiveness depends on there being a
managed world, a world to fulfil and work out his acts, a world where
the garbage is removed and where peace and home are provided for.  If
there is Odysseus, there is also Penelope and Telemachus.

Opposed to, but mutually dependent on the actor, there is the
spectator, engaged in the practice of judgment or criticism.
Disinterested, not involved, the spectator-judge will demand that
others agree with his judgments--although the others may differ and
offer judgments which they demand he agree with.   What is crucial is
that the demands are rational, founded in evidence and argument.
Disagreement is meant to lead both to mutual appeals and to rational
argument.  For there is a community, and an appeal is an appeal to its
shared or common sense.  So it is an appeal that intrinsically lays
claim to others' potential allegiance.

Judgment is not only impartial, it is also justifying--putting
everything in order.  It makes sense of the world.  In aesthetic terms
it is about the unity of a work of art; in religious terms the
justification is a provision of God's grace.  But not everything goes
or works, is rational or appealing to others, or makes sense as a

possibility. There is resistance--practical, rhetorical, conceptual--some of which is not to be overcome.

If in their decisions actors make the world so, spectator-judges take it as something. Theirs is a world that is given order through their acts of valuation. Just what the world is like and how it is taken is an achievement, not at all obvious or easily achieved.

The last practice I want to discuss is entrepreneurship, a meeting-ground of action and judgment. The entrepreneur creates things, and by finding a market for them he makes them valuable. The entrepreneur's world is ordered through both will and valuation, but that ordering is contingent. It is not determined ahead of time. It is the nature of that contingency that is of interest.

Entrepreneurs are often said to "deserve" their rewards. The rewards are deserved because the entrepreneur takes risks and evidences his skill in dealing with the (chance) unknown. And so he receives an extraordinary return on what we come to call his investment. An important function of this description of entrepreneurship is to justify these rewards or returns to the entrepreneur.

To justify ownership and the consequent exclusion of others from your property, there must be a social invention called risk-taking, where risk is understood in a probabilistic sense. Unlike biological sport or Fortune as models of contingency, in risk-taking the chances are presumably equally accessible to all, and each chance is presumably independent of the others. That you rise to the risk, take it, and then succeed, marks the returns as rewards for you. If entrepreneurship is seen as risk-taking, then one can assign a rate of return to it. And so it is an investment. Time is no longer biological or the narrative time of storytelling, but objectified calendrical time. Time becomes a commensurable realm in which comparable prospective projects can work themselves out. Entrepreneurial endeavor becomes a matter for the alternative allocation of resources.

Actually, the successful entrepreneur systematically links payoffs and probabilities, so that expectation values are not simply products of the two, but nonlinear products. Careful control and anticipation of contingency are the mark of a good entrepreneur. And large investments will make it more likely that an outcome turns out as desired. Investments are strategic, and are meant to alter the future probabilities as well as the payoffs.

Once projects become investments, then heroic action is tamed and become prudence, and critical judgment is no longer about qualities and becomes financial. Heroism is identified with success (rather than virtue). Its reward is not eternal fame but transitory wealth. Virtue becomes skill, Fortune becomes risk, and acts of appropriation becomes ownership. Entrepreneurs have made Fortune their own. And in a perverse way, the entrepreneur's world comes to be a marginalist world.


## Conclusion

Let me summarize the view of decisionmaking that I have presented here. First of all, decision themselves are remarkable events, isolated as events through social, political, and cultural arrangements. The decisions may be little, meant to be added up so as to recover the larger sequence of life. Or they may be big decisions, meant to mark that sequence with turning points, separating before and after the big decision. One might model little and big decisions using mathematical and physical pictures, or narrative, legal, and mythic ones. The second problem is to set up a situation (or find a suitable description of what is going on) in which decisionmaking is possible. I described a half-dozen such situations or practices, each of which depends on the others to make up for its limitations. Their interdependence suggests we might think of them as a culture, each practice giving an account of all the others in its own terms. In actuality some practices are much more suited than are others to the kinds of decisionmaking we are engaged in.

Thinking in terms of big and little decisions and in terms of decisionmaking allows us to consider, at one time, mathematical and religious models and legal and heroic ones. Together they provide an account of those moments when we may act as if we are making a decision. So not only does life go on, but it goes on in segmented and marked and rational ways.


Acknowledgment: This research was supported by a grant from the Russell Sage Foundation.

Bibliography:

Arendt, H. Lectures on Kant's Political Philosophy. Chicago: U. of Chicago Press, 1982.

Brown, P. Augustine of Hippo. Berkeley: University of California Press, 1969.

Caro, R. The Power Broker. New York: Vintage, 1975.

Cohen, J. "How is the Past Related to the Future," Annual Report. Center for Advanced Study in the Behavioral Sciences: Stanford, 1982.

Douglas, M. The World of Goods. New York: Basic, 1979.

Kahrl, W.L. Water and Power. Berkeley: U. of California Press, 1982.

Kirkpatrick, S., Gellatt, Jr., C.D., and Vecchi, M.P. "Optimization by Simulated Annealing," Science 220 (13 May 1983): 671-680.

Krieger, M.H. Advice and Planning. Philadelphia: Temple U. Press, 1981.

Krieger, M.H. "Modeling Urban Change," Socio-Economic Planning Sciences 5 (1971): 41-55.

Krieger, M.H. "Phenomenological and Many-body Models in Natural Science and Social Research," fundamenta scientiae 2 (1981a): 425-431.

Newhouse, J. The Sporty Game. New York: Knopf, 1982.

Ricoeur, P. Time and Narrative. Chicago: University of Chicago Press, 1984.

Schelling, T.C. Micromotives and Macrobehavior. New York: Norton, 1978.

Simon, H. Models of Man. New York: Wiley, 1957.

Thompson, M. Rubbish Theory. Oxford: Oxford University Press, 1979.

Turner, V. The Ritual Process. Chicago: Aldine, 1969.

Walzer, M. Spheres of Justice. New York: Basic, 1983, Ch. 4.

Wilson, K. "The renormalization group: Critical phenomena and the Kondo problem," Reviews of Modern Physics 47 (October 1975): 773-

Wilson, K. "Problems in Physics with Many Scales of Length," Scientific American 241 (August 1979): 158-179.

# DIFFERENT DISSOLUTIONS OF THE MAN-AND-WORLD PROBLEM

Laszlo Zsolnai[1] and Istvan Kiss[2]
[1] *Karl Marx University of Economics, Budapest, Hungary*
[2] *Bureau for Systems Analysis of the State Office for
Technical Development, Budapest, Hungary*

Naturally, there is only *one real world* but people are not directly
living in this single real world.  J. Ortega y Gasset wrote that "man
must ever be grounded on some beliefs, and that the structure of his
life will depend primordially on the beliefs on which he is grounded".
Beliefs, "always constitute a system insofar as they are effective
beliefs".  (ORTEGA Y GASSET, J. 1963:  283-284).  According to this
we can say that *belief systems* are those media by which people are
able to live in the real world.

Belief systems are imaginary pictures about the real world, or more
exactly, hypothetical ontologies, i.e. assumptions on basic structure,
characteristics, and processes of the real world.  For this reason
belief systems define certain *possible worlds*.

The classical and well-known formulation of possible worlds by D. Lewis
is as follows:  "I believe that there are possible worlds other than
the one we happen to inhabit [...].  It is uncontroversially true,
that things might be otherwise than they are.  I believe, and so do
you, that things could have been different in countless ways.  [...].
I therefore believe in the existence of entities that might be called
'ways things could have been'.  I prefer to call them 'possible worlds'."
(See Lewis, D. 1973:  84-85).

We think that each possible world accepted by a certain group of people
is in a strong interaction with the real world.  (See Figure 1).  This
interaction can be schematically summarized by a cyclical process which
consists of four steps:

(i)     People make their actions following their beliefs in the real
        world;
(ii)    Some changes occur in the real world caused by people's actions;
(iii)   People's perceptions of real changes are influenced by their
        beliefs;
(iv)    Some changes occur or not in people's belief systems.

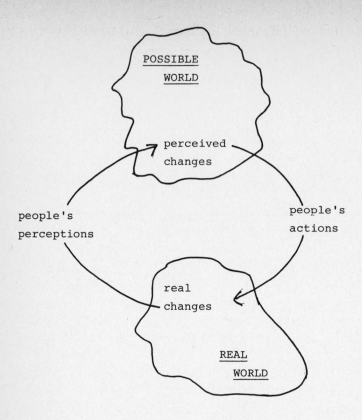

FIGURE 1:  Interaction between a possible world and the real world.

[In this schematical model we have disregarded the motivations and/or
the causal background of people's actions.]
Each belief system must *dissolve the Man & World problem*.  We use the
term 'dissolve the problem' in R.L. Ackoff's sense.  According to this
"problem dissolvers idealize rather than satisfice or optimize."
(ACKOFF, R.L. 1981:  21).  The expression 'Man & World problem' is
close to the concept of 'image of man'.  Authors of the excellent book
'Changing Images of Man' have used "image of man (or of humankind-in-
the-universe) to refer to the set of assumptions held about the human
being's origin, nature, abilities and characteristics, relationships
with others, and place in universe."  (MARKLEY, O.W. and HARMAN, W.W.
(eds.) 1982:  2).  In our intentions 'Man & World problem' refers to
the *confused and fuzzy game among Man, Nature, and Society*.  The essence of this problem is, how can we locate Man into Nature and how
can we locate Man into Society?

In every historical period of human history there were some relevant
and effective belief systems of mankind, consequently there were different interactions among different possible worlds and the real world.
(See Figure 2).  In our time the situation is the same.  E. Laszlo's
characterisation of interexistent belief systems of present-day mankind is as follows:  "the Christian vision of universal brotherhood
governed by man's love for God of all men and for his fellow human
beings.  There is Judaism's historical vision of an elected people in
whom all the families of the earth are to be blessed.  Islam has a
universal vision of an ultimate community of God, man, nature, and
society.  Hinduism envisions matter as but the outward manifestation
of spirit and urges attunement to cosmic harmony through the varied
paths of yoga.  Buddhism too, perceives all reality as interdependent,
and teaches man to achieve union with it through rejection of the
drives and desires of a separate ego.  Confucianism finds supreme
harmony in disciplined and ordered human relationships, and Taoism
finds such harmony in nature and naturalness.  The African tribal
religions conceive of a great community of living and the dead, to
which each person belongs unless he wilfully creates imbalances
between the seen and unseen forces in and around himself.
To those rejected religious beliefs and look instead to secular values
and ideals, liberal democracy offers a vision of a free society where
all may do as best suits their wishes and temperament, and where each
can find the best chances of happiness.  Communism, in turn, proposes
the ideal of egalitarian society where there is no exploitation, and
where each receives benefits according to his true needs.  (See Laszlo,
E. 1978: 29).
Different belief systems and different possible worlds are essentially
incommensurable in themselves.  We can transcend this incommensurabil-
ity when we reconstruct the dissolution the Man & World problem of
different belief systems.  In this way we can confront them with each
other.  We shall try to illustrate this inquiring of belief systems
by the example of two systems of economics.
Currently there are many different belief systems in the field of
economics, the Western, Socialist, Islamic, Buddhist, and Hindu
(Gandhist) economics.  There are also different dicrections of Alternative economics, ecological economics, bio-economics on the one hand
and human economics, ecomomic ethics on the other hand.  We think,
however, today the *Western* and the *Buddhist economics* represent the
two absolutely different economic belief systems.

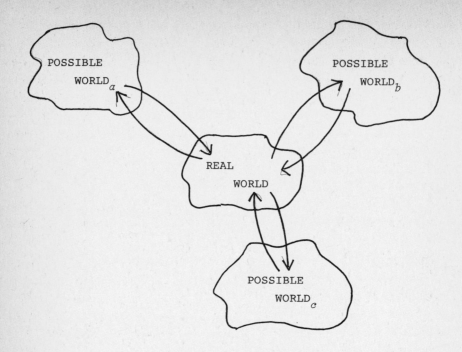

FIGURE 2: <u>Different possible worlds and the real world</u>.

Different dissolutions the Man & World problem of economic belief
systems are connected with the dimensions as follows:

(α)  *Man's attitude towards Nature*;

(β)  *type of Man's consumption*;

(γ)  *relationship between Man and Society*;

(δ)  *ethical motive of Man's economic activity*.

Dimensions (α) and (β) refer to the question, how can we locate Man
into Nature.  This is the one side of the Man & World problem.  Dimensions (γ) and (δ) are connected with the other side of this problem,
how can we locate Man into Society.

Radical critics of Western economics have already discovered the latent
and tacit assumptions of Western economic thinking.  <u>E. Fromm</u> wrote
that "The Great Promise of Unlimited Progress - the promise of domination of nature, of material abundance, of the greatest happiness for
the greatest number, and of unimpeded personal freedom - has sustained
the hopes and faith of the generations since the beginning of the industrial age".  (See FROMM, E. 1976:  1).  He has continued:  "The
failure of the Great Promise, aside from industrialism's essential
economic contradictions, was built into the industrial system by its
two main psychological premises:  (1) that the aim of life is happi-

ness, that is, maximum pleasure, defined as the satisfaction of any desire or subjective need a person may feel *(radical hedonism)*; (2) that egotism, selfishness, and greed, as the system needs to generate them in order to function, lead to harmony and peace". It is a well-known fact that the basic cause of Western Man's destructive attitude toward nature lies in Judeo-Christian traditions. From this point of view Man is ordered to dominate and rule Nature, his mastery over Nature is rightful, and Nature has no significance beyond that of a quarry for exploitation by Man. (See EHRLICH, P.R. and EHRLICH, A.N. 1972: 351; SCHUMACHER, E.F. 1973: 93).

Based on the radical critics of Western economic thinking, we can consider the dissolution of Western economics the Man & World problem as follows:

W(α)  *aggressive attitude toward Nature, Man's domination over it*;
W(β)  *hedonistic consumption*;
W(γ)  *individualism*;
W(δ)  *selfishness*.

These basic features form a very closed and strongly interrelated system. For example,'Man's domination over Nature' is a necessary condition of 'hedonistic consumption'.

E.F. Schumacher, in his well-known book 'Small is Beautiful' has presented an excellent summary of Buddhist economic thinking. Buddhist economics accept the principle of non-violence toward Nature. From the Buddhist point of view "men are men, and animals are animals, and men are far the higher. But he does not deduce from this that man's superiority gives him permission to illtreat or kill animals. It is just the reverse. It is because man is so much higher than the animals that he can and must observe towards animals the very greatest compassion, be good to them in every way he can". (See SCHUMACHER, E.F. 1973: 89). In Schumacher's opinion "Buddhist economics [...] sees the essence of civilisation not in a multiplication of wants but in the purification of human character". (See SCHUMACHER, E.F. 1973: 46). "The optimal pattern of consumption, producing a high degree of human satisfaction by means of a relatively low rate of consumption, allows people to live without great pressure and strain and to fulfil the primary injunction of Buddhist teaching: 'Cease to do evil, try to do good'. As physical resources are everywhere limited, people satisfying their needs by means of a modest use of resources are obviously less likely to be at each other's throat than people depending upon a high rate of use". (See SCHUMACHER, E.F. 1973: 48-49).

Finally, the Buddhist way of economic activity tries to transcend the egocentredness of economic actors and to consider the local communities as superior units of people's economy. (See SCHUMACHER, E.F. 1973: 45 and 49).

According to Schumacher's reconstruction of Buddhist economics, we can find the dissolution of Buddhist economic belief system the Man & World problem as follows:

B(α)   *non-violent attitude toward Nature, Man's accommodation to it;*

B(β)   *restricted consumption;*

B(γ)   *collectivism;*

B(δ)   *altruism.*

Like in the case of Western economics, these basic features are also interrelated. For example, if we accept the principle of non-violence, then we must accept the 'restricted consumption' too.

Table 1 shows the different dissolutions of Western and Buddhist economics the Man & World problem.

Western economics gives a radical *anthropocentric* approach to Man & World problem while Buddhist economics presents a radical *desanthropocentric* one. The basic value-choice of Western economics can be expressed by the Latin concept *'homo mensura'*. This means that Man is a single measure of every entity of the World. The basic value-choice of Buddhist economics can be summarized by the concept *'mensura natura'* (also in Latin). This means that Nature is a single measure of every entity of the world. Dissolutions of Western and Buddhist economics the Man & World problem are *contrary* to each other.

Gy. Lukács, the famous marxist philosopher, has declared that there are not any innocent world-view or belief systems. A certain belief system cannot absolutely but partially transform the real world. These real world transformations are destructive and/or constructive. If a belief system destroys and/or develops a certain segment of the real world, this is not indifferent for those people who live in other belief systems, because only one real world exists. Different possible worlds are interexistent through their interrelated real world transformations.

Different dissolutions the Man & World problem are natural and necessary. But it does not mean that we accept the doctrine of philosophical relativism. We do not think that all belief systems are equally right or equally false. In our opinion the *healthy plurality* of belief systems and possible worlds means that all belief systems and possible worlds which are able to satisfy certain basic value-criteria have equal rights to being.

TABLE 1: Western versus Buddhist economics according to Man & World problem

|  | Western economics | Buddhist economics |
|---|---|---|
| (α) Man's attitude toward Nature | aggressive attitude toward Nature, Man's domination over it | non-violent attitude toward Nature, Man's accommodation to it |
| (β) type of Man's consumption | hedonistic consumption | restricted consumption |
| (γ) relationship between Man and Society | individualism | collectivism |
| (δ) ethical motive of Man's economic activity | selfishness | altruism |

We would like to propose two *discriminational criteria* to evaluate belief systems and possible worlds. We think that a certain dissolution the Man & World problem *must be human centered* and *must not be counter-ecological*. We are sure it would be indispensable that people who live in different belief systems and possible worlds accept 'being human centered' and 'being not counter-ecological' as absolute and unquestionable values.

We think that the *axiological* and *evaluational approach* of belief systems and possible worlds is right and fruitful. First of all, it needs axiological studies which define the above-proposed fundamental values, both conceptually and operationally. Secondly, it needs evaluational studies which are complex evaluations of different belief systems and possible worlds in themselves and in their past and future changing processes. We think that the main features of the current belief systems and possible worlds of humankind is not enough human centered and/or is rather counter-ecological. We cannot imagine that it would be possible to create or establish some new belief systems and possible worlds for humankind. In our opinion, instead of this, we need to try to *transform* or to *change* the current belief systems and possible worlds of humankind toward their *more human centered* and *less counter-ecological versions*.

How to dissolve these problems might be challenging for IIASA as well.

## REFERENCES

EHRLICH, P.R. and EHRLICH, A.N. 1972: *Population, Resources, Environment*. W.H. Freeman and Company, San Francisco, U.S.A.

FROMM, E. 1976: *To Have or To Be?* Happer & Row, Publishers, New York, U.S.A.

LASZLO, E. 1978: *The Inner Limits of Mankind*. Pergamon Press, Oxford, U.K.

LEWIS, D. 1973: *Counterfactuals*. Harvard Univ. Press, Cambridge, Mass.

MARKLEY, O.W. and HARMAN, W.W. (eds.) 1982: *Changing Images of Man*. Pergamon Press, Oxford, U.K.

ORTEGA Y GASSET, J. 1963: "History as a System", in: R. Klibansky and H.J. Paton (eds.): *Philosophy and History*. Harper & Row, Publishers, New York, U.S.A.

SCHUMACHER, E.F. 1973: *Small is Beautiful*. Abacus.

# RATIONALITY AND EQUIVALENT REDESCRIPTIONS

Douglas Maclean
*Center for Philosophy and Public Policy, University of Maryland,
College Park, Maryland, USA*

## I

In an essay on risk perception, Kenneth Arrow writes: "The concept of rationality has been basic to most economic analysis."[1] Arrow has a specific conception of rationality in mind, a major implication of which is the expected utility hypothesis. This hypothesis says that a rational individual assesses alternative choices in terms of expected utility -- the aggregated, probability-weighted utilities of each alternative's possible consequences -- and then chooses the alternative that maximizes this amount.

The theory expressing this conception of rationality traditionally has been regarded as both a theory that explains human behavior and one that can help guide and correct it, a theory that is both predictive and normative. The history of the subject reflects strong reasons why the theory of choice should have this dual character. As James March points out, "For a variety of historical reasons, ... [w]hether one considers ideas about choice in economics, psychology, political science, sociology, or philosophy, behavioral and normative theories have developed as a dialectic rather than as separate domains."[2]

A normative theory of choice gains credibility from its predictive and explanatory power, for although empirical success itself may not constitute much of a normative argument, the theory of rational behavior is less likely to be found objectionable if rationality turns out to be widespread. The theory could then be interpreted as an idealization of common behavior. But if, on the other hand, the normative theory turns out to be incompatible with the best established behavioral theory, then the verification of the normative theory will depend entirely on the intrinsic plausibility of its axioms, and that appeal must be quite strong, strong enough to make us overcome our charitable reluctance to conclude that our actual behavior is systematically irrational.

I will argue that the conception of rationality that Arrow claims to be basic to economics is on shaky ground. The normative status of the utility axioms has never been entirely above suspicion, primarily because these axioms generate some well-known paradoxes. They prescribe certain choices, that is, which seem to fly in the face of

intuition and common sense.  Recently, moreover, the predictive claims
of utility theory have come under strong attack.  Tversky, Kahneman,
and other psychologists have carefully studied actual choice behavior,
and their findings show rather conclusively that people violate the expected utility hypothesis frequently in systematic ways, and often in
quite simple choice situations.[3]  People do not maximize expected utility; they do not act as if they were maximizing expected utility; and
when their deviant behavior in the light of the theory is explained to
them, most people stick to their choices and reject the axioms.[4]  Apparently, as Paul Samuelson once put it, most people choose to satisfy
their preferences and "let the axioms satisfy themselves."[5]  This research opens the door for competing behavioral theories to explain risk
perception and decision making.  From psychology we now have prospect
theory,[6] and from anthropology a cultural theory,[7] both of them incompatible with expected utility theory and making plausible claims to
being predictively superior to it.

We appear to be at an interesting juncture in the historical dialectic of theories of choice.  The behavioral and the normative have
come apart.

## II

If we assume that expected utility theory cannot draw support by
claiming explanatory or predictive powers, then the burden of proof is
squarely on the shoulders of those who defend the theory as a normative
account of rationality.  The weak link in the theory is well known, so
I can describe it briefly.  Then I will consider three attempts to defend the theory and explain why they do not succeed.

The axioms of expected utility theory can be thought of as expressing three assumptions about rational preferences over risky prospects.  The first, completeness, says that all alternatives can be compared and ordered.  The second is a consistency assumption, which includes transitivity of preferences.  Neither of these assumptions is
trivial, and I believe that the objections several philosophers have
made to completeness, which implies that a rational person cannot have
incommensurable values, especially deserve more attention than they
have received.[8]

But all the attention has been focused on independence, the
third assumption.  The importance of the independence assumption
(which is usually defined by more than one axiom, in Luce and Raiffa's
system, for example, by independence and substitutivity together)
can be expressed in different ways.  It implies, for instance,

that a rational person's preferences are strongly separable, in the sense that if he is indifferent to any two outcomes or prospects, then his preferences will not be affected when one is substituted for the other in any decision problem. The assumption implies that all redescriptions of a decision problem that preserve the same opportunity set -- the same set of alternative choices over probabilities and outcomes -- are equivalent and will not affect the ordering of a rational person's preferences. Most generally, perhaps, the independence assumption conceives of rationality as an orientation toward alternative choices that is independent of the contexts in which the alternatives present themselves.

The most famous paradox generated by the independence assumption was first published by Maurice Allais in 1953.[9] It has been reproduced in many variations. The following example of the paradox, I think, presents it in a way that shows most dramatically how the independence assumption can conflict with common intuitions.[10] It consists of two choices involving Russian roulette with a six-shooter. In the first case, you are playing with four bullets in the chamber, and you are asked how much you would pay to have one bullet removed. How much would you pay, that is, to reduce your risk of dying by 1/6, from 2/3 to 1/2? (Assume that you can leave no inheritance if you die.) In the second choice situation, you are playing Russian roulette with two bullets in the chamber, and you are asked how much you would pay to have them both removed. How much would it be worth to you to eliminate altogether a 1/3 risk of dying?

Many people, including those of us who are skeptical about whether expressions of willingness-to-pay in such cooked up examples mean anything at all, nevertheless feel pretty confident that removing two bullets and eliminating the risk is worth a lot more than removing just one of four bullets and reducing the risk. But according to expected utility theory, we are being irrational if we feel this way. Surprisingly, the independence assumption implies that we should be willing to pay exactly the same in both cases, because they are equivalent. How would somebody defend a rationality condition with such counter-intuitive implications? How does the argument go? Let us see, as we turn now to consider the first defense of the independence assumption and expected utility theory.

## III

The first argument was originally produced by Howard Raiffa and has been repeated recently by David Lewis.[11] It claims that the two Russian roulette cases can be shown to involve the same decision problem -- that is, the same prospects or opportunity set -- in different contexts. Once you see the problem separated from the different contexts (eliminating the "irrelevant alternatives"), you will see the equivalence and be forced to bring your preferences in line, by agreeing that you should pay the same amount to remove, in the one case, one bullet, and in the other case, two.

Thus, we can redescribe the cases in the following manner, without changing the overall prospects. Think of both Russian roulette games as being played with two six-shooters, not one, which will be fired successively. (Make the time interval between firings short enough so as not to introduce different anxiety or dread factors.) The chamber of the first six-shooter contains either no bullets or three. You have no control over this. We can think of this six-shooter as giving us the context of our decision problem, for it determines an element of risk that is outside the scope of alternative choices. The second revolver has two bullets in the chamber, and you must decide how much you would pay, if you survive the first stage of the game, to remove the two bullets.

The defense of independence now takes the following form. It should make no difference to you whether you make your decision before the first trigger is pulled or afterward. Whether that revolver has three bullets or none in its chamber, therefore, should not influence your choice. But if there are three bullets, the problem is identical to the first case (you are paying to reduce a 2/3 risk of death to 1/2), while if there are no bullets, it is identical to the second (you are paying to remove a 1/3 risk of death). Hence it is rational to regard them as the same problem.

Now, I do not find this argument at all convincing. To be sure, your overall prospects of survival are unaffected by the timing of your choice, but the appropriate description of your decision can change. One perspective opens up the possibility of acting to remove the risk, a possibility that is unavailable from the other choice perspectives. These possibilities, moreover, are relevant to some reasons for acting or choosing, though not, of course, to other reasons. For example, they do not affect the reasons that derive from our interest in surviving (or, in purely monetary versions of the example, from our interest in wealth), but they are relevant to how we explain ourselves to others and to the justification of their judgments of us. Where the risk involves a loss of something other than life, these perspective-relative differences are also important in determining the feelings of regret, elation, disappointment, and so on, that we can expect to have afterwards. It would be unreasonable to ignore any of these factors. In such ways, therefore, the context or perspective of choice partly determines the nature of our acts.

The presence of the first six-shooter in the redescription of the decision problem might serve to remind us that even if we remove a particular risk, we can never remove our risks altogether. Whenever we decide to pay to remove two bullets, other guns might, for all we know, be pointed at our heads. For that matter, I might survive the game only to be run over by a truck on my way home. These are risks, to be sure, but for certain purposes they simply do not matter. We would not be blamed, for instance, for suffering consequences like these. Nor could we be held responsible for them. Our responsibilities and duties, not to mention our reactions and feelings, do not exactly follow the contours of overall changes in risk prospects, but they are central to our reasons for acting and the reasons we give by way of explaining ourselves.

If we are rational, then, we will often have to take into account much more than overall prospects or expected utilities. Sometimes this can lead us not to take up some more detached or context-independent perspective on a problem but to appreciate instead the implications of having the perspective we find ourselves naturally to have. Some redescriptions of a choice situation, then, although equivalent in the sense of not altering the probabilities or outcomes, will nevertheless have to be rejected for social or moral or even psychological reasons, because they are inappropriate or they distort the problem.

Whether we are winning or losing can be more important than where we end up. I might gain a windfall and then gamble it away; or I might have my wallet stolen and then win back what I lost in the lottery. The result is the same, but of course there is all the difference in the world. The ordering of events will determine my own reactions, and it will justify different judgments about me that others might make. Why do men and women who have "made it" in capitalist societies so frequently continue to drive themselves hard well into old age? It seems reasonable to suppose that they have discovered that winning can be much more satisfying than wealth.

Perspective is also a determinant of responsibility. What might be good reasons to want something to happen may not provide a person with a good reason to act to bring it about. Thus, we might know that the world would be a better place if some person were dead and that killing him is the only likely way to make him dead soon, yet knowing this does not necessarily give any of us a good reason to kill him. This shows how reasons can change with the mere shifting of perspective, a shift that does not alter anything about what economists call "the opportunity set."

One of the paradoxes of deterrence also trades on this shift. We would, of course, most prefer worlds where deterrence is not necessary, but next best are the worlds where deterrence works. So we might all have reasons to want among us a credible threatener, and this could mean that we need a person who is known to be morally unscrupulous, who will carry out punishment even when no good can come of it. But though all of us might endorse such reasoning in the abstract, or from a detached perspective, none of us might be able to apply it, because our reasons for acting do not permit the cultivation of an amoral character. This paradox of deterrence is generated by the inability of either perspective rationally to dominate the other. Examples like these, which show the importance of shifting perspectives, merely illustrate a point made by Tversky and Kahneman, that "the adoption of a decision frame is an ethically significant act."[12]

The argument for the independence assumption amounts to identifying rationality with a detached point of view, one that sees things sub specie aeternatatis. It looks at choices in a timeless and contextless way. Detachment often begets greater wisdom and knowledge, of course, but we cannot entirely identify rationality with that point of view. We have our own reactions also to consider, and our relationships to others and to their judgments. We have our moral responsibilities, and most important, we have to be able to identify ourselves with our choices. A complete account of rationality, then, will not be the same as a detached one, for as the philosopher Thomas Nagel observes, "Each of us is not only an objective self, but a particular person with a particular perspective; we act in the world with that perspective, and not only from the point of view of a detached will, selecting and rejecting world-states."[13]

## IV

The second argument defends the independence assumption by drawing analogies to logical extensionality and to visual perception. Arrow claims, "A fundamental element of rationality, so elementary that we hardly notice it is, in logicians' language, its extensionality."[14] His explanation of how rationality is extensional is, unfortunately, quite brief. He says only that rational choice "depends on the opportunity set from which the choice is made, independently of how that set is described."[15] Tversky and Kahneman, who demonstrate how the framing of choices determines preferences, suggest a similar analogy to visual perspective. They write: "Veridical perception requires that the perceived relative height of two neighboring mountains, say, should not reverse with changes of vantage point. Similarly, rational choice requires that preferences between options should not reverse with changes of frame."[16]

References to opportunity sets and analogies to vision notwithstanding, it is not at all clear what it means to compare rationality with veridical perception or to call it extensional. Mountains exist independently of viewers, and the truth about relative mountain heights can be ascertained independently of perceptions and vantage points. Thus, the truth of 'A is taller than B' is logically independent of the truth of sentences like 'S believes that A is taller than B' or 'From this perspective it appears that A is taller than B.' In these latter sentences, 'A is taller than B' appears in non-extensional contexts, i.e., contexts in which the substitution of logically equivalent propositions is not truth-preserving. The criterion for veridical perception, therefore, is that 'It appears that A is taller than B' is true only if A _is_ taller than B. Mountains, that is to say, have an extension that is independent of and determines the truth of viewers' perceptions of their heights.

How are we supposed to apply this analogy to rational choice? Should we say, perhaps, that a preference for A over B is rational only if, in some sense that is objective and independent of choosers, A is better than B? That might make the analogy work, but decision theorists tend to be fiercely agnostic about such normative judgments, opting instead for preferential sovereignty. Besides, as our previous discussion suggests, any satisfactory objective normative analysis of rationality would have to include contextual elements. So it looks like this argument turns in a very small circle.

What the extensionalists must have in mind is something like this.
Two different descriptions are extensionally equivalent or are descriptions of the same problem if we can all agree upon reflection that they
describe the same set of choices.  And, of course, if they do describe
the same choices, then rationality requires that we make the same decision in each case.  But we can only hope that arguments about rationality will result in such agreement; it cannot be assumed as the
basis of those arguments.  The empirical data showing that most people
violate the independence assumption in systematic ways strongly suggest
that what counts as a redescription and what counts as changing the
problem is the central issue.  By assuming independence, then, the extensionality argument for rationality begs the question.

V

The third argument I will take up defends expected utility theory
by putting forward a modified account of it that attempts to avoid these
objections.[17]  Instead of rejecting the familiar behavior that deviates
from expected utility theory, the strategy of this argument is to modify
the theory to model that behavior more closely.  It gives up the assumption that people do or ought to choose solely to maximize the expected
utility of outcomes, by adding an attribute to the utility function that
measures the regret or delight people feel in having made the choices
they made.

Regret theory, as this new-fangled decision theory is called, wea-
kens the independence assumption by limiting the possible equivalent
redescriptions of a decision problem.  No longer is indifference assumed
to hold over the same expected outcomes.  In the revised theory, it also
matters what one gains or loses, or what one gives up to get there.  Regret theory assumes people are made happy or sad not only by what they
receive, but also by the choices they make.  This regret factor is
measured as the difference in utility between what a person gets as a
result of her choice and what she would have gotten, had she chosen
differently.

The primary motive behind regret theory is to modify utility theory
in order to make it a better behavioral or explanatory theory of human
choice.  The appearance of regret theory serves to confirm March's observation about the historical dialectic between the behavioral and the
normative.  As the empirical evidence against utility theory adds up,
the pressure to modify the theory is felt.  Normative theories of

rational choice do not stand up well against our behavior. I do not mean to suggest that regret theorists have all made a radical break with tradition. They are modifying utility theory, not abandoning it. Some regret theorists resist adopting regret theory as a normative theory of choice. They maintain a certain skepticism about the behavior they are trying to model, calling it, for instance, "normal, if not economically rational."[18] They may not be willing to concede yet that anything other than consequences ought to be a source of utility or a reason for acting.

Regret theory is more interesting, however, if we also take it as a normative theory of rationality. For one thing, it incorporates some features of the context of choice, which I claim is a good thing to do. Regret and delight are measured from the reference point of a decision maker, which means that the perspective from which choices are made is, to some extent at least, being taken into account. Moreover, regret theory resolves some of the paradoxes of utility theory that directly challenge the independence assumption, including Allais's paradox. Nevertheless, regret theory does not fully succeed in the end, even as a descriptive theory.

We can best see this by comparing regret theory with Tversky and Kahneman's prospect theory. Prospect theory explains the pervasive and systematic -- and, on expected utility theory, paradoxical -- features of how people perceive risk and make decisions in a way that is incompatible with utility theory. Prospect theory makes three basic claims about risk perception and the psychology of choice. One is about how people assign decision weights or probabilities to risky prospects. We will ignore that part of the theory here. The other two claims bear directly on the role of context or perspective. First, people evaluate prospects not in terms of assets or independently described consequences, but as gains and losses, and they evaluate gains and losses differently. They show risk aversion toward perceived gains and risk-seeking behavior to avoid losses. This is the part of prospect theory that regret theory can model.

But prospect theory makes another claim, about the determination of the neutral reference point from which gains and losses are measured. A central claim of prospect theory is that the reference point is determined not by the prospects but by how the prospects are framed or described. Regret theory must assume that this point can be determined by the prospects alone, and it usually assumes that the reference point

is the decision maker's asset position at the time of choice. The framing phenomenon turns out to be an essential component of the psychology
of choice which cannot be captured by regret theory or, so far as I can
see, by any modificaiton of expected utility theory.

VI

Tversky and Kahneman are quite concerned about the framing that is
confirmed by their research, especially, as they claim, the ease with
which decision frames can be manipulated by alternative redescriptions
of a problem, causing people to take up different perspectives from which
they view gains and losses. This is why Tversky and Kahneman embrace
extensionality as a requirement of rationality. The arbitrariness of
decision frames, they believe, is a major source of preference rever-
sals and other sorts of irrational decisions.

It is undeniable that decision frames can often be manipulated, as
advertising and public relations experts are well aware. But I believe
we must be cautious about how we generalize about human thinking processes from decision experiments carried on in the artificial settings
of psychological laboratories. In the real world, all sorts of factors
help to determine a person's perspective or decision frame, and many of
these factors might be defensible and non-arbitrary. One of the central problems for decision theorists in the future, I would think, would
be to sort out differences in the framing phenomena and to ask which
heuristics, descriptions, and other factors that cause people to take
up the perspectives they do are reasonable, and which ones are arbitrary and manipulable. Making this distinction will help us understand
better the division between rational and nonrational decisions.

There is much work to be done, then, but I don't see this kind of
work coming out of the tradition of classical utility theory. I expect,
rather, that it is more likely to emerge from research into decision
making and risk perception that looks explicitly at the contextual determinants of choice perspectives. This means looking further into the
nature and reasonableness of reactive attitudes, such as regret, disappointment, and delight, but also looking more at the social determinants of perspective, including shared meanings and values. We might
well expect, therefore, that the next breakthroughs in decision theory
will come from the social sciences that begin with the assumption that
contextual features determine a person's decision frame and what count
as reasons from that perspective, and that reasons are tied as much to
the concrete peculiarities of social values and social interactions as
to concepts like utility and asset positions.

REFERENCES

1.  Kenneth Arrow, "Risk Perception in Psychology and Economics,"
    Economic Inquiry 20 (1982), p. 1.

2.  James March, "Bounded Rationality, Ambiguity, and the Engineering
    of Choice," The Bell Journal of Economics 9 (1978), p. 588.

3.  For a description of these violations, see Amos Tversky and Daniel
    Kahneman, "The Framing of Decisions and the Psychology of Choice,"
    Science 211 (January 30, 1981), pp. 453-58; also, Kahneman and
    Tversky, "The Psychology of Preferences," Scientific American
    246 (January 1982), pp. 160-71.

4.  Paul Slovic and Amos Tversky, "Who Accepts Savage's Axioms?"
    Behavioral Science 19 (1974), pp. 363-73; and K. R. MacCrimmon
    and S. Larsson, "Utility Theory:  Axioms versus 'Paradoxes',"
    Expected Utility Hypotheses and the Allais Paradox, ed. M.
    Allais and O. Hagen (Dodrecht:  Reidel, 1979), pp. 333-409.

5.  Paul Samuelson, "Probability and the Attempts to Measure Utility,"
    The Economic Review 1 (1950), p. 167

6.  Daniel Kahneman and Amos Tversky, "Prospect Theory," Econometrica
    47 (1979), pp. 263-91.

7.  Mary Douglas, "Cultural Bias," in In the Active Voice (London:
    Routledge & Kegan Paul, 1982); and Michael Thompson, "An Outline
    of the Cultural Theory of Risk," IIASA Working Paper WP-80-177
    (Laxenburg, Austria, 1980).

8.  See Charles Taylor, "The Diversity of Goods," in Utilitarianism
    and Beyond, ed. A. Sen and B. Williams (Cambridge:  Cambridge
    University Press, 1982), pp. 129-44; Stuart Hampshire, Morality
    and Conflict (Cambridge, Massachusetts:  Harvard University Press,
    1984); and Ian Hacking, "Hume's Species of Probability," Philo-
    sophical Studies 33 (1978), pp. 21-37.

9.  Maurice Allais, "Le Comportement de l'Homme Rationnel devant le
    Risque:  Critique des Postulates et Axiommes de l'Ecole Ameri-
    caine," Econometrica 21 (1953), pp. 503-46.

10. I first encountered this version in David Lewis, "Russian Roulette,"
    (1984), unpublished mimeo.  He attributes it to Allan Gibbard.

11. Howard Raiffa, Decision Analysis (Reading, Massachusetts:  Addison-
    Wesley, 1968), pp. 80-86.  Lewis, "Russian Roulette."

12. Tversky and Kahneman, "The Framing of Decisions and the Psychology
    of Choice," p. 458.

13. Thomas Nagel, "The Limits of Objectivity," The Tanner Lectures
    on Human Values, Volume 1, ed. S. McMurrin (Salt Lake City: Uni-
    versity of Utah Press, 1980), pp. 134-35.

14. Arrow, "Risk Perception in Psychology and Economics," p. 6.

15. Ibid.

16. Kahneman and Tversky, "The Framing of Decisions and the Psychology of Choice," p. 453.

17. See, for example, David Bell, "Regret in Decision Making Under Uncertainty," Operations Research 30 (1982), pp. 961-81; Peter Fishburn, "Normative Theories of Rationality Under Risk and Under Uncertainty," Bell Laboratories, June 1983; and Mark Machina, "'Expected Utility' Analysis Without the Independence Axiom," Econometrica 50 (1981), pp. 297-323.

18. Bell, "Regret in Decision Making Under Uncertainty," p. 962.

# II.  FRAMEWORKS FOR RATIONAL DECISION MAKING

# INTRODUCTION

This section presents a group of papers that discuss existing formal frameworks for rational decision making. Two of them are not available for the Proceedings: a paper by James Vaupel on the classical prescriptive framework, and a paper *The program- and goal-oriented approach to management: recent developments, perspectives and applications to urban planning practice* by Victor Volkovich, Yuri Dubov and Alexander Schepkin. The second paper would have been of particular interest because it represents a specific formal framework for decision making motivated by the culture of planning and developed mathematically by Glushkov, Pospelov, Irikov and others for over a decade. It is markedly different from both the classical utility maximization framework and the bounded rationality and satisficing framework. However, some brief comments on this framework are given in the paper by Wierzbicki.

This group of papers was followed by a plenary discussion. The main result of the discussion was the agreement that the different axioms underlying the various formal frameworks of rationality are the results of a holistic and intuitive abstraction of deeply rooted basic values characterizing the various cultures. These should therefore be re-examined and re-evaluated from a broader comparative perspective. In other words, the very concept of rational action is not value-free and must be re-interpreted as we move from one cultural setting to another. The paradoxes that result from any formal framework for rational decision making fall into two groups. One group comprises the paradoxes that point to deficiencies of the theory or axioms within a given culture; the other group comprises the paradoxes that point to inconsistencies in the basic values of the culture itself. From this perspective, it becomes clear that the time is ripe for a much broader investigation of the premises of rational decision making.

In the first paper in this group, *Back from prospect theory to utility theory*, Raiffa makes a spirited defense of the framework of expected utility maximization. Given its cultural background, the expected utility theory is one of the most advanced formal frameworks for rational decision making. Thus to abandon it would be to write off a large intellectual investment and we should think rather about the possibilities for more sophisticated use and for constructive ways of extending it, for example, by including the impact of context in some more formal way. But if these possibilities turn out to be empty then abandon it we must. On the other hand, the discussions at the meeting have shown that it would be sensible to abandon the concept of the "normative" character of expected utility theory (a better word, suggested by Raiffa, is "abstractive"). Since the axioms of any formal framework are culturally conditioned, giving them a "normative" character implies a strong value judgement indeed. For example, the axiom of independence (of irrelevant alternatives, of reformulation, of context) implies a very individualistic stance and would not fit comfortably into Hindu culture, say, where categories of humankind and their interdependencies predominate.

The paper by Wierzbicki, *Negotiation and mediation in conflicts. II: Plural rationality and interactive decision processes*, considers the question of how we can expect agreements to be reached in cross-cultural negotiations if the parties involved have widely differing cultural and abstractive perceptions of rationality. A number of principles, including the principle of limited knowledge and interactive learning, and the principle of cultural respect, are put forward as a means of dealing with this issue. An extended formal framework for rational decision making (including some aspects of utility maximization, bounded rationality and satisficing, and goal- and program-oriented management) called the *quasi-satisficing framework* is also proposed.

Discussions about this paper at the meeting centered on the issue of conflict escalation in repetitive games with multiequilibria outcomes. Here quasi-satisficing selections of these equilibria made by players guided by adaptively formed aspiration levels may be incompatible with each other, leading to conflict escalation.

The paper *On the structure, stabilization and accuracy of decision processes* by Tietz describes recent developments in the behaviorally-oriented, bounded rationality and satisficing framework. The paper analyzes a decision process, stressing the roles of goal- and aspiration-setting, satisficing behavior in the selection of decision rules and the stability aspects of such processes, and finally turns to the question of accuracy in aspiration-based decision theory.

Some of the concepts discussed in this paper were drawn on in later parts of the meeting, particularly in the interactive decision support and experimental sessions.

The paper *Uses of experimental games* by Rapoport discusses the intricacies of the "social traps" that can result from certain variants of simple two-person games. The analysis of such social traps shows that formalized individualistic minimizing rationality cannot be defended in any situation more complex than a zero-sum game; formalized collective rationality gives quite different, and typically superior, prescriptions of behavior in such situations. Several games (such as Prisoner's Dilemma, Chicken, Top-dog - Underdog, and even some apparently conflict-free games) illustrate the differences between formalized individualistic and collective rationalities. Experimental results show that on average about 50% of players are "individualists", who would exploit the other side's cooperative behavior, and about 50% are "collectivists", who would nevertheless try to cooperate. This is true even for players who come from cultures generally regarded as individualistic. A specific "non-naive" cooperative strategy with swift retaliations for noncooperation (called "Tit-for-tat" and devised earlier by Rapoport for repetitive Prisoner's Dilemma games) has proven to be very successful in many experiments, including computer tournaments. It succeeds, not because it can beat a consciously noncooperative strategy, but because noncooperative strategies lose more by beating each other. From several such examples, Rapoport suggests that experimental games may have a high educational value by illuminating the possible consequences of individualistic and collectivist attitudes in situations that involve social traps.

For instance, in the discussions it became apparent that the principle of "strength through weakness" that emerges from these repetitive experimental games comes close to a basic principle that is recognized as evolutionarily advantageous in most societies: the best self-serving behavior in the long term is "non-naive" altruism. This principle, though common knowledge in everyday life, seems to have got squeezed out of international relations. Many participants were in favor of somehow putting it back in again.

M. Thompson
A. Wierzbicki

# BACK FROM PROSPECT THEORY TO UTILITY THEORY

Howard Raiffa
*Littauer Center, J.F. Kennedy School of Government, Harvard University,*
*Cambridge, Massachusetts, USA*

## The Empirical Reality:  What to Do About It?

People, both smart and dumb, often do not behave the way normative theorists say they should behave.  But what is even more frustrating, some (otherwise) smart people, who know how they should behave according to some impeccably beautiful normative theory, like the maximization of subjective expected utility (SEU) -- you can clearly see my biases -- nevertheless, do not always follow those guidelines.

Well, what should we do about this state of affairs if we want to help people make better, wiser decisions?  We can:

(a)   Abandon the (normative) theory (heaven forbid!)

(b)   Modify the theory.

(c)   Apply the theory in a more sophisticated manner.

(d)   Give therapy to deviators.

There are lots of researchers who gleefully want to do (a) and (b).  In this paper I shall concentrate on (c) and (d).  But some commentators who have already heard what I am about to tell you have opined that my suggestions for (c) really are tantamount to embracing (b) and advocating (a).  That's going too far!

Back in the 1950s when someone like Allais or Ellsberg concocted an ingenious example that showed that people violated the fundamental axioms of the SEU theory, I exploited such observations.  I argued that if people, in making intuitive choices, always satisfied the norms of the SEU theory, then there would be no *raison d'être* for teaching people how to choose wisely.  Just do what comes naturally!  The trouble is that after I had my say, some misguided souls still did not see the light.  There are lots of people who fully understand the normative ideas of SEU analysis but who refuse to adopt these principles in their own important decision making.  In short what I am going to argue is that in some cases some important psychological concerns of the decision makers are inappropriately ignored and these concerns should be addres-

---

* I am indebted to my· colleague, Professor David Bell, for many insight-
  ful comments that have been incorporated in this paper.

sed openly.  But also I am going to argue that sometimes therapy is the appropriate remedy.

## Some Examples Where Deviations Should Not be Tolerated

Many behavioral decision theorists that I know who really want to abandon the SEU theory would nevertheless join me in labelling certain behavior really "irrational."  The examples I have in mind have to do mostly with the probabilistic side of the ledger.  Let me illustrate a few of these.  There are gambler's fallacies:  the dice are running hot and I am now on a lucky streak; or, I better quit now while I am ahead or the law of averages will catch up with me; or, a social bridge player will graciously give up his or her hot seat to some forlorn player who has been doing miserably.  In such cases we invoke the wise observation that "a die hath neither memory nor conscience."  But it is not easy to teach this lesson.  A lot of people are swayed intellectually by such rational interventions but emotionally they feel, deep down, that these dice are in fact friendly or unfriendly.

Some other examples:  Subjects will often assign a higher probability to the joint event (A and B) than to A alone, the so-called conjunction fallacy.  Most serious observers agree, that's just an oversight or error.  There are loads of examples where there is confusion about conditionality: $P(A|B)$ is mistaken for $P(B|A)$.  An expert is asked for an assessment of A given B, and he thinks about all those cases where A prevails and reflects about what proportion are B's.  We fail students in exams for such behavior.  We don't modify the theory.  People forget about base rates in assessing probabilities.  People employ strange heuristics in updating probabilities, like: How can you infer anything about a population of 220 million from a random sample of 1000?  We apply educational therapy in such cases and we are sparse in giving recommendations to those for whom the therapy does not take hold.

## Some Examples Where Deviations are Sometimes Tolerated

But now let's move a bit towards a murkier area.  Mr. Jones prefers A to B, B to C, and insists that he prefers C to A -- an intransitivity.  Such actions can be rationalized.  But should they be tolerated and should normative theories be amended to accommodate such behavior?  Mrs. Smith prefers A to C, prefers B to C, but can not make up her mind between A and B, and therefore chooses C.  Mr. Henry prefers the freedom to choose an alternative from the set {A,B} rather than from the set {A,B,C}.  If one is worried about reversing oneself later on, we might arbitrarily restrict one's later choices.  These examples seem to contradict the rational tenets of most willful-choice theories but by reconfiguring the consequences, by adding in effort of analysis and search costs, such behavior can be accommodated in normative theories. But the question is: how far should we go?

## Prospect Theory

Kahneman and Tversky (K & T, henceforth) in their paper, "Prospect Theory: An Analysis of Decision Under Risk," brilliantly portray what's wrong with the SEU theory as a *descriptive* or predictive theory. They systematically codify behavioral departures from the normative SEU model. I have replicated many of their experiments with my own students and I obtain similar and sometimes even more dramatic departures from normative theory.

At the Harvard Business School my colleagues and I train -- better yet, we indoctrinate -- all students how to use the (prescriptive) theory of utility to make managerial decisions. If our students were to be subjects in the K & T experiments, then their responses, we believe, would strongly depend on the setting of the experiment: if administered in the course where they had been taught (brainwashed (?)) utility theory, they would not exhibit the inconsistencies of K & T subjects; if, however, the experiment were slightly masked and it were given in a course in marketing or finance, then we suspect that these very students would be prey to the same inconsistencies as the K & T subjects. This is a painful admission to make. It doesn't mean that we are wrong in trying to influence our students how to think about risky choice, but that we do not do a good enough job in getting them to think about fundamentals. We teach them to use utility theory in too mechanistic a fashion and if they do not use the formalism they do not think hard enough about their choices.

I now would like to discuss some informal attempts I have made to get subjects to change their minds or to think more deeply about choices they have made that are inconsistent with SEU theory. In some cases my therapeutic interventions have convinced some of these subjects that they have made choices that are not appropriate for their deeply held basic feelings and they actually reverse some choices. In other cases, all I succeed in doing is making some subjects uncomfortable. Who says therapy is easy. In other cases, I conclude that the subjects are right in registering so-called inconsistencies, and the theory is wrong or that the theory is being applied in too gross and insensitive a manner.

## Illustration 1

The subjects of the K & T experiments were Israelis and the payoffs were in Israeli pounds. When I discuss these problems I'll talk about dollars instead.  I am convinced that non-indoctrinated U.S. students (with dollar payoffs) behave roughly the same.

K & T start out by contrasting behavior in two choice problems:

Problem 1:    Choose between

$2500 with probability  .33
A:  $2400 with probability  .66    B:  $2400 for certain
$0 with probability  .01
                          1.00

N = 72      (18%)                              (82%)

(The last line means: of 72 subjects, 18% chose A over B and 82% chose B over A.)

Problem 2:    Choose between

C:  $2500 with probability  .33      D:  $2400 with probability  .34
    $0 with probability  .67             $0 with probability  .66
                      1.00                                 1.00

N = 72      (83%)                              (17%)

Both problems involve the same payoffs: $0, $2400 and $2500.  If the subjects were to use utility theory -- which they did not -- then there is no loss of generality if we let u($0) = 0, u($2500) =1 and u($2400) = x where $0 \le x \le 1$.  It is not difficult to see that*:

if x < 33/34  then  A < B  and  C < D
if x > 33/34  then  A > B  and  C > D
if x = 33/34  then  A ~ B  and  C ~ D.

So we see that the majority choice of A < B and C > D is inconsistent with utility theory.  Some would now say, "So much the worse for utility theory."  But wait!  Now let us think hard about problem 1.

Most subjects I imagine choose B because with B that $2400 is certain (and certainty is lovely if it involves a sure gain) and with A they risk not getting that $2400;  furthermore $2500 is so close to $2400 that $2400 and $2500 are practically the same.  In debriefing sessions I might ask a subject: "What would happen if B were held fixed and A were modified by pushing the upper prize up from $2500 to $2600 to $2700 ... to $3000 ... to $4800 to ... ."  By doing this I would want the subject to concentrate attention on the difference between $2400 and $2500.  I might ask: "Would you feel differently if in A you had a choice between a prize of $2500 or a prize of $2400 plus a $100

---

* A < B is read: "A is less preferred than B."  And so on for > and ~.

gift certificate in a store you could designate?" The purpose of this line of questioning is to focus attention on the difference between $2400 and $2500.

For those that would pick B over A I might ask: "Would you still pick B if the probabilities in A were changed from (.33, .66, .01) to (.333, .666, .001) or to (.3333, .6666, .0001)? Have you thought hard enough about the probabilities .33 and .01?" By this line of questioning, I am not in any way arguing that it is wrong to choose B over A but that first impulses should be checked when there is a certainty on one side and an uncertainty on the other side.

I would continue my probing. Let's put in an urn 100 balls that are all labelled with $2400 and let's suppose that 66 are green and 34 are orange. Imagine that you are going to pick one ball at random. Now in problem 1 the question is whether you would be willing to relabel those orange balls by adding $100 to 33 of them and subtracting $2400 from one of them. Certainly this choice should depend on the number of orange balls, but should your choice in any way depend on the number of green balls? If not, is not the essence of the problem the same to you if we get rid of those green balls altogether? This line of attack is designed to get you to think about what the essence of your choice problem really is.

Now let's go back to the urn with 34 orange balls, each labelled $2400 and now let's label the 66 green balls with the value $0 instead of $2400. Now we ask about modifications of the 34 orange balls. In the choice between C and D you are asked whether you would be willing to add $100 to 33 of the orange balls and subtract $2400 from 1 orange ball. This is the exact same modification you were asked to consider before but now the 66 green balls are labelled $0 instead of $2400. In this case does the problem depend on the number of green balls? If not, you can get rid of those distracting green balls as before and the essence is: would you be willing to modify the 34 orange balls as proposed?

If we have an urn with 34 orange balls and some green balls, then K & T have shown that it is important to most subjects to know something about the number and prizes on the green balls in judging proposed modifications of the orange balls. That's strange. Why does this happen? I think for some subjects it has to do with regret. Suppose you, the reader, are the subject. If you choose C and get $0, then you do not have much regret because D could also have yielded a $0 prize. Let's examine this more closely. Suppose C were conducted with 33 orange balls labelled $2500, one striped orange ball labelled $0 and 66 green balls labelled $0. If now you drew the striped ball, you would know

that the choice of D would have produced $2400. How would you feel
now?

A subject might respond, "When you offered me the choice between
C and D there were no colored balls. If I chose C and got a $0-ball I
would be unhappy but I would not feel regret. I suppose that I would
feel regret if you colored the balls and I happened to pick the striped
orange ball. But still not as much regret as if I got the $0 prize in
choice A."

I think that it is not unreasonable for a subject to worry *ex ante*
about the regret that he might feel *ex post*. That cognitive concern is
part of his reality. But, in my opinion, concern for regret is often
overdone. It becomes a dominating concern when it should often be only
of minor concern.

I would continue my probing. "In the choice of A in problem 1, you
say that you would feel terribly uncomfortable if you drew a $0-ball.
How serious is this concern? Would you be willing to pay $100 to mirac-
ulously eliminate this regret from your mind?" Let's say that for the
subject the stimulus [-$50 without regret] is of equal discomfort to
[$0 with the regret he would feel for having chosen A and obtained a
$0-ball]. Schematically he should be indifferent between the two choices:

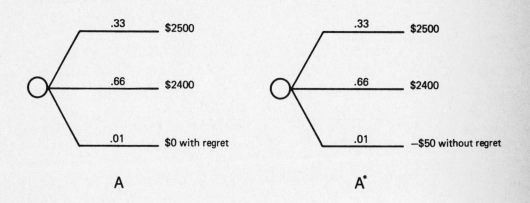

How much should the subject be willing to pay *ex ante* to remove the
regret feeling if it arose *ex post*? The regret feeling if it arises *ex
post* is worth a penalty of $50. Hence the fair actuarial insurance
value is only .01 × $50 or $.50. So let's say he would pay $1 or even
$2 *ex ante* to make a contract with Mr. Fixit who can miraculously remove
all traces of regret in the subject's mind should it arise *ex post*. Not
a big deal.

## Illustration 2

Let's push on.  K & T next contrast the choices in problems 3 and 4.

Problem 3:    Choose between

A:   $4000 with probability   .80    B:  $3000 with certainty
    $0 with probability   .20
          1.00

N = 95    (20%)          (80%)

Problem 4:    Choose between

C:   $4000 with probability   .20   D:   $3000 with probability   .25
    $0 with probability   .80       $0 with probability   .75
          1.00            1.00

N = 95    (65%)          (35%)

If we implement C and D by considering 100 appropriately labelled balls in each of two urns and if we then delete 75 balls labelled $0 that are common to the two urns, urn C would contain 20 balls labelled $4000 and 5 labelled $0, and urn D would have 25 labelled $3000.  Hence we immediately see the essential equivalence of problems 3 and 4.  The problem to be understood here is why B was so compelling in problem 3 but D not so compelling in problem 4.  As K & T illustrate, problem 4 can be depicted as in Fig. 1.

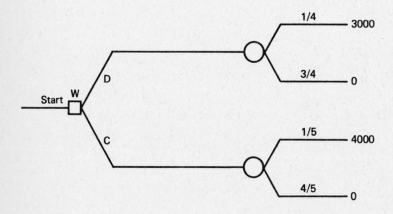

FIGURE 1   Problem 4.

Now contrast the choice in Fig. 1 with the choice in Fig. 2

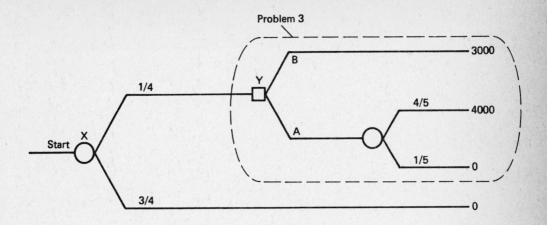

FIGURE 2   Problem 4*.

Notice that the dotted subproblem in Fig.2 is just the problem stated
in problem 3.

   Now suppose that you are like the majority of K & T subjects that
prefer B over A in problem 3 and C over D in problem 4.  Now I would
ask you about how you feel about being perched at the start of Fig.1 or
at the start of Fig.2.  The diagrams look different but if you choose
D in Fig.1 and B in Fig.2 you will be exposed to the same probabilistic
payoffs; if you choose C in Fig.1 and A in Fig.2 you also will be exposed to the same probabilistic payoffs.  If you do not quite feel sure
whether you would rather be perched at the start of Fig. 1 or 2, then how
much would you be willing to pay to go from your inferior to your superior starting position?  We hope that on reflection you would agree
that the options in Fig.2 are just as desirable -- no more, no less --
as in Fig.1.  But now how should you choose in Fig.2?  If you get to
node Y you have a choice of a certainty of $3000 (with choice B) and a
choice of an uncertain payoff (with choice A).  If at Y you agree that
you prefer B, then should you not be willing at the start of Fig.2 to

say, "I am willing to announce now that if chance leads me to a choice at Y, I will choose B." If you so assert, you are saying that in problem 4 you prefer D over C.

"But wait" you may say, "I chose B over A in problem 3 partly because with B I had a certainty of $3000. There was no uncertainty involved. When you embed problem 3 in an uncertain context, as you do in Fig.2, then I already am engaged in a gambling context. In that environment -- with the realization that I am already gambling -- I evidently want to shift from B to A."

This reasoning seems a bit strange to me but I assure you that if you feel this way, you are not alone. I would continue my probing. Suppose now you are perched at the start of Fig.2 but now we let the probability of going from node X to node Y be p instead of 1/4. Should your choice at node Y, if you arrive there, depend on p? When in problem 3 you had the choice of B or A, did you take into consideration the peculiar set of chance events that led you to be offered that choice? I think not. So on reflection would you not want to argue that your choice of B versus A at node Y does not depend on p and that you would be willing to announce this conditional choice at node X (assuming there are no time lags), and that if you were to announce B over A in problem 3, you should also announce D over C in problem 4?

Another way of forcing a subject to think more deeply about these issues is to pose the problem this way. "Suppose that tomorrow one student will be chosen at random from a pre-specified population and given the choice in problem 3. You might be that student. Think about what choice you would make if you were selected?"

In discussing this problem with the student the next day, I might ask: "Did it make any difference to you in deciding between B and A in problem 3 just how many students were in the pre-specified population?"

Most students respond that it did not even occur to them to worry about that. In other words, in Fig.2 the probability at node X did not enter into the consideration of their choice.

I have a confession to make: In experiments with my students, my ingenious protestations did not always prove to be ingenious enough. Yes, they were dazzled (and perhaps confused) but many remained unconvinced; if the chips were down, they would behave just as before.

## Illustration 3

I can be briefer with the next example offered by K & T.

Problem 5:    Choose between

A:    $6000 with probability  .45        B:    $3000 with probability  .90
          $0 with probability  .55                  $0 with probability  .10
                              1.00                                        1.00

N = 66        (14%)                                        (86%)

Problem 6:    Choose between

C:    $6000 with probability  .001      D:    $3000 with probability  .002
          $0 with probability  .999                 $0 with probability  .998
                              1.000                                       1.000

N = 66        (73%)                                        (27%)

After reducing both these problems to their essentials (i.e. by getting rid of common balls), we see that the crux of these choice problems is: Would you rather get ($3000 for certain) or get (a 50-50 lottery on $6000 or nothing). Stated this way risk-averse individuals should prefer B over A and D over C. Why, then do 73% of the subjects choose C over D? K & T state, "In this situation (problem 6) where winning is possible but not probable, most people choose the prospect that offers the larger gain." I concur, and I would not be surprised if a majority of subjects would accept C even if the $6000 were reduced to $5000 or if the probability in option D were raised from .002 to .003.

What to do about this? First people have to learn that small probabilities are treacherous. We suspect that there is a tendency for people to think in the following terms: "The only way I can win with D is to be extremely lucky. I just am not going to win unless it's my time to be rewarded by Providence. And if it is my time, I might as well get $6000 as $3000." This type of reasoning is somewhat mystical and people just have to learn to guard against these fuzzy-minded tendencies. I conjure: "Don't jump to conclusions with small probabilities because it's easy to make stupid errors."

Illustration.4

The Reflection Effect

Now let's follow K & T and consider prospects where losses are involved and where subjects flip-flop: they are risk-averse in the positive domain but risk-seeking in the negative domain.

The negative counterparts of problems 3 and 4 are exhibited on the following page.

Problem 3':   Choose between

A:
-$4000 with probability  .80
$0 with probability  .20
                     1.00

B:  -$3000 with certainty

N = 95        (92%)                                    (8%)

Problem 4':   Choose between

C:
-$4000 with probability  .20
$0 with probability  .80
                     1.00

D:
-$3000 with probability  .25
$0 with probability  .75
                     1.00

N = 95        (42%)                          (58%)

If in problem 4' we think of 2 urns, each with 100 appropriately labelled balls, and then delete the common 75 balls labelled $0, then we see the essential equivalence between the two problems.

Now let's look at problem 3' more closely. Suppose that you are like 92% of the subjects and prefer A to B. Presumably this means that if you were forced to take B and were then given the opportunity to immediately switch to A, then you would want to make the switch. If you had B in hand your asset position would be reduced by $3000. In this case if you switch from B to A you are saying the following: from the vantage point of being $3000 poorer, you would stake losing an additional $1000 for a .2 chance of regaining that $3000 loss. Looked at this way a lot of subjects, we believe, would have second thoughts about moving from B to A. But still one can give many reasons why you might want to go from B to A. For example, a loss of $3000 might mean that you cannot buy that new car you've been saving for and a loss of $4000 instead of $3000 just means a little more inconvenience. Or perhaps you might have to explain a sizeable loss to your spouse or parent or companion and it's just as embarrassing for you to account for a $3000 loss as a $4000 loss. Or perhaps with a loss of $3000 you will have to borrow money from a bank or friend and borrowing $3000 is almost as uncomfortable for you as borrowing $4000. We can give other rationalizations why you might want to switch from B to A but then in all these cases we think that these reasons should also lead you to prefer C over D in problem 4'. If a loss of $4000 is not so different to a loss of $3000 for you, why take that added 5% chance of a loss by choice of D over C?

Why do so many subjects choose A over B? Another example might help illustrate the reasons. Three miners are trapped and are sure to die (analog of B) unless a rescue attempt is made. A fourth miner could attempt the rescue but the odds are 4 to 1 that all 4 will be killed rather than all 4 will be rescued (analog of A). It's terrible

to take a sure loss without fighting back.  The decision for a rescue
attempt might be made even if the odds against were 9 to 1 rather than
a mere 4 to 1.  Now contrast this situation with:  three miners have a
1/4 chance of dying (analog of D) and a rescuer can reduce that chance
from 1/4 to 1/5 but he also runs a chance of losing his life in addition
(analog of C).  The feeling now goes that as long as there is hope that
the miners will come out safely (with D) why stake the life of an additional person for a small decrease in the probability?  Certainly from
the point of view of the decision maker who might be concerned about
his own accountability, as well as for the lives of the miners, there
would be great pressure on him to choose B over A and C over D.  Part
of the reason is the public pressure on the decision maker.  In problem
3' how can he not do anything?  If the fourth fellow also dies, at least
he tried.  In problem 4' if he sends in that fourth fellow and he also
dies, he might be held accountable for risking another life needlessly;
if all 4 survive, then maybe the three would have survived without the
rescue attempt.  So even if C results in a good outcome the decision
maker cannot take the full kudos -- unless in this last case it becomes
unambiguously clear *ex post* that the three miners would have definitely
been doomed without this noble intercession.  It should be clear from
this discussion that this formulation of the problem brings in the notion of *ex ante* concern for *ex post* accountability and it highlights the
notion of potential regret.  Some of these features, but to a lesser
extent, are also involved in the K & T problems with monetary losses.
If accountability to others and regret are major concerns, then these
concerns should be recognized by incorporating them into the description
of the consequences.  If that were done, then, for example, the $0-out-
come with choice A in problem 3' would be far different than the $0-
outcome with choice C in problem 4'.  And in terms of these enriched
consequences a choice of A in 3' and D in 4' would not be inconsistent
with the (prescriptive) utility axioms.  It should be noted, however,
that a decision maker, accountable to others, may resist formalizing
his own personal accountability and regret because that's not what a
courageous, noble decision maker should be thinking about.  That decision maker might feel that these private thoughts are better left private rather than brought out for public display.

Fig.3 depicts the miners' problem.  If p = 1, the analog is problem
3'; if p = .25, the analog is problem 4'.

CHOICE

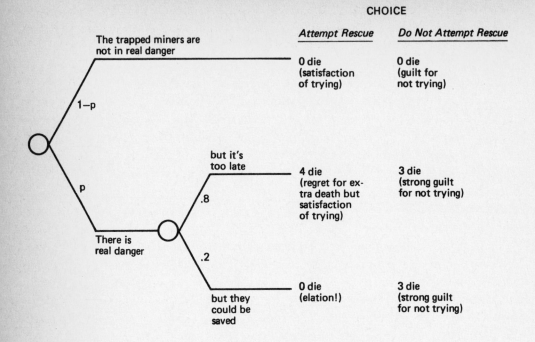

FIGURE 3   The problem of the miners.

The External and Internal Kibitzer

Imagine someone is doing a standard decision-tree type of analysis
in a marketing setting.  Imagine that at the tip of the tree a typical
consequence can be described in terms of: a net cash flow, a good-will
loss (some unsatisfied customers), and a change of market share of a
few percent.  Certainly an analysis that just considers the net cash
flow position (without even worrying about post-tax considerations) and
that ignores good-will and share of market would be naively inappropriate.  As a minimum the analysis should not only look at post-tax concerns (especially if different outcomes will be taxed differently) but
impute an after-tax adjustment to account for goodwill loss and the
change of market share.  That's standard fare.

Now let's change the problem.  Suppose that at the tip of the tree
the consequence can be described by an (after-tax) monetary flow, x,
and by a stream of snide or congratulatory remarks by a kibitzer --
a business partner, a spouse, a righteous friend.  Certainly if you
were the decision maker, stuck with this external kibitzer, you would
want to think of the whole consequence, and this includes what the ki-

bitzer might say and keep on reminding you about. Just as in this previous example, you might want to adjust outcome x to reflect the role of kibitzer.

But now what happens if the kibitzer is internalized? You are a divided self. You know when you make your choice, that you cannot prevent yourself from having *ex post* regret, disappointment, elation, envy, guilt, and so on. Shouldn't these cognitive concerns be treated just like an external kibitzer? Actually it's sometimes easier to get rid of the external kibitzer than the internal one. Well, I say, if it's an important part of your reality, it should be part of the description of your consequence.

Let me conclude with two observations. First, psychological concerns can get out of hand; they can be pathological. A subject may need therapy to get these concerns under control. Second, in formal analyses we often ignore these cognitive concerns and assume that they do not exist or are not appropriate to acknowledge. But then we may not want to be led by such an analysis since it is abstracting too much away from our reality. We could try to cost out these concerns. How much would you be willing to pay to wave that magic wand that gets rid of that regret or disappointment? I have found in a few cases that some subjects who are bothered by regret (say) realize, after they confront it openly, that they would not pay much to get rid of it. It looms large because it is unattended. In these cases confrontation may become the therapy.

If a researcher is trying to understand behavior, then there is power in simplicity. You can explain almost anything *ex post* if you have enough degrees of freedom to play with, and the introduction of regret, disappointment, envy, elation, guilt, etc. would allow an empirical observer to rationalize almost any behavior. But there would not be much predictive power in such a descriptive theory. But the same observation does not apply in prescriptive applications. The analyst can query the decision maker about what are his or her real concerns and if these cognitive concerns loom large, they can be incorporated into the analysis.

In a seminar I gave a skeptical analyst opined that she is worried that she may regret that she has acknowledged her regret. That's a good place to quit.

# NEGOTIATION AND MEDIATION IN CONFLICTS: II. PLURAL RATIONALITY AND INTERACTIVE DECISION PROCESSES

Andrzej Wierzbicki

*International Institute for Applied Systems Analysis, Laxenburg, Austria*
*and Institute of Automatic Control, Technical University of Warsaw, Warsaw, Poland*

## 1. INTRODUCTION

In many multi-actor decision situations the parties involved do not share the same perception of rationality, the same basic values or the same information. This could be because the actors come from different cultural backgrounds (Thompson, 1984). Yet even quite culturally diverse actors can achieve agreement if they recognize their diversity, are willing to learn and exchange information, and agree on the legitimacy of some negotiation procedure or on some principles of fairness for use in mediation. These concepts seem difficult to formalize; yet, as shown later, formalization or abstraction is an important part of the cognition process, and thus necessary for a deeper understanding of the problem.

This paper attempts to formalize these concepts by recognizing the existence of plural rationality, comparing several formal frameworks for rational decision making and considering the possibility of combining them. Work on the formalization of mediation processes begun in the first part of this paper (Wierzbicki, 1983b) is continued.

## 2. PLURAL RATIONALITY

### 2.1. *The role of value judgment in decision analysis*

Following Weber (see, e.g., Weber, 1968), many decision theorists take it for granted that any serious scientific analysis must be value-free — although any actions based on this analysis are typically value-dependent. In order to better understand this apparent paradox we must return to some reservations made by Weber himself. He admits that any concept or assumption used in scientific analysis, and indeed the choice of subject itself, might be influenced by value-judgments. However, he considers these reservations to be minor. On the other hand, the development of the theory of cognition after Weber has stressed the very basic dependence of concepts on language and thus on deeply rooted cultural values. On this basis, it should not appear surprising that the very concept of rational behavior might be quite different in different cultures. Therefore, Weber's postulate of value-free science must be understood as a methodological ideal worth striving for, but typically achieved to only a limited degree. These reservations, although not really minor, do not imply a totally relativistic attitude; some values, such as global responsibility, tolerance, the pursuit of truth, understanding, and learning are upheld throughout the community of scientists. Therefore, our purpose should be to *understand* plural perceptions of rationality rather than to judge them.

## 2.2. *The dialectical triad of cognitive processes*

Much attention has recently been paid to the distinction between the *descriptive*, normative (a better word might be *abstractive*, see Raiffa, 1984) and *prescriptive* schools of decision analysis. This is a very important distinction, since every process of human cognition involves observation and description, then abstraction (in order to identify the important features of the observed phenomenon), and finally prescription (in order to test or utilize the acquired knowledge). Individual researchers attach different importance to these stages, some concentrating on abstraction, others on observation and critical analysis, and yet others on tests and utilization. However, we could equally well speak about passively empirical, theoretical, and actively empirical stages; most sciences treat these three stages as iterative steps necessary for progress, in the sense of the dialectical triad of thesis, antithesis and synthesis. Examples abound: empirical knowledge of the limited speed of light motivated Einstein to work on relativity theory, and the theoretical understanding acquired in this way prompted not only observations of the deflection of solar radiation by Mercury, but also many other experiments of an even more active nature.

A mature science uses all these three stages of research. Therefore, we cannot use this distinction as evidence of plural rationality — although it is true that a number of perceptions of rationality with different emphases have been developed. As decision analysis matures, however, we might expect these three stages of research to be accepted as equals.

## 2.3. *Several abstractive frameworks for rationality*

When trying to classify various methods of rational decision making, we must first distinguish between *holistic* and *analytical* ways of making a decision. The holistic approach is based on the decision maker's reaction to the situation as a whole; it is not necessary to identify elements or information before making the decision (Dreyfus, 1984). Purist decision theorists may question whether such a method of decision making is rational at all, since heuristic assumptions and intuition could play a significant role. This leads us to the question of what we mean by "rationality". A broad concept of this type can be restricted by the development of mathematical theory that analyzes only chosen aspects of the concept (e.g., catastrophe theory). However, such a restriction might be detrimental to the development of an applied science; hence, we prefer to use the word 'rationality' in its broader, more conventional sense. A rational decision does not have to be based on all the available information, nor does it have to be optimal. It should only take into account the possible consequences of the decision and be intended not to be detrimental to the interests of the decision maker. As a reasonable compromise, we can define various degrees of rationality: *super-rationality* (ability to deal with the paradoxes of rationality), *optimizing rationality, satisficing rationality, procedural rationality* (Dobell, 1984), and so on. Using this broader definition, an adaptively formed decision rule or procedure can lead to quite rational decisions; the effectiveness of various decision rules is a very interesting subject for study (Rapaport, 1984). Moreover, it can be argued that most day-to-day decisions are made in a holistic way (Dreyfus, 1984) and even that the holistic approach is often superior in the long run, as shown by computer tournaments of repetitive prisoners' dilemma games.

However, decisions based on inadequate experience or involving new issues often require an analytical approach to decision making, i.e., a systematic evaluation of possible alternatives and related outcomes before making a decision. Several frameworks for analytical decision making have been developed: very loosely and without implying any value judgment, we can say that the *utility maximization framework* originated from a study of ideal markets and Adam Smith's 'invisible hand' concept, while the *satisficing framework* is based on a description of decision processes in large enterprises. Less well known is the *goal- and program-oriented action (management) framework* (programno-celovye upravlenye) developed in the USSR by Glushkov (1972), Pospelov and Irikov (1976) and others from a study of planning decisions.

*The utility maximization framework* has the strongest theoretical and mathematical foundations, and is therefore widely accepted as a reasonable framework for analytical decision making. However, this framework leads to paradoxes both in theory and in empirical testing. Some of the paradoxes imply that maximizing behavior cannot be consistently rational in any non-zero-sum multi-actor situation. Others imply that one of the cornerstones of utility theory, the axiom of independence of irrelevant alternatives, cannot be justified either by empirical verification or by deeper analysis. Here we shall consider only one of many possible arguments. The analytical approach to decision making is typically adopted when a somewhat novel situation presents itself. Thus, the decision maker must first *learn* from the analysis, and we learn mostly by making mistakes or by considering alternatives that are later classified as inferior. A decision maker may therefore *change* his utility function after analyzing inferior alternatives; this process could be considered a necessary element of analytical decision making, thus violating the above axiom (which implicitly equates inferior with irrelevant). There are two ways of incorporating this argument into utility theory. One is to say that the decision maker has a potential utility function which he does not perceive at the beginning, but which slowly reveals itself during the decision process. However, this leads to the question of how we know when the decision maker has learned enough to recognize his potential utility function. The other way is to modify the axiom and to admit that the utility function is basically non-stationary, that it changes as the decision maker learns. This possibility will be pursued further in subsequent sections.

*The satisficing framework* (Simon, 1958, and others) grew out of an empirical criticism of the maximizing framework: most real decision makers (managers, engineers, customers, etc.) do not actually optimize because they do not have the time or information. Instead they form *aspiration levels* that they try to achieve by making "good enough" (satisficing) decisions. This framework also has some mathematical foundations, mostly oriented towards prescription. These include goal programming techniques (Charnes and Cooper, 1977) and related theoretical developments such as the theory of the displaced ideal (Zeleny, 1976). However, the mathematical foundations of this framework have not been developed consistently, mostly because of the unclear nature of the role played by optimization. The original criticism of optimization has lost some of its strength with recent advances in computer technology and other fields. Ways of dealing with uncertainty and lack of information have also been improved. Thus, optimization can certainly be used as a *tool* to help people make decisions; the issue is whether it should be used as a *goal*, as a description of human behavior.

Other things being equal, a decision maker would typically try to exceed an aspiration level if this requires no additional effort and has no obvious disadvantages. He might have a different attitude to maximization above and below his aspiration level, but he would still have some tendency towards maximization. Thus the assumption that overachievement is generally undesirable (as accepted in such formal expressions of satisficing behavior as goal programming) is not justified in practice.

On the other hand, the fact that people do form aspirations and use them to guide their decisions has since been confirmed by extensive experimental and theoretical research (see, e.g., Tietz, 1983). Therefore, we shall describe human decision-making behavior as *quasi-satisficing*, by which we mean that *the decision maker has a tendency towards maximization, but might, for some good reason, lose this tendency after attaining his (adaptively formed) aspiration levels*. This direction of research has been pursued by the present author (Wierzbicki, 1980, 1982, 1983a,b, 1984a).

*The program- and goal-oriented action (management) framework* assumes that some goals or programs (aspirations) have greater priority and must be reached; the question is how to allocate or increase resources, overcome obstacles, and modify other aspirations in order to achieve these high-priority goals. Although its mathematical formalization was largely developed in the Soviet Union, this framework is a good model of the rational, purpose-oriented behavior of many groups throughout the world — for example, social action groups in the United States (Umpleby, 1983). Formally, this framework is not inconsistent with utility maximization (we could always use the high-priority goals as constraints and maximize utility over the allocations of resources and efforts), but in actual fact it represents quite a different approach which is more closely related to satisficing methods (suitably modified goal programming techniques could be used to model goal- and program-oriented action). However, this framework can also be incorporated into the quasi-satisficing model if we assume that some aspirations are hierarchically dominant and less adaptive than others.

### 2.4. Postulates of plural rationality

If even the formal frameworks for decision making reflect different culturally-based methodological perceptions of what is rational, how can we ever expect to reach agreement in international negotiations? Evidently, there must be something more to reaching agreement than we have considered so far. We shall try to capture the essence of this additional factor in the form of four *postulates of plural rationality*:

(a) *The postulate of limited knowledge and interactive learning*. When negotiating, one should never assume perfect knowledge or rational expectations; rather, one should accept that one's own knowledge is limited, be humble about one's own ignorance, and be prepared to learn interactively from others with the aim of establishing a commonly acceptable information base. Any formalization of decision processes in a situation involving plural rationality should stress the interactive learning aspect.

(b) *The postulate of cultural respect*. Learning situations involving plural rationality must be based on respect for the cultural values and perceptions of the other participants. In particular, any formalization of decision processes in such situations should admit parallel interpretations in terms of the different perceptions of rationality of the participants. Nobody should take his own perception of rationality for granted. For example, the common holistic perception of the world as a zero-sum game ('if he wins, I lose') and the mini-max perception of uncertainty ('prepare for the worst') can both lead to a dangerous escalation of conflict in such situations.

(c) *The postulate of legitimate organization*. In situations involving plural rationality, some agreement on the institutional or organizational aspects of a given situation is a necessary prerequisite for obtaining mutually acceptable solutions. For example, if one side in bilateral negotiations insists on a leading position (in the Stackelberg sense, for instance) and the other side does not accept this, there is no chance of any agreement. Thus, the organizational structure of any multi-actor situation should not be taken for granted, but carefully specified and agreed upon.

(d) *The postulate of fair mediation*. If a mediator or mediating technique is to be used in a situation involving plural rationality, the principles of fairness on which such mediation would be based should be carefully specified and agreed upon.

The role of these postulates will be illustrated later in the paper.

## 3. TOWARDS A SYNTHESIS OF DECISION-ANALYTICAL FRAMEWORKS

A unified framework based on the assumption of quasi-satisficing behavior has already been introduced in earlier papers by the present author. Here we present a summary of earlier findings and some new results that stress the usefulness of such a framework in plural rationality situations.

As is usual in analytical decision theory, we assume that two spaces are given: the space of decisions (actions, alternatives) denoted here by $E_x$, and the space of outcomes (objectives, attributes) denoted by $E_q$. Both spaces are assumed to be normed, although not necessarily finite-dimensional, since we could include objectives which change over time or probability distributions. The set of admissible decisions $X_o \subset E_x$ may be defined by listing its elements (discrete alternatives), by implicit relations (constraints in mathematical programming) or by some other means. A completely specified though not necessarily deterministic mapping $f : E_x \to E_q$ is assumed to be given. This mapping defines the set of attainable outcomes $Q_o = f(X_o) \subset E_q$. The essence of analytical decision theory is to find ways of selecting decisions that correspond to specific desirable outcomes $\hat{q} \in Q_o$.

To do this, we assume that the elements of the space $E_q$ have a partial preordering $\leqslant$ which has some natural interpretation (in terms of increasing gains, decreasing losses, improving quality, etc.). In most cases, the space $E_q$ can be defined such that the partial preordering can be represented by means of a positive (closed, convex, proper) cone $D \subset E_q$:

$$q'' \leqslant q' \iff q' - q'' \in D . \tag{1}$$

We could strengthen the preordering relation by defining $q'' < q'$ as $q' - q'' \in \tilde{D} = D \setminus (D \cap -D)$, or strengthen it even further by taking $q'' \ll q'$ as $q' - q'' \in \mathring{D} = \text{int } D$ (if the cone $D$ has an interior). We could also weaken the preordering relation in various ways: for example, generalizing the concept of proper efficiency (Geoffrion, 1968), we could introduce an $\varepsilon$-neighborhood $D_\varepsilon = \{q \in E_q : \text{dist}(q, D) \leq \varepsilon \|q\|\}$ of $D$ in $E_q$, and define $q'' \leqslant_\varepsilon q'$ as $q' - q'' \in D_\varepsilon$, $q'' <_\varepsilon q'$ as $q' - q'' \in \tilde{D}_\varepsilon = D_\varepsilon \setminus (D_\varepsilon \cap -D_\varepsilon)$, and $q'' \ll_\varepsilon q'$ as $q' - q'' \in \mathring{D}_\varepsilon = \text{int } D_\varepsilon$ (the cone $D_\varepsilon$ always has an interior for positive $\varepsilon$ even if $D$ does not). If a decision maker is strictly satisficing (over-achievement is as bad as under-achievement), then the concept of partial preordering is not needed and the distance or metric implied by the norm suffices: he would select the outcome that is closest to an aspiration level $\bar{q} \in E_q$. However, if a decision maker wishes to maximize his objectives (as in the utility framework) or at least has a tendency towards maximization (as in the quasi-satisficing framework), the selected outcome $\hat{q}$ should be nondominated (or efficient), i.e., belong to the set:

$$\hat{Q}_o = \{\hat{q} \in Q_o : Q_o \cap (\hat{q} + \tilde{D}) = \phi\}, \quad \tilde{D} = D \setminus (D \cap -D). \tag{2}$$

For analytical purposes, we can also consider the (larger) weakly nondominated set $\hat{Q}_o^w = \{\hat{q} \in Q_o : Q_o \cap (\hat{q} + \mathring{D}) = \phi\}$ and the (smaller) $\varepsilon$-nondominated set $\hat{Q}_o^\varepsilon = \{\hat{q} \in Q_o : Q_o \cap (\hat{q} + \tilde{D}_\varepsilon) = \phi\}$.

Now, the utility framework assumes that the actual selection is made by maximizing (over $Q_o$) a utility function $u : E_q \to \mathbf{R}^1$ which is given by the decision maker, and which is not subject to any modification due to learning or changing context (this reservation, though not usually made explicit in utility theory, is nevertheless implied by its axioms). *In contrast to this, the quasi-satisficing framework assumes that the selection is guided by aspiration levels, $\bar{q} \in E_q$, which are established in the course of a learning process; a plausible model for the development of aspiration levels might be*

$$\bar{q}_{t+1} = \bar{q}_t + \alpha_t (q_t - \bar{q}_t) , \tag{3}$$

*where $q_t$ is an observed (although not necessarily accepted) outcome and $\bar{q}_t$ is the aspiration level. Starting from an aspiration level $\bar{q}$, the actual choice is made, as in the utility framework, by trying to maximize over outcomes $q \in Q_o$ a quasi-utility function (called an achievement function) s : $E_q \times E_q \to \mathbf{R}_1$ of the form $s(q,\bar{q})$, which depends explicitly not only on the outcomes but also on the aspiration levels.*

The underlying axioms and properties of various achievement functions have already been analyzed by the present author (Wierzbicki, 1982, 1983a, 1984a). In addition to the requirement of *order preservation* or monotonicity (which results in the selection of nondominated outcomes, as in utility theory), achievement functions should also have the property of *order representation*:

$$\{q \in E_q : s(q,\bar{q}) \geq 0\} = S_{o\bar{q}} = \bar{q} + D , \quad \text{for all } \bar{q} \in E_q \tag{4}$$

or, since an order-representing function cannot be strictly monotonic (and thus could have weakly nondominated outcomes as maxima), at least *order approximation*: for some $\varepsilon > 0$

$$\bar{q} + D \subset \{q \in E_q : s(q,\bar{q}) \geq 0\} = S_{o\bar{q}} \subset \bar{q} + D_\varepsilon , \tag{5}$$

which is compatible with strict monotonicity and hence nondominated outcomes. The property of order approximation reflects the fact that a decision maker typically attaches different weights to over-achievement and under-achievement, and his quasi-utility or achievement function is thus usually nondifferentiable at $q = \bar{q}$ (although differentiable approximations of achievement functions, obtained by modifying requirement (5), are also possible (Wierzbicki, 1984a)). However, *the property of order approximation has an important theoretical consequence: if the aspiration level is $\varepsilon$-nondominated, $\bar{q} \in \hat{Q}_o^\varepsilon$, then the decision maker does not need to consider other outcomes when maximizing an order-approximating achievement function $s(q,\bar{q})$, since its maximum over $q \in Q_o$ will be attained at $q = \bar{q}$* (Wierzbicki, 1982). This is not only a constructive necessary condition for $\varepsilon$-nondominance (which also holds for nonconvex $Q_o$), but also implies that the decision maker has full control of $\varepsilon$-nondominated outcomes, i.e., can select any of them merely by changing his aspiration levels without modifying the achievement function. Thus, aspiration levels are sufficiently strong to describe the dependence of the decision maker's preferences on context and learning.

If $E_q = \mathbb{R}^n$ and $D = \mathbb{R}_+^n$, then a suitable form for an achievement function might be:

$$s(q,\bar{q}) = \min_{1 \leq i \leq n} (q_i - \bar{q}_i) + \frac{\chi}{n-1} \sum_{i=1}^{n} (q_i - \bar{q}_i), \tag{6}$$

where $\chi > 0$ is a parameter related to the parameter $\varepsilon$ used above. Ideally, a standard *aspiration-induced scaling of outcomes* should be incorporated into (6):

$$s(q,\bar{q}) = \min_{1 \leq i \leq n} \left[ \frac{q_i - \bar{q}_i}{\tilde{q}_i - \bar{q}_i} \right] + \frac{\chi}{n-1} \sum_{i=1}^{n} \left[ \frac{q_i - \bar{q}_i}{\tilde{q}_i - \bar{q}_i} \right], \tag{7}$$

where $\tilde{q} = (\tilde{q}_1,...,\tilde{q}_i,...,\tilde{q}_n)$ is a *scaling point* — a utopia or ideal point composed of the maxima of individual objectives, or any upper bound point *accepted by the decision maker as a reference for forming aspirations* ($\bar{q}_i < \tilde{q}_i$ implied). Achievement function (7) has two important properties. First, the parameter $\chi$ (more precisely, the value of $\chi(1 + \frac{\chi}{n-1})$) characterizes the weight or importance of average over-achievement compared to the worst possible under-achievement on some standard scales. Second, the standard scales are chosen to reflect the average weighting of the various outcomes implied by the choice of the aspiration point compared to the scaling point. If the decision maker chooses a smaller value for $\tilde{q}_i - \bar{q}_i$ than for $\tilde{q}_j - \bar{q}_j$, this means that he prefers outcomes with $\tilde{q}_i - q_i$ smaller than $\tilde{q}_j - q_j$. This is reflected by the weighting coefficients $1/(\tilde{q}_i - \bar{q}_i)$ and $1/(\tilde{q}_j - \bar{q}_j)$, which should be interpreted as averages since the function $s(q,\bar{q})$ is nondifferentiable and they determine the direction in which its points of nondifferentiability lie.

In the above sense, an achievement function can be interpreted as a rough approximation to any utility function, including nondifferentiable and nonstationary functions. Operationally, information about the more specific properties of a utility function is contained in the aspiration levels or their position relative to a scaling point.

Now we can consider the question: does the quasi-satisficing framework encompass the different perceptions of rationality described in the previous section? We shall first show that this framework is not incompatible with plural rationality postulates (a) and (b).

This framework is in fact constructed to satisfy the postulate of limited knowledge and interactive learning. Consider a decision situation in which several decision makers decide to share some knowledge about the *substantive* aspects of a problem. Suppose that this information includes a characterization of the sets of admissible decisions and attainable outcomes; the space of outcomes might contain more than the actual outcomes of concern and we do not need to assume, at this stage, that any information about the *judgmental* aspects of the problem is shared. With a formal, substantive model of $X_o$, $f$ and $Q_o$, the decision maker can first define his own partial preordering (identifying his outcomes of interest, deciding whether to maximize or minimize or even satisfice them), possibly choosing a subspace of, or even enlarging, the space $E_q$. He could then use a technical device based on the maximization of an achievement function to obtain a nondominated outcome $\hat{q}$ and the decision $\hat{x}$ corresponding to any given aspiration level $\bar{q}$ (Lewandowski and Grauer, 1982). In this way, he can learn about the implications of various decisions, the properties of the nondominated boundary of the set of attainable outcomes $Q_o$, and adjust his aspirations accordingly. He does not require all the available information about the problem when first approaching it; he only needs enough information to define his own outcome space with its preordering and his initial aspirations. Any further information could be supplied by another decision maker (sharing information), by experts, or by the substantive model itself.

In single-actor situations, this learning process can actually lead to a final decision.

Turning now to the postulate of cultural respect, we shall show that the quasi-satisficing approach can be used by decision makers following any of the formal frameworks for rational decision making described in the previous section.

Strict satisficing assumes that over-achievement is as undesirable as under-achievement. However, since the partial preordering of the space of outcomes depends only on the decision maker, he can choose a positive cone that contains only zero for any outcome component that must be satisfied strictly. For all such components $\hat{Q}_o = Q_o$, and the requirements of order approximation (5) simply state that an achievement function should topologically approximate the norm of the outcome space. The form of such an achievement function could be

$$s(q,\bar{q}) = -\left(\max_{1\le i\le n} |\frac{\bar{q}_i - q_i}{\tilde{q}_i - \bar{q}_i}| + \frac{\chi}{n-1}\sum_{i=1}^{n} |\frac{\bar{q}_i - q_i}{\tilde{q}_i - \bar{q}_i}|\right), \tag{8}$$

which is a negative weighted sum of the $l_1$ and $l_\infty$ (Tchebyshev) norms; alternatively, we could use separate variables and scaling factors for under- and over-achievement, thus obtaining a variant of the goal programming technique. Thus, strict satisficing and goal programming can both be regarded as special cases within the quasi-satisficing framework.

The changing of aspirations in the quasi-satisficing framework leads to the following proposition:

**Proposition 1.** *Assume that $Q_o \subset R^n$ is such that $(\bar{q} + D) \cap Q_o$ is bounded and convex for any $\bar{q} \in R^n$. Let $\hat{q}(\bar{q}) = \arg \max\limits_{q \in Q_o} s(q, \bar{q})$ be uniquely determined, where $s(q, \bar{q})$ is a strictly order-preserving and order-approximating function for some $\varepsilon > 0$. Consider a process of aspiration formation:*

$$\bar{q}_{t+1} = \bar{q}_t + \alpha_t(\hat{q}(\bar{q}_t) - \bar{q}_t) ; \quad \bar{q}_o \text{ given,} \tag{9}$$

*where $\alpha_t \to 0$, $\sum\limits_{t=0}^{\infty} \alpha_t = \infty$. Then the process converges to $\bar{q}_\infty \in \hat{Q}_o$ with $\hat{q}(\bar{q}_\infty) = \bar{q}_\infty$.*

The proof (Wierzbicki, 1984b) is a modified version of quasi-gradient convergence arguments. The proposition can be understood as stating that a decision maker following the learning process (9) ends up by choosing a nondominated outcome and the corresponding decision. A theorem with a similar interpretation but quite different assumptions (consistent modification of preference cones) was given by Volkovich (see, e.g., Volkovich, 1984).

The goal- and program-oriented action framework assumes the hierarchical dominance of certain outcomes or aspiration components. We can always assume $E_q = E_{q^1} \times E_{q^2}$, where $q^1 \in E_{q^1}$ denotes the (lexicographically) dominating outcomes and $q^2 \in E_{q^2}$ all other outcomes. Let $\bar{q}^1$ be a goal in the space of dominating outcomes, and be *attainable* if $Q_o \cap \bar{Q}_1 \neq \phi$, where $\bar{Q}_1 = \{q \in E_q : q^1 = \bar{q}^1\}$, and let $D = D_1 \times D_2$, where $D_1 = \{0\} \subset E_{q^1}$, $D_2 \subset E_{q^2}$. Choose any strictly order-preserving and order-approximating functions $s_1 : E_{q^1} \times E_{q^1} \to R^1$ and $s_2 : E_{q^2} \times E_{q^2} \to R^1$; from the argument given above, $s_1$ is topologically equivalent to the norm of $q^1 - \bar{q}^1$ in $E_{q^1}$. Let $\rho(q)$ denote the indicator function of the set $\bar{Q}_1$ (equal to 1 if $\bar{q}^1 = q^1$, and 0 otherwise). Then the following proposition holds:

**Proposition 2.** *If the goal $\bar{q}^1$ from the pair $(\bar{q}^1, \bar{q}^2) \in E_q$ is attainable, then*

$$\operatorname{Arg} \max\limits_{q \in Q_o} (s_1(q^1, \bar{q}^1) + \rho(q) \cdot s_2(q^2, \bar{q}^2)) \subset \hat{Q}_o . \tag{10a}$$

*If, additionally, $(\bar{q}^1, \bar{q}^2) \in \hat{Q}_o^\varepsilon$, then*

$$(\bar{q}^1, \bar{q}^2) \in \operatorname{Arg} \max\limits_{q \in Q_o} (s_1(q^1, \bar{q}^1) + \rho(q) \cdot s_2(q^2, \bar{q}^2)) . \tag{10b}$$

*If $q_1$ is not attainable and $s_1(q^1, \bar{q}^1) = -\|q^1 - \bar{q}^1\|$, then*

$$\operatorname{Arg} \max\limits_{q \in Q_o} (s_1(q^1, \bar{q}^1) + \rho(q) \cdot s_2(q^2, \bar{q}^2)) \subset \operatorname{Arg} \min\limits_{q \in Q_o} \|q^1 - \bar{q}^1\| . \tag{10c}$$

The proof is elementary, being based on the properties of achievement functions given above (Wierzbicki, 1984b). However, the function maximized in (10) is discontinuous (this is generally the case for functions that scalarize lexicographical orderings). Thus, for practical applications it might be useful to assume that goals $\bar{q}^1$ have some flexibility and to use achievement functions either of the form $s'(q,\bar{q}) = s_1(q^1,\bar{q}^1) + \rho \cdot s_2(q^2,\bar{q}^2)$ or of a form similar to (7):

$$s''(q,\bar{q}) = \min \left( s_1(q^1,\bar{q}^1) , \rho s_2(q^2,\bar{q}^2) \right) + \chi(s_1(q^1,\bar{q}^1) + \rho s_2(q^2,\bar{q}^2)) . \tag{11}$$

Here $\rho$ is a small positive constant reflecting the importance of achieving aspirations $\bar{q}^2$ relative to aspirations $\bar{q}^1$. In both cases, however, goal- and program-oriented action can be considered as lying within the quasi-satisficing framework.

The utility maximization framework could be analyzed in its original form, without including the effects of learning, nonstationarity and the possible nondifferentiability of the utility function. However, this can be considered as a special case of the following more general situation: a decision maker has a utility function which might be nondifferentiable and which he does not perfectly recognize; he might make mistakes when comparing given alternatives; he might change his preferences in time; but he is learning, and hence the nonstationarity and his mistakes vanish with time. The range of these assumptions appears formidable, but recent results obtained by Yastrembski and Michalevich (1980) and Ermoliev and Gaivoronski (1982) can be reformulated to prove the following proposition:

**Proposition 3.** *Consider a sequence $\{u^t\}_{t=0}^{\infty}$ of utility functions, $u^t : E_q \to R^1$, where $E_q \subset R^m$, with one of the following properties: either*

(a) $u^t(q) \to u(q)$ *uniformly on $E_q$ (uniform cardinal convergence), or*

(b) $d_t = \sup\limits_{q \in E_q} |u^t(q) - u^{t+1}(q)| \to 0$ *(cardinal convergence), or*

(c) $\Delta_t \to 0$, *where:*

$$\Delta_t = \sup_{q \in E_q} \max \left\{ \begin{array}{l} \sup\limits_{z_1 \in Y^t(q)} \inf\limits_{z_2 \in Y^{t+1}(q)} \|z_1 - z_2\| , \\ \sup\limits_{z_1 \in Y^{t+1}(q)} \inf\limits_{z_2 \in Y^t(q)} \|z_1 - z_2\| \end{array} \right\} \tag{12a}$$

*and*

$$Y^t(q) = \{y \in E_q : u^t(y) \geq u^t(q)\} \tag{12b}$$

*(ordinal convergence).*

*Suppose that the utility functions $u^t$ are convex and uniformly bounded on $E_q$, that they are strictly monotonic but not necessarily differentiable, and that, for all $\bar{q} \in E_q$, the sets $(\bar{q} + D) \cap Q_o$ are bounded and convex.*

*Suppose that the utility functions characterize a maximizing decision maker who is aided by a modified quasi-satisficing framework in the following iterative procedure (where $s(q,\bar{q}^t)$ represents the negative (Euclidean) norm $-\|q - \bar{q}^t\|$ ):*

*(i) given some $\bar{q}^t$, compute $\hat{q}^t = \hat{q}(\bar{q}^t) = \arg \max_{q \in Q_o} s(q, \bar{q}^t)$;*

*(ii) select a vector $\xi^t$ from the uniform distribution on the unit cube in $\mathbf{R}^n$;*

*(iii) select a vector $\zeta^t$ from the uniform distribution on the unit ball in $\mathbf{R}^n$;*

*(iv) present alternatives $\breve{q}^t = \hat{q}^t + \alpha_t \xi^t$ and $\tilde{q}^t = \breve{q}^t + \beta_t \zeta^t$, $\tilde{\tilde{q}}^t = \breve{q}^t - \beta_t \zeta^t$ to the decision maker for comparison. If $u^t(\tilde{q}^t) > u^t(\breve{q}^t)$, then $\bar{q}^{t+1} = \tilde{q}^t$; if $u^t(\tilde{\tilde{q}}^t) > u^t(\breve{q}^t)$, then $\bar{q}^{t+1} = \tilde{\tilde{q}}^t$; in both cases return to step (i), setting $t:t+1$. If neither of the alternatives is preferred, return to step (ii) without increasing $t$.*

If, additionally, the coefficients $\alpha_t$ and $\beta_t$ satisfy the following conditions:

(1) $\alpha_t \to 0, \beta_t \to 0, \beta_t / \alpha_t \to 0, \sum_{t=0}^{\infty} \beta_t = \infty$;

(2) if (b), then $d_t / \beta_t \to 0$;

(3) if (c), then $\Delta_t / \beta_t \to 0$;

then $u(\hat{q}^t) \to \max_{q \in Q_o} u(q)$ in case (a), $u^t(\hat{q}^t) - \max_{q \in Q_o} u^t(q) \to 0$ in case (b), and $\inf_{\hat{q} \in \hat{Y}_t} \|\hat{q} - \hat{q}^t\| \to 0$, where $\hat{Y}_t = \{\hat{q} \in \hat{Q}_o : u^t(\hat{q}) \geq u^t(q)$ for all $q \in Q_o\}$, in case (c).

The proof of this proposition is a simple modification of the proof given by Ermoliev and Gaivoronski (1982).

Clearly, if instead of a sequence $\{u^t\}_{t=0}^{\infty}$ we consider a fixed utility function $u$, the theorem would hold with obvious simplifications. However, by considering a sequence of utility functions, we allow the decision maker to make mistakes (interpreted as momentary changes in his utility) and take into account the fact that he might learn as the session proceeds. Requirements (b), (c) and (2), (3) specify only that he must learn in time to suppress mistakes, i.e., faster than the coefficients $\beta_t$ of this procedure converge. The coefficients $\alpha_t$ are needed only to deal with the possible nondifferentiability of the utility function (if it is differentiable, we can take $\alpha_t = 0$).

Proposition 3 *has an important interpretation in the quasi-satisficing framework: this framework can be used consistently by any decision maker following the principle of utility maximization, and the aspiration levels $\bar{q}^t$ are sufficient (in the form of a sequence of achievement functions $s(q, \bar{q}^t)$ ) to approximate any monotonic utility function.* In fact, Proposition 3 could be modified by somewhat stronger requirements: if the decision maker could specify the directions of change of his aspirations $\zeta^t$ that, on average, belong to the subdifferential of his utility function, he could guide the changes in his aspirations himself and not rely on random perturbations and pairwise comparisons (in this case, more general classes of achievement functions could also be used).

Thus, we can say that the quasi-satisficing framework satisfies the postulate of cultural respect, at least with regard to the three culturally-based formal frameworks for rational decision making considered here.

## 4. MULTI-ACTOR DECISION SITUATIONS IN A QUASI-SATISFICING FRAMEWORK

The postulate of legitimate organization means that a decision theorist should first check what the actors in a decision situation consider to be a legitimate organization or procedure in their case; he might suggest some models of such organizations, but should not try to impose such an organization upon them. Many different types of legitimate organizational structures are encountered in practice (see, e.g., Wierzbicki, 1983b), many of them involving hierarchies. Hierarchical decision structures have not received much attention as yet, although many specific problems have been investigated in considerable detail — examples include the theory of single-objective hierarchical optimization and control, (Findeisen et al., 1980) and the theory of single-objective hierarchical games (Germeer, 1976). The question is which of the analytical frameworks for rational choice would be most suitable for an analysis of decision making in such organizations, in particular negotiation and mediation processes in hierarchies. The results presented above seem to indicate that the quasi-satisficing framework might be the best-adapted to this purpose.

However, we shall limit our attention here to two basic types of nonhierarchical multi-actor decision situations. One, typically analyzed in decision theory or the theory of cooperative games, is the case of group decision making or *concentrated decisions*: there are many actors, but either the nature of the problem or a legitimate agreement require that the final decision should be joint. For example, when allocating shared resources, there should be no possibility that the actors involved would try to implement minority decisions. When developing a transportation system, the legitimacy of concentrated decisions depends upon the financing scheme and agreements: if the financing is decentralized, actors could implement minority decisions, but they could also agree that the only legitimate decisions are those made jointly. The other type of decision situation we shall consider is concerned with *distributed decisions* and is typically the subject of game theory: each actor is legitimately entitled to implement his own decisions whether the others agree or not. Even in this case, however, the actors may have different rights. If, for example, one actor has sufficient authority to assume the role of a leader and the others accept the role of followers, a legitimate hierarchical organization develops; however, we shall consider here only the case in which there is no legitimate hierarchical structure.

Both concentrated and distributed decisions are important in international negotiation and mediation: the first when reaching multilateral or bilateral agreements on joint benefits, the second when avoiding conflict escalation through unilateral action. The usefulness of the quasi-satisficing framework in both cases was demonstrated in the first part of this paper (Wierzbicki, 1983a). If some actors adopt the strictly maximizing perception of rationality and their model contains multiple noncooperative equilibria then conflicts can escalate. In contrast, when choosing (quasi)-satisficing multiple game equilibria it is possible to display constructive, hidden destructive, strictly maximizing or openly destructive behavior; only constructive choices can help to de-escalate conflicts, while the others typically contribute to conflict escalation. These concepts can be used to construct formal models of mediation processes for the de-escalation of conflicts by unilateral action; similar concepts can be used for mediation in multilateral agreements.

The postulate of fair mediation means that the proposed mediator should be accepted as impartial by all parties involved. In order to achieve this, it is advisable to specify in advance a set of principles of fairness which apply to a given case. The concept of fairness has more of a historical and cultural meaning than an absolute interpretation: *something that is fair does not in principle favor any side (although it might have this effect) and is accepted as such by all sides*. A particular rule for fair mediation, proposed first by Raiffa and then by Kalai and Smorodinsky (1975) for single-objective games, was analyzed in the first part of this paper. Unlike most concepts of cooperative game solutions, it can also be extended to multiobjective games. Here we concentrate on the development of this mediation rule through the analysis of various types of control coefficients.

### 4.1. Conflict coefficients in multiobjective optimization or cooperative games

Consider a decision situation with several outcomes which can be treated as maximized objectives, or a cooperative game in which the objectives of various players are to be maximized; then $E_q = \mathbf{R}^n$ and $D = \mathbf{R}^n_+$. Consider the bounds on the individual objectives obtained by successive maximization of each objective separately:

$$q_i^{(j)} = \min_{x \in A_j} (q_i = f_i(x)) \; ; \quad A_j = \text{Arg} \max_{x \in X_o} (q_j = f_j(x)) \; . \tag{13a}$$

The upper bound (utopia, ideal point) is then defined by:

$$\hat{q} = (\hat{q}_1,...,\hat{q}_i,...,\hat{q}_n) \; ; \quad \hat{q}_i = q_i^{(i)} = \max_{1 \le j \le n} q_i^{(j)} \tag{13b}$$

and the lower bound (nadir point) by:

$$\check{q} = (\check{q}_1,...,\check{q}_i,...,\check{q}_n) \; ; \quad \check{q}_i = \min_{1 \le j \le n} q_i^{(j)} \; . \tag{13c}$$

If we take $\Delta q_i = \hat{q}_i - \check{q}_i$ as the scaling factor, we can define the Tchebyshev distance of any outcome $q \in Q_o$ from the ideal point as follows:

$$d_\alpha = \max_{1 \le i \le n} \frac{\hat{q}_i - q_i}{\Delta q_i} \; . \tag{14a}$$

This distance is then minimized according to the Raiffa mediation rule:

$$d_{am} = \min_{q \in Q_o} \max_{1 \le i \le n} \frac{\hat{q}_i - q_i}{\Delta q_i}. \tag{14b}$$

Now let us introduce a nonlinear transformation of this distance such that the result of this transformation, $c = \mathcal{E}(d)$, called the *conflict coefficient*, will be $c = 0$ if $d = 0$, $c = 2$ if $d = 1$, and $c = 1$ if the nondominated set is contained in a hyperplane (i.e., is linear), in which case it is easy to show that $d_{am} = (n-1)/n$. This transformation makes the conflict coefficient independent of the dimensionality of the outcome space:

$$c = \mathcal{E}(d) = 2d + \frac{n(n-2)}{n-1} d(d-1). \tag{15}$$

(The idea of this nonlinear transformation was suggested by Tomasz Kreglewski.)

We have chosen the simplest quadratic function here, since the requirements do not specify the transformation uniquely. We shall call $c_a = \mathcal{E}(d_a)$ the *absolute conflict coefficient* for a given solution, and $c_{am} = \mathcal{E}(d_{am})$ the *minimum absolute conflict coefficient*. The properties of the latter are summarized in the following proposition:

**Proposition 4.** *Let* $E_q = R^n$, $D = R^n_+$, *and sets* $(\bar{q} + D) \cap Q_o$ *be bounded for all* $\bar{q} \in E_q$. *Then* $c_{am} = 0$ *iff* $\hat{q} \in Q_o$, $0 \le c_{am} \le 1$ *if* $Q_o$ *is convex*; $c_{am} = 1$ *if* $\hat{Q}_o$ *is contained in a hyperplane; and* $1 < c_{am} \le 2$ *indicates that* $Q_o$ *is nonconvex*.

The proof is elementary. Now consider some modifications of the concept of the conflict coefficient. A *lower relative conflict coefficient* is obtained if we accept some attainable aspiration point $\bar{q} \in Q_o$ as the status quo point and lower bound, and define the relative bounds as

$$q_i^{(j)}(\bar{q}) = \min_{x \in A_j(\bar{q})} (q_i = f_i(x)) \; ; \; A_j(\bar{q}) = \underset{x \in X_{oj} \; f(x) \ge \bar{q}}{\text{Arg max}} (q_j = f_j(x)) \tag{16a}$$

$$\tilde{q}_i(\bar{q}) = q_i^{(i)}(\bar{q}) \; ; \; \check{q}_i(\bar{q}) = \min_{1 \le j \le n} q_i^{(j)}(\bar{q}) . \tag{16b}$$

the scaling coefficients as $\Delta q_i = \tilde{q}_i(\bar{q}) - \check{q}_i(\bar{q})$, and take

$$d_r = \max_{1 \le i \le n} \frac{\tilde{q}_i(\bar{q}) - q_i}{\Delta q_i} \; ; \; c_r = \mathcal{E}(d_r) \tag{16c}$$

$$d_{rm} = \min_{q \in Q_o \cap (\bar{q} + R^n_+)} \max_{1 \le i \le n} \frac{\tilde{q}_i(\bar{q}) - q_i}{\Delta q_i} ; \; c_{rm} = \mathcal{E}(d_{rm}) . \tag{16d}$$

The *minimum lower relative conflict coefficient* has properties very similar to those described in Proposition 4. However, the relative conflict $c_r$ can be much greater than 2, thus indicating the possibility of conflict de-escalation. It might therefore be used by a mediator when starting from any status quo point.

Similarly, it is possible to define the *upper relative conflict coefficient* by accepting a nonattainable but component-wise attainable aspiration point $\bar{q} \in \hat{\hat{q}} - R_+^n$ as an upper bound.

### 4.2. Conflict coefficients in noncooperative games

When trying to characterize conflicts in noncooperative multi-equilibria games, it is useful to introduce conflict coefficients corresponding to noncooperative (Nash) equilibria rather than to nondominated (Pareto) solutions. Let $Q_N = f(N)$ be the image of the set $N$ of multiobjective Nash equilibria in the outcome space (Wierzbicki, 1983b) and assume that each player selects his strategy by choosing some equilibrium from this set. Typically, the resulting overall strategy is not an equilibrium strategy, and the corresponding outcomes are much worse than expected. Take these outcomes as the status quo point and lower bound, $\bar{q}$, and define the relative bounds as in (16a), (16b) (substituting $Q_N$ for $Q_o$), the scaling coefficients as described earlier, the relative distance and conflict coefficient as in (16c) and the minimum relative distance and conflict coefficient as in (16d) (substituting $Q_N$ for $Q_o$). Examples of conflict escalation given by Wierzbicki (1983a) show that the value of the conflict coefficient can be much greater than 2 because the disequilibrium point defined by the incompatible choices of equilibria may be far from the Nash set. Such a numerical measure of conflict might be useful in convincing players of the need for de-escalation.

The characterization of the point that results in the greatest possible conflict poses an interesting theoretical question; one possible answer is to relate this point to openly destructive choices of equilibria. Another open question is whether these destructive choices are necessarily of Stackelberg type when adopted by all players. In a multiobjective game, however, the definition of both destructive and Stackelberg-type decisions depends on the achievement or utility functions assumed by one player to characterize the others; thus the above theoretical questions could be studied more easily in single-objective games with multiple equilibria.

## 5. CONCLUSIONS

While we cannot say that any analytical framework for rational decision making is universal, the quasi-satisficing framework discussed here represents a first step in this direction. This framework, taken together with the concept of quasi-satisficing selection of game equilibria and the idea of a conflict coefficient, can also be used to increase our understanding of conflict escalation processes and thus help us to prevent conflict escalation by mediation or negotiation.

# REFERENCES

Charnes, A. and W.W. Cooper (1977). Goal programming and multiobjective optimization. *European Journal of Operational Research* 1: 39—54.

Dobell, R. (1984). Group decision processes: three examples from Canadian government. Presented at the Summer Study on Plural Rationality and Interactive Decision Processes, Sopron, 16—26 August 1984.

Dreyfus, S. (1984). Beyond rationality. This volume, pp. 55—64.

Ermoliev, Yu. and A. Gaivoronski (1982). Simultaneous non-stationary optimization, estimation and approximation procedures. Collaborative Paper CP-82-16, International Institute for Applied Systems Analysis, Laxenburg, Austria.

Findeisen, W. et al. (1980). *Control and Coordination in Hierarchical Systems*. John Wiley, Chichester.

Geoffrion, A.M. (1968). Proper efficiency and the theory of vector maximization. *Journal of Mathematical Analysis and Applications* 22: 618—630.

Germeer, Yu.B. (1976). *Games with Non-Opposing Interests* (in Russian). Nauka, Moscow.

Glushkov, V.M. (1972). Basic principles of automation in organizational management systems (in Russian). *Upravlayushchee Sistemy i Mashiny* 1.

Kalai, E. and M. Smorodinsky (1975). Other solutions to the Nash bargaining problem. *Econometrica* 43: 513—518.

Lewandowski, A. and M. Grauer (1982). The reference point optimization approach — methods of efficient implementation. Working Paper WP-82-019, International Institute for Applied Systems Analysis, Laxenburg, Austria.

Pospelov, G.S. and V.A. Irikov (1976). *Program and Goal-Oriented Planning and Management* (in Russian). Sovietskoe Radio, Moscow.

Raiffa, H. (1984). Back from prospect theory to utility theory. This volume, pp. 100—113.

Rapaport, A. (1984). Use of experimental games. This volume, pp. 147—161.

Simon, H. (1958). *Administrative Behavior*. MacMillan, New York.

Schwarz, M. and M. Thompson (1984). Beyond the politics of interest. This volume, pp. 22—36.

Tietz, R. (1983). Aspiration Levels in Bargaining and Economic Decision Making. *Lecture Notes in Economics and Mathematical Systems*, Vol. 213. Springer-Verlag, Heidelberg.

Umpleby, S.A. (1983). A group process approach to organizational change. In H. Wedde (Ed.), *Adequate Modeling of Systems*. Springer-Verlag, Berlin.

Volkovich, V. (1984). Methods of constructing interactive procedures in multicriteria optimization problems. Presented at the Summer Study on Plural Rationality and Interactive Decision Processes, Sopron, 16—26 August 1984.

Weber, M. (1968). *Methodologische Schriften*. Frankfurt/Main.

Wierzbicki, A.P. (1980). Multiobjective trajectory optimization and model semiregularization. Working Paper WP-80-181, International Institute for Applied Systems Analysis, Laxenburg, Austria.

Wierzbicki, A.P. (1982). A mathematical basis for satisficing decision making. *Mathematical Modelling* 3: 391—405.

Wierzbicki, A.P. (1983a). A critical essay on the methodology of multiobjective analysis. *Regional Science and Urban Economics* 13: 5—29.

Wierzbicki, A.P. (1983b). Negotiation and mediation in conflicts. I: The role of mathematical approaches and methods. Working Paper WP-83-106, International Institute for Applied Systems Analysis, Laxenburg, Austria. Also in H. Chestnut et al. (Eds.), *Supplemental Ways of Improving International Stability*. Pergamon Press, Oxford.

Wierzbicki, A.P. (1984a). Interactive decision analysis and interpretative computer intelligence. In M. Grauer and A. Wierzbicki (Eds.), *Interactive Decision Analysis*. Springer-Verlag, Heidelberg.

Wierzbicki, A.P. (1984b). Negotiation and mediation in conflicts. II: Plural rationality and interactive processes (extended version of this paper). IIASA Working Paper (in preparation).

Yastrembski, A.I. and M.B. Michalevich (1980). Stochastic search methods for most preferred elements and their interactive interpretation (in Russian). *Kibernetika* pp. 90–94.

Zeleny, M. (1976). The theory of displaced ideal. In M. Zeleny (Ed.), *Multiple Criteria Decision Making — Kyoto*. Springer-Verlag, Berlin.

# ON THE STRUCTURE, STABILIZATION AND ACCURACY
# OF THE DECISION PROCESS

Reinhard Tietz
*University of Frankfurt, Frankfurt, FRG*

## 1. LIMITED RATIONAL DECISION MAKING BASED ON ASPIRATION LEVELS

For an improvement of human relations within and between nations a better understanding of interactive human decision making is needed. In economic research concerned with decision making there are two contrasting approaches: the classical theory of the absolute rational decision maker, who maximizes his utility function, and the behavior oriented theory of the limited rational decision maker, who searches for a satisfying alternative.

Both theories have their own domain of application. The first, as a static theory, has a simple structure, but a complicated evaluation part reduces the applicability in differentiated situations. The second theory has simple evaluation rules but, as a dynamic process theory, it has a complicated structure that makes case-specific modifications necessary. The first theory has a unique solution concept and allows a manifoldness of utility assessments. In addition to that evaluation manifoldness, the second theory allows a manifoldness of solution processes. This point of view takes into account the limitations of the human abilities to perceive, to memorize, and to compute information.

The human limitations limit the scope of applicability of theories that assume strict rational behavior. If there are many decision alternatives with many characterizing dimensions, the decision situation is too complex for a maximizable utility function to be established. Only when the complexity is reduced by neglection of some aspects does the decision problem become soluble. This step of simplification is not a part of the traditional maximization theory but has to be made outside this theory. A realistic descriptive theory of decision making, however, should include rules of simplification.

A realistic theory that describes each single step of the decision process of limited rational decision making is of interest for explanation of observed behavior and for the prognosis of future behavior. In

addition, a realistic theory delivers the interfaces for methods of
decision support, which will be the more successful the more they use
natural points of the decision process as interfaces to the human
thinking. Since aspiration levels are used as such a tool in multicriteria decision support systems (WIERZBICKI 1984), it may be useful
to consider aspiration-oriented decision making also under behavioral
aspects (cf. TIETZ 1983b).

An important step of simplification is the use of an aspiration
grid which divides the continuous decision space into a few aspiration
ranges. For such an aspiration grid only few discrete aspiration levels for potential situations have to be formed. The aspiration levels
may serve as operational subgoals. They may be ordered in the direction of preference. Since in most decision situations a goal is the
more difficult to attain the more preferable it is, the attainability
direction is opposed to the preference direction. The difference between two adjacent aspiration levels varies with the attainability of
the upper one (TIETZ 1975, pp. 47 f.).

The exploration of the process of human decision making is the
more successful the more steps of the decision process are revealed
and can be observed. This is the case in bargaining situations in
which the  i n t r a personal decision process has to be interrupted
by phases of  i n t e r personal communication. Since the bilateral
negotiation is one of the simplest interpersonal relations it is
often used as an experimental paradigm. The progress of the theory
of bargaining, seen as an aspiration-oriented decision process, is
based on bilateral negotiation experiments (SAUERMANN 1972, 1978;
TIETZ 1983a).

The decision process has a hierarchical structure. The result of
the decision process depends on the sequence in which criteria are
applied as "decision filters". This contrasts with the simultaneous
solution approach of the traditional decision theory. In addition,
the bargaining and decision variables may form a hierarchy by their
importance.

For the stability of human, economic, or political relations it
is of great importance that both sides see the bargaining results as
fair solutions of conflicting interests. Otherwise, often-changing
partnerships would result; this would reduce the general level of
trust and would increase the decision cost. The "aspiration balancing

principle" is an important fairness principle for negotiations. Agreements should allow each bargaining partner to reach nearly the same aspiration level (TIETZ/BARTOS 1983).

In order to come to a fair agreement balanced in aspiration levels, the negotiators have to follow fair decision rules already during the bargaining process. The "aspiration securing principle" is such a decision rule. It postulates that a concession of the opponent is rewarded by the negotiator only if the opponent guarantees or "secures" to the negotiator as aspiration level at least as high as the negotiator's last offer does to the opponent (TIETZ 1975, p. 51; TIETZ/WEBER 1978, pp. 66 f.).

The comparison of the secured aspiration levels determines also which negotiator starts the concession process. Because of the discrete character of the aspiration levels, such rules result sometimes in ambiguity. For a definite decision to be made, additional decision filters, e.g., the comparison of "tactical reserves", have to be tested. The coincidence of such filters determines the situational bargaining strength of the first concession maker. The more filters select the same person as concession maker the weaker is his bargaining position and the larger are the concessions he must make in order to come to a fair agreement (TIETZ 1976).

## 2. DECISION MAKING AS A CYBERNETIC PROCESS

An attempt to generalize limited rational decision making as a cybernetic process is presented in Fig. 1 (cf. TIETZ 1982; KIRSCH 1970/71). The decision process can be seen as consisting of subprocesses or phases which may overlap each other. The arrows stand for forward influences and feedbacks, which occur also within subprocesses.

The goal formation process (G) leads to the formulation of goals within an organization. It may result in the formation of aspiration levels, which serve as operational subgoals. The phase of information gathering and processing (I) includes the search for information relevant to the decision. The information is condensed to causal models of the environment. These "inner" models serve to build expectation and to make conditional forecasts. In the planning process (P) the decision maker searches for decision alternatives. The alternatives are evaluated by the goal system, which may be simplified by the use of aspiration levels.

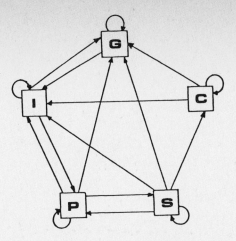

Fig. 1: The recursive decision process

G goal formation process
I information gathering and processing
P planning process
S selection process
C control process


In the selection process (S) one or more favorable alternatives
are selected which fulfill certain criteria as given by aspiration
levels. Possibly, the selection process includes a coordination with
other decision makers by means of negotiations. As long as not exactly
one alternative remains after the selection process, feedbacks occur
to the proceeding phases G, I, or P, which have to narrow or to widen
the range of selection.

Finally, the control process (C), in which the level and the
degree of aspiration fulfilment are realized, influences the phases
G and I. For subsequent decisions, phase G adapts the goals and aspiration levels and phase I improves the "inner" model.

After this short description of the phases of the decision process, we may ask which parts we can identify in the classical decision
theory and which we are missing. First of all, feedbacks do not occur,
neither between nor within the subprocesses. No goal formation process
(G) is needed, since the goal variable is the utility, which is to be
maximized. If, in the extreme case, all the information is available,
no information processing is needed. However, there are some newer

approaches regarding the search for information and its costs. From
the planning process only the evaluation part for utility assessment
remains. In addition, we may have the probability assessment, which is
made simultaneously for all alternatives. The selection part consists
of the calculation of the maximum of the utility function. The control
process we are missing entirely. There are extensions of the strict
rational theory with additional aspects (cf. e.g., LESOURNE 1977,
pp. 43 ff.). Nevertheless, the decision making itself does not become
a network of processes with feedbacks but at best has a linear sequential structure.

$$\boxed{I} \rightarrow \boxed{P} \rightarrow \boxed{S}$$

## 3. THE STRUCTURE OF THE DECISION PROCESS

Both extremes, the maximizing simultaneous approach and the satisfying process approach, have their domains in which they may be applicable and appropriate. However, the reality of the decision process
may lie somewhere in between. An overview on possible influences on
its structure is given in Fig. 2.

The number and the organization of the decision makers (field 1)
influence the decision interdependence (2) and the objective complexity of the decision situation (5) with indefinite signs of the influence;
the simplest economic situations are, as everybody knows, the extreme
cases of monopoly and pure competition. The length and the variety of
chains of causal relations (3), which form the causal network and finally influence the outcome of the decision, have a positive influence
on the objective complexity (5). They also influence the relevant
volume of information (4). The irregularity of the former development
(6), positively influenced by (3), (4), and (5), influences, together
with (5), the uncertainty of expectations (8). The aspects (5), (6),
and (8) increase the subjectively perceived complexity of the decision
situation (9). The higher the problem-oriented cognitive capacity of
the decision maker (7), the more will this complexity be reduced. The
relative importance of the decision problem (10), e.g., the proportion
between a purchase and the decision maker's income, has positive im-
pacts on the subjective complexity (9) and on the fineness of evaluation on the preference scale (12). This fineness has to be the more
reduced the more the situation is perceived as complex (9) and the
less decision time is available (11).

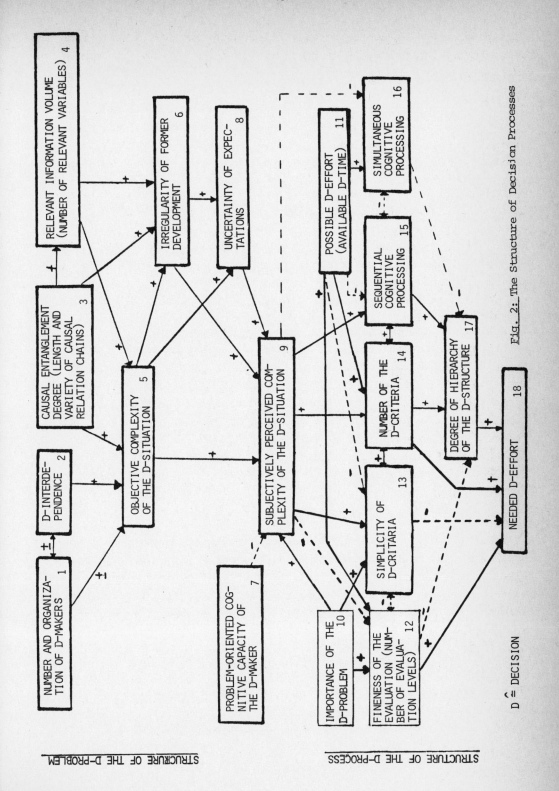

Fig. 2: The Structure of Decision Processes

D ≙ DECISION

STRUCTURE OF THE D-PROBLEM

STRUCTURE OF THE D-PROCESS

Whether decisions, especially in the information, planning, or selection processes, are made more sequentially (15) or more simultaneously (16), depends on the subjective complexity (9), the available decision time (11), and the simplicity (13) and the number (14) of decision criteria used. The degree of hierarchy of the decision structure (17) is influenced by these variables. Finally, the needed decision effort (18) depends on this degree and on (12), (13), and (14).

Although simultaneous cognitive information processing (16) may be seen as a type of sequential processing with many inner loops, the distinction between simultaneous and sequential processing seems to be appropriate. This view is based on the postulation that the results of this "quasi-simultaneous" processing should be consistent and independent of the chronological order of considerations. These qualities are not postulated for a sequential processing in the sense of a limited rational theory.

The order of the criteria applied during the decision process is deduced from the task of coming to a solution with an appropriate decision effort. Especially, in interpersonal relations, simple criteria are used prior to more complicated ones for the reduction of complexity; they need less computational effort and are better suited to coordinate expectations of both sides, since they are more prominent and more salient (SCHELLING 1960, pp. 53-80). The simpler the criteria are, the less selective they are, the more of them are needed, and the higher becomes therefore the degree of hierarchy of the decision structure.

The art of decision making may be seen in the ability to decompose by simple rules a complex decision problem into simpler subproblems and to establish an appropriate chronological hierarchy to handle and to solve them. Rationalized decision making is a compromise between simplification and accuracy.


4. THE STABILIZATION OF BEHAVIOR- AND DECISION-RULES

To develop a descriptive theory of limited rational decision behavior, we have to consider the following aspects. Instead of the unique rule of utility maximization there are many suboptimal rules thinkable which could lead to satisfying results. To construct a realistic theory we have to search for observable regularities of behavior. Regularity of behavior means that there exists an equilibrium of behavior- and decision-rules. This concept may be subsumed under a general idea of equilibrium in a modified definition:

A rule equilibrium is a situation in which the decision maker(s) has(have) no reason to change his(their) rule(s).

There is no reason to change the rules as long as they have proved to be good. The rule equilibrium is a prerequisite of a decision equilibrium normally used in economic theory.

Besides simple decision rules, there may be rules which decide on the application of other rules; thus we may distinguish lower- and higher-order rule equilibria. It is more a philosophical question than an observable fact, whether humans sometimes or always behave in such a higher-order rule equilibrium. Independently of this question, a prerequisite for testing a descriptive theory of a certain order is that a rule equilibrium of at least the same order prevail in reality. In other words, the possibility of observing or testing a theory or parts of it depends on the degree of intensity and stabilization of a behavior- or decision-rule (or of the whole decision process) used by one or more decision makers (intra- or interpersonal degree).

The most important influences on this stabilization degree (1) are shown in Fig. 3. They are:

(2) the degree of communication,
(3) the suitability of a behavior- or decision-rule to coordinate expectations,
(4) the benefit of a rule, or the degree to which a rule proved to be useful,
(5) the relevancy in the sense of a functional suitability,
(6) the strategic suitability,
(7) the fairness of the rule with respect to other decision makers,
(8) the frequency of handling the decision problem before,
(9) the experience with the decision problem and with the other decision makers,
(10) the stage of development and stabilization of the "inner" model of the environment.

The more a decision rule is stabilized (1), the more it becomes a habit (12), unless an important decision problem (11) is to be solved.

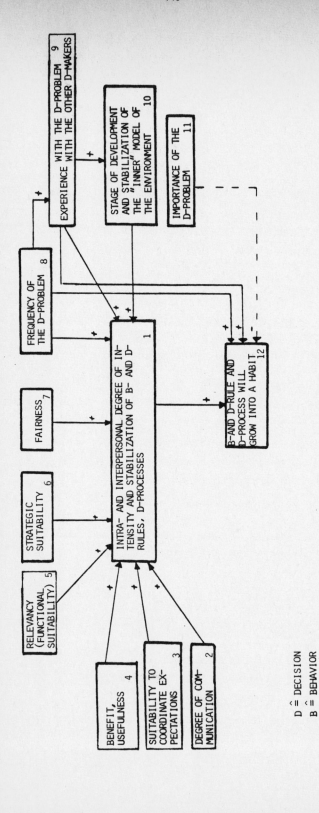

Fig. 3: Stabilization of Behavior and Decision-Rules

D ≙ DECISION
B ≙ BEHAVIOR

An unexperienced decision maker has a flat frequency distribution over the decision rules used for a certain topic. The distribution becomes more and more concentrated on the most suitable rule during the stabilization process (Fig. 4).

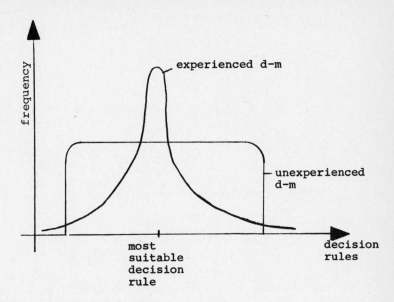

<u>Fig. 4:</u> The frequency distribution of decision rules of experienced and unexperienced decision makers

## 5. ON THE ACCURACY OF A DISCRETE BARGAINING THEORY

One possible simplification of complexity is the thinking in discrete alternatives rather than in a continuum of possibilities. It is an interesting question how accurate discrete theories may be if their prediction misses the correct result by not more than the smallest possible error. The smallest possible error depends on the point of the decision process at which real behavior differs from theory. The decision maker's ability and/or willingness to differentiate the decision situations varies within the decision process.

In the context of an aspiration-oriented bargaining and decision theory the following steps of considerations may be helpful to formulate some hypotheses on the accuracy. These aspects can outline only tendencies and are not yet implemented in a bargaining theory.

*(1) The average niveau of decision b*

The average niveau (b) of the problem which is up for decision influences the numeric accuracy in general. Although considering constant relations between accuracy measures and the level of decisions, we do not postulate an analogy to the law of WEBER/FECHNER (cf. e.g., LUCE/GALANTER 1963).

*(2) The global decision area g*

The global decision area is that area in which the decision maker believes the solution can be found. This area is limited by the human capacity of information processing. To limit this area is reasonable behavior, too.

Assuming a constant relation between the area g and the niveau of the decision b, one may write

$$g = \frac{b}{c} \, , \qquad\qquad\qquad (5.1a)$$

where $c \in N$ and N is the set of natural numbers. The weaker formulation

$$g = g \, (b, \ldots) \qquad\qquad\qquad (5.1b)$$

allows also for additional influences.

*(3) The number of aspiration levels n*

The number of aspiration levels of an aspiration grid, formed during the planning phase of the decision process, is limited to $n (n \in N)$. This follows from the limited human ability of imagination. Before negotiations one cannot imagine more than about four or five different situations with different behavioral consequences.

*(4) The aspiration range r*

The aspiration range (r) is the range between two adjacent aspiration levels. Whereas the upper and the lower aspiration levels are distinct points, the alternatives within the range are not distinguished by preference and attainability considerations made during the planning phase. In addition, the decision maker is unable to project too many different situations into the same range; we assume that his ability is limited to the number $d \in N$.

Combining the foregoing points, we can write the average aspiration range $\bar{r}$ as follows:

$$\bar{r} = \frac{g}{n-1} , \quad \text{for} \quad n > 1, \text{[1]} \tag{5.2a}$$

or less accurately

$$\bar{r} = \bar{r} \ (g,n,\ldots) . \tag{5.2b}$$

The number of distinguished situations within the global area g is
then

$$(n-1)d + n = (n-1)(d+1) + 1 . \tag{5.3}$$

An additional limitation of the aspiration range is given by
attainability considerations (a). The closer two adjacent aspiration
levels are the more attainable the upper level is felt to be. Then the
individual aspiration range r amounts to:

$$r = a\,\bar{r} , \tag{5.4}$$

$$\text{with} \quad 0 \leq a \leq n-1 .$$

*(5) The prominence standard p*

The use of prominent numbers follows from the limited capacity
of memorizing and transfering information. The prominence principle,
first discussed by SCHELLING (1960), simplifies interpersonal and
intrapersonal communication. There are certain numbers, that, together
with their multiples, are used more often than others. These numbers,
which seem to be preferred by the decision maker as prominent, are
called prominence units. One can try to establish a prominence order
within a sample of observations (VIDMAJER 1977, TIETZ 1984). We may
define the prominence standard p as the most preferred prominence
unit. [2]

One can assume that the prominence standard p is more or less
strongly connected with the aspiration range $\bar{r}$ through the number of
distinguished situations d:

$$p \approx \frac{\bar{r}}{d+1} \tag{5.5a}$$

$$\text{or} \quad p = p(\bar{r},d,\ldots) . \tag{5.5b}$$

---

1) n = 1 is equivalent to g = 0 and $\bar{r}$ = 0. (5.1) would then not hold.
2) A more precise definition of p is given in TIETZ 1984.

*(6) The threshold of perceptibility* φ

If two values differ not more than the threshold of perceptibility φ, the just-noticeable difference, they are regarded as equal:

$$x = y \ , \ if \ \ |x-y| < \phi \ .$$  (5.6)

The use of a threshold is not only suitable for the assumption of
limited human perceptional capacity (LUCE/GALANTER 1963), but also
serves simplification.

With regard to decision making it is reasonable to choose this
threshold as a prominent value. Thus one can write:

$$\phi = \frac{p}{k} \ , \ \ with \ \ k \in N.^{1)}$$  (5.7)

It is an interesting question, whether the following relation between
the threshold and the niveau of the decision can be found empirically

$$\phi = \frac{b}{k \cdot (d+1)(n-1) \cdot c}$$  (5.8a)

$$or \quad \phi = \frac{1}{k} \ p(\bar{r}(g(b,\dots),n,\dots),d,\dots) \ .$$  (5.8b)

*(7) The smallest possible error e and the accuracy f*

Obviously, a theory predicting an aera is less accurate than a
point-predicting theory. But an area-predicting theory has a greater
chance to cover reality.

As an example of such an area theory, the aspiration balancing
principle of negotiation postulates agreements by which both partners
reach nearly the same aspiration level (cf. TIETZ/BARTOS 1983). That
means the difference is not greater than one aspiration range $\bar{r}$. Thus,
the accuracy f amounts to

$$f = \pm \bar{r} \ .$$  (5.9)

The smallest possible error which can be made within this theory would
occur when each partner's estimation of the opponent's reached aspiration level deviates just by $e = \bar{r}$. Thus, the accuracy regarding this
error amounts to

$$f_e = \pm 2 \bar{r} \ .$$  (5.10)

---

1) In a wage negotiation experiment we found values of p = .5% and
φ = .05% wage increase, thus k = 10 follows. Cf. TIETZ 1975; 1978,
esp. footnote 15 on p. 439.

An example of a point-predicting theory is the market-negotiation
theory of CROESSMANN (CROESSMANN/TIETZ 1983). This theory allows only
price concessions of 1, 2, or 3 price units.[1] Thus, one can conclude
that the prominence standard p is equal to one price unit. In this
process theory the aspiration levels of both bargaining partners are
compared already during negotiation according to the aspiration securing principle. The possible two consequences of the result of this
comparison are that the first counterconcessions are made with 1p or
2p.[2] If at this point the negotiator in estimating the opponent's
secured aspiration level makes the smallest possible error of $e = \bar{r}$,
then the final bargaining result will differ from the theory not by $\bar{r}$,
but by p. The accuracy is then

$$f_e = \pm\, p \ . \tag{5.11}$$

These tentative considerations show that the judgment of the
accuracy of discrete theories has to be made with regard to the smallest possible error. Besides a point-predicting theory, we need a
sequence of related theories, derived by taking into account the possible errors which could be made during the decision process. This
follows from the concept of limited rationality, since even goal-
oriented behavior is not always perfect.

REFERENCES

Croessmann, H.J./ Tietz, R. (1983): Market Behavior Based on Aspiration
    Levels, in: R. Tietz (1983a), pp. 170-185.

Kirsch, W. (1970/71): Entscheidungsprozesse, Wiesbaden.

Lesourne, J. (1977): A Theory of the Individual for Economic Analysis,
    Vol. 1, Amsterdam-New York-Oxford.

Luce, R.D./ Galanter, E. (1963): Discrimination, in: R.D. Luce/ R.B.
    Bush/ E. Galanter (eds.): Handbook of Mathematical Psychology,
    Vol. 1, New York et al., pp. 191-243.

Sauermann, H. (ed.)(1972): Contributions to Experimental Economics,
    Vol. 3, Tuebingen.

Sauermann, H. (ed.)(1978): Bargaining Behavior, Contributions to Expe-
    rimental Economics, Vol. 7, Tuebingen.

Schelling, T.C. (1960): The Strategy of Conflict, Cambridge-Mass.

Tietz, R. (1975): An Experimental Analysis of Wage Bargaining Behavior,
    in: Zeitschrift für die Gesamte Staatswissenschaft 131,pp. 44-91.

---

1) Fig. 6 and 7, CROESSMANN/TIETZ 1983, p. 182-183.
2) h10 and Fig. 7, ibid., p. 182 f.

Tietz, R. (1976): Der Anspruchsausgleich in experimentellen Zwei-Personen-Verhandlungen mit verbaler Kommunikation, in: H. Brandstätter/ H. Schuler (eds.): Entscheidungsprozesse in Gruppen, Beiheft 2 der Zeitschrift für Sozialpsychologie, Bern-Stuttgart-Wien, pp.123-141, reprinted in: H.W. Crott/ G.F. Müller (eds.): Wirtschafts- und Sozialpsychologie, Hamburg 1978,pp. 140-159.

Tietz, R. (1978): Entscheidungsprinzipien der bilateralen Anspruchsanpassung, in: E. Helmstädter (ed.): Neuere Entwicklungen in den Wirtschaftswissenschaften, Schriften des Vereins für Socialpolitik, N.F. Bd. 98, Berlin,pp. 431-453.

Tietz, R. (1982): Verhandlungsprozesse als Bausteine ökonomischer Systeme, in: R. Pfeiffer/ H. Lindner (eds.): Systemtheorie und Kybernetik in Wirtschaft und Verwaltung, Berlin,pp. 389-400.

Tietz, R. (ed.)(1983a): Aspiration Levels in Bargaining and Economic Decision Making, Lecture Notes in Economics and Mathematical Systems, Vol. 213, Berlin-Heidelberg-New York-Tokyo.

Tietz, R. (1983b): Aspiration-Oriented Decision Making, in: R. Tietz 1983a, pp. 1-7.

Tietz, R. (1984): The Prominence Standard, Part I, Frankfurter Arbeiten zur experimentellen Wirtschaftsforschung, Discussion Paper A 18.

Tietz, R./ Bartos, O.J.(1983): Balancing Aspiration Levels as Fairness Principle in Negotiations, in: R. Tietz 1983a, pp. 52-66.

Tietz, R./ Weber, H.-J.(1978): Decision Behavior in Multivariable Negotiations, in: H. Sauermann 1978, pp. 60-87.

Vidmajer, U. (1977): Zur Prominenz von Anspruchsänderungen, Frankfurter Arbeiten zur experimentellen Wirtschaftsforschung, Discussion Paper No.D4.

Wierzbicki, A.P. (1984): Negotiation and Mediation in Conflict II: Plural Rationality and Interactive Processes, in this volume.

# USES OF EXPERIMENTAL GAMES

Anatol Rapoport
*University of Toronto, Toronto, Ontario, Canada*

The distinction between a descriptive or predictive theory on the one hand and a prescriptive or normative one on the other is sufficiently clear.  Still there is a region
of overlap between them.  Generally speaking, a descriptive theory deals with what
is and a prescriptive one with what ought to be.  But "ought" can be understood in
two senses:  in terms of a value system and in terms of an idealized situation.  Questions of value do not enter the realm of physical science.  Nevertheless we can speak
of normative theories of physical phenomena in the sense of our expectations of what
we should observe under idealized conditions, such as in perfect vacuum, thermodynamic
equilibrium, etc.  In fact, since physical theories consist for the most part of
mathematical models of physical phenomena, they are, strictly speaking, normative
theories, dealing with how things "ought" to behave under idealized conditions, rather
than with how they actually behave.  What makes physical theory also descriptive (and
predictive) is the circumstance that the mathematical models are often very good
approximations to reality, so that "what is" turns out to be quite close to "what ought
to be."

In the social sciences, in spite of what proponents of "value free" science maintain, values are frequently incorporated into theory and to that extent theories become
normative.  But even if values do not enter models of social phenomena explicitly, the
theories retain a strong normative component, because the idealizations (without which
no theory can be constructed) are usually considerably removed from reality.  Descriptive theories in the social sciences are seldom based on models, and predictive
theories derive their predictive potential from inductive rather than deductive reasoning.

Such is the situation in decision theory.  The distinction between a normative
and a descriptive (or predictive) decision theory is quite sharp.  The values that
enter normative decision theory revolve around the concept of rationality and of
utility.  Normative decision theory purports to prescribe to an actor how he is to
choose among a set of alternatives if utilities can be assigned to them and if he is
rational.  A descriptive theory would purport to describe how actors actually choose
among alternatives in a given situation.  An area of overlap between "what is" and
"what ought to be" would exist, if the existence of actors sufficiently similar to
rational actors governed by sufficiently consistent utility assignments to alternatives could be demonstrated.  Those of us who have worked in the field know how

difficult it is to exhibit a rational actor with consistent utilities on a sufficiently strong scale. For this reason, decision theory must remain divided in two branches: a normative theory, logically elegant and providing opportunities for utilizing sophisticated mathematical apparatus, and a descriptive theory, heavily dependent on masses of data, forcing the investigator to face the problem of making sense of them and of finding a basis for some semblance of generality.

## Points of Contact between Normative and Predictive Decision Theories

The gulf that separates normative and descriptive decision theory is narrower in some areas of investigation and wider in others. I would venture to say that the two theories come closest where the concept of rationality can be most clearly defined and where utility can be most naturally linked to observable quantities. Such an area is that of risky choices iterated many times, where utilities are expressible in money. Gambling and insurance come immediately to mind.

In this way, a connection can be established between a prescriptive and a predictive decision theory. If the decision of a "rational actor" in a given situation can be specified, then such a decision can be used as a base line with which actual decisions of real actors can be compared. And so a measure of rationality can be established for a given actor in terms of the discrepancy between his decisions and the prescribed "rational" decisions. Corroborated hypotheses about the presumed causes of the discrepancies can be put at the foundation of a predictive theory. This is one way in which experimental games can be used, for example as so-called "games against nature" involving a single decision-maker in a chancy environment or a pair of decision-makers playing a zero-sum game.

If the payoffs in a decision problem are not naturally measurable quantities, such as money, or if the decision problem involves monetary payoffs but occurs only once, the situation is more complex. Here a predictive theory necessitates a preliminary establishment of a utility function on the outcomes of decisions. Except when an ordinal utility scale suffices, the problem of determining a utility function can be quite difficult. Note that it will not do to define utility tautologically, as it were, as "that which is maximized by a rational player." For in that case, the establishment of a utility function is based on the assumption that every actor is rational at least in situations used to determine his utility function. To be sure, such a function, once determined, could be used in further experiments to predict decisions. The difficulty is that in many instances a utility function satisfying certain apparently innocuous consistency criteria cannot be established to begin with. The investigator who is interested not in an actor's utility function per se but rather in his decision behaviour is left with no choice but to by-pass the utility problem altogether and work with the actual payoffs used in the experiments, for instance, money. But then he must give up the idea of formulating a prescriptive theory (since he does not know the actor's utilities, if any). He must confine himself to mere descriptions of behaviour in experimental games. If he is lucky, he may detect regularities in patterns of such behaviour which may suggest the beginnings of a predictive theory.

## Social Traps

This approach seems to be the only feasible one in situations that transcend the confines of games against nature and of two-person zero-sum games. The most salient situations of this sort are so-called "social traps." Here the concept of "rationality" is no longer unambivalent. To be of use as a reference point in decision analysis, it must be refined. In particular, individual, better said, individualistic and collective rationality must be clearly distinguished, since the prescriptions of the two kinds of rationality in social trap situations conflict. In fact, a social trap is defined as a situation in which "rational" pursuit of own interest by each player results in an outcome that no one is satisfied with in the sense that the participants would unanimously prefer another attainable outcome.

In studies involving social traps, the problem of utility measurement and of quantitative comparisons between actual and optimal outcomes assumes a secondary importance. In fact the absence of an unambivalent definition of a "rational outcome" (without further qualification) often precludes such comparisons altogether. The more interesting questions are those related to the players' choices between individually rational and collectively rational courses of action.

For instance, in the well known Prisoner's Dilemma game, a typical question to be answered by experiment is that of relative frequencies of choices of the "cooperative" (collectively rational) and of the "defecting" (individually rational) strategy. Maximization of real numbers does not enter this picture, since the distinction between individually rational and collectively rational outcomes requires the payoffs to be given, as a rule, on scales no stronger than the ordinal.

Cardinal payoffs can be introduced, but whether utilities are linear functions of the payments (e.g., money) is not important, because the behaviour of subjects in such experiments is not compared with some ideal standard, representing rationality in terms of the maximization of utility. Rather, variations of subjects' behaviour correlated with some imposed variation of the payoffs (whatever be the wherewithal of payment) are interesting in their own right.

## Prisoner's Dilemma

As an example, consider the game called Prisoner's Dilemma, shown in its general form as a symmetric game represented by Matrix 1.

|  | $C_2$ | $D_2$ |
|---|---|---|
| $C_1$ | R, R | S, T |
| $D_1$ | T, S | P, P |

Matrix 1

Player 1, called "Row" chooses between $C_1$ and $D_1$. Player 2, called "Column," chooses between $C_2$ and $D_2$. The first entry in each cell is the payoff to Row, the second to Column. Prisoner's Dilemma is characterized by the inequality $T_i > R_i > P_i > S_i$ (i=1,2).

In experiments with this game it is found that when the game is played just once, some subjects choose C, others D. If the game is repeated many times, the same subject sometimes chooses C sometimes D. Thus, the frequency of C choices becomes a naturally prominent dependent variable. The cardinal values of T, R, P, and S can be used as independent variables. No a priori hypotheses based either on assumed "rationality" of players and so on some maximization procedures suggest themselves. At this stage a theory of such a game can be only descriptive. On the basis of observed regularities, however, predictions might be made about how frequencies of observed C choices will vary with each of the independent variables. Indeed, it is found that frequencies of C choices increase with R and S and decrease with T and P. This finding, being strongly expected on common sense grounds or in terms of some conditioning learning model (in iterated plays) is for this reason not very interesting. However, it would be interesting to know which of the payoffs has the greater effect on variations of frequency, since the answer is difficult to guess on a priori grounds and also because the answer can be interpreted in psychological terms.

One can, for example, ask which is numerically larger $\partial C/\partial T$ or $\partial C/\partial S$, where C is the frequency of C choices. As has been said, both derivatives are observed to be negative. The first can be interpreted as a measure of the "temptation" to try to obtain the largest payoff. The second can be interpreted as a measure of the "fear" of getting the "sucker's" (i.e., the lone cooperator's) payoff. Given sufficiently large volumes of data, this question could be answered quite reliably (i.e., with sufficient statistical significance) for a given population of players. Given even larger masses of data, the question can be answered for different populations, e.g., men or women, people in various social categories, of various cultural backgrounds, and so on, who would thereby be psychologically differentiated. It is these opportunities that brought experimental games, especially the best known of them--Prisoner's Dilemma--to the attention of social psychologists.

## The Game of Chicken

As has been said, Prisoner's Dilemma is a prime example of a social trap. There are others. Consider the so-called game of "Chicken." If the payoffs are labeled as in Matrix 1, Chicken is characterized by inequalities $T > R > S > P$, so that the worst payoff for both players is in the lower right hand corner of the payoff matrix. Since it is the smallest payoff, its numerical magnitude is not restricted by the inequality that defines the game. It can be a huge negative number. An example is shown in Matrix 2.

|  | $C_2$ | $D_2$ |
|---|---|---|
| $C_1$ | 1, 1 | -10, 10 |
| $D_1$ | 10, -10 | -100, -100 |

Matrix 2

The game of Chicken with large punishment for double defection (both players choosing D).

The game could also be called "Brinkmanship" or a game of pre-emption. The definition of a game in normal form demands that the players choose their strategies simultaneously, i.e., in ignorance of each other's choice. If the rules specify that one of the players must choose first and the choice is made known to the other, the matrix representing simultaneously chosen strategies no longer represents the normal form of the game, for in that case, the second player's strategies must be defined as conditional on the first player's choices. For example if the original game is a 2 x 2 game (two players with two strategies each), then requiring one player to choose first and to make his choice known to the other would make four strategies available to the second player. In the case of the two games just considered, these would be: (1) Choose C regardless of the first player's choice; (2) Choose the same as the other; (3) Choose the opposite of what the other chooses; (4) Choose D regardless of how the other chooses.

Since, however, we are discussing experimental situations suggested by the theory of games rather than formal game theory, let us ignore this implication of non-simultaneous choices. In particular, let us assume that in the game of Chicken, one of the players can somehow manage to choose his strategy first and to make his choice known to the other. He then has the opportunity to "pre-empt." The pre-emption refers not to a "pre-emptive strike," much discussed in strategic circles, but to a pre-emptive threat, emphasized by prominent civilian strategists of the American defence community, in particular, by Thomas Schelling and by Herman Kahn. The latter gave a picturesque description of a pre-emptive threat in the context of the game of Chicken as it was actually played by spirited American youngsters in the 1950's. Possibly the game was inspired by the then publicized concept of "brinkmanship," advanced by Eisenhower's Secretary of State, John Foster Dulles.

One way of playing chicken is for two drivers to rush at each other straddling the white line that divides the directions of traffic. If neither driver swerves in time, both are killed in a head-on collision. According to Herman Kahn, who used this game as a model of international relations, a way to insure a win is to yank one's own steering wheel off and to throw it away. If the driver of the other car sees this, he will know that now the first driver could not swerve even if he wanted to. Consequently, the opponent must swerve (if he does not want to die) and, in doing so, is labeled "Chicken" (American slang for "coward") conceding victory to the reckless driver. This strategy is sure to work if the opponent is "rational," in which case the reckless, that is the "irrational" driver wins. Indeed the advantage of being thought crazy has been frequently pointed out in strategic circles.

The absurdity of Kahn's recommendation becomes obvious when one takes into account that his advice applies equally to both players. In fact, Kahn recognizes this when he says in the very next paragraph of his book On Escalation (Kahn, 1965), that it may happen that just as the creatively reckless driver yanks his steering wheel off, his opponent is inspired by the same idea. Thus, "showing resolve" can have disastrous consequences.

## Strategic vs. Non-strategic Approaches to Game-theoretic Models

Social traps (of which the game of Chicken is also an example) are traps precisely because conventional strategic analysis provides no satisfactory way out. By conventional strategic analysis I mean an analysis oriented toward optimization of decisions by one party. This is overwhelmingly, perhaps exclusively, the point of view underlying all strategic analysis in which present day decision-makers are interested in. I am referring to the decision-makers in the so-called "Man's world," predominantly the world of business, competitive politics, and war. Social traps are either excluded from the conceptual repertoire of the actors in that world or else are subjected to the same sort of analysis that is relevant to games against nature and to two-person zero-sum games, namely strategic analysis directed toward discovering optimal strategies that can be recommended to a single actor. The late Yuri Germeier, in his book Igry s nieprotivopolozhnymi interesami (non-antagonistic games) has made this orientation quite explicit. He says specifically that his analysis is conducted from the point of view of one of the players involved in a game, whom he calls "dieistvuyush-chaia storona," that is, "the actor." As a result, the most salient problems raised by the analysis of social traps assume a secondary importance or are by-passed altogether. It is to restore the saliency of these problems, in particular their glaring relevance to the horrendous dangers with which humanity is currently faced that some investigators in so-called "peace research" have turned to experimental games.  The principal objectives in this programme is not that of training decision-makers to make "optimal" decisions, as is the case in most business games and in all war games used for training purposes.  The objective is, rather, to see how people behave in social trap situations and to use these findings in educational programmes aimed at promoting enlightenment in areas where obscurantism, hand-me-down conventional wisdom, and dangerous delusions have been entrenched.

## Experimental Techniques

Let us return to Prisoner's Dilemma, which, as has been said, is the best known and most explored social trap game.  Experiments with this game can be conducted in three formats:  (1) the one shot game; (2) the iterated game with two bona fide players; and (3) the iterated game with one bona fide player and one "stooge." Each format brings out a different aspect of the game.  The dilemma is most salient in the one-shot format.  One would think that if the game is iterated many times, a pair of players might eventually "learn" to cooperate.  The purpose of the one-shot experiment is actually to exclude the effects of learning and the effects of interaction.  The question raised is what the subject will do, when he must make a single decision, where he understands that one of his available strategies is dominant and thus governed by the sure-thing principle, while the other is collectively rational and, if adopted by both players, leads to a Pareto-optimal outcome.

Difficulties in conducting one shot experiments are those of cost effectiveness. It becomes costly in time and money to recruit a pair of subjects, to schedule them, to deal with the "no show" problem, to spend a half hour or so to instruct them in the rules of the game, to explain the implications of their decisions, and for all that trouble to obtain at most two bits of information:  the choices of one or the other strategy by each of the players.  In the iterated game this problem does not arise since the same two subjects can provide much more information.  As we have seen, however, the iterated game brings in effects of learning and interaction, which it is desirable to exclude in observing behaviour of people in a social trap when it is presented in its crassest form.

In attempting to make single shot experiments more cost effective, my colleagues and I at the University of Toronto designed a procedure where each subject indicates his decision in many different 2 x 2 games, each played with no announcement of the outcome.  Specifically, each subject is given a booklet containing hundreds of game matrices, each with a different strategic structure.  He/she is assigned the role of one of the players and is asked to indicate his/her choice of strategy, having been told that each of his/her choices will be matched at random with that of another subject in the role of the co-player and that they will be paid in money in accordance with the payoffs indicated in each matrix when they bring the filled out booklets back to us.

In a way, the procedure proved to be highly satisfactory, since there was no need to bring the subjects into the laboratory, the "no show" problems did not arise, and the subjects could take all the time they wanted to think about their decisions. Another problem, however, arose. There were strong indications that the subjects, faced with the task of making several hundred decisons, simply adopted an across-the-board decision rule, for example, the maximim or maximization of expected gain, as-suming equiprobability of the co-player's choices, or something of this sort. Thus, it was the subjects that could be categorized according to the (inferred) decision rule they used. We, however, were interested in categorizing the games according to their strategic structure.

A neat solution of the problem of conducting one-shot experiments cost-effectively was found by D. Hofstadter (1983). He conducted his experiment on one-shot Prisoner's Dilemma by mail. Obtaining some financing from Scientific American, where his results were subsequently published, he could make the game worthwhile by paying off in dollars instead of in pennies as has been usual in laboratory experiments. Hofstadter sent a letter to 20 of his colleagues, explaining the rules of Prisoner's Dilemma and soli-citing their decision. He told each prospective player that his response would be matched with each of the others' and that he would be paid the total amount thus obtained. Specifically, each of twenty players would get $3.00 for each C response and nothing for each D response if he chose C. If he chose D, he would get $5.00 for each C response and $1.00 for each D response. If we denote the number of C and D responses respectively by C and D, the situation can be depicted thus, where $U_c$ and $U_d$ are payoffs to a C player and to a D player respectively:

$$U_c = 3C$$
$$U_d = 5C + D = 4C + N$$

If the game is presented in this way, the dominance of D over C is glaring. Yet it is in everyone's collective interest to choose C, since $U_c$ increases linearly with C. To be sure, $U_d$ also increases linearly with C. However, if everyone played C, everyone would receive 3C = 3N dollars, while if everyone played D (i.e. C = 0), everyone would receive 0 + N = N dollars.

## Experimental Results

Assuming that a choice of C reflects a higher degree of social awareness (i.e., aware-ness of collective interest), Professor Hofstadter's disappointment with the result of his experiment is understandable. Out of his twenty subjects only 8 chose C. This result, however, is in line with several results obtained in one-shot Prisoner's Dilemma games in different experimental situations. Roughly 50% of naive subjects choose C. Far from disappointing, I find this result rather encouraging, since it demonstrates that individualistic rationality, the solid rock on which all classical economics and most of operations research rest, does not, at any rate not yet completely dominate the consciousness of ordinary people. Apparently, confronted with a Prisoner's Dilemma game, quite a number of them look to see which outcome is most advantageous to both players and choose accordingly.

It can be argued, of course, that many naive subjects choose C not because they are socially sophisticated but because they are strategically naive. They have not internalized the idea of strategy and erroneously assume that they are in a position to choose an outcome. There may be something in that argument. Let us see what a pair of strategically sophisticated players would do if they had to play Prisoner's Dilemma 100 times, the outcome of each play being announced. Elementary strategic analysis shows that the individualistically rational thing to do is to play D all 100 times. This is so, because whatever be the first 99 outcomes, the outcome of the hundredth play is a foregone conclusion. Neither player has any cause to fear retaliation for choosing D and hence can choose D with impunity. He should be motivated to do so because D gets him more than C regardless of how the co-player chooses on the last play. But if the outcome of the last play is a foregone conclusion, the next-to-the-last play becomes the "last play" and the analysis leads to the same result. The number of plays does not matter so long as it is finite and known to both players. It follows that a pair of strategically sophisticated players will attain the DD outcome (which is worse for both than the CC outcome) whether the game is played 100 times or 1,000,000 times. The implication of this result in evaluating the nature of strategic sophistication in the "games" played in the international arena should be obvious. Unfortunately it is effectively obscured by the primacy of strategic thinking.

Experiments with iterated Prisoner's Dilemma show a very different picture. In long sequences of iterated plays, the unilateral outcomes $C_1D_2$ and $C_2D_1$ eventually become rare. Typically, both players "lock" in on either CC or on DD. The former have learned that "cooperation pays" and reap the benefits thereoff. The latter are caught in a social trap, like both superpowers, and suffer the consequences. Neither dares to break out of the trap. "Unilateralism" is anathema to the strategists of both sides. To play C while the other continues to play D amounts to rewarding the other for his adamance and being punished for one's attempt to initiate cooperation, hence unacceptable in the world where "realism" is a deeply entrenched component of conventional wisdom. It is interesting to observe that in iterated Prisoner's Dilemma experiments, initiatives of this sort are reciprocated about one third of the time on the average which attests to some (but not enough) awareness of collective interest in those contexts.

Iterated Prisoner's Dilemma in which both players are bona fide subjects has been the format most frequently used in the laboratory. The questions of interest in this context are mostly about the dynamics of learning in situations with dual control.

The third format mentioned above is an experiment with only one bona fide subject in an iterated game, the other being a "stooge," i.e., a programmed subject. Here the center of interest is the real player's response to the other's strategy, which now plays the role of the independent variable. As an example, consider an experiment where the stooge uses one of the following five strategies in a long sequence of iterated Prisoner's Dilemma. (1) The completely uncooperative strategy, i.e., unconditional D; (2) The 50% responsive strategy, i.e., one that always "punishes" the subject's D with D on the following play but "rewards" the subject's C 50% of the time; (3) "Tit-for-tat," which always rewards the subject's C and always punishes the subject's D; (4) The 50% retaliatory strategy, one that always rewards C but punishes D with probability 50%; (5) the completely cooperative (100% C) strategy (Chammah, 1969).

The results of that experiment are interesting. As expected, the unconditionally uncooperative strategy elicits very little cooperation from the subjects -- about 6% C responses, respresenting probably some futile attempts to get out of the social trap. More interesting is the average frequency of cooperation in response to the unconditionally cooperative strategy, namely 50% C responses. This mean frequency, however, is not modal. The distribution of the C frequencies in a population of subjects is strongly bi-modal: about half the subjects respond with full cooperation to the stooge's unconditional cooperation, but the other half fully exploit the unconditional cooperator.

Most cooperation is elicited by the Tit-for-tat strategy, about 75% C responses on the average. The psychologically interesting aspects of this result is that the players who play against the Tit-for-tat strategy are almost never aware of this. At any rate, they do not give the correct answer to the question, "What do you think was the pattern of choices used by your co-player?" The high level of cooperation elicited by the Tit-for-tat strategy can be attributed to simple instrumental conditioning: the cooperative response is immediately rewarded; the uncooperative one punished. What the subjects do not realize is that the co-player is a mirror image of themselves, that it is really they themselves who completely determine the behaviour of the co-player. The relevance of this observation and of the unawareness of the mirror image in international relations should be obvious to present day diplo-military strategists, but unfortunately this circumstance is also obscured by the hegemony of the strategic orientation.

## Tit-for-Tat:  Strength through Weakness

The idea that a strategy in playing iterated Prisoner's Dilemma could reflect to a greater or lesser degree an awareness of the problems set by this game crystallized in a contest arranged by Professor Robert Axelrod of the University of Michigan

(Axelrod, 1984). In the first contest of this sort 15 computer programmes were entered with the understanding that the contest would be a "round robin," that is, every programme would be matched with every other submitted programme (including itself) and the programme that got the largest total payoff would be declared the winner.

That contest was won by Tit-for-tat. The results were announced and a second contest was arranged. This time there were 63 entries from six countries submitted by persons active in a large variety of disciplines. Tit-for-tat was submitted again and again won.

This may seem somewhat surprising if one assumes that the success of Tit-for-tat in the first contest stimulated contestants to submit programmes designed to "beat" Tit-for-tat. Whether they were so designed or not, the fact is that Tit-for-tat did not "beat" a single one of the submitted programmes when matched with each of them in turn. It did, however, get once again the highest score for the simple reason that the "smart" programmes, which did beat Tit-for-tat in one-vs-one encounters had also to be matched <u>against each other</u>, whereby they reduced each other's scores. One would assume that the obvious "moral" in this story, namely that "in weakness there is strength" makes no impression in the "defence communities."

## What Can Be Learned from Experimental Games

This brings me to the central point I hope to make in this presentation, the answer to the question of the value experimental games for decision theory. Their principal value is educational but in a way different from the way most simulation games are used educationally in business or military circles. Almost invariably, the format of simulation games provides for the conception of strategically optimal decision. That is to say, optimality is considered from the point of view of each participant as an individual in the sense of representing a single set of interests. The object of the training is that of inculcating the participants with strategic sophistication. As can be seen from the examples of experimental games discussed here, these serve a different purpose. The center of interest is the limitation of individualistic rationality in most conflict situations, specifically in conflict situations that transcend the format of the two-person zero-sum game in which maximization of utility accruing to <u>one</u> of the players (and therefore minimization of the opponent's utility) can be defended as a principle of rationality. This is not true of social traps. But the hegemony of zero-sum game mentality is itself a social trap. It is the sort of mentality that makes the defence communities of both superpowers a horrendous threat to civilization and perhaps to humanity itself. The two-person zero-sum game mentality embodies the cardinal principle of strategic thinking in the military profession, expressed in the maxim, "Not the preferences or intentions but the <u>capabilities</u> of the opponent" should guide the design of strategy."

The educational value of experimental games is in the way they shed light on the limitations of this view of "strategic sophistication." The object is not to "train" the participants in techniques of effective decision-making, which is the objective of practically all business and military simulation games, but rather to enlighten the participants, to stretch their conceptual repertoires and so (one hopes) to make at least some of them immune to the lures of social traps.

Social psychologists have been attracted by the experimental potentialities of Prisoner's Dilemma because of the way it illustrates the dialectic opposition between individual and collective rationality, between competition and cooperation or between conflict and conflict resolution, if you will. It is, in a way, unfortunate that because of these opportunities, the attention of social psychologists using experimental games as a research tool has been riveted on this particular game. If one approaches experimental games from an opposite point of view, as it were, not from the point of view of finding a game to fit a particular social situation but by investigating the strategic structures of the simplest games systematically in the abstract, as it were, and only then looking for social situations that may be modeled by the various structures, one gets a much better idea of the richness of this approach.

Assume that the payoffs of a 2 x 2 game are given only on an ordinal scale and that the four payoffs of each player are strictly ordered. Then the strategic structure of each of the 2 x 2 games can be defined in terms of a pair of inequalities expressing the preference orderings of the respective players for the outcomes. It turns out there are 78 strategically inequivalent 2 x 2 games (Rapoport and Guyer, 1966). If the payoffs are only weakly ordered, the number of inequivalent games is 732 (Guyer and Hamburger, 1968).

So far we have mentioned only two such games. An idea of how entirely different motivational pressures can operate in a 2 x 2 game can be gotten by analyzing the game shown in Matrix 4.

|  | $S_2$ | $T_2$ |
|---|---|---|
| $S_1$ | 0, 5 | 5, 0 |
| $T_1$ | -2, -1 | -1, -2 |

Matrix 4

The Top Dog-Underdog Game

In this game, both Row and Column have dominating strategies. Individual rationality, therefore, dictates the outcome $S_1S_2$. Moreover, the outcome is Pareto-optimal, so that the paradox noted in Prisoner's Dilemma does not arise. Other problems, however, arise instead. In a long sequence of iterations one could expect that Row will not be satisfied in obtaining 0 as his payoff play after play, while Column gets 5. From Row's point of view, it would be "fair" if Column alternated between $S_2$ and $T_2$, while he, Row, would continue to play $S_1$. In this way Row would also get the benefit of positive payoffs. The question now arises what is a "fair" distribution of Column's choices between $S_2$ and $T_2$. Another question is what, if anything, Row can do about the situation if Column refuses to "share" and if explicit communication is not possible. For example, does it make sense for Row to "strike" by switching from $S_1$ to $T_1$, thereby "punishing" Column (but incidentally also himself) in the expectation that Column, in order to forestall further "strikes," will shift to $T_2$, thus giving Row the opportunity to effect outcome $S_1T_2$ and obtain the largest payoff? After this, Column has the power to re-establish the status quo at $S_1S_2$. What will happen then? Answers to questions such as these cannot be obtained from a normative theory. The best we can hope for is a descriptive theory which might develop into a predictive theory if enough of "relevant" independent variables can be singled out, be they cardinal payoffs, cultural background or personalities of players, dynamics of learning in iterated plays, strategies prescribed to a programmed player or what not.

With regard to the latter, two interesting questions suggest themselves immediately. Suppose the programmed player is Column (who is "top dog" in this asymmetric game) and he uses the "adamant" strategy--unconditional $S_2$. How frequently will Row resort to "striking," i.e., switching to $T_1$ if the tactics appear to be futile? How persistent will he be in sticking to $T_1$, if Column never yields? Again, consider Row (the "underdog") as the programmed player, to whom $S_1$ has been assigned as the unconditional strategy. What will be Column's response to this unilaterally "pacifist" strategy? Will he exploit the "underdog" to the hilt, sharing nothing, or will he share voluntarily and, if so, how much? There is experimental evidence in answer to the latter question. Again as in the population playing against the unilaterally cooperating player in Prisoner's Dilemma, the distribution is strongly bimodal. About half the subjects in the role of "top dog" exploit the "underdog" fully. The other half share. Of these a large majority share 50%. No one has ever been observed to give away more than 50%. Incidentally the Nash solution of this game regarded as a cooperative game is 40% for the "underdog" and 60% for the "top dog."

Of considerable psychological interest is the game shown in Matrix 5.

|  | $C_2$ | $D_2$ |
|---|---|---|
| $C_1$ | 20, 20 | -10, 10 |
| $D_1$ | 10, -10 | 5, 5 |

Matrix 5

This is a so-called "no conflict game." If the payoffs represent the actual utilities of the players, it is in the interest of each to choose C, since each gets the largest payoff in CC. If, however, the concrete payoffs (e.g., money) do not represent the actual utilities, the situation is different. Suppose, for example, Row values his relative advantage over Column more than the absolute magnitude of his payoff. Then Row is motivated to choose D. The same applies to Column. If both choose D, DD results to the disadvantage of both. This social trap is somewhat similar to Prisoner's Dilemma but is not identical with it. In Prisoner's Dilemma, strategy D dominates C. In Matrix 5, this is not the case. Can we conclude that if the payoffs in Matrix 5 represent the players' actual utilities, the Pareto-optimal outcome CC will obtain? Not necessarily, because the outcome depends not only on the utilities of the players but also on their perceptions of each other's utilities or motivations. For suppose the payoffs do represent the true utilities but one of the players suspects that the other is competitively oriented. Then he will assume that the other will choose D. hence he himself must choose D "in self-defence," as it were, to avoid getting the worst payoff. Nor is this all. Even though a player may not attribute the competitive orientation to his co-player, he may imagine that the other attributes such an orientation to him. If so, he must suppose that the other will play D not because he is competitively oriented but because he believes that the other believes that he himself is oriented. In this case the player who attributes this belief (rightly or wrongly) to the other must play D.

Now the most important result of game theory, sometimes called the Fundamental Theorem provides an escape from this vicious cycle of "He thinks that I think that he thinks..." reasoning by introducing the concept of mixed strategy. This concept provides a rationally defensible solution to all two-person constant sum matrix games. But it does not eliminate the paradoxes inherent in social traps.


Concluding Remarks

The uses of the experimental games described above depart radically from the uses of so-called "gaming." In both approaches, the major goals are educational. However, the knowledge that is supposed to be imparted by gaming is quite different from the knowledge that one might hope to be generated by the so-called "mixed motive" games. In the former case, knowledge is supposedly translatable into strategic skills. One learns how to play effectively, whereby effectiveness is almost always measurable in terms of "how well one does." Predominantly, "rationality" in this context is conceived as individualistic rationality. That is, a particular actor, be he a person, a firm, or a nation, is supposed to optimize the outcome of a process involving interactive decisions from his own point of view. To be sure, processes of this sort may involve the formation of coalitions. But this simply means that several actors coalesce into one. The coalition becomes an actor, who does better or worse depending on his strategic skills.

The knowledge one hopes to impart by the use of the simplest experimental games is of a different sort.  One is supposed to learn not how to play effectively but what happens when actors are motivated in different ways.  One is supposed to see the situation not through the eyes of some player but from a more detached position, the position of someone watching the whole process of interactive decisions and drawing conclusions about what sort of creatures the decision-makers are, how they are motivated and how their motivations and the implementations of the goals so generated or so perceived affect them all.

If this sort of knowledge has a normative as well as a descriptive aspect, the prescriptions must be addressed to all the participants collectively, not to each participant separately.  The hope is, of course, that also the individual participants may thereby become somewhat wiser in the light of the insights imparted by the detached point of view.

## REFERENCES

Axelrod, R. 1984.  The Evolution of Cooperation.  New York:  Basic Books.

Chammah, A.M. 1969.  "Sex Differences, Strategy and Communication in a Mixed Motive Game (doctoral dissertation).  Ann Arbor:  University of Michigan.

Guyer, M. and H. Hamburger.  1968.  "A Note on the 'Taxonomy of 2 x 2 Games'." General Systems, 13:  205-19.

Hofstadter, D.R. 1983.  "Metamagical Themes:  Computer Tournament of the Prisoner's Dilemma Suggests How Cooperation Evolves." Scientific American 248 (No. 5):  16-26.

Kahn, H. 1965.  On Escalation:  Metaphors and Scenarios.  New York:  Frederick A. Praeger.

Rapoport, A. and M. Guyer.  1966.  "A Taxonomy of 2 x 2 Games." General Systems.  11: 203-14.

# III. GROUP DECISION MAKING

# INTRODUCTION

This section contains several papers dealing with the issues of group decision making and negotiation. Not all of the papers presented at the meeting have been included - papers by Michel Balinski on discrete proportionality, Rod Dobell on examples of group decision processes taken from Canadian government, and Subhash Narula on pre-emptive hierarchical programming problems, were unfortunately not available.

The paper *Plausible outcomes for games in strategic form* by Shubik presents an in-depth analysis of the assumptions underlying various game-theoretical concepts. It is shown that the applicability of such concepts depends very much on the context and the conditions under which a game is played. There is a small subclass of games (including zero-sum games and mass market games) in which history, personality and institutions might not matter - in all other cases they do. Language and time, survival values, psychological limits and sociopsychological phenomena can all exert a significant influence on the plausible outcomes of games.

Further discussions at the meeting led to the conclusion that the plausible outcomes for games with nonunique equilibria tend to be disequilibrium results (this would occur if each player selected a course of action corresponding to a different equilibrium); a special equilibrium selection process is therefore needed to achieve a compatible combination of nonunique equilibria.

The paper *Game and bargaining solutions for group decision problems* by Fandel deals with the applicability of various solution and bargaining concepts in organizational group decision-making situations where a unique Pareto-optimal decision must be obtained. The author concludes that the Nash bargaining solution and the Contini-Zionts bargaining model might provide a suitable basis for organizational group decision making.

The paper *Interactive group decision making by coalitions* by Isermann presents an interactive decision support system for group decision making by coalitions. The system employs a mediation procedure and is based on adaptive increases in the lowest acceptable values of the coalition members' criteria. This paper reflects some of the more recent trends in the application of group decision theory to the design of decision support systems.

The paper *On the role of dynamics and information in international
negotiations: the case of fishery management* by Kaitala and Hämäläinen
reviews the applications of dynamic game theory to fishery management.
It points out that the real players in such a game can have quite
different perceptions of rationality (related to different planning
horizon, for example) and that such games typically have multiequilibria properties.  Thus, the purpose of negotiations is to encourage
some shared perception of rational fishery management and to prevent
conflict escalation, which can lead to the overexploitation of resources.

Finally, an essay *Macromodels and multiobjective decision making*
by Peschel stresses the role of aggregated macromodels of evolutionary
type in problems involving many agents.

This group of papers was followed by a discussion.  The conclusions were that research into such aspects of group decision making as
uncertainty, dynamic processes, negotiation and mediation processes
and decision support, should be intensified.

A. Wierzbicki

# PLAUSIBLE OUTCOMES FOR GAMES IN STRATEGIC FORM

Martin Shubik

*Department of Economics, Yale University, New Haven, Connecticut, USA*

## 1.  INTRODUCTION

This is the first in a projected series of papers on solutions to games in matrix and extensive form.  The predominant solution concept in the literature is that of the noncooperative equilibrium put forward by Nash (1951).

The major virtue of a noncooperative equilibrium is that it satisfies a form of circular stability or self-fulfilling prophecy.  If i thinks that j will follow his noncooperative equilibrium strategy then i's best response is to select his noncooperative equilibrium strategy and vice versa.

The well-known Prisoner's Dilemma game provides both an easy example and considerable experimental evidence that the noncooperative equilibrium strategies are frequently selected.

II

| I | 1 | 2 | | 1 | 2 | | 1 | 2 | | 1 | 2 |
|---|---|---|---|---|---|---|---|---|---|---|---|
| 1 | 5,5 | -1,6 | 1 | 5,5 | -63,60 | 1 | 5,5 | -5,20 | 1 | $b_1,b_2$ | $d_1,a_2$ |
| 2 | 6,-1 | 0,0 | 2 | 50,-45 | 0,0 | 2 | 20,-5 | 0,0 | 2 | $a_1,d_2$ | $c_1,c_2$ |

|        (a)        |        (b)        |        (c)        |        (d)        |

TABLE 1

This work relates to Department of the Navy Contract N00014-77-C-0518 issued by the Office of Naval Research under Contract Authority NR 047-006.  However, the content does not necessarily reflect the position or the policy of the Department of the Navy or the Government, and no official endorsement should be inferred.

Four versions of the Prisoner's Dilemma or "near Prisoner's Dilemma" [1(c)] are shown in Table 1. The games portrayed in 1(a) and 1(b) have a unique equilibrium point with payoffs of (0,0) arising from strategies (2,2). Game 1(d) also has a unique equilibrium point if $a_1 > b_1 > c_1 > d_1$; $a_2 > b_2 > c_2 > d_2$; $a_1 + d_1 < 2b_1$ and $a_2 + d_2 < 2b_2$. In game 1(c) $a_i + d_i = 20 - 5 > 2b_i = 15$ has one pure strategy equilibrium point like the others plus a correlated mixed strategy equilibrium where the players play (1,2) or (2,1) with equal probabilities if they can precommit.

Even limiting ourselves to the $2 \times 2$ matrix game it is easy to construct games with 1, 2, 3 or 4 pure strategy equilibria. Table 2 provides examples.

II

I

| | 1 | 2 | | 1 | 2 | | 1 | 2 | | 1 | 2 |
|---|---|---|---|---|---|---|---|---|---|---|---|
| 1 | 5,5 | 4,3 | 1 | 2,1 | 0,0 | 1 | 3,6 | 4,6 | 1 | 6,8 | 3,8 |
| 2 | 3,4 | 2,2 | 2 | 0,0 | 1,2 | 2 | 3,6 | 0,0 | 2 | 6,4 | 3,4 |
| | (a) | | | (b) | | | (c) | | | (d) | |

TABLE 2

In Game 2(a) there is a jointly optimal pure strategy equilibrium at (1,1) yielding (5,5). Game 2(b) has two pure strategy equilibria and a mixed strategy equilibrium where I uses a mixed strategy of (2/3, 1/3) and II uses (1/3, 2/3) and the expected payoff to each is (2/3, 2/3). If they could correlate their strategies so that they could play (1,1) and (2,2) each with 1/2 they could obtain a payoff (3/2,3/2).

Game 2(c) has a class of equilibria where I uses his first strategy and II mixes with probabilities (p,1-p) where $0 \le p \le 1$; and similarly II uses his first strategy and I mixes with (p,1-p) where $0 \le p \le 1$.

In game 2(d) any mix for either player will be an equilibrium strategy. All four pure strategy pairs form noncooperative equilibria.*

Table 3 shows games with equilibria which dominate others.

In 3(a) there are three pure strategy noncooperative equilibria at (1,1), (2,2) and (3,3) with payoffs (10,10), (5,5) and (1,1). Game 3(b) has the same equilibria. However, in game 3(a) the safety

---

* Frequently we shall use the abbreviation NCE for noncooperative equilibrium.

|   | 1 | 2 | 3 |
|---|---|---|---|
| 1 | 10,10 | 0,0 | 0,0 |
| 2 | 0,0 | 5,5 | 0,0 |
| 3 | 0,0 | 0,0 | 1,1 |

|   | 1 | 2 | 3 |
|---|---|---|---|
| 1 | 10,10 | -6,0 | -6,0 |
| 2 | 0,-6 | 5,5 | 0,-6 |
| 3 | 0,-6 | -6,0 | 1,1 |

(a)  (b)

TABLE 3

level associated with any equilibrium is zero but in game 3(b) the
safety level associated with (1,1) is -6 but the safety level with (2,2)
is zero.

We may observe from the above examples that the NCE may or may not
be unique, symmetric or Pareto optimal.

Table 4 illustrates that the existence of an NCE is not perturbed
by considerable changes in the structure of the payoff matrix.  A matrix
of general size m × n is illustrated.  Suppose that $a_{ij}$ is the largest
element in the row i and $b_{ij}$ is the largest element in the column j.
Then regardless of any changes made to the mn - m - n + 1 elements
which do not appear in either row i or column j the pair of strategies
(i,j) form an equilibrium pair with payoffs ($a_{ij}$, $b_{ij}$).

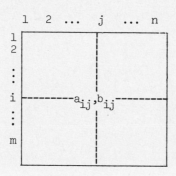

TABLE 4

The changes in the payoffs elsewhere may create new NCEs whose
payoffs could dominate the payoffs ($a_{ij}$,$b_{ij}$) but even this would not
disturb the stability of (i,j) as an NCE unless stability conditions
beyond that of self-fulfilling prophecy are specified.

## 2.  WHAT DO WE WANT OF A SOLUTION?

### 2.1. Normative or Behavioral Solutions

Traditionally game theory solutions have been divided into normative and positive or behavioral solutions.  The first set of solutions are prescriptive.  Rational people are advised to behave in a particular way, or to accept certain axioms of behavior as a guide.  For example the value proposed by Shapley (1955) offers axioms for fair division. Various bargaining procedures have been axiomatized.

The core (see Shubik, 1982, Ch.6) has been suggested as a solution which satisfies subgroup rationality for all sets of players in a game.

In contrast with the core and Shapley value, much of the discussion concerning the noncooperative equilibrium solution has stressed best response as being a reasonable way to behave in situations with no direct communication.  Furthermore some evidence can be mustered that under-graduates, or engineers or others tend to play one-shot Prisoner's Dilemma games in such a way that the NCE is a reasonably good predictor (see Rapoport and Chammah, 1965).  Yet although this is true there is overwhelming evidence that as the entries in even a 2 × 2 matrix are varied, the briefings manipulated and a host of other factors controlled, the NCE as a predictor leaves much to be desired (see Rapoport *et al.*, 1975).

In contrast with a behavioral defense of the NCE, Harsanyi and Selten (1982) offer a resolutely normative argument for the "rational selection of a single equilibrium point."

### 2.2. The Game and Rational Players

Without going into detail, there are four major game representa-tions used in most investigations.  The various solutions which have been suggested, in general, are related to one or possibly two of these representations.  Underlying each is a large set of implicit and explicit assumptions.  In essence the parts of Schelling's perceptive book (1960) which criticize game theory are in fact devoted to a critique of the inappropriate use of game models for the study of some strategic prob-lems where certain implicit and explicit assumptions do not apply.

The four major representations of a game of strategy are:

1. The finite extensive form
2. The strategic or normal form
3. The cooperative or coalitional form
4. Some variant of an infinite extensive form.

The cooperative form is not a process model. Von Neumann and Morgenstern (1944) explicitly abstracted any considerations of cost or timing of bargaining in their discussion of the characteristic function. Edgeworth (1881) in his discussion of bargaining did the same. In essence the cooperative form is noninstitutional. There is no way one can deduce the specific form of the rules of the game from the cooperative form.

All three other representations noted are process oriented. The two extensive form representations spell out moves and information. The strategic form suppresses a great deal of structure but nevertheless explicitly reflects the rules of the game.

None of the representations are able to treat adequately the role of language. In many aspects of human behavior there is a delicate interplay between words and deeds. Items such as contract, threat and bluff depend upon this interplay and the strategic modeler is faced with the problem that in many of the strategic situations of society the rules are not rigid but depend upon the broader context in which the game is embedded.

The first three representations noted address situations with a well-defined beginning and end. Board games or card games fit nicely into this category. But many aspects of politics, economics and life in general do not. There is no definite end, and the beginning may be lost in history. The fourth game representation, which allows for the possibility of games of indefinite length, opens up the possibility of considering neither normatively cooperative nor noncooperative solutions, but quasi-cooperative solutions whose stability is due to the assumption that there will be enough time left to settle accounts.

Associated with the cooperative form are the value, core, stable set, nucleolus, kernel and bargaining set solutions. Associated with the finite extensive form and strategic forms are many variants of noncooperative equilibrium and minimax solutions. The infinite horizon extensive form opens up the possibility of defining and describing many quasi-cooperative and behavioral solutions.

Underlying virtually all of formal mathematical game-theoretic analysis is an extremely austere nonsocialized abstract model of the intelligent, calculating rational decisionmaker. Without passion, the *homo ludens* of much of game theory is a colorless, sexless, classless, ageless calculating device who knows what it wants and what constitutes its set of strategies. The assumption of *external symmetry* made explicitly or implicitly states that any feature distinguishing Player A from Player B must be formally modeled in the game otherwise all

features are assumed to be the same.  Thus when the game theorist is contrasted with the social psychologist we find that the former tends to be
concerned with predicting the outcomes resulting from situations involving identical individuals with different resources and positions while
the latter tends to consider outcomes involving different individuals
who may start with the same resources.

Much of game theory has been devoted to suggesting what an individually rational, intelligent, nonsocialized, calculating, consciously goal-
oriented individual should do when confronted with a well-defined game of
strategy.

How successful or useful this approach is cannot be answered without reference to context.  Hence we turn to an explicit consideration of
both the context and purpose of the models.

## 3.   WHAT ARE THE CONTEXTUAL ASSUMPTIONS?

### 3.1. Noninstitutional Statics

Much of the success of modern economic theory and political science
has been in the investigation of situations involving faceless crowds
of individual agents.  In particular the attractiveness and apparent
power of the modern theory of the price system and mass markets comes
from the attenuation of much personal interaction.  The essence of decentralization is that individuals need not think about other individuals, but plan their actions against a mechanism called the market.
Personality is irrelevant, individual power except to inflict self-harm
is nonexistent and special information is of fleeting worth.

Under the appropriate assumptions a large array of different models
and solutions all lead to the mass market price system (for a survey see
Shubik, 1984).  It is possible to construct game models in both strategic and cooperative form and have the NCE, value, core and other solutions predict the same set of outcomes in what appears to be a virtually
institution-free context.

Unfortunately what may hold for a mass market under special circumstances does not hold if there is even one agent of substantial size.
The various structures of the mechanism influence outcome, and the
possibilities for individual signaling and threat may appear.

### 3.2. Finite Process Models

If one is to understand the structure of strategic interaction
even for as few as two individuals the salient features of the game
must be spelled out.  The extensive form does this in detail and the
strategic form does it in a somewhat aggregated manner via the concept
of strategy.

In the context of a society, polity or economy the construction
of a game in extensive form requires the implicit specification of the
institutions and laws of the society.  They are described in the rules
of the game.  Thus when we try to model trade as a game in extensive or
strategic form we can start to identify the basic features which distinguish and describe markets, banks, clearing houses and other economic
institutions.

When the situation to be modeled is a diplomatic negotiation, a
revolution or a mass march we tend to find that our lack of substantive
knowledge and the difficulties encountered in sorting out psychological,
socio-psychological, economic, legal, political and other factors make
the task of specifying a plausible extensive form difficult and even of
dubious worth.  The perceptive essay or even a simulation may provide
better tools for analysis.

Because of the difficulty in constructing extensive form models
of many "soft science processes" we run the danger of gross over-
simplification in order to force them upon our methodological Procrustean
bed.  In particular it is for this reason that we must approach all
interpretations of results from simple experimental games such as the
Prisoner's Dilemma with great circumspection.

Von Neumann and Morgenstern (1944) in the first chapter of their
book warned that the construction of game theory dynamics might pose
considerable difficulties.  They stressed that they felt it desirable
to explore the statics first.  They stressed a cooperative theory.
But in doing so not only did they suppress the dynamics; they also
removed the description of the rules of the game by the device of using
the characteristic function.

Before one tries to develop full dynamics, the description of the
game in strategic or extensive form provides an understanding of the
structural bounds on play.  The strategic form which by the device of
the strategy collapses the finite extensive form into a matrix or one-
shot game suppresses much of the structure, but not as much as the coalitional form.  The noncooperative equilibrium solution applied to a game
in strategic form may be regarded as a static solution.  All move simultaneously -- beyond that time plays no role and the path of play is
irrelevant.

## 3.3. The Infinite Future:  Markovian Dynamics

The von Neumann-Morgenstern theory deals with games with a specific
beginning and finite end.  The analogy with formal games has already
been noted.  If we wish to construct models which appear to be better

approximations of many societal, political and economic processes we need to extend the horizon to an indefinite future. The cost of doing so is to complicate the concept of solution and change the mathematical requirements.

Two natural classes of model which have been considered are repeated games with a stochastic ending or with a discounted payoff. The repeated matrix game offers experimental possibilities in either of these forms. An attractive candidate for a solution to a stochastic game (see Heyman and Sobel, 1984) is an NCE involving strategies which are only dependent on the current state.

When we consider applications of stochastic games, however, we must ask what phenomena can be best represented. I suggest that in virtually all applications there are several important distinctions which should be made. They are:

Two person:    face-to-face
Two person:    anonymous
Two institutions
One individual and an institution
Few individuals:    face-to-face
Few individuals:    anonymous
Many individuals:    anonymous without group identity or affiliation
Many individuals:    anonymous with group identity or affiliation

The formal models most amenable to analysis are two-person games and many-person games. It is hard to justify, except on an *ad hoc* basis, the assumption that in situations involving two individuals interacting over time anonymity is reasonable and history and personality do not matter.

Fortunately for the applications of duels and antagonistic games, the assumptions are justified in general. Furthermore, if we believe that the assumption of a mass market with no large agent is justified in economic analysis, then the dynamics of such a market may be studied as though it were a collection of individuals each facing his own dynamic program.

In virtually all other instances history, personality and institutions appear to matter. These cannot be ignored even by the experimenter using the simplest of matrix games. The players bring their personalities, mindsets, socialization and training with them, and both these and the initial briefing must be taken into account.

Partially in jest, partially seriously, John Kennedy of the Department of Psychology at Princeton noted that given control of the briefing an experimenter should be able to get virtually any results he wants.

## 3.4. The Infinite Past:  History Matters

In experimenting with as simple a game as that shown in Table 5,
some individuals acting as Player 1 select the first strategy and others

|          |   | 1        | 2        |
|----------|---|----------|----------|
| Player   | 1 | 2,1      | 0,0      |
|          | 2 | 0,0      | 1,2      |

TABLE 5

select the second.  Each easily supplies a rationalization; one of the
variety "strategy one is best for me", the other "I think my opponent
may be greedy hence I am safer playing strategy two in order to get some
payoff."

A briefing telling all players that their competitors are greedy
and stubborn appears to influence the outcome.

How are we to control or initialize the initial expectations or
subjective probabilities of players concerning the nature and behavior
of their competitors?  One way of doing this is by the initial briefing
and this may involve telling a player that he has taken over from a
previous player while his competitor is still the same.  The new player
is then supplied with a history of k periods of play.  For example, one
briefing for the game in Table 5 might be: "During the last 100 periods
(2,2) has been played all the time." Another briefing would be "(1,1)
and (2,2) have been played alternately for as long as we can remember
and (1,1) was played last time."

How far back into history we want to go or need to go appears to be
a matter of understanding the problem and its context.  It is not merely
a problem in methodology or mathematics.  It is here that revenge, national pride and other factors regarded as irrelevant, irrational or
uninteresting in an economics-oriented decision theory appear.

## 3.5. Does Language Matter?

One school of thought has it that a "barking dog never bites" and
"sticks and stones will break my bones but names will never hurt me."
Another school takes threat, slander, innuendo and promises seriously.
Many of the examples in brinksmanship and bargaining used by Schelling
(1960) depend delicately upon words as deeds.  Sometimes deeds are best
interpreted as part of the conversation.  Someone is shot with a foot
over the border just to convey the message that we mean that we do not
want anyone to cross the border.

Formal game theory does not provide us with a way to encode speech
and gesture as moves.  In a mass market you cannot argue with the tape,
but in a thin market you can argue with the sellers.  In a disarmament
conference words and gestures are part of the play.

We do not know how to code language into strategies.  But at least
in experimental games we can introduce a limited set of messages as
formal moves.  For example, consider the game portrayed in Figure 1.

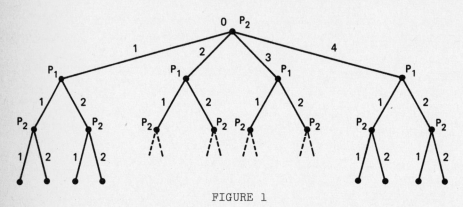

FIGURE 1

We may interpret the first four moves as messages from Player 2 to
Player 1 concerning what he intends to do if Player 1 selects 1 or 2.
They can be read as:

If $P_1$ selects 1 then $\frac{1}{2}$; if $P_1$ selects 2 then $\frac{1}{2}$.

We might also include a fifth alternative in which no message is
sent.  If we include this then the total number of strategies available
to $P_2$ is $5 \times (2)^{10}$ or 5,120.

Griesmer and Shubik ran a pilot study of a game with this structure
in 1962 but I am not aware of the results of any systematic study of
games with messages.

It must be noted that in a two-person, constant-sum game, language
plays only a psychological role.  The only words are deeds.  In mass
societies individuals can still send simple signals to large groups by
wearing badges, campaign buttons, concentration camp numbers or uniforms.
Even with large numbers there are many binary interactions between two
individuals who have to find out if they are friend, foe or neutral.

4.   THE SOCIAL SCIENCE SHOPPING LIST

In this section a sketch is given of some of the factors we need
to consider when we try to apply strategic analysis to a host of different conflict and cooperation scenarios.

## 4.1. Historical, Biological, Chronological and Ordinal Time

Cooperative game theory is timeless. This is one of the major reasons why interpreting experiments based on the characteristic function is so difficult. If negotiations take several hours this expenditure of effort may influence perceived payoffs.

The finite game in strategic form is timeless. All players have one (possibly enormously complex) move and all move simultaneously.

The finite game in extensive form has ordinal time. Moves are sequenced but there is no measure of elapsed time. In essence the game tree is event oriented. Actions and the sequencing of actions count, not the time involved.

Yet chess championship games have time limits. Furthermore we frequently wait for decisions to mature or tempers to cool or even for time to heal wounds and to soften or obliterate some memories.

Repeated games or stochastic games tend to be represented with a fixed clock. Each period measures some unspecified $\Delta t$ and there may be many periods. When a discount factor is introduced, as is the case for business games and many economic models, the (usually fixed) time period is a quarter or a year.

A key factor distinguishing many problems in the behavioral sciences is the length of time involved in a process. Elapsed time appears to be related to whether decisions or acts are instinctive, consciously thought through, unconscious or habit guided. Qualitatively new problems have been posed by the existence of nuclear missiles, where decisions to loose mass destruction must be made by a handful of individuals in less time than most people need to decide to buy a new lawnmower.

The bias of many economists and operations researchers has been towards decision problems lasting for a relatively short time, say a few weeks to a few years. In this zone many environmental factors, habits, customs and laws can be regarded as constant. The decision-making takes place within the arena of the economy and for the most part concentrates on conscious decisionmaking.

Decisions to marry, have children, commit suicide, kill, declare war, found the National Socialist party, go on a hunger strike, move the tribe westward from the Urals, or die at Massada all may have some element of conscious economic decisionmaking to them. But there is more: the time scale, scope and context of each is significantly different from the others. The will of a group or a species or a set of genes to survive may be measured on an even longer time scale and may depend far more on instinctive than calculated decisionmaking.

To be more specific, how long does it take to form trust, respect

and consistent beliefs in individual and international relations?  How
long does it take to destroy them and rebuild them?  It has been said
that "if your friend betrays you once it is his fault, if he betrays
you twice it is your fault."  Is this merely a matter for ordinal time
Bayesian updating or is a more complex process description called for?

## 4.2. Players and Population

One of the most powerful and useful assumptions in the construction
of game-theoretic models is the assumption of external symmetry.  All
personal attributes not specified are assumed to be the same.  For many
problems the model of the player without personal attributes acting as
a principal in an institution-free environment may be a reasonable
approximation.  But for virtually any political or international strategic problem the players are fiduciaries acting through bureaucracies.
We use phrases such as "the Russians want" or "the State Department
intends."  It is easy to deal with such phrases in rhetoric or in essay
form but it is extremely difficult to produce useful formal models of
the State Department as a player with preferences.

In the literature of operations research we can find titles such
as "Solveable Nuclear Wars" (Dalkey, 1965) or "The Statistics of Deadly
Quarrels" (Richardson, 1960).  The simple model or special statistic
serves to call attention to and provide analysis for a special and possibly important point.  But nuclear wars are not solveable and deadly
exchanges may be grossly misrepresented by body counts.  How usefully
we can represent whole nations as actors depends heavily upon the question at hand.

The basic distinction concerning individuals is whether they are
acting as principal agents or as fiduciaries for others.  But in the
study of strategic behavior the simplification made regarding what constitutes a player is critical.  Political scientists study "the games
nations play."  Are institutions actors or should we model them as games
within games, set in a larger context?  At the very least we need to
distinguish the individual, the informal group, the formal group, various institutions and nations.

One possible modification to the assumption of external symmetry
among the players is to consider a population with different arrays of
attributes such as hawk or dove.  Then, as has been considered in biological models, we might interpret mixed strategy equilibria as arising
from chance encounters with different behavioral types.  The recent
work of Axelrod (1983) is oriented in this way.

## 4.3. Preferences

Much has been written about individual preferences.  Only three points are stressed here.  The first concerns how to describe preferences for organizations or institutions if they are to be treated as players.

The second point appears to be of importance both in the context of political and economic life and in military matters.  This is the distinction between personal risk and risk taken on when acting as an agent or fiduciary for other people's money and lives.  The economic theory of agency attempts to explain the behavior of agents strictly in terms of economic organizational structure, which provides the structure of incentives.  Yet the socio-psychological and sociological features of loyalty, honesty, morals, responsibility, pride and other factors appear to play an important role in determining the behavior of generals, civil servants and corporate presidents.  The responsibility assumed in sending troops into battle does not appear to be usefully portrayed primarily in terms of economic analysis.

The third point is that in my opinion not enough stress has been laid upon the importance attached to survival in individual preferences.

## 4.4. Psychological Limits

The survey on decisionmaking and decision theory of Abelson and Levi (1983) provides a relatively comprehensive coverage of some of the problems seen by the psychologist in analyzing decisionmaking.  These include limits to memory, limits to calculation, faulty perception and the importance of problem representation in influencing decisions.

Possibly the most important open question at the core of strategic analysis is how individuals form subjective probability estimates and how they update them.  The experimental evidence that they do not appear to use Bayesian updating does not invalidate the logic of Bayes, but suggests two hypotheses.  Individuals may be somewhat less than logical and could benefit from training.  The way individuals often use new information is not merely to update and modify old information, but to reorganize their perceptions of the causal structure of the system being considered.

## 4.5. Socio-psychological and Other Criteria

In our search for solutions we need to ask what considerations must be taken into account.  How rich must the models be to account for the phenomena we feel to be of critical significance in a process.  For example, in much of economic theory evaluation and judgment are taken as given, or if there are two individuals with equal resources and risk

| Individual Psychological Factors | Socio-Psychological Factors | Political Factors | Sociological Factors | Mathematical & Philosophical Solution Properties |
|---|---|---|---|---|
| preference | specific concern for others | political belief | social conscience | domain of decision |
| risk & uncertainty pref. | envy | | social position | payoff transformation |
| tolerance of ambiguity | revenge | nationalism | wealth | local/global solution |
| self-concern | hate | militarism | nationalism | union of games |
| fear | love | | militarism | uniqueness |
| judgmental bias | trust | ideology | bureaucracy | independence of games |
| self-control | greed | | religion | symmetry |
| motivation | honesty | power | | safety level |
| aspiration | suspicion | patriotism | hero/martyr | external symmetry |
| instinctive behavior | sacrifice for young | | | certainty equivalence |
| survival | | | | insufficient reason |
| age | | | societal norms & values | irrelevant alternatives |
| sex | signalling | | | continuity |
| habit | coordination | | loyalty | ordinal/cardinal utility |
| faith | cooperation | | custom | limit behavior |
| sloth | | | justice | |
| knowledge | | | tradition | value |
| coding & editing | | | | |
| memory | | | | efficiency/optimality |
| span of attention | | | | |
| intelligence | | fiduciary norms | fiduciary norms | stability |
| rationality | | | | equilibrium & best response |
| "cleverness" | | | | |
| talent | | | | |
| experience | | | | |
| commitment | | | | |
| determination | | | | |

TABLE 6

preferences the one who has less uncertainty concerning evaluation will perform better. Yet the best securities analysts do not appear to be the best investors. Perception and calculation do not appear to be the same as perception, calculation, commitment and decisiveness. Yet even in economics it is precisely where the numbers are few and the stakes are high that factors such as the courage of one's convictions count.

It is a monument to the success of economic theory that so much can be squeezed from the parsimonious assumptions of given preferences, many rational actors, initial wealth and technology. But it appears that, in spite of the economic components to society, politics and war, the parsimony of economic theory is not sufficient to provide good explanations elsewhere.

The informal list presented in Table 6 indicates some of the factors which are regarded by different social scientists as relevant to decisionmaking. Many of the words, such as loyalty, hope, faith, are catchall names for a highly complex set of attributes. Yet when we try to explain strategic behavior there is some context in which each item noted is a factor of consequence. Revenge and envy may not enter into consideration when buying a pound of bacon; but they do when the decision is made to continue a vendetta.

The shopping list is clearly even larger -- for example, health and demographic features (such as a species' innate drive to reproduce) have not been included. The overall psychological concerns on perception and cognition are only partially covered.

An important constructive use of theory and gaming experiments is to isolate why and where intuitively important concepts fit into our models and explanation of behavior. Thus we may take a concept such as revenge or envy and ask what is the simplest game in which we would be able to attribute motivation to such factors. It is with this in mind that I suggest that the very success of much of game-theoretic thought and experimental gaming may come from their apparent lack of success in being able to identify a solution of high predictive value for how individuals will play a one-shot or many-period, two-person matrix game.

There is no paradox and no pessimism to this observation. We have a language, a methodology and the possibility to perform some experiments of interest. The noncooperative equilibrium and minimax solutions do not appear to be particularly useful as predictors in general, even though they may be quite good in certain contexts. Our problem is to find better solutions and to justify or explain the influence of different contexts.

## 4.6. A Caveat on Purposeful Modeling

Good modeling calls for (1) clarity of purpose, (2) parsimony, (3) relevance and (4) analytical feasibility. Analogy and example can offer considerable aid in gaining insight. But they can also be devices to mislead by false analogy and special or pathological example. In the context of game-theoretic reasoning these dangers are easy to illustrate. It is well-known among social psychologists that the running of a simple game with the same mathematical structure in each instance but with different scenarios will lead to different behavior (see the Ph.D thesis of R. Simon, 1967). It is also clear that whole books and hundreds if not thousands of articles have been devoted to the Prisoner's Dilemma game with little discussion of how typical or valuable an experimental game it is and how generalizable are results obtained from experiments using it.

Experimental games may only reflect a few of the factors in command and control systems for nuclear weapons. These systems may manifest a competitive decision structure which is quite different to that in political conflict and certainly in competition in mass markets.

Game theory offers abstract models for the study of conflict and cooperation. But the abstraction sufficient to illustrate mass markets may not stretch to mass warfare, murder or even to a Potlach. The development of solution concepts for context-free games played by hypothetically personality-free players is a useful exercise in normative game theory but it is not the only approach. Even at the philosophical level individuals are at best idealized as machines with some finite capacity, and hence there are basic problems to be faced in even defining individual rational behavior.

## 4.7. Death, Triumph and Disaster

Prior to discussing matrix games, one further basic warning is in order. When using matrix games even as analogies in the discussion of topics such as war or diplomacy, or any situation involving high or low risk and matters of vital importance, the very basis of justification for assigning expected subjective valuation of outcomes is in question. Kahneman and Tversky (1973) have suggested a $\pi$ function for subjective probabilities which is not well-behaved at the extreme ranges, overestimates low probabilities and underestimates high probabilities.

The act of formulating an abstract matrix game and presenting it to experimental subjects without a detailed discussion of what the abstract von Neumann-Morgenstern expected utilities mean to the players

hides many of the key problems in understanding the linkages between
psychological socio-psychological and cultural phenomena and the abstractions of game theory.

## 5.   THE SEARCH FOR MEASURES

The remarks here are confined to games in matrix form played by
individuals acting on their own behalf.  Do we have a reasonable theory
as to how they will be played if they are played only once?

The question being asked here is considerably less ambitious than
any of the burning questions concerning military, political or organizational behavior.  As a start it is not even at the level of complexity
of "do Russian, Chinese, English and American students play matrix games
differently?"

There are only a few postulates that can help us to determine the
probable outcome of a game when the noncooperative equilibrium is non-
unique.  There have been many attempts to formulate such postulates,
but most of them do not give satisfactory answers.  Nash suggested that
the following conditions should be satisfied (1) *best response;* (2) *equal
value;* (3) *interchangeability of strategies*.  But we can give simple
examples of games where none of these conditions can be satisfied.  We
might add another condition: (4) *a probable equilibrium should be selected from those NCEs which are nondominated by other NCEs*.  However, this
condition does not necessarily have any predictive strength.  Another
possible condition might be: (5) *the other player will select any of his
NCE strategies with equal probability*.  However, this assumption cannot
be justified on socio-psychological grounds.  Socio-psychologically, we
can state: (6) *in a symmetric two-person game, the only socio-psychologically neutral NCE is a symmetric one*.  In non-symmetric games, interpersonal comparisons might be very important, and hence there is a large
difference between the following two assumptions: (7a) *cardinal but not
comparable utilities are assumed, i.e. games are left unchanged by linear
transformations of utility scales;* and (7b) *cardinal utility scales and
interpersonal comparisons are assumed*.  Thus, socio-psychological phenomena appear to be quite important, which is strongly supported by the
experimental evidence.

The mathematical and philosophical shopping list for extra criteria
has been summarized in Table 6.  A few general observations can be made
on the possible formalization of socio-psychological phenomena.  Several
approaches are described in the literature; however, for example,
Harsanyi in his work both on games with incomplete information and his
tracing procedure (see Harsanyi, 1975) as well as in his work with Selten

on the selection of a unique NCE (see Harsanyi, 1982) is resolutely non-psychological and non-socio-psychological. Another general point is that the literature usually stresses conscious individualistic behavior with little attention to such phenomena as concern for others, compassion, greed, spite and revenge, etc. A possible means of formalizing some of these aspects would be to average outcome utilities with weighting coefficients interpreted as measures of concern for the welfare of others. In repetitive games, such phenomena as envy and revenge could also be illustrated and possibly formalized.

## 6. WHERE TO FROM HERE?

The development of economic game theory, especially for mass markets, has been to some extent an essay in the study of strategic decisions in which psychology and socio-psychology are of minimal importance. Much of the search for solution concepts for n-person games has had a normative bent based upon the abstraction of the culture-free, personality-free, society-free, rational individual.

A cogent argument for utilizing this model of the decisionmaker is that it is analytically easier and better defined than models with limited capacity and perception. In spite of the rhetorical attractiveness of Simon's "Satisficing man" there is a Will-o-the-Wisp quality to attempts to produce formal models and to define the meaning of rational behavior for the decisionmaker as a finite device interacting with other finite devices. We are forced to raise many of the basic questions posed in artificial intelligence and must confront the possibility that, as soon as we postulate individuals who can never know as much as society as a whole, cultural norms and societal conventions become necessary devices to code into manageable size the vast body of data, information and knowledge which the single individual cannot master.

My suggestion is that the time is ripe for the development of *context-specific* theories of decisionmaking, with stress upon the distinctions and links between estimates of exogenous and endogenous uncertainty and the actual taking of responsibility for decisions. In particular, the use of context-free game-theoretic models in the study of international relations, arms control and other areas for negotiation must be done with great circumspection. The use of simple analogies may obliterate or distort or distract from our understanding of the process at hand.

In parallel with the emphasis upon context, the very pathological simplicity of the matrix game provides an experimental device for the

posing of questions and design of experiments not in game theory alone
but also in the array of other behavioral aspects associated with strategic decisionmaking.

I suspect that the way to blend strategic behavior with behavioral
bias is to consider players as managers running idiosyncratic agents who
they do not fully control. The manager is strategic but some of his
agents may be behaviorally limited in their choices.

REFERENCES

Abelson, R. P., and A. Levi (1983), "Decision making and decision the-
    ory," in G. Lendzey and E. Aronson (Eds.), *Handbook of Social Psy-
    chology*. Reading, Mass.: Addison-Wesley.

Axelrod, R. (1983), *The Evolution of Cooperation*. New York: Basic Books.

Dalkey, N. (1965), "Solveable nuclear wars," *Management Science*, 11:
    783-791.

Edgeworth, F. Y. (1881), *Mathematical Psychics*. London: Kegan Paul.

Harsanyi, J. (1975), "The tracing procedure: A Bayesian approach to
    defining a solution for n-person games," *International Journal of
    Game Theory*, 4: 61-94.

Harsanyi, J. C. (1982), "Solutions for some bargaining games under the
    Harsanyi-Selten solution theory," *Mathematical Social Sciences*, 3:
    179-191.

Heyman, D. P., and J. M. Sobel (1984), *Stochastic Models in Operations
    Research*, Vol. II. New York: McGraw-Hill.

Kahneman, D., and A. Tversky (1973), "On the psychology of prediction,"
    *Psychological Review*, 80: 237-251.

Nash, J. F., Jr. (1951), "Noncooperative games," *Annals of Mathematics*,
    54: 289-295.

Rapoport, A., and A. M. Chammah (1965), *Prisoner's Dilemma*. Ann Arbor,
    Michigan: University of Michigan Press.

Rapoport, A., M. J. Guyer and D. G. Gordon (1975), *The 2 × 2 Game*. Ann
    Arbor, Michigan: University of Michigan Press.

Richardson, L. F. (1960), *The Statistics of Deadly Quarrels*. Chicago,
    Ill.: Quadrangle Books.

Schelling, T. C. (1960), *The Strategy of Conflict*. Cambridge, Mass.:
    Harvard University Press.

Shapley, L. S. (1953), "A value for n-person games," in H. Kuhn and
    A. W. Tucker (Eds.), *Contributions to the Theory of Games*, Vol. 2.
    Princeton, N.J.: Princeton University Press.

Shubik, M. (1982), *Game Theory in the Social Sciences*. Cambridge, Mass.:
    M.I.T. Press.

Shubik, M. (1984), *Game Theory in the Social Sciences*, Vol. II. Cambridge, Mass.: M.I.T. Press.

Simon, R. (1967), *The Effects of Different Encodings on Complex Problem Solving*, Ph.D. Thesis, Yale University, New Haven, Connecticut.

von Neumann, J., and O. Morgenstern (1944), *Theory of Games and Economic Behavior*, Princeton, N.J.: Princeton University Press.

# GAME AND BARGAINING SOLUTIONS FOR
# GROUP DECISION PROBLEMS

Günter Fandel
*Fernuniversität Hagen, Hagen, FRG*

*Decision processes in organizations can formally be described as group decision pro-*
*blems, i.e. as decision problems with several decision makers and different utility*
*functions. Game and bargaining approaches have to be taken into account as solution*
*methods. They are characterized by the actual decision rule which describes, or rather*
*determines, the decision behaviour of the group members. For this rule certain require-*
*ments are set up, the fulfilment of which gives information, how far the presented ap-*
*proaches are useful for determining optimal decisions in groups.*

## 1. Introduction

When in the beginning of the fifties SIMON (1952/1953), for the first time, systematically tried to analyze decisions in organizations with a view to concluding from this
to the necessary quantitative solution instruments, it had rashly been expected that
the formal foundations of an organization theory with respect to business administration would be created very soon. In view of the developments which have in the mean-
time taken place in the fields of game and bargaining theory, and considering the
knowledge obtained from the theory of multiple criteria decision making it seems reasonable today to make another attempt to find out how far quantitative economic concepts of this kind can be used for or contribute to the formulation and solution of
decision problems in organizations, looking at these organizations as groups of independent decision makers with different utility functions. Thus, cooperative games with
or without side payments as well as non-cooperative games come into consideration. As
to the application of the theory of bargaining to decision problems in groups, two
qualitatively different procedures have been developed, namely the approaches based
on the game theory and the concessive models of bargaining formulated on the basis of
spontaneous elements of behaviour.

## 2. Description of the Decision Situations in Groups

For the formal description of group decision problems let

$\mathbb{N}$     be the set of the natural numbers,

$\mathbb{R}$     be the set of the real numbers,

n     $\in [N] = \{1,\ldots,N\}$ be the decision makers - units or persons - in the group,
$N \in \mathbb{N}$ and $N \geq 2$,

$A \subset \mathbb{R}^N$ be the set of decision alternatives $a = (a_1,\ldots,a_N)$ of the group, and

$U \subset \mathbb{R}^N$ be the set of utility vectors $u = (u_1, \ldots, u_N)$ of the group which develop as a mapping of A under the individual utility functions $u_n = u_n(a)$, $n \in [N]$, of the decision makers, that is to say $U = u(A)$.

In order to obtain a reasonable economic and mathematical formulation of the problem let us further assume that the set of decision alternatives A is convex, bounded and closed, and that the utility functions $u_n$, $n \in [N]$, are concave, continuous and different from each other, that is to say, $u_n \neq u_{n'}$ is true for n, $n' \in [N]$ and $n \neq n'$ in particular. Without loss of generality we further suppose that every decision maker n controls one and only one decision component $a_n$ of a vector a, where $a_n \in A_n$ and $a \in A = A_1 \times \ldots \times A_N$; $A_n$ designates the set of decision alternatives of the n-th decision maker.

Then the group decision problem consists of choosing alternatives $a \in A$ or, equivalently, in determining utility vectors $u \in U$ that the decision makers will regard as solutions to their decision process. The common decision rule of the group members determines the choice of such $a \in A$ or $u \in U$. This rule can at the same time serve to characterize the solution approach used. In this connection, the notion of decision rule means an operation $Q: \mathbb{R}^N \to \mathbb{R}^N$, which for each utility set $U \subset \mathbb{R}^N$ chooses a subset $L_Q \subset U$, and thus for each decision set $A \subset \mathbb{R}^N$ a subset of decision alternatives $A_Q$ with $u(A_Q) = L_Q$. $L_Q = \{u' \in U | u' = Q[u(a)], a \in A\}$ can be designated as set of the Q-optimal solutions to the group decision problem.

For practical reasons the solution $L_Q$ of the decision problem is to fulfil the following requirements:

(A1) $$L_Q \neq \emptyset,$$

that is to say, there must exist at least one solution to each decision problem.

(A2) $$L_Q \subset U,$$

that is to say, only such utility vectors will be suitable for solutions which can be obtained by corresponding feasible decision alternatives.

Designate $M(U) := \{u \in U | u \geq \bar{\bar{u}}\}$, where the utility vector $\bar{\bar{u}}$ indicates the utility level $\bar{\bar{u}}_n = \max\limits_{a_n} \min\limits_{\bar{a}_n} u_n(a_n, \bar{a}_n)$, $\bar{a}_n = (a_1, \ldots, a_{n-1}, a_{n+1}, \ldots, a_N)$, $(a_n, \bar{a}_n) \in A$ and $n \in [N]$ which the individual decision makers can at least obtain within the group, then let

(A3) $$L_Q \subset M(U).$$

Thus postulate (A3) requires the solutions to be individually rational (LUCE/RAIFFA 1958, pp. 192/193).

Let $P(U) = \{u \in U \mid w \geq u \wedge w \in U \Rightarrow w = u\}$ be the set of all Pareto-optimal utility vectors of U. Then, the solution is to satisfy the condition

(A4)                              $L_Q \subset P(U)$,

that is to say, consider efficient results only.

(A5)                              $L_Q$ is a one-element set

insures the uniqueness of the solution.

The conditions (A1) - (A5) allow a comment on the quality of the solution proposals still to be presented, that means, a comment with respect to their contribution to the optimal decision in organizations. In this connection, existence, feasibility and individual rationality of the solution are quite obvious postulates derived from plausibility assumptions. From the economic point of view the requirement of Pareto-optimality corresponds to the use of synergic effects which can emerge in groups due to the joint effort of several members. Under the conditions (A1) - (A4) the necessity of a unique solution results from the following fact: If there exist several Pareto-optimal solutions then some decision makers will profit more from one result vector than from another, and vice versa, so that with interests conflicting, a final solution to the decision problem has not yet been found. Furthermore, uniqueness is necessary for a stable or equilibrated decision behaviour of the persons involved (HARSANYI 1963, p.219; FRIEDMAN 1971, p.7).

## 3. Organization-theoretic Notions of Solution

The organization-theoretic notions of solution which have been historically developed in the literature are attributable to the effort to restrict the utility set U already ex ante by eliminating obviously bad result vectors, without at the same time determining unique solutions or even definitely establishing the decision rule of the organization.

a) SIMON (1952/53, p.42ff.) designates the set

$$L_Q = V(U) = \{u \in U \mid u(a) \geq \bar{u}, \ a \in A\}$$

as viable solutions.

Here $\bar{u}_n$, $n \in [N]$, indicates the utility of the n-th decision maker, which he can also obtain without being a member of the organization, for example by joining another organization. The decisions made by the organization must yield at least these utility levels in order to insure the existence of the organization. The fulfilment of the postulates (A1) - (A5) by the viable solutions is dependent on the special location of $\bar{u}$ and is realized if and only if $\bar{u} \in P(U)$ holds, hence is located on the efficient border of U. Generally, however, the viable solutions, if they exist, will be neither Pareto-optimal nor unique so that, as a rule, this notion of solution is not sufficient for determining an optimal decision in the organization. The solutions which will be considered in the following are always assumed to be viable.

b) The Pareto-optimal solutions result from

$$L_Q = P(U),$$

hence are described by the efficient border of the utility set U. Unless for special problem structures this border consists of one point only, the Pareto-optimal solutions will violate the postulate of uniqueness (A5), and, as a rule, not definitely solve the organizational decision problem.

c) By individually maximal solutions SIMON (1952/53, p.42ff.) understands

$$L_Q = I(U) = \bigcup_{n=1}^{N} I_n(U) \text{ with } I_n(U) = \{u \in U \mid u_n = \max_{a \in A} u_n(a)\}, \; n \in [N],$$

that is, they comprise all result vectors which imply a maximal utility for one decision maker. Evidently, the individually maximal solutions need not be Pareto-optimal, that is to say, the notion of solution underlying I(U) is generally incompatible with postulate (A4). Furthermore, with interests of the organization members conflicting, I(U) normally is not a one-element set, so that in this case also the uniqueness postulate (A5) is violated. Thus, I(U) is not generally acceptable as a solution to the organizational decision problem.

d) A solution may be called organizationally maximal if

$$L_Q = \{\hat{u} = u(a), \; a \in A\} \text{ with } \hat{u}_n = \max_{a \in A} u_n(a) \text{ for all } n \in [N],$$

that is to say, if there exist decision alternatives which maximize the utility of all organization members simultaneously. The existence of such a solution is very strongly dependent on the particular problem structure and, therefore, cannot generally be assumed, so that (A1) need not be fulfilled. If, however, there exists an organizationally maximal solution, then it fulfils all postulates (A1) - (A5). But in this case, analogous to a perfect solution (GEOFFRION 1965, p.2) in decision situations with multiple objectives, there no longer exists an organizational decision problem.

The properties of the organization-theoretic notions of solution dealt with are sometimes unsatisfactory with respect to the requirements (A1) - (A5), which can mainly be ascribed to the fact that they largely dispense with the formulation of a decision behaviour common to all organization members. Approaches taking this requirement into account in different ways will be discussed more thoroughly in the following section.

## 4. Game- and Bargaining-theoretic Contributions to the Solving of Organizational Decision Problems

### 4.1 Game-theoretic Solution Approaches

a) For two-person cooperative games without side payments NASH (1953, p.136ff.) has indicated an axiomatically founded solution which can be extended to N persons and is then characterized as follows:

$$L_Q = \{u^* \in U \mid \prod_{n=1}^{N} (u_n^* - t_n) = \max_{a \in A} \prod_{n=1}^{N} [u_n(a) - t_n], \, t \in U\}.$$

In this expression $t \in U$ designates a disagreement vector - which is not Pareto-optimal - from the interior of U; t may be given definitely by the rules of the game, or be determinable by threat strategies (HARSANYI 1963, p.195ff.) of the players. The optimal solutions $u^*$ are then characterized by the fact that they maximize the product of all utility increases with respect to the disagreement vector $t \in U$ for the decision makers involved. Obviously, this so-called cooperative NASH solution satisfies the requirements (A1) and (A2), as well as postulate (A3) after the construction of t. On account of the strictly monotonically increasing and strictly convex goal precept which follows from the underlying axioms, the $u^*$ are Pareto-optimal and with the possible unique choice of the disagreement vector $t \in U$ also unique, that is to say, they satisfy the conditions (A4) and (A5). Thus, as a whole, the cooperative NASH concept is well suitable for solving group decision problems. Furthermore, it has the properties which are desirable for utility-theoretic considerations, that the solution $u^*$ is invariant with respect to linear utility transformations, symmetric with respect to the decision makers and independent of irrelevant decision alternatives.

b) For solving of N-person cooperative games with side payments and transferable utilities SHAPLEY (1953) has formulated the value $\varphi(v)$ of a game. Being defined on the characteristic function v which describes the game it assigns the payoff $\varphi_n(v)$ to each of the decision makers $n \in [N]$ at the end of the game. In this connection $v : P[N] \to \mathbb{R}$ is a mapping of the power set of [N] into the real numbers, and for each coalition $\bar{S}$, $\bar{S} \in P[N]$ or $\bar{S} \subset N$, $v(\bar{S})$ indicates the common payoff under transferable utilities, which it can obtain by the maximin strategy at the expense of the coalition $\bar{N} - \bar{S}$ of the other players:

$$v(\bar{S}) = \max_{a^{\bar{S}}} \min_{a^{\bar{N}-\bar{S}}} \sum_{n \in \bar{S}} u_n(a^{\bar{S}}, a^{\bar{N}-\bar{S}}), \text{ for all } \bar{S} \subseteq N, \ a = (a^{\bar{S}}, a^{\bar{N}-\bar{S}}) \in A; \quad (1)$$

$\bar{N}$ designates the coalition consisting of all group decision makers. Because of the axiomatic requirements which, according to SHAPLEY, the mathematical structure of $\varphi$ has to satisfy it can be shown that there exists a unique function $\varphi$ describing the value of the game for each player $n \in [N]$ and reading as follows:

$$\varphi_n(v) = \sum_{\bar{S} \subseteq N} \frac{(S-1)!(N-S)!}{N!} [v(\bar{S}) - v(\bar{S} - \{n\})], \ n \in [N], \ S = \|\bar{S}\| \text{ and } N = \|\bar{N}\|. \quad (2)$$

The solution corresponding to the SHAPLEY value can be formally represented as follows:

$$L_Q = \{u^* \in U \mid u^* = \varphi(v)\}.$$

With regard to expression (1) existence and uniqueness of the solution $u^*$ follow directly from formula (2). Pareto-optimality of $u^*$ is guaranteed by the axiomatic construction of $\varphi$, since the maximal payoff which can be jointly obtained for all players will be distributed fully to them due to the solution vector $u^*$, that is to say, $\sum_{n=1}^{N} u_n^* = v(\bar{N})$ holds. $u^*$ continues to be individually rational since the function $\varphi$ satisfies the conditions $\varphi_n(v) \geq v(\{n\})$ for all $n \in [N]$. The feasibility of $u^*$ is ascribable to the classification of the considered game by admitted side payments and transferable utilities, since the utility set is then characterized by

$$U = \{u \mid \sum_{n=1}^{N} u_n \leq v(\bar{N})\} \quad (3)$$

and $u^* \in U$ holds because of Pareto-optimality. Thus, in case of a possible equivalent mapping of the group decision problem by the game situation discussed here, all requirements (A1) - (A5) for its solution are satisfied, so that in this sense the SHAPLEY value can serve as a concept of solution. Its workability in real cases, however, is questionable due to the fact that it can only be used for solving games with transferable utilities in which side payments take place. Under practical aspects these assumptions are critical and clearly limit the efficiency of the SHAPLEY value with respect to the solution of decision problems in organizations.

c) SHAPLEY himself has indicated a way which allows the extension of his solution idea to cooperative games without side payments; thus it is made more attractive for the application to organizational decision problems. As opposed to the concept of value of the game this proposal is referred to as evaluation of a game (SHAPLEY 1964; SHAPLEY/SHUBIK 1969). The starting point for deriving the SHAPLEY evalution once more is the characteristic function v which, however, is now given by the mapping v: $P[N] \rightarrow \mathbb{R}^S$, $S \in [N]$, since there are no side payments. It assigns to each coalition $\bar{S} \subseteq \bar{N}$ a subset $v(\bar{S}) \subset \mathbb{R}^S$, $S = \|\bar{S}\|$, of feasible payoff vectors. The sets $v(\bar{S})$ are subsets of the utility set $U = v(\bar{N}) \subset \mathbb{R}^N$, that is to say, $v(\bar{S}) \subseteq v(\bar{N})$ for all $\bar{S} \subseteq \bar{N}$; they are assumed to be convex, closed and nonempty. Its vectors $u^{\bar{N}} = (u_n)_{n \in \bar{S}} \in v(\bar{S})$ result from the projection of corresponding $u \in U$ into $\mathbb{R}^S$, and consequently contain just as many components as there are members in the coalition $\bar{S}$. In order to extend the SHAPLEY approach represented in b) to game situations of this kind the following procedure is taken for determining the SHAPLEY evaluation:

1. By rescaling the utility functions of the decision makers by a vector

$$\lambda = (\lambda_1, \ldots, \lambda_N) \geq 0, \quad \lambda \neq 0, \tag{4}$$

   the utility set $U = v(\bar{N})$ of the cooperative game without side payments will be transformed into the utility set $U' = v'(\bar{N}) = \{u' | u' = (\lambda_1 u_1, \ldots, \lambda_N u_N) =: > \lambda, u <, u \in U\}$ of another cooperative game without side payments, where

$$v'(\bar{S}) = \{u'^{\bar{S}} | u'^{\bar{S}} = > \lambda^{\bar{S}}, u^{\bar{S}} <, u^{\bar{S}} \in v(\bar{S})\}, \quad \bar{S} \subseteq \bar{N} \text{ and } \lambda^{\bar{S}} = (\lambda_n)_{n \in \bar{S}} \tag{5}$$

   holds.

2. The cooperative game without side payments with the transformed characteristic function v' is now treated as a corresponding cooperative game with side payments and transferable utilities. The latter then possesses the characteristic function v"(S).

3. On the basis of v" compute the SHAPLEY value

$$\varphi(v'') = \tilde{u} \tag{6}$$

   according to (2).

4. If now $\tilde{u} \in U' = v'(\bar{N})$ holds, that is to say, if there exists a $u^* \in U = v(\bar{N})$ with the property

$$\varphi(v'') = \tilde{u} = > \lambda, u^* <, \tag{7}$$

   then $\tilde{u}$ – and consequently $u^*$ – can be obtained also without drawing on side pay-

194

ments. $u^* \in U$ which, after rescaling the utility functions, corresponds to $\tilde{u} \in U'$ on returning to the original cooperative game without side payments is to be regarded as the solution of this game, that is to say, let

$$L_Q = \{u^* \in U \mid > \lambda, u^* < = \varphi(v'')\}.$$

$\lambda \cdot u^*$ is referred to by SHAPLEY as the evaluation of a game if and only if $\lambda$ and $u^*$ satisfy the requirements (4) and (7).

The SHAPLEY evaluation $\lambda \cdot u^*$ fulfils the existence postulate (A1) for any finite N-person cooperative game without side payments (SHAPLEY 1964); according to its construction the appropriate solution vector $u^*$ will then also obey the requirements (A2) - (A4). As opposed to the SHAPLEY value, in this case the uniqueness is dependent on the possible unique choice of the scaling vector $\lambda$, so that the fulfilment of (A5) cannot generally be insured. Precisely this deficiency, however, gives rise to the strongest objections as regards the practical use of the SHAPLEY evaluation for solving organizational decision problems. An additional difficulty is the fact that the relative utility positions of the decision makers shift in the solution vector $u^*$ when the relative utility weights are changed by the choice of $\lambda$ (FANDEL 1979, p.52). Therefore, in higher-dimensional problems it is hardly any longer possible to predict in which way solution $u^*$ will behave in case of variation of $\lambda$ if there exist several evaluations $\lambda \cdot u^*$ for a cooperative game without side payments.

d) Extending the minimax criterion developed for two-person zerosum games NASH (1951) designates the set of equilibrium decisions $a^*$ in common N-person non-cooperative games as their solution. This socalled non-cooperative NASH solution formally reads as follows for the considered group decision situation

$$L_Q = \{u^* \in U \mid u^* = u(a^*), \ a^* \in A, \text{ and } u_n(a^*) = \max_{a_n \in A_n} u_n(a_n, \bar{a}_n^*) \text{ for all } n \in [N]\}.$$

NASH has shown that each non-cooperative game of this kind possesses at least one equilibrium vector $a^* \in A$. Such equilibria are at the same time feasible and individually rational. As opposed to these positive statements with respect to the postulates (A1) - (A3) the requirements (A4) of Pareto-optimality and (A5) of uniqueness cannot normally be insured for the non-cooperative equilibria (LUCE/RAIFFA 1958, p.106ff.; SHUBIK 1960). Therefore, the non-cooperative NASH concept cannot generally be considered to be a satisfactory approach to the solution of group decision problems.

e) In order to come from nonefficient equilibria in non-cooperative games to such equilibria with Pareto-optimal utility vectors FRIEDMAN (1971) starts from the formulation of a supergame consisting in the infinite periodical repetition of a given normal game. To deal with it, a new class of non-cooperative supergame equilibria is introduced by definition, first assuming that the normal game possesses only a (non-efficient) equilibrium $c \in A$. In this connection for each decision maker $n \in [N]$ a super-game strategy $\sigma_n'$ on the basis of a decision vector $a' \in A$ which strictly dominates the normal equilibrium $c$ with respect to the utility – that is to say, for which $u(a')$ $>>u(c)$ holds – may be constructed as follows:

$$\sigma_n' = (a_{n1}, a_{n2}, \ldots, a_{nt}, \ldots) \text{ with } a_{n1} = a_n',$$

$$a_{nt} = \begin{cases} a_n', & \text{if } a_{n'\tau} = a_{n'}', \ n \neq n', \ \tau = 1, \ldots, t-1, \ t > 1, \\ c_n & \text{otherwise.} \end{cases} \tag{8}$$

Allowing (8), the supergame stategy $\sigma^{a'} = (a', a', \ldots)$ represents a noncooperative equilibrium if it fulfils the condition

$$\sum_{t=1}^{\infty} \alpha_n^{t-1} u_n(a') > u_n(\bar{a}_n', b_n) + \sum_{t=2}^{\infty} \alpha_n^{t-1} u_n(c) \text{ for all } n \in [N]. \tag{9}$$

$\alpha_n$ designates the discount rate of the decision maker $n$; it is constant for all periods $t$. $u_n(\bar{a}_n', b_n) = \max\{u_n(\bar{a}_n', a_n) \mid a_n \in A_n\}$, $n \in [N]$, indicates the maximal yield which he can achieve at the expense of all other players by deviating once from $a'$. Since condition (9) after splitting, applying the sum formula and regrouping, is equivalent to

$$u_n(a') > u_n(c) + (1 - \alpha_n)[u_n(\bar{a}_n', b_n) - u_n(c)] \equiv u_n^+(a'), \ n \in [N], \tag{10}$$

the class of the non-cooperative supergame equilibria can now be described in the utility space by the following set $U_G^{\sigma'} \subset U$:

$$U_G^{\sigma'} = \{u \in U \mid u(a') >> u^+(a') \text{ and } u(a') >> u(c), \ a' \in A\}. \tag{11}$$

If (10) is transformed into (12)

$$\frac{\alpha_n}{1 - \alpha_n}[u_n(a') - u_n(c)] > u_n(\bar{a}_n', b_n) - u_n(a'), \ n \in [N], \tag{12}$$

it can be seen that the supergame strategy $\sigma^a = (a, a, \ldots)$, resulting from the infinite repetition of a strategy $a \in A$ of the normal game dominating the equilibrium $c$ belongs to $U_G^{\sigma'}$, if for each decision maker the single net gain obtainable by deviating from $a$ – right hand side of the inequation (12) – is smaller than the cash value of the permanent utility losses to be expected on account of the reaction of the partners – left hand side of the inequation (12). According to (8) any other supergame strategy $\sigma_n$ for player $n$ is weakly dominated either by $\sigma_n' = (a_{n1}, a_{n2}, \ldots)$ or $\sigma_n'' = (b_n, c_n, c_n, \ldots)$.

Now, in order to particularly mark a Pareto-optimal $\sigma^{a^*}$ in the sense of (8) as solution among the equilibria of the supergame, FRIEDMAN proposes that the temptation to deviate from $a^*$ is to be equally large for all players, that means

$$L_Q = \{u^* \in U \mid u^* = u(a^*) \in P(U_G^{\sigma'}) \text{ and } v_n(a^*) = v_{n'}(a^*) \text{ for all } n, n' \in [N]\}.$$

The temptation to deviate $v_n(a^*)$ is defined by:

$$v_n(a^*) = \frac{u_n(\bar{a}_n^*, b_n) - u_n(a^*)}{u_n(a^*) - u_n(c)} \quad , \quad n \in [N]. \tag{13}$$

The existence of such a decision alternative $a^*$ is not generally guaranteed since the set $U_G^{\sigma'}$ - and thus also $L_Q$ - can become empty according to condition (10) in case of small discount rates (that is high time preferences) of the decision makers. For suf-ficiently high discount rates, however, the fulfilment of postulate (A1) can be in-sured. In this case $a^*$ will also satisfy the requirements (A2) - (A4). The uniqueness of the solution, however, cannot be guaranteed at the same time (FRIEDMAN 1971, p. 8 ff.), which means that on account of a possible violation of (A5) the FRIEDMAN concept can be used for solving the group decision problem in special cases only.

## 4.2 Bargaining-theoretic Solution Approaches

a) The N-person bargaining model developed by HARSANYI (1963) is based on the idea to generalize the cooperative NASH solution (NASH 1950 and 1953) which has been concei-ved for two-person decisions. As opposed to the determination of solution described in 4.1 a) the N-person decision in the HARSANYI model, however, must first be de-composed into a set of two-person subgames between all possible pairs n and n' from [N] according to the mathematical concept of the theory of bargaining. Allowing for their interdependence the resulting subgame will then have to be formulated so mutu-ally consistently with respect to the partial conditions of solution that subsequently, the total solution of the group decision problem can be composed of them in the form of an equilibrium strictly taking two-person subgames as a basis.

Let the function $f(u)=0$ describe the efficient border $P(U)$ of the utility set $U$ in parametric form, and let it be differentiable. With the analytic properties of the cooperative NASH solution for the two-person decision problem the optimal total solu-tion to the general N-person bargaining problem

$$L_Q = \{u^* \in U \mid u^* = u^{\bar{N}}\}$$

which in the HARSANYI model has successively been composed of the solutions to two-party subgames can then be characterized by the following system of necessary condi-tions (HARSANYI 1963, pp. 214/215):

$$f(u^{\bar{N}}) = 0 \ ; \tag{14.1}$$

$$c_n = f_n(u^{\bar{N}}) = \partial f / \partial u_n \mid u^{\bar{N}}; \ n \in \bar{N}; \tag{14.2}$$

$$u_n^{\bar{S}} = u_n(a^{\bar{S}^O}, a^{\bar{S}'^O}); \ n \in \bar{S}, \ \bar{S} \subset \bar{N}, \ \bar{S}' = \bar{N} - \bar{S}; \tag{14.3}$$

$$t_n^{\bar{S}} = \sum_{\substack{\bar{R} \subset \bar{S} \\ n \in \bar{R}}} (-1)^{s-r+1} u_n^{\bar{R}}; \ n \in \bar{S}; \ \bar{S} \subseteq \bar{N}, \ s = \|\bar{S}\| > 1, \ r = \|\bar{R}\|; \tag{14.4}$$

$$c_n(u_n^{\bar{N}}-t_n^{\bar{N}})=c_{n'}(u_{n'}^{\bar{N}}-t_{n'}^{\bar{N}}) \text{ for all } n,n'\in\bar{N};$$ (14.5)

$$\begin{cases} \sum_{n\in\bar{S}}c_n u_n^{\bar{S}}-\sum_{n'\in\bar{S}'}c_{n'}u_{n'}^{\bar{S}'} \\\\ =\sum_{n\in\bar{S}}c_n u_n(a^{\bar{S}^O},a^{\bar{S}',O})-\sum_{n'\in\bar{S}'}c_{n'}u_{n'}(a^{\bar{S}^O},a^{\bar{S}',O}) \\\\ =\max_{a^{\bar{S}}\in A^{\bar{S}}}\min_{a^{\bar{S}'}\in A^{\bar{S}'}}[\sum_{n\in\bar{S}}c_n u_n(a^{\bar{S}},a^{\bar{S}'})-\sum_{n'\in\bar{S}'}c_{n'}u_{n'}(a^{\bar{S}},a^{\bar{S}'})], \ \bar{S},\ \bar{S}'\subset\bar{N},\ A^{\bar{S}}=\underset{n\in\bar{S}}{X}A_n; \\\\ \text{subject to: } c_n(u_n^{\bar{S}}-t_n^{\bar{S}})=c_k(u_k^{\bar{S}}-t_k^{\bar{S}}),\ n,\ k\in\bar{S}; \\\\ \qquad\qquad c_{n'}(u_{n'}^{\bar{S}'}-t_{n'}^{\bar{S}'})=c_1(u_1^{\bar{S}'}-t_1^{\bar{S}'}),\ n',\ 1\in\bar{S}'. \end{cases}$$ (14.6)

Conditions (14.1), (14.2), (14.5) and (14.6) are expressive of the fact that for a consistent construction of the bargaining result according to the cooperative NASH concept, the criteria of optimality of the total solution must be of prime importance for all two-person or two-party subgames, too. According to (14.3) the utility of the decision maker n in the coalition $\bar{S}$ is dependent on the choice of optimal threat strategies $a^{\bar{S}^O}$ and $a^{\bar{S}',O}$ by the two coalitions $\bar{S}$ and $\bar{S}'$. When he joins this coalition his disagreement payoff, however, according to (14.4) will consist of the cumulated utility increases achieved by him in all subcoalitions $\bar{R}\subset\bar{S}$ of which he was a member previously.

The optimal solution $u^{\bar{N}}$ of the problem (14.1) - (14.6) which, in its formulation, tries to make the most perfect use of the NASH axioms for two-person cooperative games with respect to the theory of bargaining in general, fulfils the requirements (A1) - (A4). Difficulties, however, in unrestrictedly accepting $u^*=u^{\bar{N}}$ as optimal solution to the organizational decision problem may arise from the fact that the disagreement payoffs are variable on account of threat strategies, so that the solution $u^{\bar{N}}$ need not necessarily be unique. This violation of (A5) is, however, avoidable by uniquely presetting $t_n^{\bar{S}}$.

Other bargaining-theoretic approaches on the basis of the cooperative NASH concept have been formulated by LEMAIRE (1973), MIYASAWA (1964) and ISBELL (1960). Further game-theoretically founded solution proposals with regard to the bargaining problem which start out from systems of axioms different from those of NASH may be found in KRELLE (1975).

b) As an alternative to such game-theoretically founded approaches of the theory of bargaining CONTINI and ZIONTS (1968) have conceived a concessive bargaining model in which the solution to the group decision problem is simultaneously determined by agreement of all group members. This agreement is reached under threat of an imposed solution $y \in U$ by means of a process of concession which is continuous with respect to time and leads to the solution

$$L_Q = \{u^* \in U \mid u^* \geq z(t) \geq y\}.$$

Here $z(t)$ designates the decision makers' aspiration levels at time $t$, declining in the course of the process of concession. At the beginning let $z(0) = \hat{u}$, that is to say, let the aspiration levels tally with the individual utility maxima of the group at time $t=0$. The concession behaviour of the decision makers which is achieved by the threat of an imposed solution is described by the following system of conditions:

$$dz_n(t)/dt = \begin{cases} k_n(t) < 0, & \text{if } L_Q = \emptyset \text{ and } z_n(t) > y_n, \\ & \qquad\qquad\qquad\qquad n \in [N]. \\ 0 & \text{otherwise,} \end{cases} \qquad (15)$$

Consequently, every decision maker is ready to make concessions only as long as no feasible solution has been found and his aspiration level remains above the payoff which would be yielded to him in case of the imposed solution. If one of the conditions does no longer apply, then the concession rate $k_n(t)$ will become equal to zero.

In order to insure according to the postulate (A1) the existence of a solution, that is to say $L_Q \neq \emptyset$, the functions $k_n(t)$ are subjected to the following additional sufficient conditions that for every $k_n(t)$ there exists a $t_n'$, $0 \leq t_n' < \infty$, with

$$-\int_0^{t_n'} k_n(\tau) d\tau = \hat{u}_n - y_n, \quad n \in [N]. \qquad (16)$$

Thus, even if the condition $L_Q = \emptyset$ in (15) is neglected the concession path $z(t)$ for a finite $t' = \max \{t_n' \mid n \in [N]\}$ would at any rate have at least to lead to the imposed solution $y \in U$ as stationary solution. With the existence the feasibility requirement (A2) is at the same time fulfilled by the solution $u^*$. The individual rationality (postulate (A3)) of $u^*$, however, is not automatically given; it is rather dependent on the clever choice of the imposed solution $y$. Sufficient for the guarantee of individually rational solutions is $y \geq \hat{u}$. Pareto-optimality and uniqueness of the solution $u^*$, as well, cannot generally be insured without additional conditions. CONTINI and ZIONTS have shown that (A4) and (A5) are fulfilled if the utility set is strictly convex. It is also sufficient if for the location of the imposed solution $y \in U$ $\eta(y) \cap R(U) \subseteq P(U)$ holds with $\eta(y) = \{u \in \mathbb{R}^N \mid u \geq y\}$ and $R(U)$ as border of the utility set $U$ (FANDEL 1979, p. 115).

It is evident that the concessive bargaining model developed by CONTINI and ZIONTS can be

used for solving the group decision problem on certain additional conditions only, the
existence of which must always be separately examined. Nevertheless, this concept
with its spontaneous elements of behaviour - expressed in concession rates - may by
all means be regarded as a practice-oriented alternative to the axiomatically founded
solution approaches. The question, however, in how far the concession rates of the decision makers can rationally be accounted for, remains still to be answered. This problem will be treated in the next section concluding this paper.

## 4.3 On the Rationalizing of the Concession Behaviour

It is unsatisfactory, that so far there are only two-person concepts available for rationally elaborating the concession behaviour characterized according to (15) (FANDEL
1979, p.120ff.). Their ability to give information about the solution of the group decision problem is limited correspondingly; yet, they indicate possibilities of development with respect to elaborating the rational foundations of the concessive bargaining models under the aspect of their usefulness in practice.

Most of the approaches can be reduced to the idea of the bargaining theorem developed
by ZEUTHEN (1930, chapter 4). According to this theorem the concession behaviour for
jointly determining a Pareto-optimal solution vector $u^* \in P(U)$ depends on the subjective
probabilities of conflict which can maximally be accepted by the two bargaining partners; the former result from the Pareto-optimal proposals and counterproposals which
are made by the two players in the course of the process of concession. At the beginning let $u^1$ and $u^2$, $u^1 \neq u^2$, be the proposal and counterproposal of the first and the
second decision maker, respectively. Let $\bar{u} \in U$ represent the disagreement or conflict
point, and let $U' = \{u \in U \mid u \geq \bar{u}\}$. Then the following conclusions can be drawn with respect
to the first decision maker:

1. He can definitely achieve the utility $u_1^2$ if he accepts the counterproposal $u^2$ of
the second decision maker (action 1).

2. If, however, he rejects $u^2$ persisting in his proposal $u^1$ (action 2) the expected
value of his utility will be $\bar{u}_1 \pi + u_1^1 (1-\pi)$, where $\pi$ indicates the probability that decision maker 2 will risk a conflict.

The subjective conflict probability $p_1$ which is maximally acceptable for decision
maker 1 and with which he is just able to keep up his proposal then results from the
indifference between the two actions indicated, that is to say, if one has

$$u_1^2 = \bar{u}_1 p_1 + u_1^1 (1-p_1) \quad \text{or} \quad p_1 = (u_1^1 - u_1^2)/(u_1^1 - \bar{u}_1) \ . \tag{17}$$

Correspondingly, for the second decision maker one obtains:

$$p_2 = (u_2^2 - u_2^1)/(u_2^2 - \bar{u}_2). \tag{18}$$

According to ZEUTHEN now a concession is made by the decision maker $n \in \{1,2\}$ for whom

$$p_n \leq p_{n'}; \quad p_n, p_{n'} > 0 \quad \text{and } n,n' \in \{1,2\}, \ n \neq n', \tag{19}$$

holds, that is to say, by that decision maker who is not able to cope with a greater probability of conflict than his bargaining partner. The concession consists of a new proposal (e.g. $\hat{u}^2$ instead of $u^2$) which causes the probability of conflict maximally endurable to become greater again than that of the contrahent, thus forcing the latter to make concessions for his part. This process is iteratively continued until a common agreement solution $u^* \in P(U')$ is obtained. If, allowing for the expressions (17) and (18) condition (19) is transformed into the equivalent inequation

$$(u_n^n - \bar{u}_n)(u_{n'}^n - \bar{u}_{n'}) \leq (u_n^{n'} - \bar{u}_n)(u_{n'}^{n'} - \bar{u}_{n'}); \ n,n' \in \{1,2\}, \ n \neq n', \tag{20}$$

for N=2, it can be seen that the rationalizing of the concession behaviour in the bargaining theorem by ZEUTHEN is identical with the axioms of the cooperative NASH solution (see section 4.1 a)). The embedding of a concession behaviour thus rationalized in the system (15) of the bargaining model by CONTINI and ZIONTS is quite obvious now if there the process is discretized by proposals and counterproposals $u^n(t) \in P(U')$, $n \in \{1,2\}$, at times t, t=0,1,2,.... Using the old symbols we then have: $y = \bar{u}$, $z_n(0) = \hat{u}_n = \max \{u_n | u \in U'\} = u_n^n(0)$ and

$$z_n(t+1) - z_n(t) = \begin{cases} k_n(t) < 0, \text{ if } L_Q = \emptyset \text{ and } \prod_{r=1}^{2} [u_r^n(t) - \bar{u}_r] \leq \prod_{r=1}^{2} [u_r^{n'}(t) - \bar{u}_r], \\ \\ 0 \text{ otherwise,} \\ \\ n,n' \in \{1,2\} \quad \text{and} \quad n \neq n', \end{cases}$$

with

$$\begin{cases} k_n(t) = u_n^n(t+1) - u_n^n(t) \text{ and } u^n(t+1) \text{ with the property that no } u \in P(U') \\ \text{exists with } u_n > u_n^n(t+1) \text{ and } \prod_{r=1}^{2}(u_r - \bar{u}_r) > \prod_{r=1}^{2}[u_r^n(t+1) - \bar{u}_r], \\ n \in \{1,2\} \quad \text{and} \quad t \in \{0,1,2,...\}. \end{cases} \tag{15'}$$

The extension of the thus described rational concession behaviour according to (20) or (15') to N persons, N>2, is obvious, but it can no longer formally be concluded from the bargaining theorem by ZEUTHEN (condition 19). The above remarks show, however, that the combination of game-theoretic axioms and concessive bargaining models which are based on spontaneous elements of behaviour may yield valuable suggestions for the solving of group decision problems.

## References

CONTINI, B. and ZIONTS, S.: Restricted Bargaining for Organizations with Multiple Objectives, in: Econometrica, 1968, pp.397-414.
FANDEL, G.: Optimale Entscheidungen in Organisationen, Berlin-Heidelberg-New-York 1979.
FANDEL, G. and WILHELM, J.: Zur Entscheidungstheorie bei mehrfacher Zielsetzung, in: Zeitschrift für Operations Research, 1976, pp.1-21.
FRIEDMAN, J.W.: A Non-cooperative Equilibrium for Supergames, in: Review of Economic Studies, 1971, pp.1-12.
GEOFFRION, A.M.:A Parametric Programming Solution to the Vector Maximum Problem, with Applications to Decisions under Uncertainty, Stanford/California 1965.
HAPSANYI, J.C.: A Simplified Bargaining Model for the n-Person Cooperative Game, in: International Economic Review, 1963, pp.194-200.
ISBELL, J.R.: A Modification of Harsanyis Bargaining Model, in:Bulletin of the American Mathematical Society, 1960, pp.70-73.
KRELLE, W.: A New Theory of Bargaining, Applied to the Problem of Wage Determination and Strikes, Institut für Gesellschafts- und Wirtschaftswissenschaften der Universität Bonn, Wirtschaftstheoretische Abteilung, Nr. 70, Bonn 1975.
LEMAIRE, J.: A New Value for Games without Transferable Utilities, in: International Journal of Game Theory, 1973, pp. 205-213.
LUCE, R.D. and RAIFFA, H.: Games and Decisions, New York 1958.
MIYASAWA, K.: The n-Person Bargaining Game, in: DRESHER, M., SHAPLEY, L.S. and TUCKER, A.W. (eds.): Advances in Game Theory, Princeton/New Jersey 1964, pp.547-575.
NASH, J.F.: The Bargaining Problem, in: Econometrica, 1950, pp.155-162.
NASH, J.F.: Noncooperative Games, in: Annals of Mathematics, 1951, pp.286-295.
NASH, J.F.: Two Person Cooperative Games, in: Econometrica, 1953,pp.128-140.
SHAPLEY, L.S.: A Value for n-Person Games, in: KUHN, H.W. and TUCKER, A.W. (eds.): Contributions to the Theory of Games, Volume II, Princeton /New Jersey 1953, pp.307-317.
SHAPLEY, L.S.: Values of Large Market Games: Status of the Problem, Memorandum RM-3957-PR, The Rand Corporation, Santa Monica/California, February 1964.
SHAPLEY, L.S. and SHUBIK, M.: Pure Competition, Coalitional Power and Fair Division, in: International Economic Review, 1969, pp.337-362.
SHUBIK, M.: Games Decisions and Industrial Organization, in: Management Science, 1960, pp.455-474.
SIMON, H.A.: A Comparison of Organization Theories, in: The Review of Economic Studies, 1952/53, pp.40-48.
THIRIEZ, H. and ZIONTS, S. (eds.): Multiple Criteria Decision Making, Berlin-Heidelberg-New York 1976.
ZEUTHEN, F.: Problems of Monopoly and Economic Warfare, London 1930.
ZIONTS, S., (ed.): Multiple Criteria Problem Solving, Berlin-Heidelberg-New York 1978.

# INTERACTIVE GROUP DECISION MAKING BY COALITIONS

Heinz Isermann

*Faculty of Business Administration and Economics, University of Bielefeld,
Bielefeld, FRG*

ABSTRACT

This paper addresses some aspects of group decision making by coalitions.
In Section 2 we analyse and illustrate efficiency concepts with regard to group
decision making. Section 3 - which is the main part of the paper - is devoted
to the design of an interactive decision support system for group decision making by coalitions. This interactive decision support system is not based on the
assumption that individual or collective preference systems can be represented
by preference functions.

## 1. INTRODUCTION

In this paper we explore some of the difficulties inherent in attempting to
determine a compromise alternative for a multiple objective planning model with
respect to multiple decision makers (DMs). In the course of a collective decision
process intrapersonal as well as interpersonal conflict situations have to be mas-
tered  by the DMs involved in the collective decision process. The intrapersonal
conflict situation of each individual DM may be characterized by the impossibility to achieve all his or her objectives simultaneously: some alternative provides
an acceptable criterion value for one criterion but unsatisfactory values for the
remaining criteria whereas other alternatives provide acceptable criterion values for some of the latter criteria but fall behind acceptable criterion values
with respect to other criteria. The interpersonal conflict situation arises as
the criterion values which are accepted by the indivudial DMs lead to the selection of alternatives which are mutually incompatible.

Many decisions in both the public and private sectors are made via majority
voting. In these situations an agreement on an alternative is not demanded from
all DMs involved in the collective decision process but from a defined majority
of DMs. This majority forms a coalition of J out of K DMs. If an unanimous agreement on an alternative is necessary then all K DMs form this coalition. Thus the
structure of collective decision processes where all DMs have to agree on an alternative may be regarded as a special case of collective decision making via
majority voting.

Attempts to characterize a welfare function for the coalition of $J \leq K$ DMs
and then to maximize this welfare function might be considered a reasonable approach to resolve the collective decision problem. However, such a social welfare function does not generally exist, as shown by ARROW (1). KERSTEN et al.
(8,9) propose a collective decision support system for a linear multiple objective planning model with respect to several DMs which is based on the assumption
that the individual DMs' preference systems can be represented by a linear utility function. WENDELL (12) views the collective decision process as a majority

voting game. He implicitly assumes that each individual DM has stable preferences in the course of the whole decision process and that his preference system can be represented by a utility function with specified properties. However, our own experiments support the hypothesis that the formation of the individual DM's valuation system is neither complete nor definite at the beginning of the decision process (cf. e.g. (3,7)). Rather the formation of the DM's implicit valuation system develops in the course of the decision process and it was observed in our experiments that the formation process of the individual DM's valuation system is attended by consecutive modifications of one or more objectives. Thus we shall desist from designing a decision support system which is based on the prior assumption that the individual DM's valuation system can be represented by a scalar-valued utility or preference function. Our approach is keyed to an interactive collective decision support system which provides for both, resolving intrapersonal and interpersonal conflict situations. The structure of the collective decision support system will be based on the concept of mediation (11). In some recent papers by GRAUER and WIERZBICKI (4,13,14) we also find the concept of mediation integrated in a collective decision support system.

The structure of the collective decision support system we are going to present will become subject of an empirical investigation. In the course of this empirical inquiry we want to test the suitability of the proposed structure with regard to resolving practical multi-DMs decision problems.

## 2.    MULTIPLE OBJECTIVE PLANNING MODELS WITH RESPECT TO MULTIPLE DECISION MAKERS

We assume that K DMs are members of a committee which has to select an alternative x from a set of alternatives X. Let $k = 1,...,K$ be the index set of the DMs. Each alternative is to be evaluated in terms of its performance on several criteria. Let $i = 1,...,I_k$ be the index set of the finite number of attributes the k-th DM considers relevant with regard to the current decision problem. We assume that each DM $k = 1,...,K$ can give ordinal or cardinal scores $z_{ki}(x)$ for each alternative $x \in X$ on each attribute $i = 1,...,I_k$. Without loss of generality we assume that for each attribute i each DM k prefers higher scores to lower scores. Let $z_k(x) = (z_{k1}(x),...,z_{kI_k}(x))^T$ be the vector valued criterion function of the k-th DM. Then the multiple objective planning model with respect to a committee of K DMs may be formulated as:

$$\text{"maximize" } z_1(x)$$
$$\vdots$$
$$\text{"maximize" } z_K(x)$$
$$\text{s.t.} \tag{1}$$
$$x \in X.$$

In the sequel we shall assume that all DMs involved in the collective decision problem agree that (1) adequately represents the problem under consideration.

As long as all K DMs have to agree on a final compromise alternative this alternative which is to be unanimously chosen from the set of alternatives has to be an efficient alternative. $x^* \in X$ is called efficient alternative for (1), if and only if, by definition there is no alternative $x' \in X$ such that

$$z_k(x') \geq z_k(x^*) \qquad \text{for all } k = 1,...,K$$
and $\quad z_k(x') \geqq z_k(x^*)$ [1] $\qquad$ for at least one $k \in \{1,...,K\}$.

---
[1]
$$z_k(x') \geqq z_k(x^*) \iff z_k(x') \geq z_k(x^*) \text{ and } z_k(x') \neq z_k(x).$$

Let $X_E$ denote the set of all efficient alternatives for (1). Thus $X_E$ contains the set of nominees for a compromise alternative which is to be unanimously selected by all K DMs of the committee.

As soom as in the course of the collective decision process the concept of unanimity is repleaced by a majority concept the above efficiency concept is no more appropriate (5, pp. 17). Let $K_J = \{k_1,\ldots,k_J\} \subset \{1,\ldots,K\}$ be a coalition with J DMs ($K/2 < J \leq K$). Obviously, an alternative on which all members of a coalition $K_J$ have to agree has to be efficient with respect to all objective functions of the members of $K_J$ but no more with respect to the objective functions of the other DMs who are not members of the coalition $K_J$. $x^* \in X$ is called $K_J$-efficient alternative for (1), if and only if, by definition there is no alternative $x' \in X$ such that

$$z_k(x') \geqq z_k(x^*) \quad \text{for all } k \in K_J$$

and
$$z_k(x') \geq z_k(x^*) \quad \text{for at least one } k \in K_J.$$

Let $X_E(K_J)$ denote the set of all $K_J$-efficient alternatives for (1). Each $x \in X_E(K_J)$ is a nominee for a compromise alternative which is to be unanimously selected by the J members of the coalition $K_J$.

A further useful efficiency concept with respect to collective decision making via majority voting is the concept of J-efficiency. Let $J > K/2$. $x^* \in X$ is called J-efficient alternative for (1), if and only if, by definition $x^*$ is $K_J$-efficient for at least one coalition $K_J \subset \{1,\ldots,K\}$. Let $X_E(J)$ denote the set of all J-efficient alternatives for (1). Hence $X_E(J)$ contains the set of nominees for a compromise alternative which is to be unanimously selected by at least J out of K DMs. In other words: $X_E(J)$ contains the set of nominees for the J-majority core (cf. e.g. (10)).

## 3. OUTLINE OF AN INTERACTIVE COLLECTIVE DECISION SUPPORT SYSTEM

### 3.1 Mediation of Interpersonal Conflicts

The complexity of the collective decision process calls for a structure of of the decision support system which provides for an alternation of individual and collective decision stages. Typically the criterion values that one DM regards as acceptable at the end of an individual decision process would result in selecting an alternative which is different from those alternatives which other DMs would like to see implemented. Let $(z^R_{k1},\ldots,z^R_{kI_k})$ be the vector of criterion values which has been accepted by the k-th DM at the end of the R-th stage of his individual decision process,

$$X^R_k := \{x \in X \mid z_{ki}(x) \geq z^R_{ki} \quad (i = 1,\ldots,I_k)\}$$

be the set of alternatives which meet the criterion values $z^R_{ki}$ $(i = 1,\ldots,I_k)$ and let $K_J$ be a coalition of J DMs ($K/2 < J \leq K$). If

$$\bigcap_{k \in K_J} X^R_k \neq \emptyset$$

then an alternative which is mutually acceptable by all members of $K_J$ exists.

When negotiating problems of comparable complexity the negotiating individual DMs often join a mediator in a joint-problem-solving quest for a reasonable
compromise solution. The mediator may accumulate information from each individual DM in a balanced way and provide analytical, problem-solving skills in order to help the DMs to solve the joint problem (11). The mediator concept will
be a substantial component of the structure of the collective decision support
system we are going to present in this section. The collective decision process
will be decomposed into individual decision phases where the individual DMs engaged in the collective decision process try to resolve the intrapersonal conflicts subject to constraints which have been imposed by the mediator in order
to facilitate a commom agreement. If an agreement on a compromise alternative
has to be reached by a coalition $K_J$ the role of the mediator may be even more
comprehensive as the composition of the final coalition $K_J$ as well as the compromise alternative on which the members of $K_J$ agree become the main issues of
the collective decision process.

Typically, a coalition may not be known at the beginning of the collective
decision process, and in the course of the collective decision process some DMs
may leave a tentative coalition while others may want to join a coalition. In
order to facilitate the formation process of a coalition $K_J$ the mediator may
consider a tentative coalition $K_L \subset \{1,\ldots,K\}$ of $L \geq J$ DMs during the initial
stages of the collective decision process and successively reduce $K_L$ to some
appropriate $K_J$ as the collective decision process terminates.

The negotiation process within a coalition is easier to support if no DM
involved in the collective decision process has to renounce the full realization
of the accepted criterion values. The mediator may therefore offer to the individual DMs only a proportion $\alpha_{ki}$ of the true criterion values $z_{ki}$ in the course
of the individual decision process and hold out a prospect of further increases
of criterion values in the course of the collective decision process. During the
initial stages of the collective decision process the values of the $\alpha_{ki}$ should
not be close to 1 in order to allow for a "smooth" process of negotiations.


## 3.2 Structure of the Decision Support System for the Individual Decision Maker

The collective negotiation process is easier to support if no DM involved
in the collective decision process has to renounce the full realization of the
currently accepted criterion values. Thus the mediator should be prepared to
suggest joint imporovements to the currently accepted criterion values in order
to facilitate the collective decision process. This can be accomplished if the
individual DMs are offered only a proportion of the true criterion values.
Let

$$\hat{z}_{ki}^{o} = \max \ \{z_{ki}(x) \mid x \in X\} \qquad (i = 1,\ldots,I_k; \ k = 1,\ldots,K),$$

n denote the current stage of the collective decision process and $K_L$ denote a
subset of $\{1,\ldots,K\}$ with $L \geq J$ DMs.

Moreover, let $\hat{y}$ be an optimal solution for

$$\min y$$
$$\text{s.t.} \quad z_{ki}(x) / \hat{z}_{ki}^{o} + y \geq 1 \qquad i = 1,\ldots,I_k; \ \forall \ k \in K_L$$
$$y \geq 0$$
$$x \in X$$

With $\bar{y} > \hat{y}$ be fixed by the mediator the initial "feasible" set for the L DMs engaged in the collective decision process is (with n = 1):

$$X^n := \{x \in X \mid z_{ki}(x) \geq (1-\bar{y}) \, \hat{z}^0_{ki} \quad (i = 1,\ldots,I_k; \; \forall \, k \in K_L)\}.$$

For n > 1 the "feasible" set for the L DMs will be constructed in a different way. Let r be the stage-index of the interactive decision process for the k-th DM and R denote the final stage for given n. Moreover let $(z^R_{k1},\ldots,z^R_{kI_k}) \; \forall \, k \in K_L$ be the vectors of criterion values accepted by the L members of $K_L$ in stage (n-1) of the collective decision process, $\hat{\beta}$ be an optimal solution for

$$\max \beta$$
$$\text{s.t. } z_{ki}(x) - \beta z^R_{ki} \geq 0 \qquad i = 1,\ldots,I_k; \; \forall \, k \in K_L$$
$$x \in X$$

and $\beta^n \leq \min \{1, \, \hat{\beta}\}$ be fixed by the mediator. The "feasible" set in stage n > 1 of the collective decision process is:

$$X^n := \{x \in X \mid z_{ki}(x) \geq \beta^n \, z^R_{ki} \quad (i = 1,\ldots,I_k; \; \forall \, k \in K_L)\}.$$

Recall that the value of $\hat{\beta}$ provides the mediator with some information about the potential mutual agreement within the tentative coalition $K_L$.

In the course of the interactive decision process of the k-th DM at the beginning of each new decision stage r (see also (2)) one or more vectors of criterion values $(z^r_{k1},\ldots,z^r_{kI_k})$ are presented to the k-th DM. The DM is asked whether

(i) he or she dislikes all currently presented criterion values $z^r_{ki}$ (i = 1,..., $I_k$) and thus wants to terminate the decision proces without accepting any currently offered vector of criterion values;

(ii) he or she accepts all criterion values of a presented vector of criterion values $(z^r_{k1},\ldots,z^r_{kI_k})$;

(iii) he or she accepts some criterion values of a presented vector of criterion values $(z^r_{k1},\ldots,z^r_{kI_k})$ and wants to continue the interactive decision process by stating lower bounds on some criterion values and/or reconsidering lower bounds on criterion values fixed in earlier stages of the decision process. Based on the DM's response the system which generates vectors of criterion values to be proposed to the k-th DM is updated and new criterion vectors $(z^{r+1}_{k1},\ldots,z^{r+1}_{kI_k})$ are generated by the system on the basis of the partial information provided so far by the k-th DM about his or her preference system.

In order to describe the individual decision process in more detail we introduce the following notation:

$$\hat{z}^n_{ki} := \max \{z_{ki}(x) \mid x \in X^n\} \qquad (i = 1,\ldots,I_k; \; \forall \, k \in K_L)$$

$\tilde{z}^r_{ki}$ : current lower bound on the criterion value $z_{ki}(x)$ which has been fixed by the k-th DM in the course of the first (r-1) stages of the interactive decision process.

$D_k^r$ : current index set of those criteria for which the k-th DM has not yet specified a lower bound $\tilde{z}_{ki}^r$ in the course of the first $(r-1)$ stages of the interactive decision process.

$\alpha_{ki}^n$ : proportion of the true criterion value $z_{ki}(x)$ which is revealed to the k-th DM by the mediator in the n-th stage of the collective decision process.

The applied model which generates the criterion-vectors to be presented to the k-th DM in the course of his individual decision process reads:

$$\min y - \epsilon \sum_{\substack{i \in I_k \\ k \in K_L}} z_{ki}(x)$$

$$\text{s.t. } z_{ki}(x) / \hat{z}_{ki}^n + y \geq 1 \qquad \text{for all } i \in D_k^r$$

$$\alpha_{ki}^n z_{ki}(x) \geq \tilde{z}_{ki}^r \qquad \text{for all } i \notin D_k^r \tag{2}$$

$$x \in X^n$$

with $\epsilon$ being a sufficiently small but positive scalar. Let $x^r$, $y^r$ be an optimal solution for (2). Then the criterion values $z_{ki}^r = \alpha_{ki}^n z_{ki}(x^r)$ $(i = 1,\ldots,I_k)$ are presented to the k-th DM in stage r of his individual decision process.

The interactive decision support system for the individual member $k \in K_L$ is outlined as follows:

Step 1: Initialization

Step 2: In order to generate a proposal for the k-th DM we determine an optimal solution $x^r$, $y^r$ for (2) and present the criterion values $z_{ki}^r = \alpha_{ki}^n z_{ki}(x^r)$ $(i = 1,\ldots,I_k)$ to the DM.

Step 3: If $r = 1$ go to Step 5; otherwise go to Step 4.

Step 4: Does the k-th DM want to modify one or more lower bounds $\tilde{z}_{ki}^r$ in order to provide for more attractive values for the criterion values $z_{ki}(x)$ $(i \in D_k^r)$? If "yes", go to Step 9. If "no", go to Step 5.

Step 5: Does the k-th DM accept the criterion values $z_{ki}^r$ for all $i = 1,\ldots,I_k$? If "yes", go to Step 12. If "no", go to Step 6.

Step 6: Does the k-th DM accept for at least one $i \in D_k^r$ the criterion value $z_{ki}^r$? If "yes", go to Step 7. If "no", go the Step 13.

Step 7: The k-th DM is asked to specify $\tilde{z}_{ki}^r < z_{ki}^r$ for at least one $i \in D_k^r$ which imposes a lower bound on $z_{ki}(x)$.

Step 8: Actualize $D_k^r$ and program (2). Go to Step 11.

Step 9: The k-th DM is asked to reconsider the lower bounds $\tilde{z}_{ki}^r$ and specify actualized values for $\tilde{z}_{ki}^r$ $(i \notin D_k^r)$.

Step 10: Actualize program (2).

Step 11: $r := r+1$ and go to Step 2.

Step 12: $r := R$. The k-th DM continues the collective decision process with the acceptance of the criterion values $(z_{k1}^R,\ldots,z_{kI_k}^R)$. Stop.

Step 13: The multiple objective planning model does not provide acceptable criterion values for the k-th DM. If the mediator increases $\alpha_{ki}^n$ for some $i \in \{1,\ldots,I_k\}$ actualize the parameters $\alpha_{ki}^n$ in (2) and go to Step 2. Otherwise set $K_L := K_L \smallsetminus \{k\}$ . Stop.

## 3.3 Structure of the Mediator-Supported Collective Decision Process

At the beginning of each stage of the collective decision process the DMs involved in the collective decision process determine simultaneously an acceptable vector of criterion values $(z_{k1}^R,\ldots,z_{kI_k}^R)$ in the course of an interactive decision process as outlined in Section 3.2. As the formation of a coalition in the course of a collective decision process may have to be supported by the mediator we shall first indicate how the mediator may be assisted in identifying those DMs which - on the basis of their currently accepted criterion values $(z_{k1}^R,\ldots,z_{kI_k}^R)$ - may be regarded as potential members of the coalition. With respect to the formation of a coalition 3 cases have to be distinguished:

(i) $K_J$ is not known at the beginning of the collective decision process:

  1. Determine $X^1$ with $K_L := \{1,\ldots,K\}$

  2. Let the DMs $1,\ldots,K^* \leqq K$ terminate their individual decision process by accepting a criterion vector $(z_{k1}^R,\ldots,z_{kI_k}^R)$. A tentative proposal for $L \geq J$ nominees for a coalition $K_J$ is generated by means of the program

$$\max \beta + \varepsilon \sum_{k=1}^{K^*} \sum_{i=1}^{I_k} \lambda_k z_{ki}(x)$$

$$\text{s.t. } z_{ki}(x) - \beta z_{ki}^R \lambda_k \geqq 0 \qquad \begin{array}{l} i = 1,\ldots,I_k; \\ k = 1,\ldots,K^* \end{array} \tag{3}$$

$$x \in X$$

$$\sum_{k=1}^{K^*} \lambda_k \geq L$$

$$\lambda_k \in \{0,1\} \qquad k = 1,\ldots,K^*$$

with $\varepsilon$ being a sufficiently small but positive scalar. Let $\hat{x}$, $\hat{\beta}$, $\hat{\lambda}_1,\ldots,\hat{\lambda}_K$ be an optimal solution for (3). Then a tentative proposal for the composition of $K_L \supset K_J$ would be $K_L := \{k \in \{1,\ldots,K\} \mid \hat{\lambda}_k = 1\}$. Note that $\hat{x}$ is a $K_L$-efficient solution for (1).

(ii) $K_J$ is known and a stable coalition in the course of the collective decision process: No support by the mediator is necessary.

(iii) $K_J$ is not stable in the course of the collective decision process:

  1. Each DM who may be considered to become nominee for membership in the coalition is asked to determine an acceptable criterion vector $(z_{k1}^R,\ldots,z_{kI_k}^R)$ with respect to $X^n$.

2. Let $L^1$ be the index set of those DMs who in all cases will be members of the coalition and $L^2$ be the index set of those DMs who may be considered to become members of a coalition and have terminated their individual decision process by accepting a criterion vector $(z_{ki}^R,\ldots,z_{kI_k}^R)$. A tentative proposal for $L \geq J$ nominees for a coalition $K_J$ may be generated by means of the program

$$\max \beta + \varepsilon \sum_{k \in L^1 \cup L^2} \sum_{i=1}^{I_k} \lambda_k z_{ki}(x)$$

$$\text{s.t.} \ z_{ki}(x) - \beta z_{ki}^R \lambda_k \geq 0 \qquad\qquad \begin{matrix} i = 1,\ldots,I_k, \\ \forall k \in L^1 \cup L^2 \end{matrix} \qquad (4)$$

$$x \in X$$

$$\sum_{k \in L^1 \cup L^2} \lambda_k \geq L$$

$$\lambda_k = 1 \qquad \forall k \in L^1$$

$$\lambda_k \in \{0,1\} \qquad \forall k \in L^2$$

with $\varepsilon$ being a sufficiently small but positive scalar. Let $\hat{x}, \hat{\beta}, \hat{\lambda}_k$ $(k \in L^1 \cup L^2)$ be an optimal solution for (4). Then a tentative proposal for the composition of $K_L$ would be $K_L := \{k \in L^1 \cup L^2 \mid \hat{\lambda}_k = 1\}$. Recall that $\hat{x}$ is a $K_L$-efficient solution for (1).

In the course of the collective decision process the mediator controls the process of approaching a $K_J$-efficient alternative which has to be mutually accepted by the members of a coalition $K_J$. The formation of a coalition is adjusted to the degree of unanimity with respect to the current values of the criterion vectors $(z_{k1}^R,\ldots,z_{kI_k}^R)$. The value of $\hat{\beta}$ in program (3) and (4) expresses which proportion of $(z_{k1}^R,\ldots,z_{kI_k}^R)$ the marginal member of $K_L$ can realize if the respective alternative $\hat{x}$ is unanimously accepted by all $k \in K_L$. Other members of $K_L$ may realize a higher proportion than $\hat{\beta}$. The more DMs are included in $K_L$ the smaller will be the optimal value of $\beta$ in (3) and (4), respectively. If $\hat{\beta} \geq 1$ then no member of $K_L$ has to renounce the full realization of the currently accepted criterion values $(z_{k1}^R,\ldots,z_{kI_k}^R)$.

Recall that the parameters $\alpha_{ki}^n$ which state the proportion of the true criterion values to be revealed to the k-th DM in stage n of the collective decision process are to be fixed by the mediator. The optimal solution $\hat{x}$ for (3) or (4) provides the mediator with an approximate upper bound for $\alpha_{ki}^n$: Let $\bar{\beta}_{ki}$ be the maximal value for $\beta_{ki}$ such that

$$z_{ki}(\hat{x}) - \beta_{ki} z_{ki}^R \geq 0 \qquad\qquad i = 1,\ldots,I_k$$

holds. As $z_{ki}^R = \alpha_{ki}^{n-1} z_{ki}(x^R)$ we obtain $\bar{\beta}_{ki} \alpha_{ki}^{n-1}$ as an approximate upper bound for $\alpha_{ki}^n$.

The mediator-supported collective decision process has the following structure:

0. Initialization

1. Set $n := n+1$. Determine $x^n$ and $\alpha_{ki}^n$ $(i = 1,\ldots,I_k; k \in K_L)$ and ask the DMs which are members of $K_L \supset K_J$ to select an acceptable criterion vector $(z_{k1}^R, \ldots,z_{kI_k}^R)$ in order to continue the collective decision process.

2. Have at least J DMs terminated the decision process with the selection of a criterion vector $(z_{k1}^R,\ldots,z_{kI_k}^R)$? If "yes", go to 3. If "no", go to 6.

3. Is $x^n$ "small" enough to propose a $K_J$-efficient alternative to all DMs currently engaged in the collective decision process? If "yes", go to 4. If "no", go to 5.

4. Set $L = J$. Solve program (3) or (4) and propose a $K_J$-efficient alternative $\hat{x}$ with $(z_{k_1}(\hat{x}),\ldots,z_{k_J}(\hat{x}))$ to the members of $K_J$.

   If all J DMs accept this proposal the collective decision process terminates. Otherwise go to 5.

5. Solve program (3) or (4) with $L \geqq J$ and go to 1.

6. Ask potential nominees for membership in $K_J$ to select an acceptable criterion vector $(z_{k1}^R,\ldots,z_{kI_k}^R)$ and go to 7.

7. Have at least J DMs terminated the decision process with the selection of a criterion vector $(z_{k1}^R,\ldots,z_{kI_k}^R)$? If "yes", go to 3. If "no" increase the current set $x^n$ or increase some values of $\alpha_{ki}^n$ $(i \in \{1,\ldots,I_k\}, k \in \{1,\ldots,K\})$ and go to 1 or terminate the collective decision process.

   It is hoped that the presented structure of a mediator-supported collective decision process produces a compromise alternative which is mutually accepted by the members of a coalition $K_J$ if the DMs behave constructively. An empirical analysis will provide the necessary information about the suitability of the proposed structure.

## REFERENCES

1. Arrow, K.J.. Social Choice and Individual Values. 2nd Edition. New York: Wiley 1954
2. Benayoun, R., De Montgolfier, J., Tergny, J., and O. Laritchev. Linear Programming with Multiple Objective Functions: STEP-Method (STEM). Mathematical Programming 1, pp. 366 - 375, 1971
3. Dinkelbach, W. and H. Isermann. Resource Allocation of an Academic Department in the Presence of Multiple Criteria - Some Experience with a Modified STEM-Method. Computers & Operations Research 7, pp. 99-106, 1980
4. Grauer, M., Bischoff, E., and A. Wierzbicki. Mediation in Long-Term Planning. International Institute for Applied Systems Analysis, Laxenburg, 1983
5. Isermann, H. Lineare Vektoroptimierung. Doctoral Dissertation, University of Regensburg, 1974
6. Isermann, H. The Enumeration of the Set of All Efficient Solutions for a Multiple Objective Linear Program. Operational Research Quarterly 28, pp. 711 - 725, 1977.

7. Isermann, H. An Analysis of Decision Behavior of Individual Decision Makers in the Course of a Computer-Assisted Interactive Decision Process. Paper presented at the VIth International Conference on Multiple-Criteria Decision Making, Cleveland, Ohio, 1984

8. Kasprzyca, H., Kersten, G. and A. Olszewska. Production Planning and Profit Distribution. Group Decision Making Support System NEGO1, Management Organization and Development Institute, University of Warsaw, 1984

9. Kersten, G. Interactive Computer System for Solving Group Decision Problems. Management Organization and Development Institute, University of Warsaw, 1984

10. McKelvey, R.D. and R.E. Wendell. Voting Equilibria in Multidimensional Choice Spaces. Mathematics of Operations Research 1, pp. 144 - 158, 1976

11. Raiffa, H. The Art and Science of Negotiation. Cambridge, Mass.: Harvard University Press, 1982

12. Wendell, R.E. Multiple Objective Mathematical Programming with Respect to Multiple Decision-Makers. Operations Research 28, pp. 1100 - 1111, 1980

13. Wierzbicki, A. Negotiation and Mediation in Conflicts I: The Role of Mathematical Approaches and Methods. International Institute for Applied Systems Analysis, Laxenburg, 1983

14. Wierzbicki, A. Negotiation and Mediation in Conflicts II: Plural Rationality and Interactive Processes. International Institute for Applied Systems Analysis, Laxenburg, 1984

# ON THE ROLE OF DYNAMICS AND INFORMATION IN INTERNATIONAL NEGOTIATIONS: THE CASE OF FISHERY MANAGEMENT

Veijo Kaitala and Raimo Hämäläinen

*Systems Analysis Laboratory, Helsinki University of Technology, Espoo, Finland*

## 1. Introduction

Fishery resource management is an intrinsically dynamic problem where current harvest decisions affect the possibilities of harvesting in the future. Moreover, in the case of two or more harvesting agents, the harvesters face a complicated dynamic game problem the solution of which depends on the behavioural strategies adopted (cooperative or non-cooperative management, myopic or foresighted optimization etc). Decision making in such an environment means negotiations and bargaining on the management strategies as well as on the planning horizon considered. These questions will be discussed in Section 2. In Section 3 we will illustrate problems which are related to the practical negotiation policies in international fishery management.

## 2. On dynamic interactions and negotiations

### 2.1. A model framework for resource management

Consider a two-agent resource management problem, where the resource dynamics is described by a differential equation model of the form

$$\dot{x}(t) = G(x(t)) - h_1(t) - h_2(t) \ , \ x(0) = x_o \ , \quad (1)$$

where the dot ( $\dot{}$ ) denotes the time derivative. The state variable representing the n substocks of fish in different fishing grounds is denoted by the vector $x = (x_1, \ldots, x_n)$. The function $G(.)$ includes the resource growth and the interdependence of the subfisheries on each other. The harvest rate of agent i in substock j is $h_{ij}$ and the total harvest is given by vector $h_i = (h_{i1}, \ldots, h_{in})$, i = 1,2. The harvest rates are assumed to depend on the stock, $x_j$, and on the related fishing effort, $E_{ij}$, and

$$h_{ij}(t) = f_{ij}(x_j(t), E_{ij}(t)). \qquad (2)$$

The instantaneous revenue flow to an agent i from the fishery, $R_i(x, h_i, h_j)$, depends on the stock, and on the harvest rates. Over a fixed time interval $[0,T]$, the total net revenue for an agent i is

$$J_i^T = \int_0^T e^{-s_i t} R_i(x, h_i, h_j) dt, \quad i,j=1,2, \ i \neq j \ , \quad (3)$$

where $s_i$ is the discount rate of agent i. The agents represent countries or independent fishing fleets of different nationalities. The interest in mutual negotiations among the agents arises due to the agents' interdependence through the resource dynamics (eq. (1)) and to the joint interests in the marketing (eq. (3)). Moreover, another type of possible interdependence is the crowding effect because the effort of one fleet can affect the harvesting of the other fleet. These interdependencies make a resource exploitation problem a dynamic multiagent decision making problem (see e.g. 3,4, 6-10, 14,15,17-20,25). The consequences of different behavioural patterns of the agents can be effectively analysed by the theories of dynamic games and bargaining.

In the analyses of the resource management and negotiation problem each agent needs to make a decision about the following questions all of which are closely related to the problem's dynamics:

1) Resource's growth law and each others utility functions (models (1) - (3)).
2) The time horizon of planning.
3) Framework for cooperation:
   a) What happens in the case of no agreement, what is the status quo?
   b) Practical and credible ways of quaranteeing cooperation over the whole planning horizon.

The modelling of the exploitation dynamics (1) - (3) is not a simple problem. In practice, such a modelling process is based on extensive field research and data collection carried out by national fishery research institutes. Only very seldom one could expect to find a generally accepted stock model. The population models tend to change following the improvement in the understanding of the fishery.

When the planning time horizon is considered, the possibilities available can be roughly divided into three categories: myopic decision making, decision making over a fixed and finite time horizon, and decision making over an infinite time horizon. The planning horizons of the agents need not always be the same (for a development of this topic, see (10)). For clarity, we shall restrict our treatment to myopic decision making and agreements made over an infinite time horizon.

## 2.2. Myopic decisions

Myopic decision makers are either unwilling (e.g. infinite discount rate) or unable to take into account the development of the resource in the future. A myopic agent i optimizes the current instantaneous revenue flow due to the harvest

$$\text{Max}_{h_i} \ R_i(x, h_i, h_j) \ , \ i, \ j = 1,2, \ i \neq j. \tag{4}$$

Necessary conditions for myopic interior solutions of non-cooperative optimization problems are

$$\partial R_i / \partial h_i \ = 0 \ , \ i=1,2 \ . \tag{5}$$

Thus, on each stock level $x(t)$ the agents face a static decision making problem, which changes over time due to changes in the resource stock. However, the future growth potential of the resource is not taken into account in the current decisions.

The agents can also agree on cooperation in a myopic sense. In this case the myopic cooperative solution is obtained by solving the problem

$$\text{Max}_{h_1, h_2} \ \alpha_1 R_1 + (1 - \alpha_1) R_2 \ . \tag{6}$$

and bargaining over the weight $\alpha_1$ at each time instant. Usually the solution of (6) differs from the non-cooperative solution of (4). The agreement will then depend on the current value of the state, $x(t)$. Moreover, a myopic cooperative agreement is vulnerable to cheating in the same sense as the dynamic solution (see discussion

below). Since myopic decisions do not depend on the future growth
potential of the resource, threats cannot be used to support the
agreements in the same way as they can be used in dynamic
optimization.

## 2.3. Dynamic bargaining

The analysis of multiagent decision making is complicated due to the
nonuniqueness of the possible rationality concepts of the agents,
even when each agent has a single decision criterion. Besides the
choice between cooperative and non-cooperative agreements, we usually
encounter non-unique equilibrium solutions depending e.g. on the
choice of decision or control variables (8,25). Moreover, cooperative
solutions are affected by the choice of the bargaining schemes (1) as
well as by the choice of disagreement solutions.
In mathematical economics optimization problems are traditionally
formulated over infinite time horizons (see e.g. (23) ). This
causes some theoretical difficulties. First, it may happen that the
integral to be maximized, such as the net revenues due to resource
exploitation, grow to infinity when time tends to infinity. This is
the case especially when discount rates are zero. For this reason,
new optimality concepts have been developed (5,12). Second, when we
apply the necessary conditions of the maximum principle for an
optimal solution of an infinite time horizon optimization problem (5)
the transversality conditions are not determined. We seldom find
explicit solutions, and the solutions need to be characterized by
their asymptotic properties (5,6,12,15).
Yet another set of difficulties is due to the fact that when a
bargaining agreement has been established in a dynamic game setting,
the related cooperative solution does not have an equilibrium
property in the original information structure (11). This appears
generally as a temptation to deviate onesidedly from the agreement,
i.e. cheating. A closely related problem to this is that of
sustainability. If an agreement is such that none of the agents has a
reason to require rebargaining during the game, it is sustainable.
However, this is not the case in general, since the outcomes of
bargaining depend on the initial state.
The first question that the bargaining agents have to answer is, what
will happen if no agreement can be reached. The outcome of this
no-agreement is called the status quo point. In many papers on

fishery bargaining, open-loop (Nash) equilibria have been considered as potential status quo policies (6,7,15). Although one would consider only open-loop equilibria as status quo policies, the problem of non-uniqueness of disagreement behaviour still remains left. It has been shown (see e.g. (8,14,25)) that a change in the property rights or control variables also changes the status quo and hence the outcome of the bargaining process. The choice of an open-loop equilibrium solution to represent the status quo is not the only possibility. For example, in the theoretical papers of Haurie and Tolwinski (13) and Tolwinski (24) status quo has been described through feedback equilibria and mini-max threat policies. In high sea fisheries, a natural status quo is unregulated open-access harvesting. In a duopoly case this problem can be considered as a myopic non-cooperative problem (eq. (4)). Under the assumption that a status quo policy can be agreed upon and that both it and the Pareto-optimal solutions can be solved (analytically or by computational methods) in a normal form, a single Pareto-optimal solution can be picked up by applying some bargaining scheme to determine the agreement (1,16,21,22). However, as was noted above, in a dynamic game setting an agreement made in an open-loop framework at one time point leaves a temptation for each agent to deviate onesidedly from the agreed policy during the remaining time period. What can we then do to avoid cheating? In practice it is realistic to assume that cheating can be detected after a finite time period. (Under this assumption we must give up the open-loop formulation of the problem and consider memory strategies.) One idea is to use threats to eliminate the temptation to cheat. The purpose of a threat of potential punishment (which is announced in advance to follow cheating) is to guarantee that the total utility from the game cannot be increased by cheating. Thus, the temptation to cheat disappears, and the Pareto-optimal agreement has the equilibrium property. This equilibrium solution also dominates non-cooperative equilibrium solutions. For this reason, it should be emphasised that in general there will not be any reasons for the agents to implement the punishments. It has been shown by Tolwinski (24) and Haurie and Tolwinski(13) that in dynamic games all the feasible solutions (including Pareto-optimal solutions) can usually be transformed into equilibrium solutions. This theory was then tested on fishery games by Hämäläinen, Haurie and Kaitala (6,7). These studies demonstrate numerical results on the topic.

## 3. Problems in international resource negotiations

International organizations make strong efforts in attempting to establish guiding principles for the exploitation of marine resources and for the resolution of conflict situations occurring in these areas. There exist regional organizations which annually carry out negotiations in order to determine catch quotas and other measures for countries involved in particular fisheries. For example, the International Baltic Sea Fishery Commission has been founded for the management of Baltic fishery resources. The commission includes representatives from Denmark, Finland, FRG, GDR, Poland, Sweden and the USSR. This commission negotiates each year an agreement, and the negotiation procedure is supported by scientific research work carried out in each member country.

Recently, United Nations published The Law of the Sea (17). Among other things, the law tells the countries to enter into negotiations and to cooperate whenever there is joint interest in the resources. The following quotation is concerned with the high sea areas where the access to the resources is free for all the countries: "States whose nationals exploit identical living resources, or different living resources in the same area, shall enter into negotiations with a view to taking the measures necessary for the conservation of the living resource conserned" (17, Article 118).

The concept of bionomic equilibrium (used extensively in fishery economies) predicts the exploitation of resources, which are open to all the countries (for refs., see e.g. (2)). The prediction is that the total harvest of competitive fishing fleets and the stock growth stabilize to a level where the economic rent of the resource is dissipated. General understanding is that the practice of competitive exploitation in open-access fisheries should be changed. The Law of the Sea proposes the countries a goal for cooperation in the following way: "In determining the allowable catch and establishing other conservation measures for the living resources in high seas, States shall: (a) take measures which are designed, on the best scientific evidence available to the States concerned, to maintain or restore populations of harvested species at levels which can produce the maximum sustainable yield, as qualified by relevant environmental and economic factors,..." (17, Article 119). This statement needs some notes, that are related to the practical establishment of cooperation.

First, cooperation does not necessarily mean Pareto-optimality from the economic point of view, since the maintenance of the population does not require it. Thus some safe satisficing policies could also be well acceptable. One should note that non-cooperative equilibria can also maintain the population at a biologically desirable level. In many cases countries could prefer "safe" non-cooperation to risky Pareto-optimal cooperation, which is vulnerable to cheating (6,11). This can be the case especially when there are no effective ways of implementing threats to support the agreements. The condition for non- cooperation is, however, that it does not lead to the escalation of the conflict, which would destroy the fish population or the fishing fleets. Secondly, maintaining a population is a difficult practical question in itself. The ecological and economic problems are quite different. For example, we can have a herring stock which is not subject to extinction in an ecological sense but it can be a nonexisting stock from the economic point of view. Thirdly, the concept of maximum sustainable yield can be understood as the maximum harvest rate (e.g. in the sense of biomass produced) or as a maximum economic rent available from the fishery. It has been clearly shown that these two criteria give different management policies.

We shall conclude this section by considering multinational management of coastal fisheries. According to the current international jurisdictional practice and the Law of the Sea, every coastal country has the right to establish an exclusive economic zone, where it can utilize the resources by itself. However, if the coastal country does not have the capacity to harvest or process entirely the catch available, it should give other countries access to the surplus catch (17). The international allocation of catch constitutes a whole new set of problems since the conditions under which it should take place is by no means clear. Moreover, in the allocation of the surplus catch the countries should take into account especially the requirements of the developing and land-locked countries. For example: "Land-locked States shall have the right to participate, on an equitable basis, in the exploitation of an appropriate part of the surpluss of the living resources of the exclusive economic zones of coastal States of the same region..." (17, Article 69). Such land-locked and especially developing countries do not usually have a fishing fleet of their own, which in this case should be rented from a third country.

There are over a hundred places in the world, where the coasts of two countries are so close to each others that no open sea remains between the exclusive economic zones. If a resource stock is divided by the exclusive economic zones, both of the countries have a right to utilize the resource in an optimal way. However, it has been shown in ref. (8) that such a "divided fishery" problem can have several different but acceptable non-cooperative and cooperative solutions, even if the countries use the same management criteria.


4. Conclusions

In this paper we have presented dynamic control and game theoretic views on the modelling and analysis of resource and decision dynamics in international negotiations. In dynamic formulations of resource management problems emphasis needs to be put on the choice between different rationality concepts. Moreover, the ways of reaching Pareto-optimal equilibrium agreements, which are not vulnerable to onesided deviations by a contracting party, are of great importance.

References

1.      Cao, X.R., Preference functions and bargaining solutions, Proceedings of the 21st IEEE Conference on Decision and Control, Vol. 1, pp. 164-171, Orlando, Fa., 1982.

2.      Clark, C.W., Mathematical Bioeconomics: The Optimal Management of Renewable Resources. New York, Wiley-Interscience, 1976.

3.      Clark, C.W., Restricted access to common-property fishery resources: A game theoretic analysis. In: P.Liu (ed.), Dynamic Optimization and Mathematical Economics, New York, Plenum Press, pp. 117-132, 1980.

4.      Fischer, T.R., An hierarchical game approach to fishery resource management, IEEE Transactions on Systems, Man, and Cybernetics, Vol. SMC-11, pp. 216-222, 1981.

5.      Halkin, H., Necessary conditions for optimal control problems with infinite horizon, Econometrica, Vol. 42, pp. 267-273, 1974.

6.      Hämäläinen, R.P., Haurie, A. and Kaitala, V., Equilibria and threats in a fishery management game, Helsinki University of Technology, Systems Research Report A3, 1983. Accepted for publication in Optimal Control Applications & Methods.

7.    Hämäläinen, R.P., Haurie, A. and  Kaitala, V., Bargaining on whales: A differential  game  model  with  Pareto  optimal equilibria, Operations Research Letters, Vol. 3, No. 1, pp. 5-11, 1984.

8.    Hämäläinen, R.P. and Kaitala, V.,  A game  on  the choice of policy  variables  in  a  dynamic  resource management game. Proceedings  of  the  21st  IEEE  Conference on Decision and Control, Vol. 1, pp. 181-185, Orlando, Fa., 1982.

9.    Hämäläinen, R.P., Ruusunen, J. and Kaitala, V., Myopic Stackelberg equilibria and social coordination in a share contract fishery. Helsinki University of Technology, Systems Research Report A9, May 1984.

10.   Hämäläinen, R.P., Ruusunen, J. and Kaitala, V., Cartels and dynamic contracts in sharefishing.  Helsinki University of Technology, Systems Research Report A10, May 1984.

11.   Haurie, A.,  A note on  nonzero-sum differential  games with bargaining  solution,  Journal of  Optimization Theory and Applications, Vol. 18, pp. 31-39, 1976.

12.   Haurie, A. and Leitmann, G., On the global asymptotic stability of equilibrium solutions for open-loop differential games, to appear in Large Scale Systems.

13.   Haurie, A. and Tolwinski, B., Acceptable equilibria in dynamic bargaining games, in Drenic, R.F. and Kozin, F. (eds.), System Modelling and Optimization, Proceedings of the 10th IFIP Conference, New York, September 1981.

14.   Kaitala, V. and Hämäläinen, R.P., A differential game model of the  non-cooperative management of an international fishery. Proceedings  of  the First International Conference Applied Modelling  and  Simulation, Life, men and societies, Vol. V, pp. 183-186, Lyon, France, September 7-11, 1981.

15.   Kaitala, V., Hämäläinen, R.P. and Ruusunen, J., On the analysis of equilibria and bargaining in a fishery game. To appear in: G. Feichtinger (ed.), Economic Application of Control Theory, Proceedings of the Second Viennese Workshop, May 1984, North-Holland.

16.   Kalai, E. and Smorodinsky, M.,  Other  solutions to  Nash´s bargaining problem, Econometrica, Vol. 43, pp. 513-518, 1975.

17.   The Law of the Sea. United Nations Convention on the Law of the Sea with Index and Final Act of the Third United Nations Conference of the Law of the Sea. UN, New York (USA), 262 pp., 1983.

18.   Levhari, D. and Mirman, L.J., The great fish war: An example using a dynamic Cournot-Nash solution,  The Bell Journal of Economics, Vol. 11, pp. 322-334, 1980.

19.   Mirman, L.J. and Spulber, D.F. (eds.), Essays in the Economics of Renewable Resources, Amsterdam, New York, Oxford,  North-Holland, 1982.

20.  Munro, G.R., The optimal management of transboundary renewable resources, Canadian Journal of Economics, Vol. 12, pp. 355-376, 1979.

21.  Nash, J., The bargaining problem, Econometrica, Vol. 18, pp. 155-162, 1950.

22.  Roth, A.E., Axiomatic Models of Bargaining, Berlin, Springer-Verlag, 1979.

23.  Sethi, S.P. and Thompson, G.L., Optimal Control Theory: Applications to Management Science, Martinus Nijhoff Publishing, Boston, 1981.

24.  Tolwinski, B., A concept of cooperative equilibrium for dynamic games, Automatica, Vol. 18, pp. 431-447, 1982.

25.  Vincent, T.L., Vulnerability of a prey-predator model under harvesting, in Vincent, T.L. and Skowronski, J.M. (eds.), Renewable Resource Management, New York, Springer-Verlag, pp. 112-132, 1980.

# MACROMODELS AND MULTIOBJECTIVE DECISION MAKING

Manfred Peschel

*Division of Mathematics and Cybernetics, Academy of Sciences of the GDR, Berlin, GDR*

## 1. Macromodels

A macromodel should have the following features:
- Both the structure and the function of the system should be reflected in the mathematical properties of the macromodel.
- A suitable formalization of a macromodel may be obtained using abstract automata theory. Every module has a description of the form

$$(z^i)' = G(z^i, y^i, p^i)$$

$$x^i = F(z^i, y^i, q^i)$$

  with inputs $y^i$, outputs $x^i$ and states $z^i$. A macromodel also has overall inputs (controls) and outputs (global indicators).
- All of the models considered (including macromodels) should be robust against amplitude-bounded stochastic disturbances.
- A macromodel should be based on a systems concept obtained through some compromise between the following dialectical contradictions: global/local; static/dynamic; discontinuity/continuity; randomness/necessity; cooperation/competition; autonomy/control.
- Macromodels are usually highly nonlinear dynamical systems with eigen-dynamics and eigen-preferences.

We should not try to control a macrosystem against its eigendynamics.

The main use of macromodels is to forecast the behavior of a system under specific control conditions. Reliable forecasting requires good models of the driving forces (evolution models), and can be hindered by the presence of chaos or strange attractors.

## 2. The Significance of Evolution Models (especially Growth Models) for Macromodels

Macromodels of evolutionary systems show growth and structural development. Growth observed at a high level of aggregation can be described using the evolon model (see Fig. 1) [1].

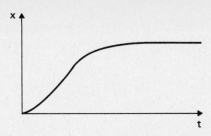

FIGURE 1:  The evolon model

One suitable description of an evolon is based on the hyperlogistic
differential equation

$$\frac{dx}{dt} = Kx^k(B-x^W)^\ell \quad .$$

This is obviously a generalisation of the logistic growth function
(with $k = w = \ell = 1$).

   In evolutionary systems, structure is a precondition for growth;
conversely, growth is a precondition for structural development.  The
feasibility of the evolon concept has been demonstrated for a number
of examples, including the growth of world population [2], the growth
of energy production [2], and the growth of European cities [3].

   It seems that the Lotka-Volterra equations offer a promising
approach to the modelling of growth processes in macromodels.  We have
the following
*Structural demands:*  the structure consists mainly of chains and
cycles; and
*Functional demands:*  the function is based on elementary functions
following the rate-coupling principle, i.e.,

$$Fx = Ky \ , \quad F = \frac{d}{dt}(\ln) \quad .$$

Based on these restricting demands, we have proposed a Structure Design
Principle [4], which says that a macromodel described by a set of
ordinary differential equations can be transformed into the classical
Lotka-Volterra equations by introducing additional state variables
[5,6].  This means that a complex interaction structure (for example,
that of a macroeconomic model) can be reduced by the introduction of
virtual actors (additional state variables) into a set of binary interactions (predator-prey interactions).

A macromodel given by a set of Lotka-Volterra equations can be reformulated by appropriate coordinate transformations

$$x_i = \underset{r}{\Pi} u_r^{t_{ir}}$$

into the so-called Riccati representation:

$$\frac{du_i}{dt} = K_i \underset{r}{\Pi} u_r^{k_{ir}} \underset{s}{\Pi} n_s^{\ell_{is}} \quad .$$

This representation demonstrates the universality of the concept of Cobb-Douglas production functions (this is a more general form of the version usually encountered in econometric models).

Under some special conditions the Lotka-Volterra equations exhibit very interesting eigen-dynamics. To demonstrate this we shall write the Lotka-Volterra equation in the following vector form:

$$\frac{d\xi}{dt} = \sum_j x_j G._j \quad ,$$

where $\xi_i = \ln x_i$ and $G._j$ represents the column vectors. Let H denote the operation of taking the convex hull, and assume that

$$0 \notin H(G._j, \ j = 1,2,\ldots,n) \quad .$$

Then $k = H(0,H(G._j, \ j = 1,2,\ldots,n))$ defines a convex cone k which acts as an eigen-preference cone (in the multiobjective optimization sense) for the trajectories of the system. For every reference point $\xi(0)$ the trajectory of the system must enter the corresponding preference cone k and remain within it for the forseeable future. This situation is shown schematically in Fig. 2. Obviously the behavior of such a system is quite similar to the behavior of the world according to the theory of special relativity, except that we have to deal with the so-called "light cone" instead of the cone k.

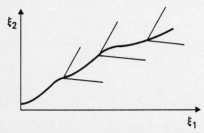

FIGURE 2:  Examples of preference cones k for given reference points

Applying the Structure Design Principle to the evolon growth model

$$\frac{dx}{dt} = Kx^k(B-x^w)^\ell \quad ,$$

we obtain the following Lotka-Volterra description:

$$Fx_0 = x_1 \ , \quad F = d \ \ln/dt \ , \quad x_0 = x(t)$$

$$Fx_1 = (k-1)x_1 - w\ell x_2$$

$$Fx_2 = (k+w-1)x_1 - w(\ell-1)x_2 \quad .$$

Figure 3 shows the corresponding Lotka-Volterra structure.

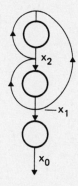

FIGURE 3:   The Lotka-Volterra structure of the model

The shift-cone construction for the case $k > 1$, $\ell > 1$ is illustrated in Fig. 4.

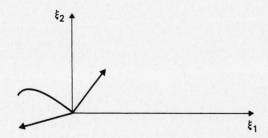

FIGURE 4:   The shift-cone construction for $k > 1$, $\ell > 1$

From this it immediately follows that $\xi_1 \to -\infty$.  It can easily be shown that for the case $k > 1$, $\ell > 1$ we also have $\xi_2 \to -\infty$.

Important growth models can be constructed from exponential chains based on the recursion

$$Fx_i = K_i x_{i+1} \quad i = 0,1,2,\ldots \quad .$$

It can easily be shown that the evolon model based on the hyperlogistic equation does not obey such a chain expansion. However, it makes sense to base a chain expansion on more aggregated base modules, namely

$$\frac{dx_i}{dt} = K_i x_i^{k_i} x_{i+1} \quad i = 0,1,2,\ldots \quad .$$

The problem then arises as to how to identify the best values for the exponents $k_i$. We use the following identification procedure (which however is not always successful):
From the chain expansion we derive the following expression

$$H_i(t) = \frac{F\dot{x}_i}{Fx_i} = k_i + \lambda_i t \quad ,$$

where $\lambda_i(t) = Fx_{i+1}/Fx_i$. The signs of the expressions $\lambda_i(t)$ are clearly constant for all chain expansions under consideration.

We then have the following identification condition:
If sign $\lambda_i(t) = +1$ and there exists a $t_0$ such that $\lambda_i(t_0) = 0$, then $k_i = \text{Min } H_i(t)$;
If sign $\lambda_i(t) = -1$ and there exists a $t_0$ such that $\lambda_i(t_0) = 0$, then $k_i = \text{Max } H_i(t)$.
This rule can be used for an evolon model based on the hyperlogistic differential equation and leads in this case to the following result:

$$\frac{dx_0}{dt} = Kx_0^k x_1 \ , \quad x_1 = (B - x_0^w)^\ell$$

$$\frac{dx_1}{dt} = K_1 x_1^{(2\ell-1)/\ell} x_2 \ , \quad K_1 = -w\ell K \ , \quad x_2 = x_0^{w+k-1}$$

$$\frac{dx_2}{dt} = K_2 x_2^{(w+2k-2)/(w+k-1)} x_1 \ , \quad K_2 = K(w+k-1)$$

Figure 5 shows the corresponding structure.
Obviously the hypercycle of order $r = 2$ in Fig. 5 can be replaced by a chain formed by a repeating sequence of the pair of modules within the hypercycle structure.

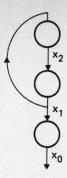

FIGURE 5:  The structure of a hyperlogistic model of order $r = 2$

## 3.  Links between Multiobjective Decision Making and Macromodels [7]

There are a number of situations in which decision making can be aided by the use of a macromodel:

- when a number of decision makers with different objectives are dealing with the same global macromodel;
- when the whole system is decomposed into sectors coupled together, and different decision makers are responsible for decisions in each sector.

It can be very useful to have decision support systems connected to macromodels.  These usually operate in the following way:

- the users (decision makers) specify certain virtual control actions;
- the corresponding macromodel is run for one step of the virtual control;
- the outcomes are analyzed, reporting the consequences to some or all decision makers.

The sequence above can then be repeated a given number of times.  After this, each decision maker applies one real control step to the model or the concrete system within the bounds of his particular responsibility.

We believe that operational gaming is important, especially when this takes the form of a combination of a macromodel with a group of decision makers as players.

From the methodological point of view all control sequences are obtained through a multidimensional search process, in which (for example) stochastic methods and evolution strategies are of importance.

All search processes rely on the following basic mechanisms:

mutation (generation of alternatives)

selection (evaluation of the alternatives).

This represents an application of Darwin's ideas to systems analysis.

## References

1. W. Mende and M. Peschel. Problems of fuzzy modelling, control and forecasting of time-series and some aspects of evolution. IFAC Symposium on Control Mechanisms in Bio- and Ecosystems, Plenary Paper, Leipzig, 1977.

2. U. Kriegel, W. Mende and M. Grauer. An analysis of world energy consumption and world population in terms of a hyperlogistic evolution model. *Syst. Anal. Model. Simul.* 1(1984) 225-236.

3. K.F. Albrecht and W. Mende. A new possible description and interpretation of population growth data in German towns. *Syst. Anal. Model. Simul.* 1(1984) 237-249.

4. W. Mende and M. Peschel. Strukturentwurf für instationäre und nichtlineare Systeme. *Mess.-Steuern-Regeln* 10(1981).

5. V. Volterra. *Lecons sur la théorie mathématique de la lutte pour la vie.* Gauthier-Villars, Paris, 1931.

6. M. Peschel and W. Mende. *Leben wir in einer Volterra-Welt?* Akademie-Verlag, Berlin, 1983. *(Predator-Prey Models: Do we live in a Volterra World?* Springer Verlag and Akademie-Verlag, Berlin, 1985).

7. M. Peschel. *Ingenieurtechnische Entscheidungen-Modellbildung und Steuerung mit Hilfe der Polyoptimierung.* VEB Verlag Technik, 1980.

# IV. INTERACTIVE DECISION SUPPORT

# INTRODUCTION

During the past decade there has been increasing activity in the field of interactive decision support. Research in this area can be seen on the one hand as coming from management information systems and on the other hand from optimization-based decision support. The contributions in this section are mostly concerned with the second strand of research, and focus on interactive multiple-criteria decision support systems. Such systems are based on the recognition that decision making is not simply concerned with one simple objective such as profit. They give the user the chance to explore the efficient solutions of his multicriteria problem, confining his attention to the region in which he seems most interested at any particular stage of the decision process. Nakayama, in his contribution *On the components in interactive multiobjective programming methods*, identifies the three main components necessary for such a system: (1) preference information elicited from the decision maker, (2) scalarizing functions and (3) numerical methods for auxiliary scalar optimization. After discussing these elements individually, the author presents a numerical method based on the aspiration level approach.

The paper *An integrated programming package for multiple-criteria decision analysis* by Grauer, Messner and Strubegger describes an approach based on the interactive multiple-criteria decision support system DIDASS. The use of the system is demonstrated by three examples. In the first example, three important objectives in energy planning (minimization of costs, imported energy, and emissions) are optimized using an energy model for Austria. The second application describes the development of a model covering the main aspects of natural gas trade in Europe, which by no means follows purely economic rules. In the third example a system of models is presented which could help in an analysis of the factors linking consumers, the economy, the energy system and the government.

The paper *A trajectory-oriented extension of DIDASS and its applications* by Lewandowski, Rogowski and Kręglewski describes recent developments in DIDASS methodology and implementation. It outlines the software written for trajectory decision analysis which is then demonstrated by application to a flood control problem (see Section V).

When implementing a new technology there are two critical resources: investment and completion time, which constitute a two-dimensional criteria space. Górecki, Dobrowolski, Ryś, Więcek and Żebrowski offer a supporting tool for this type of problem in their paper *Decision support on the skeleton method - the HG package*.  The idea is outlined and the software for the linear case is explained.

In his contribution *A principle for solving qualitative multiple-criteria problems*, Korhonen describes a method which helps the decision maker to find the most preferred ranking of alternatives evaluated on the basis of several qualitative or quantitative criteria with a hierarchical structure.  It is assumed that the decision maker is able to make at least pairwise comparisons between alternatives.  The final ranking of alternatives is achieved through the construction of the preference strength matrix.

The paper *A decision support system for planning and controlling agricultural production with a decentralized management structure* by Makowski and Sosnowski describes some of the work carried out by the authors within a project aimed at constructing a model of Polish agriculture.  The authors outline linear sectoral models and give a description of the structure of the decision support system.

Unfortunately, for reasons of space, it was not possible to include all of the papers presented under this heading at the meeting in the Proceedings.  The Editors therefore regretfully decided to exclude those papers with some overview character; however, the main points of these papers are summarized below.

*Some applications of multiobjective decision making methods on finite sets*, by J. Gouevski, B. Danev, G. Slavov and B. Mettev. The paper summarizes some methods of multiobjective estimation and choice of elements from a finite set and describes the computer implementation and applications of such methods in Bulgaria.

*About some methods and applications in multicriteria decision making*, by J. Ester. The author gives an overview of the work done in this area in the GDR, especially at the Technical University of Karl-Marx-Stadt.  The overview includes computational methods and applications ranging from problems in the design of freezing systems for foods, through design problems in the textile industry, to multiple-criteria control problems.

*Interactions in decision support systems:  division of labor in DSSs*, by Z. Paprika and I. Kiss. The authors present an analysis of decision support systems (DSSs), taking the management of information as the first generation of DSSs. On the basis of a comparison of six different DSSs, they draw some conclusions about the future involvement of computers in the decision process.

*Roles and motivations in decision support systems of organizations*, by J. Vecsenyi and A. Vari.
This paper puts forward the idea that the design of decision support systems should be based not only on the characteristics of the decision problem, and the available decision analytical tools, but also on the social background of the whole decision-making process in the organizational context.

*Use of MIDA (a Multiobjective Interactive Decision Aid) in the development of the chemical industry*, by G. Dobrowolski, J. Kopytowski, T. Ryś and M. Żebrowski.
Even when narrowed to a single industry, the problem of industrial development is very broad and complex, involving consideration of socio-economic, technological, environmental and political phenomena. The authors present a Multiobjective Interactive Decision Aid (MIDA) for tackling such a problem and apply it to the development of the chemical industry.

Most of the contributions in this section served as introductions to experimental sessions. Some of these sessions are described in more detail in the next section.

M. Grauer

# ON THE COMPONENTS IN INTERACTIVE MULTIOBJECTIVE PROGRAMMING METHODS

Hirotaka J. Nakayama

*Department of Applied Mathematics, Konan University, Kobe, Japan*

## 1. Introduction

Interactive programming methods are composed of three main factors, i.e., (1) preference information elicited from the decision maker, (2) scalarization functions and (3) numerical methods for auxiliary scalar optimization. In developing interactive programming methods, it seems very important to make effective use of various devices in these three factors. Above all, aspiration levels are promising as the preference information elicited from the decision maker, since they are easy and intuitive to answer. Moreover, the weighted Tchebyshev norm can be effectively used as a scalarization function for obtaining a Pareto solution. In this paper, we discuss each components in interactive multiobjective programming methods.

## 2. Interactive Multiobjective Programming Methods for CAD

CAD (Computer Aided Design) is now applied to various fields of industrial design problems. However, the primary attention in CAD at the present stage is paid to drawing by computers, but not to design itself. On the other hand, interactive multiobjective programming methods have been highly developed in recent years, and it seems that they can be effectively applied to many industrial design problems. However many practical problems can not be so easily solved even if they are formulated as scalar optimization problems, since they are highly nonlinear and nonconvex, and sometimes have a large number of criteria functions. In particular, in design problems of structures such as bridges, function forms of many criteria, for example, stress and displacement, can not explicitly be given, but are evaluated by some complex structural analysis. Similarly, in camera lens design problems various kinds of aberration can be evaluated only by a simulation of ray trace. These difficulties become more serious in the formulation of multiobjective programming, because some number of auxiliary scalar optimization are inevitable for obtaining a Pareto solution. Therefore, in order to overcome the difficulties, we need some device in the three components in interactive multiobjective programming methods (i.e., preference information elicited from the decsion maker, scalarization functions and numerical methods for scalar optimization) respectively. We shall discuss this in the following in more detail.

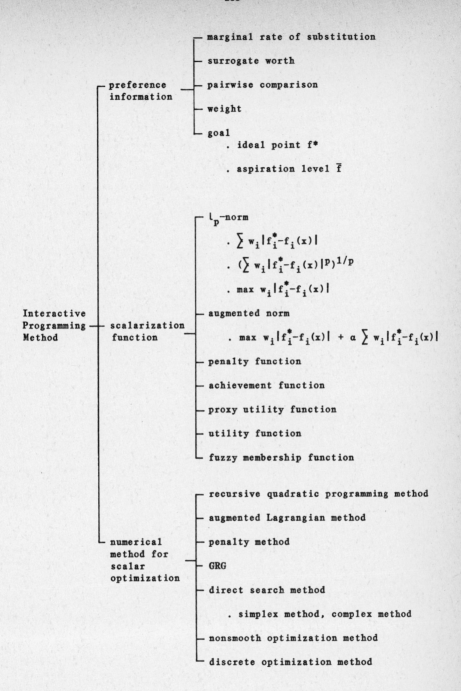

marginal rate of substitution

surrogate worth

pairwise comparison

weight

goal

    . ideal point $f^*$

    . aspiration level $\bar{f}$

preference information

$L_p$-norm

    . $\sum w_i |f_i^*-f_i(x)|$

    . $(\sum w_i |f_i^*-f_i(x)|^p)^{1/p}$

    . $\max w_i |f_i^*-f_i(x)|$

augmented norm

    . $\max w_i |f_i^*-f_i(x)| + \alpha \sum w_i |f_i^*-f_i(x)|$

penalty function

achievement function

proxy utility function

utility function

fuzzy membership function

scalarization function

recursive quadratic programming method

augmented Lagrangian method

penalty method

GRG

direct search method

    . simplex method, complex method

nonsmooth optimization method

discrete optimization method

numerical method for scalar optimization

Interactive Programming Method

Fig. 2.1    Components in Interactive Multiobjective Programming Methods

## 3. Preference Information

At the early stage of development of interactive multiobjective programming methods, Geoffrion-Dyer-Feinberg suggested to use the well known Frank-Wolfe method in an interactive way [2]: where the marginal rate of substitution (MRS) of the preference of the decision maker is used as an information deciding the search direction. As many researchers pointed out [8], however, it is very difficult to elicit MRS from the decision maker due to the limitation of perceptual ability of human beings. For example, it has widely observed that human beings can not recognize a small change within some extent. Such a threshold of recognition is called JND (Just Noticeable Difference) [5]. Due to JND, it seems impossible to answer MRS which corresponds to differentials in the usual calculus. Therefore, even if the decision maker answered MRS, it should have been interpreted as a difference approximation.

Of course, the difference approximation to gradients can be effectively used in ordinary mathematical programming, when the exact information of gradient can not be available. In ordinary mathematical programming, as long as the search direction assures to improve the objective function, the convergence to the solution can be guaranteed by an appropriate line search. However, this is not necessarily expected in interactive programming methods, because JND in the line search makes sometimes a termination at a wrong solution (Fig. 3.1). In Fig. 3.1, if JND of the attribute X is $x_B-x_A$, in evaluation of MRS we can not access further from the point B to the point A, which implies that MRS represents the direction d. When the difference between A and C is within JND along the direction d, the decision maker answers A is most preferred along the direction. Namely, the optimization process terminates at the point A, which differs from the true optimum (if any) and possibly even from the satisfactory solution. This example shows that a merely parallel tansformation of ordinary optimization methods to interactive programming can not produce a good effect so long as the characteristics of human factors is not taken into account. MRS seems to be inadequate as the preference information in interactive programming methods, because it is too difficult to answer and its accuracy is questionable.

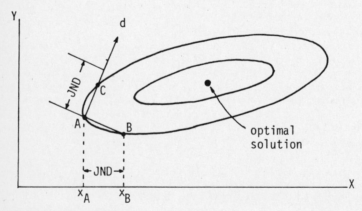

Fig. 3.1.  An Example in which GDF-method does not work well.

In the surrogate worth trade-off method suggested by Haimes-Hall-Friedman [4], the decision maker is required to answer the surrogate worth as a score assigned to each sampled Pareto solution. In this case, the burden of the decision maker is decreased a little in comparison to the Geoffrion-Dyer-Feinberg method. Even so, since the evaluation of surrogate worth includes that of MRS implicitly, it is difficult to answer surrogate worths with a consistency in the whole decision process. Moreover, the fact that the number of auxiliary scalar optimization is large in general makes also the method difficult.

Pairwise comparison is relatively easy to judge for human beings, and it can be effectively used in some cases with a few discrete alternatives. However, its judgment is sometimes too local to be consistent and usually requires too many number of similar questions which make the decision maker bored.

These observations show that the optimization with respect to the decision maker's preference can be realized only in some limited cases. For many multiobjective programming problems in practice, the optimization seems very difficult. Now we arrive at a question 'Is it really necessary to make a decision by optimization ?'. H. Simon asserted that human behaviors in many cases are based on 'satisficing' rather than optimization. In cases that higher levels of criteria are more desirable, the satisficing can be represented by a problem finding a solution to

$$f_i(x) \geq \bar{f}_i \qquad i=1,..,r$$

where $\bar{f}$ is the aspiration level of the decision maker. It has been ovserved that aspiration levels are very easy and intuitive to answer, because other preference informations are something 'should be' with a consistency, while aspiration levels are flexible with tolerance, and the rigidity in their consistency is not required so much. In some literatures, the aspiration levels are defined as one of goals. In the early stage of goal programming, goals are defined as levels $\bar{f}$ which the decision maker wants to attain, i.e. $f(x) = \bar{f}$. Recently, it is also extensively defined as the ideal level $f^*$ such that $f_i^* = \max f_i(x)$ ($i=1,...,r$), or as the aspiration level $\bar{f}$, i.e., the decision maker wants to find a solution $x$ such that $f(x) \geq \bar{f}$.

Aspiration levels are recognized differently depending on people. Optimists answer their aspiration levels close to the ideal value, while pessimists answer them as if they were minimum allowable levels. Even in intrapersonal judgment, they may vary over some range. However, we can utilize this characteristics of aspiration level in interactive multiobjective programming methods as follows: The decision maker is asked to change his aspiration level adaptively unless he agrees with the suggested solution, i.e.,

$$\bar{f}^{k+1} = ToP(\bar{f}^k)$$

where $\bar{f}^k$ represents the aspiration level at the k-th iteration. The operator $P$ selects the Pareto solution nearest in some sense to the given aspiration level $\bar{f}^k$. The operator $T$ is the trade-off operator which changes the k-th aspiration level $\bar{f}^k$ if the decision maker does not compromise with the shown solution $P(\bar{f}^k)$. Of course, since $P(\bar{f}^k)$ is a

Pareto solution, there exists no feasible solution which makes all criteria better than $P(\bar{f}^k)$, and thus the decision maker has to trade-off among criteria if he wants to improve some of criteria. Based on this trade-off, a new aspiration level is decided as $ToP(\bar{f}^k)$. Similar process is continued until the decision maker obtain an agreeable solution.

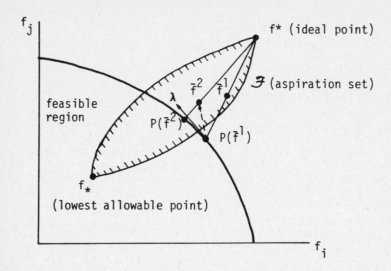

**Fig. 3.2   Interaction Process in the Satisficing Trade-off Method**

## 4. Scalarization Functions

In the previous section, we have seen that $P$ is an operator which finds the Pareto solution <u>nearest</u> <u>in some sense</u> to the aspiration level $\bar{f}^k$. This can be done by using some scalarization function. The sense of 'nearest' strongly depends on what kind of the scalarization function we shall use. We impose the following requirements on the scalarization functions:

$1^o$. They can cover all Pareto solutions.

$2^o$. Solutions to the auxiliary scalar optimization should be Pareto solutions.

$3^o$. Solutions to the auxiliary scalar optimization should be satisfactory, if the aspiration level is feasible.

Since our decision making solution is a satisfactory Pareto solution, the scalarization function should hold the property that we can select any Pareto solution by maximizing or minimizing it with an appropriate parameter in order to show a Pareto solution as the decision making solution whatever the problem may be and whatever the preference of the decision maker may be. Further the solution to the auxiliary scalar optimization for the scalarization function should be nothing but a Pareto solution, because our aim is to find a (satisfactory) Pareto solution.

Finally, if the aspiration level is feasible, then there exists a satisfactory Pareto solution. Therefore, it would not make sense to show the decision maker a nonsatisfactory solution when the aspiration level is feasible. These observations make the above three requirements to be reasonable.

Unfortunately, it should be noted, however, that there is no scalarization function satisfying all these requirements: It is well known that $l_1$-norm can not necessarily yield any Pareto solution if the problem is nonconvex. Even if we use $l_p$-norm $(1<p<\infty)$, we can not always get all Pareto solution depending on the degree of nonconvexity of the problem. In Fig. 3.1, we can see that the only norm (scalarization function) which can yields any Pareto solution in any problems is the weighted Tchebyshev norm. However, the weighted Tchebyshev norm violates the requirement $2^o$. Namely, the weighted Tchebyshev norm produces not only Pareto solutions but also weak Pareto solutions. For weak Pareto solutions, there exists another solution which improve some criteria while other criteria being unchanged, and hence weak Pareto solutions seem to be inadequate as a decision making soution. We can get a Pareto solution from a weak Pareto solution as follows:

$$\text{Maximize} \quad \sum_{i=1}^{r} \varepsilon_i$$

subject to

(P)

$$f_i(x) - \varepsilon_i = f_i(\hat{x})$$

$$\varepsilon_i \geq 0 \qquad (i=1,\ldots,r)$$

$$x \in X$$

where $\hat{x}$ is a (weak) Pareto solution. If all $\varepsilon_i$ for the solution to (P) are zero, then $x$ itself is a Pareto solution. If there are some $\varepsilon_i \neq 0$, then the solution $\tilde{x}$ to the problem (P) is a Pareto solution.

Like this, we can get a Pareto solution from a given weak Pareto soluiton by solving an auxiliary optimization problem. However, in some cases such as structure design problems and camera lens design problems it is expensive to optimize such an auxiliary optimization. In order to avoid such an additional scalar optimization problem, some researchers suggested to use some kinds of augmented norms. One of typical examples is given by

$$S_a = \max_{1 \leq i \leq r} w_i |f_i^* - f_i(x)| + a\sum_{i=1}^{r} w_i |f_i^* - f_i(x)| \qquad (4.1)$$

For any $0<a<\infty$, the solution obtained by minimizing $S_a$ is guranteed to be a Pareto solution. However, it can be easily seen that the augmented norm $S_a$ violates the requirements $1^o$ and $3^o$. (Fig. 4.1) Observe here that $l_\infty$-norm satisfies the requirement $3^o$.

## Theorem 4.1

Suppose that for any $x \varepsilon X$

$$f_i^* \geq f_i(x), \qquad i=1,\ldots,r. \tag{4.2}$$

If we set for a given aspiration level $\bar{f}$

$$w_i = \frac{1}{f_i^* - \bar{f}_i}, \qquad i=1,\ldots,r \tag{4.3}$$

then the solution $\tilde{x}$ to the Min-Max problem

$$\text{Minimize} \quad \underset{1 \leq i \leq r}{\text{Max}} \ w_i |f_i^* - f_i(x)| \quad \text{over} \quad x \in X \tag{4.4}$$

is a satisfactory Pareto solution in case of $\bar{f}$ being feasible, while it is assured to be a Pareto solution even in case of $\bar{f}$ being infeasible.

Proof: It is well known that the solution to the Min-Max problem (4.4) is a weak Pareto solution. Hence, we shall show that if the aspiration level $\bar{f}$ is feasible, then the solution $\tilde{x}$ to the Min-Max problem becomes a satisfactory solution, namely, $f(\tilde{x}) \geq \bar{f}$.

Let

$$\rho(y) := \underset{1 \leq i \leq r}{\text{Max}} \ w_i |f_i^* - y_i|$$

and define the level set at $\bar{f}$ by

$$L := \{y=(y_1,\ldots,y_r) \mid \rho(y) \leq \rho(\bar{f})\}.$$

Further, setting

$$S := \{y=(y_1,\ldots,y_r) \mid y_i \geq \bar{f}_i, \quad i=1,\ldots,r\},$$

we have

$$L \subset S. \tag{4.5}$$

In fact, the way of setting the weight $w_i$ yields $w_i |f_i^* - \bar{f}_i| = 1$ $(i=1,\ldots,r)$, and hence for any $y \varepsilon L$ and $i=1,\ldots,r$

$$w_i |f_i^* - y_i| \leq w_i (f_i^* - \bar{f}_i),$$

which yields $y_i \geq \bar{f}_i$ $(i=1,\ldots,r)$.

Now note that if $\bar{f}$ is feasible, then there exists a $\hat{x} \varepsilon X$ such that $f_i(\hat{x}) \geq \bar{f}_i$ for all $i=1,\ldots,r$. Then

$$w_i |f_i^* - f_i(\hat{x})| = w_i (f_i^* - f_i(\hat{x}))$$

$$\leq w_i (f_i^* - \bar{f}_i),$$

thereby

$$\{f(x)|x \in X\} \cap L \neq \emptyset. \qquad (4.6)$$

The relations (4.5) and (4.6) implies that the solution to $\underset{x \in X}{\text{Min}} \, \rho(f(x))$ belongs to the set S.

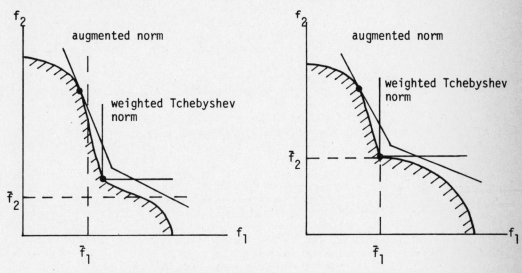

Fig. 4.1   Some Characteristics of the Weighted Tchebyshev Norm
and the Augmented Norm

From the above discussion, the weighted Tcheyshev norm seems very attractive, in particular, in view of the fact that it satisfies the requirement $3^o$. However, in cases where the auxiliary scalar optimization is too difficult to solve, the compensation for the requirement $2^o$, (i.e., getting a Pareto solution from a weak Pareto solution) is too expensive. In this case, it should be noted that under relatively mild condition, the augmented norm can give a Pareto solution arbitraily close to the solution to the minimization of the weighted Tchebyshev norm. In fact, the following holds:

**Theorem 4.2**

Suppose that all $f_i^*$ (i=1,...,r) are continuous. Let $w_i = 1/(f_i^* - \bar{f}_i)$. Further let $f(\alpha)$ be the function value at the solution to

$$\text{Minimize} \quad \underset{1 \leq i \leq r}{\text{Max}} \, w_i |f_i^* - f_i(x)| + \alpha \sum_{i=1}^{r} w_i |f_i^* - f_i(x)|$$

and let $f(0)$ be that of the Min-Max problem (4.4). Then

$$\lim_{\alpha \to 0} \, f(\alpha) = f(0).$$

Proof:  See, for example, [7].

Threfore, although the augmented norm violates the requirement $1^O$ and $3^O$, it can be effectively used on behalf of the weighted Tchebyshev norm, particularly in cases where the auxiliary scalar optimization is expensive. Note that in order for the augmented norm to satisfy $3^O$ in a sense of approximation, it is necessary to make a positive paramerter $\alpha$ sufficiently small.  However, we can not know in advance how small is enough.  In some special cases, any positive $\alpha$ can not yield a desirable solution (Fig. 4.1).  This is the only drawback of the augmented norm.

Other scalarization functions have been suggested by utilizing the well known penalty functions in ordinary mathematical programming, or as achievement functions [3].  However, in nonlinear problems, it seems from our experience that the weighted norm or the augmented norm are most simple and convenient in view of the requirements $1^O$-$3^O$.  Unless we need to find an optimal solution with respect to the decision maker's preference, it seems redundant to use (proxy) utility functions as scalarization functions.  Goals or aspiration levels are originally fuzzy and flexible. In DIDASS and the satisficing trade-off method, this characteristic is used in such a way that the decision maker can change his aspiration level adaptively according as the situation.  In other words, the fuzziness of the decision maker's judgment  is treated implicitly in the interaction with the decision maker.  In these methods, therefore, we do not need to invoke to membership functions in the fuzzy analysis.  Utility functions and membership functions can be effectively used in cases that we want to decrease the number of interaction and iteration for finding the solution rather than in interactive programming methods.


## 5. Numerical Methods for Scalar Optimization

Both the weighted Tchebyshev norm and the augmented norm are nonsmooth. However, we can convert them into smooth ones:  For example, suppose that $f_i^* \geq f_i(x)$ for all $x \in X$.  Then, as is well known, for the augmented norm the following two minimization are equiuvalent:

(I)  $$\text{Minimize} \quad \underset{1 \leq i \leq r}{\text{Max}} \; w_i |f_i^* - f_i(x)| \; + \; \alpha \sum_{i=1}^{r} w_i |f_i^* - f_i(x)|$$

(II)  $$\underset{x, \, \xi}{\text{Minimize}} \quad \xi + \alpha \sum_{i=1}^{r} w_i (f_i^* - f_i(x))$$

subject to

$$w_i (f_i^* - f_i(x)) \leq \xi \qquad i = 1, \ldots, r$$

$$x \in X$$

Therefore, we can use the RQP method and other effective methods for smooth optimization for solving the problem (II) which is equivalent to (I). Another merit of transforming (I) into (II) may be seen in the following theorem:

**Theorem 5.1**

Let $(\tilde{x},\tilde{\xi})$ be a solution to the problem (II) and let $\tilde{\lambda}=(\tilde{\lambda}_1,...,\tilde{\lambda}_r)$ be the optimal Lagrange multipliers. If $\tilde{x}$ is of the interior to the set $X$ and each $f_i$ has appropriate smoothness, then we have

$$\sum_{i=1}^{r} \tilde{\lambda}_i = 1, \qquad \tilde{\lambda}_i \geq 0, \qquad i=1,...,r \qquad (5.1)$$

$$\sum_{i=1}^{r} (\tilde{\lambda}_i+a)w_i \nabla f_i(\tilde{x}) = 0. \qquad (5.2)$$

Moreover, if the problem (II) is convex, namely, if each $f_i$ is concave and the set $X$ is convex, then for any $x \varepsilon X$

$$\sum_{i=1}^{r} (\tilde{\lambda}_i+a)w_i(f_i(x) - f_i(\tilde{x})) \leq 0. \qquad (5.3)$$

Proof:    The relations (5.1) and (5.2) immediately follow from the well-known Kuhn-Tucker theorem for the Lagrangean

$$L(x,\xi:\lambda) = \xi + a\sum_{i=1}^{r} w_i(f_i^* - f_i(x))$$

$$+ \sum_{i=1}^{r} \lambda_i(w_i(f_i^* - f_i(x)) - \xi).$$

In addition, the well-known theory of convex programming provides that for the solution $(\tilde{x},\tilde{\xi})$ and $\tilde{\lambda}$

$$L(x,\xi:\tilde{\lambda}) \leq L(\tilde{x},\tilde{\xi}:\tilde{\lambda}),$$

from which the relation (5.3) follows by virtue of $\sum_{i=1}^{r} \tilde{\lambda}_i=1$.

From Theorem 5.1, the relation (5.1) can be used to check whether or not the obtained solution is optimal. The relations (5.2) and (5.3) are helpful for the decision maker to trade-off. Decision makers tend to want to improve the unsatisfactory criteria much more strongly than they agree to sacrifice others. In the original version of the satisficing trade-off method [6], the deision maker is asked both how much he wants to improve unsatisfactory criteria and in return how much he can relax other criteria. In the trade-off, he can utilize the information of (5.2) and (5.3): Let $I_I$ be the set of indices of criteria which he wants to improve and let $I_R$ be that of criteria which he can relax in return. If he wants to improve $f_i$ by $\Delta f_i$ ($i \in I_I$), then he must relax $f_j$ by $\Delta f_j$ ($j \in I_R$) satisfying (5.3). Therefore, the decision maker consider his trade-off in his mind so that the relation (5.2) may hold (Fig. 3.2).

In the recent revised version of the staisficing trade-off method, however, he can use the assignment of sacrifice for $f_j$ ($j \in I_R$) automatically set in the equal proportion to $(\tilde{\lambda}_i + \alpha)w_i$, namely, by

$$\Delta f_j = \frac{-1}{N(\tilde{\lambda}_j + \alpha)w_j} \sum_{i \in I_I} (\tilde{\lambda}_i + \alpha)w_i \Delta f_i$$

where N is the number of elements of the set $I_R$. By doing this, in cases where there are a large number of criteria, the burden of the decision maker can be decreased so much. Of course, if the deicion maker does not agree with this quota $\Delta f_j$ laid down automatically, he can modify them in a manual way.

## 6. Concluding Remarks

We have discussed the components in interactive multiobjective programming methods. The aspiration level, the weighted Tchebyshev norm, the augmented norm and RQP-like methods are observed very attractive as these components. DIDASS and the satisficing trade-off method use them effectively for finding a satisfactory Pareto solution. It is of course possible to develop another methods incorporating other components for another decision rule. The important thing is to synthesize these components effectively taking characteristics of the problem and the decision rule into account.

## REFERENCES

[1]    Dyer, J.S. 'The effect of errors in the estimation of the gradient on the Frank-Wolfe algorithm, with implicxations for interactive programming', Operations Research 22, 160-174 (1974)

[2]    Geoffrion, A.M., J. S, Dyer and A. Feinberg, 'An Interactive Approach for Multi-criterion Optimization, with an Application to the Operation of an Academic Department', Management Sccience 19, 357-368 (1972)

[3]    Grauer, M., A. Lewandowski and A.P. Wierzbicki, DIDASS- Theory, Implementation and Experiences, in M. Grauer and A.P. Wierzbicki (eds.) Interactive Decision Analysis, Proceeding of an International Workshop on Interactive Decision Analysis and Interpretative Computer Intelligence, Springer, 1984

[4]   Haimes, Y.Y., W.A. Hall and H.B. Freedman, Multiobjective
      Optimization in Water Resources Systems, The Surrogate Worth
      Trade-off Method, Elsevier Scientific, New York (1975)

[5]   Luce, R.D., 'Semiorders and a theory of utility discrimination',
      Econometrica 24, 178-191 (1956)

[6]   Nakayama, H. and Y. Sawaragi, Satisficing Trade-off Method for
      Interactive Multiobjective Programming Methods, in M. Grauer and
      A.P. Wierzbicki (eds.) Interactive Decision Analysis, Proceeding of
      an International Workshop on Interactive Decision Analysis and
      Interpretative Computer Intelligence, Springer, 1984

[7]   Sawaragi, Y., H. Nakayama and T. Tanino, Theory of Multiobjective
      Optimization, Academic Press, forthcoming.

[8]   Wallenius, J., 'Comparative evaluation of some interactive approaches
      to multicriterion optimization', Management Science 21, 1387-1396
      (1973)

## Appendix

For reference, we shall show in the following an example of the
interaction process in the revised version of the satisficing trade-off
method. The example is the same problem as the one that was illustrated in
[6]: A river basin in the middle-western part of Japan is modeled: there
are three branches in the upper-stream and one in the lower-stream. One of
three branches in the upper-stream is so clear that the treatment of used
water is not necessary. Each of other two branches in the upper reach have
its own treatment-plant which is supported by a local government in the
upper reach. Another local government around the lower reach takes care of
a treatment-plant in the lower reach. Under this situation, we have three
objectives to be minimized:

1)   treatment cost in the upper reach

$$f_1(x) = 287.58 + 2295.59(x_1 - 0.45)^2 + 404.46(x_2 - 0.45)^2 \quad (10^4 \text{yen/day})$$

2)   treatment cost in the lower reach

$$f_2(x) = 1050.73 + 10035.34(x_3 - 0.45)^2 \quad (10^4 \text{yen/day})$$

3)   BOD concentration at the inflow point into the sea

$$f_3(x) = 36.03 - (8.05x_1 + 1.04x_2 + 24.00x_3) \quad (\text{ppm})$$

Here $x_1$, $x_2$ denote the percent treatment to be used at the two treatment
plants in the upper reach, and $x_3$ denote the one in the lower reach. Our
constraints are as follows:

$$0.45 \leq x_1, \ x_2, \ x_3 \leq 1.0$$

It is natural to consider that the two local governments are both decision makers in this problem who share the cost for maintaining clear water. However, suppose here that we have a central authority who is responsible for the final decision.

One of results of our experiment is as follows: The ideal point is set as $(f_1^*, \ f_2^*, \ f_3^*) = (0.0, \ 0.0, \ 0.0)$. The initial aspiration level was given by $(\bar{f}_1^1, \ \bar{f}_2^1, \ \bar{f}_3^1) = (700.0, \ 3000.0, \ 5.0)$.

```
******** PARETO SOLUTION BY MIN-MAX METHOD ( 1) ********

             PARETO SOL.     ASP. LEVEL      LAG.MULTIPLIER
      -------------------------------------------------------
   F( 1)    0.78906D+03    0.70000D+03     0.18087D+00
   F( 2)    0.33817D+04    0.30000D+04     0.48999D+00
   F( 3)    0.56361D+01    0.50000D+01     0.32914D+00

  DO YOU COMPPOMISE WITH EACH F(I) ? (Y/N)? N


******** CLASSIFICATION OF CRITERIA ********

  PLEASE CLASSIFY THE CRITERIA INTO THREE GROUPS (I,R,A):

      I: IF YOU WANT TO IMPROVE F(I)
      R: IF YOU MAY RELAX F(I)
      A: IF YOU ACCEPT F(I), AS IT IS

  F( 1) ?
        = R

  F( 2) ?
        = R

  F( 3) ?
        = I



******** CONFIRMATION ********

   CRITERIA WHICH YOU WANT TO IMPROVE
     F( 3)= 0.56361D+01

   CRITERIA WHICH YOU MAY RELAX
     F( 1)= 0.78906D+03
     F( 2)= 0.33817D+04

   CRITERIA WHICH YOU ACCEPT, AS IT IS
     NONE

  SURE?  (Y/N)? Y
```

```
******** TRADE OFF ********

     ----- PLEASE IMPROVE -----

     F( 3)= 0.56361D+01        SENSITIVITY( 3)= 0.65829D-01
  NEW ASPF= ? 5.0


WHICH WAY DO YOU WANT TO USE FOR TRADE-OFF, A OR M ?

  A:  AUTOMATIC
  M:  MANUAL

? A



              NEW ASP.        STATUS QUO        PREVIOUS ASP.
  ----------------------------------------------------------------
   F( 1)    0.87009D+03     0.78906D+03      0.70000D+03
   F( 2)    0.35099D+04     0.33817D+04      0.30000D+04
   F( 3)    0.50000D+01     0.56361D+01      0.50000D+01



DO YOU AGREE WITH THIS TRADE-OFF ? (Y/N)   Y



******** FEASIBILITY CHECK ********

  NOT FEASIBLE --- AS LINEAR APPROXIMATION

WHICH DO YOU WANT TO GO TO 1, OR 0 ?

   0:  MIN-MAX PROBLEM
   1:  TRADE-OFF AGAIN

? 0



******** PARETO SOLUTION BY MIN-MAX METHOD ( 2) ********

              PARETO SOL.     ASP. LEVEL       LAG.MULTIPLIER
  ----------------------------------------------------------------
   F( 1)    0.87093D+03     0.87009D+03      0.19030D+00
   F( 2)    0.35133D+04     0.35099D+04      0.50920D+00
   F( 3)    0.50049D+01     0.50000D+01      0.30050D+00

  DO YOU COMPPOMISE WITH EACH F(I) ? (Y/N)? Y
END OF GO,SEVERITY CODE=00
```

# AN INTEGRATED PROGRAMMING PACKAGE FOR
# MULTIPLE-CRITERIA DECISION ANALYSIS

Manfred Grauer[1] , Sabine Messner[2] and Manfred Strubegger[2]

[1] *Division of Mathematics and Cybernetics, Academy of Sciences of the GDR, Berlin, GDR*
[2] *International Institute for Applied Systems Analysis, Laxenburg, Austria*

## 1. INTRODUCTION

A number of recent developments (for example, the rapid deterioration of European and North American forests, or the increasing conflict between the trade unions, industrial managers and the government over issues such as unemployment, the national debt, wages, etc.) have highlighted the severe shortcomings of the conventional modeling techniques (e.g., econometric models or technoeconomic approaches) used as a basis for decision making.

Econometric models describe the future development options of a system from an analysis of its past behavior. However, this excludes the possibility of modeling the response of the system to events that have never taken place before. In addition, it is assumed that the parameters of economic development depend very strongly on events that occurred in the past.

Technoeconomic models combine the technical and economic features of a system into a consistent picture of its future development. In general they look for solutions that are both technically feasible and economically optimal — however, they do not meet the present need to include social or environmental objectives, such as the reduction of pollutant emissions.

This paper describes a different approach based on the interactive multiple-criteria decision support system DIDASS [1] and gives some examples of its use. In the first example, three important objectives in energy planning are optimized using an energy model for Austria. These objectives are minimization of costs, minimization of import dependence, and minimization of $SO_2$ emissions.

The second application describes research currently underway at IIASA. The aim is to develop a model that covers the main aspects of gas trade in Europe, which by no means follows purely economic rules.

In the third example an integrated system of models is presented, which could, in its final stage, help in an analysis of the factors linking consumers, the economy, the energy system and the government (e.g., taxes).

Before considering the examples, however, it is necessary to outline the modeling approach and describe the implementation of the computer codes.

## 2. THE MODEL SET

The set of models is based on the dynamic linear programming model MESSAGE II [2]. The codes used in this interactive model system are MXG (the matrix generator of MESSAGE II), an interactive linear programming solver based on MINOS [3], and CAP (the post-processing program of MESSAGE II), which allows interactive evaluation of model results. All these codes are implemented on the VAX 11/780 at IIASA, and are accessible via telecommunications networks.

### 2.1 The Model MESSAGE II

MESSAGE II is an extended version of the IIASA energy supply model MESSAGE [4], which is described in some detail in a companion paper by M. Grauer [5]. (Readers are advised to refer to this paper for details of both the model MESSAGE and the interactive DIDASS package.) The main differences between MESSAGE II and its predecessor are the following:

— MESSAGE II allows modeling of the entire energy chain, from resource extraction via central conversion (e.g., electricity and district heat production), energy transmission and distribution to on-site conversion (e.g., heating systems) and hence to ultimate consumption (e.g., as heat, light, motive power).

— MESSAGE II permits variable period lengths.

— MESSAGE II can incorporate demand elasticity functions, so the model can react to changing energy prices.

— MESSAGE II allows user-defined constraints: the user can incorporate any additional factors influencing the development of the energy system, such as pollution control, restrictions on the use of resources other than energy (e.g., water, steel) or maximum import shares.

— Depending on the LP-solver used, MESSAGE II can cope with mixed integer programming and a non-linear objective function.

In addition, MESSAGE II supports conventional multiobjective optimization. That is, variables other than those directly related to the costs of the energy system can be included in the objective function and weighted accordingly. Such variables could be used to penalize pollution or other activities. For a more detailed description see the *User's Guide to the Matrix Generator of MESSAGE II* [2].

### 2.2 Adaptation of MESSAGE II to the Reference Point Optimization Method

In order to avoid the rather time-consuming procedure of problem formulation as described in [5] (generation of a matrix by MESSAGE, generation of additional information by LPMOD and restructuring of the matrix by the pre-processor LPMULTI), MESSAGE II was extended so that the restructuring step could be omitted. All constraints and variables necessary for the reference trajectory optimization approach are generated during the matrix generation step, using dummy variables for the reference trajectories and scaling factors. The correct values are then entered during the next step, as described below.

## 2.3 The Interactive LP-solver IMM

The interactive LP-solver is based on MINOS [3]. The routines described in [6] were added and others (Driver, Minos) extended to call various additional routines so that the necessary matrix manipulations can be performed (see Figure 1).

After the matrix has been read successfully, the user can enter the reference trajectories. These take the form of a vector of targets for each objective, and can be inserted into the matrix directly. If the "utopia" trajectories are not known for all goal trajectories the user has to supply scaling factors (as in LPMOD). However, as it is useful to know the "utopia" and "nadir" trajectories, and hence the range for decisions, the model makes it possible to calculate these values. The "utopia" and "nadir" trajectories are calculated by optimizing a weighted single objective for each time step of each trajectory. The weights are set to 1 for the trajectory being optimized, to 1000 for the current time step, and to 0.001 for the other trajectories. Then the best (utopia trajectory) and the worst (nadir trajectory) values are determined for each element. The user is then presented with the range of possible values and the solution of the dynamic problem for each objective (i.e., each trajectory is optimized over the whole time horizon). Once the reference trajectory has been defined, the scaling factors are calculated as the inverse of the distance between the reference trajectory and the corresponding "utopia" trajectory (see Figure 2 for a two-dimensional static example). This procedure avoids the arbitrary setting of scaling factors.

The actual problem is then solved by optimizing the single-criterion equivalent, an objective defined by the reference trajectories and scaling factors.

The definition of this single-criterion objective was revised to provide a better reflection of the dynamic nature of the problem: it is now formulated for each time step separately, and these single objectives then summed over all time steps.

In this case, the revised objective has the form:

$$\min \left[ \sum_t (\max_i \frac{y_{i,t} - \bar{y}_{i,t}}{\alpha_{i,t}}) + \varepsilon \sum_{i,t} \frac{y_{i,t} - \bar{y}_{i,t}}{\alpha_{i,t}} \right] ,$$

where $t$ is an index representing the time steps

$i$ is an index representing the objectives

$\bar{y}_{i,t}$ is the reference point corresponding to the value $y_{i,t}$ of objective $i$ in step $t$

$\alpha_{i,t}$ is the scaling factor for objective $i$ in step $t$.

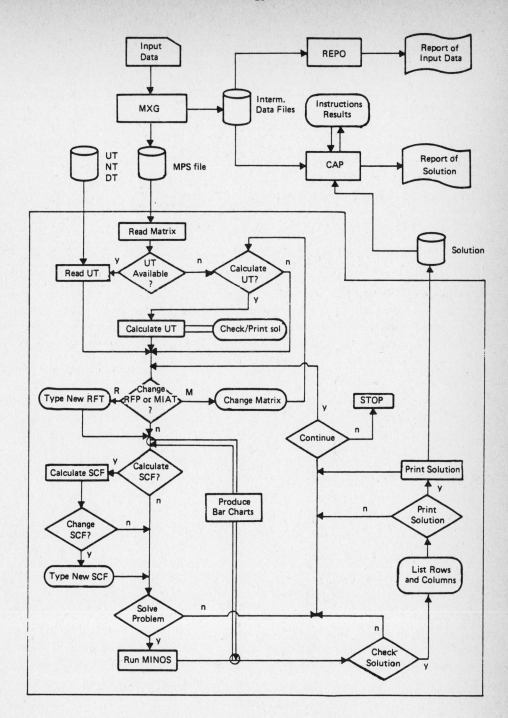

**Figure 1.** The interactive solver (IMM).

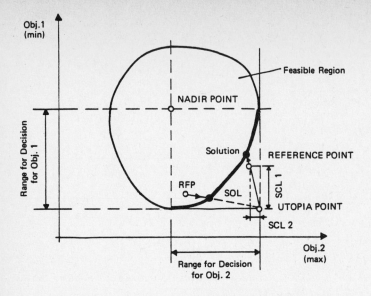

**Figure 2.** An example of a static problem with two objectives.

This reformulation is useful because in MESSAGE II the different time steps may be related only very loosely, so that use of the (single) minimax criterion yields counter-intuitive results.

After solving this problem, the present result can then be compared with those obtained during earlier iterations, and the solution analyzed. In addition the user may access the values of all constraints and variables interactively. If a detailed analysis of the results is required, the solution can be printed and processed using the post-processing program CAP [7].

Based on the analysis of the solution, the user may now change the reference trajec-tories and solve the resulting new problem. The user also has access to the matrix and can alter any element, bound or right-hand side interactively. In most cases recalcula-tion of the "utopia" trajectories is then necessary.

The interactive procedure outlined above has the great advantage of reducing the amount of time (in many cases by a factor of 100) otherwise necessary for input/output operations. This reduction of the time between defining the reference trajectories and investigating the solution makes this approach even more attractive. In addition, the machine-independent interface to the user was improved by introducing an option which displays bar charts for the different trajectories.

# 3. APPLICATIONS

The following sections present some applications of the procedure outlined above. The first describes an application to a model of the Austrian energy supply system, while the second deals with a gas trade model for Europe. Finally, current attempts to develop an energy/economy interaction model for Austria are presented.

## 3.1 SEMA: An Energy Model for Austria

The energy model described here is a relatively aggregated representation of the present Austrian energy supply system and its possible future development. The simplifications were mainly concerned with end-use, where, for example, the different temperature requirements for industrial heat were ignored and the demand for liquid fuel for transportation was supplied by a fixed mix of gasoline and diesel oil. Figure 3 shows the representation of the energy system studied. This model covers the years from 1980 to 2000, with a resolution of four years up to 1992 and eight years thereafter. The results of this model will then be used as guidelines in another, more disaggregated, model* that takes cost minimization as the decision criterion.

At present three trajectories are defined: minimization of total system costs; minimization of energy imports; and minimization of $SO_2$ emissions.

Initially the dynamic optima for the single objectives were taken as reference trajectories. This can be interpreted as meaning that every participant in the decision process wishes to reach the highest possible value for his own objective, regardless of the implications for the other objectives.

Figure 4 shows the resulting composition of primary energy consumption for the year 2000. Simple cost minimization (case 1) yields an import dependence of roughly 60%, while the other two objectives, minimization of imports (case 2) and minimization of $SO_2$ emissions (case 3), both result in a lower import dependence. The reason is clear in case 2, while in case 3 the reduction in $SO_2$ emissions is achieved by increased use of (domestic) hydropower. Use of natural gas is also considerably higher in these cases than in case 1. The reason is the higher end-use efficiency and thus lower import requirements associated with natural gas in case 2 (as well as the possibility of drilling for extremely expensive (domestic) deep gas), and the low sulfur content of natural gas in case 3.

In the multicriteria case (case 4), domestic energy production reaches a respectable 50%, while the share of natural gas (which is mainly imported and costly to distribute to remote areas) is considerably lower than in cases 2 and 3, and almost the same as in case 1.

---

*Currently under development.

254

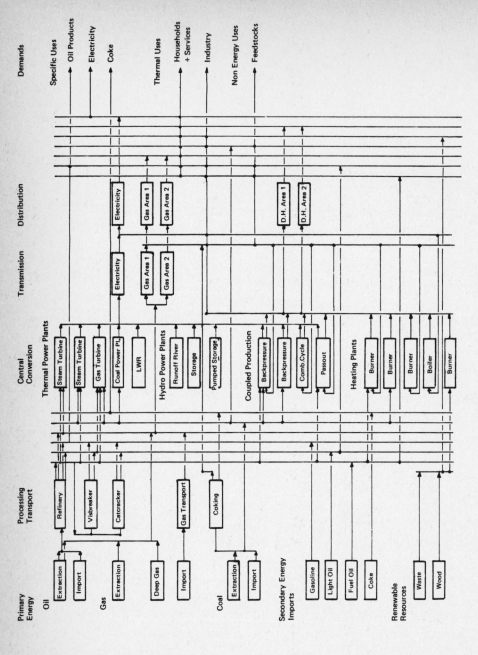

**Figure 3.** The SEMA energy system.

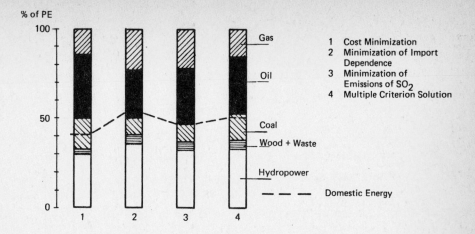

**Figure 4.** Shares of primary energy use in the year 2000 assuming different objective functions in SEMA.

The difference between the system costs resulting from minimization of system costs and minimization of $SO_2$ emissions is relatively small ("only" 4%, which amounts to roughly $160 billion per year), while minimization of import dependence could increase the cost by 20%.

In this case the multiple trajectory optimization approach can help to find a compromise solution with lower costs than in case 2, with $SO_2$ emissions 12% less than in the cost minimization case (but still nearly 80% more than the best possible reduction) and with a high share of domestically produced energy.

### 3.2 GATE: A Gas Trade Model for Europe

The question addressed by this model is: How do different strategies in the various European regions influence the gas trade between these regions and with the rest of the world? To answer this question, Europe was divided into four regions, namely North, Central, South, and East. Four gas exporting regions are also considered: the USSR, the Norwegian North Sea gas fields, The Netherlands + Denmark, and North Africa. In this context North Africa is just a synonym for the rest of the world, since projects such as a gas pipeline from the Middle East or LNG imports from any conceivable exporter could be included in this part of the model. Oil exporters were also included to give consumers an alternative to buying gas. The oil exporting regions considered are the Norwegian and UK North Sea fields, the USSR and others (including OPEC). The regions studied are summarized in Table 1.

Each of the four European regions is then represented in a framework similar to that shown in Figure 3, taking into account regional differences where necessary (see [8] for a more detailed description). The gas exporters which are assumed for the purposes

**Table 1**. The groups considered in GATE.

| Energy consumers | Gas exporters | Oil exporters |
|---|---|---|
| North Europe | Netherlands + Denmark | UK North Sea |
| Central Europe | Norwegian North Sea | Norwegian North Sea |
| South Europe | USSR | USSR |
| East Europe | North Africa (and others) | Others (e.g., OPEC) |

of this study to have inexhaustible resources (namely the USSR and North Africa) are modeled using simple ranges for price/production levels. In the case of The Netherlands and the North Sea, the gas supply options are modeled explicitly as drilling technologies and gas reserves in different cost categories. The oil producers were treated in a similar way. The suppliers in the North Sea face high investment costs and declining availability of resources, while the members of OPEC can continue their production without any such problems.

The decision criteria chosen for this complex model are listed in Table 2. The energy consumers generally wish to minimize the cost of their energy system. The gas exporters wish to maximize their income, with The Netherlands and Norway also trying to minimize their investment in infrastructure, while the USSR and North Africa want to minimize the amount of gas exported. The oil exporters have similar objectives to the gas exporters.

**Table 2**. The objectives of the regions considered in the model.

| Region | Objective |
|---|---|
| *Energy consumers* | |
| Central, North, South, East Europe | Minimize the cost of the energy system |
| East Europe | Minimize import dependence |
| *Gas exporters* | |
| Netherlands + Denmark, Norway | Maximize profits |
| USSR, North Africa | Maximize income |
| USSR, North Africa | Minimize export volume |
| *Oil exporters* | |
| UK, Norway | Maximize profits |
| USSR, OPEC | Maximize income |

The first runs with this model setup produced very promising results: three multiple trajectory optimization runs, which differ in their scaling relative to a "base case", will be discussed in some detail below. Figure 5 summarizes the results, i.e., the gas imports of western Europe in the year 2010, disaggregated by region of origin.

In a simple cost-minimization run (case 1), the gas resources in the Norwegian North Seas count as domestic supplies, so that extraction is profitable even at high costs. However, the multiobjective "base case" run (case 2) shows that the revenues from such expensive sources of gas are not sufficient to cover the high investment costs.

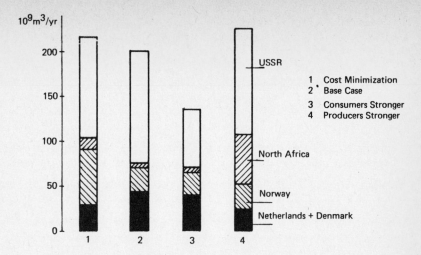

**Figure 5**. Gas imports of western Europe by region of origin, 2010.

This is emphasized by the ability of both the other gas exporters and the oil exporters to undercut the price of Norwegian gas. A comparison between cases 1 and 2 also shows that the oil exporters can — given their flexibility in pricing — keep the gas exporters out of the market.

This situation becomes even more marked if the energy consumers become more powerful (reflected in the model by a change in scaling), as in case 3. The consumers replace the imported gas by domestic gas (the extraction of which is abandoned in the base case) and an 8% increase in oil imports. If, however, the producers' "bargaining position" is strengthened by scaling (case 4), North African gas improves its position quite considerably. Not only does it open a larger market for gas, but it also displaces a significant proportion of the Dutch share.

The variations in these results seem quite dramatic, and in the cases of The Netherlands and Norway they represent considerable changes. On the other hand, the difference in the volume of gas required between cases 3 and 4 is only 5% of the total primary energy use in western Europe.

A more complete description of these tentative model runs with GATE were presented at an IIASA Workshop on Gas Issues in autumn 1984. The participants at the Workshop — particularly those from industry — rated this new approach very highly.

### 3.3 Energy/Economy Interactions: The Case of Austria

The energy/economy model described below is currently being developed to investigate options for the future development of the Austrian economy. Although the model is not yet complete, we include a preliminary description to demonstrate the capabilities of our approach.

The model consists of four modules running in sequence. These are:

— a dynamic input/output (I/O) model, based on the vintage production theory

— a dynamic energy supply model (SEMA, as described above)

— an econometric consumer demand model

— an interactive taxing and monetary redistribution accounting framework.

The I/O and energy modules are contained in a common linear programming model, in which the industrial energy demand is determined from the activity of each of the economic sectors considered in the I/O model. The energy demand is expressed as useful energy needed per unit of output produced. In turn, the energy model demands capital and intermediate goods from the rest of the economy. Thus each of the technologies included in the energy model must contain information about the structure of investment for new installations. The investment and intermediate goods needed by the rest of the economy are endogenously determined in the I/O model.

Each of the economic sectors is represented by its intermediate and investment demands as well as by other indicators (e.g., labor demand, emissions, value-added produced, or a minimum demand for imported goods). The different economic sectors are not represented as one activity but as a number of different activities having different investment, primary and/or intermediate input structures. This leads to an I/O matrix with more columns than rows. The mix of options actually used depends on the particular objectives considered. As proposed by the vintage production theory (putty–clay hypothesis), the input structure of each installation is kept constant for the entire lifetime of the installation. This hypothesis is not, of course, valid for the variable factors of production, such as labor and intermediate consumption of goods and services, but holds for the relation between these factors. The overall economic structure varies over time due to the changing mix of options offered and the varying utilization of the different installations.

The final demand for the goods and services included in the model is determined exogenously. From the model results one can determine the average and marginal prices for all goods and services as well as the total GNP produced. With this information, and assumptions on government expenditure and exports, it is possible to determine the household income. An econometric model (e.g., a linear expenditure model, or translog functions) can then be used to estimate the final private demand for the chosen consumption sectors. Using a bridge matrix, these demands may be transformed into demands for goods and services as defined in the I/O model.

These three parts of the model are then solved iteratively until an equilibrium between demand and supply is obtained.

The I/O and energy modules are solved using the reference trajectory optimization approach as described above. This means that the objectives of different decision makers can be taken into account. These objectives could include environmental criteria (reduction of emissions), producers' interests (cost minimization, minimization of labor force, etc.), political issues (balance of imports and exports, employment rate, etc.) and private interests (increasing income and thus the consumption of goods and services).

The other modules provide interactive assistance in defining different strategies for taxation, monetary redistribution and the like. The consumption module may be a specific model, or the demand for the various commodities could be given completely exogenously in order to investigate the effects of different behavioral expectations.

This model is clearly a useful tool for decision making. It requires different decision makers to agree to a common framework which can then be used to arrive at a common proposal for the future development of the economy. As with all models, it should not be seen as a crystal ball for forecasting the future, but rather as a tool for investigating various alternatives and determining the conditional expectations of possible future events.

## 4. FINAL REMARKS

The interactive decision support system presented in the previous sections has been shown to be useful in analyzing the power and consistency of energy and other linear programming models. The possibility of an interactive sensitivity analysis helps to reveal inconsistencies in the data quite rapidly. However, a truly interactive operating system such as UNIX 4.2 is necessary, so that running programs can be controlled remotely but also redirected to a terminal if necessary.

## REFERENCES

1. M. Grauer, A. Lewandowski, and A.P. Wierzbicki. DIDASS — theory, implementation and experiences. In M. Grauer and A. Wierzbicki (Eds.), *Interactive Decision Analysis*. Springer-Verlag. Berlin, 1984.

2. S. Messner. *User's Guide to the Matrix Generator of MESSAGE II*. Working Paper WP-84-71, International Institute for Applied Systems Analysis, Laxenburg, Austria, 1984.

3. Bruce A. Murtagh and Michael A. Saunders. MINOS/Augmented User's Manual. Technical Report SOL 80-19, Stanford University, June 1980.

4. L. Schrattenholzer. *The Energy Supply Model MESSAGE*. RR-81-31, International Institute for Applied Systems Analysis, Laxenburg, Austria, 1981.

5. M. Grauer. Interactive decision analysis in energy planning and policy assessment. In G. Fandel and J. Spronk (Eds.),*Readings in MCDM*. Springer-Verlag, Berlin, 1984.

6. P. V. Preckel. *Modules for Use with MINOS/AUGMENTED in Solving Sequences of Mathematical Programs*. Technical Report SOL 80-15, Systems Optimization Laboratory, November 1980.

7.  M. Strubegger. *User's Guide to the Post Processor of MESSAGE II.* Working Paper WP-84-72, International Institute for Applied Systems Analysis, Laxenburg, Austria, 1984.

8.  H.-H. Rogner, S. Messner, and M. Strubegger. *European Gas Trade: A Quantitative Approach.* WP-84-44, International Institute for Applied Systems Analysis, Laxenburg, Austria, 1984.

# A TRAJECTORY-ORIENTED EXTENSION OF DIDASS AND ITS APPLICATIONS

A. Lewandowski, T. Rogowski and T. Kręglewski
*Institute of Automatic Control, Technical University of Warsaw, Warsaw, Poland*

## 1. INTRODUCTION

The purpose of this paper is to describe recent developments in DIDASS methodology and implementation. The DIDASS system, which is based on the paradigm of satisficing decision making and the theory of multiple criteria optimization, has been the subject of numerous papers and reports. The principles of the method and selected applications were presented by Grauer et al. (1984).

The existing versions of DIDASS are oriented towards decision problems in which the quality of a particular decision can be characterized by a vector. In many practical problems, however, the system behavior has to be described by a set of trajectories and the goal of the decision maker is to ensure that these trajectories have the proper shape. DIDASS methodology can be successfully applied in this case, see e.g. Grauer et al. (1982), and standard software (Lewandowski, 1982; Kręglewski, 1983) can be used for this purpose. However, the existing software was not designed to be used for trajectory optimization. This causes some technical problems in the manipulation of the reference trajectories and the interpretation of the results. For these reasons a new version of DIDASS was developed which makes the reference - trajectory decision analysis much simpler. This paper describes both the new version of DIDASS and the application of this software to a flood control problem.

## 2. TRAJECTORY - ORIENTED EXTENSION OF DIDASS (T-DIDASS)

The core of T-DIDASS consists of the standard software already used in the non-trajectory version. The special feature of the new version lies in the modified user-computer interface. The interaction module was extended - new trajectory definition and trajectory interpretation modules were implemented. These allow us to define any group of performance vector components as a trajectory; the only restriction is concerned with the name of the trajectory - all components of the same trajectory have to be identified by a unique sequence of alphanumeric characters. This must be taken into account when creating the description file.

The syntax of the trajectory definition command is straightforward:

TRJ {Sequence of trajectory names}.

The trajectory interpretation module is menu-driven. This module makes it possible to display selected trajectories, and modify the reference trajectory and other data (e.g. scaling factors) in a simple way. Selected trajectories can be plotted using low-resolution graphics terminals. The structure of the extended system is presented in Fig. 1.

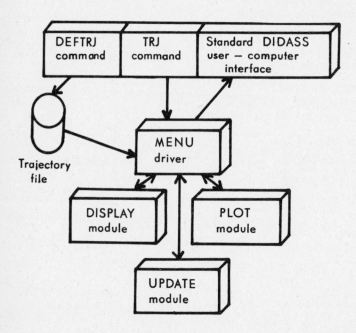

Fig. 1. Structure of the trajectory-oriented extension of DIDASS

The basic difficulty is connected with the calculation of the utopia trajectory. This is caused by the large number of trajectory components - if there are N trajectories, each characterized by n components, it is necessary to perform nN single optimization runs in order to calculate the utopia trajectory. This is usually more than in the non-trajectory case - in practical problems the number of runs can vary between 10-1000. Therefore it is necessary to use some approximation procedure.

Unfortunately there is still no proper approximation procedure.

Some ad-hoc methods have been proposed; one of the most straightforward of these consists of the following steps:

- divide the trajectory into m equal segments;
- select a segment $S_i$, $1 < i < m$;
- treat all of the components of the trajectory that lie outside $S_i$
  as free variables (this is easily done using standard DIDASS
  mechanisms);
- for all components within $S_i$ select a reference point equal to infinity;
- repeat this sequence for all segments and all trajectories.

    Using this procedure it is only necessary to perform N·n/m opti-
mization runs.

    Nothing is known about the accuracy of approximation, so some
numerical experiments were carried out. These experiments show that
for n/m in the range 2-5, the approximation error varies between 0-30%.
In most practical cases this provides sufficient information about the
properties of the problem.


3.  FLOOD CONTROL PROBLEM

    The software described above and the DIDASS methodology were used
for decision support in a flood control problem. The structure of the
system under study is presented in Fig. 2. This is a simplified sub-
system of the upper Vistula river in Poland.

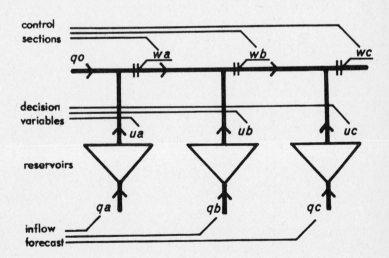

Fig. 2.  Structure of the river network.

The system consists of 3 general-purpose reservoirs supplying water to the main river reach. The goal of the system dispatcher is to operate the reservoirs (by speeding-up or delaying the flood peak on each river) such that the flood peaks on the main river do not coincide. In other words, the flood peaks in the control sections on the main river should be minimized.

It is evidently possible to formulate the above problem as a single-criterion optimization problem. Computational experiments show, however, that the resulting solution is usually not acceptable to the system dispatcher. This is because the height of the flood peak is not the only quality factor which must be taken into account. A number of other factors, some of which are very difficult to formalize, also play an essential role in the decision process. Therefore the system operator formulates his goals in terms of trajectory shape rather than performance index. In addition, a natural ordering can be introduced in the trajectory space - a small flood is evidently better than a large one. Thus the DIDASS methodology seems to be an ideal tool for solving this problem.

## 4. APPLICATION OF DIDASS METHODOLOGY TO A FLOOD CONTROL PROBLEM

The basic difficulty in applying DIDASS in this case is due to the complexity of the flood transient model.

It is shown in the literature that this process can be described with satisfactory accuracy by the following linear PDE of parabolic type (Cunge, 1980):

$$\frac{\partial Q_i}{\partial t} + C_i \frac{\partial Q_i}{\partial x} = D \frac{\partial^2 Q_i}{\partial x^2} \quad . \tag{1}$$

This can be derived from the Saint-Venant equation. In the equation above $Q_i$ denotes the water discharge in the i-th river reach. We also have the following set of boundary conditions:

$q_a$ - inflow to the system,
$u_a, u_b, u_c$ - release of water from reservoirs (decision variables).

The continuity equations in each node of the river must also be formulated.

The differential equations describing the reservoirs are straightforward:

$$\frac{dx_i}{dt} = q_i - u_i \quad , \tag{2}$$

where $x_i$ denotes the amount of water stored in reach i

$q_i$ denotes the inflow to the reservoir,

$u_i$ denotes the outflow from the reservoir.

In order to use DIDASS methodology to solve the problem, it is necessary to formulate the discrete-time equivalent of the system equations and the corresponding LP problem.

Unfortunately it is not possible to use the finite difference technique to transform the differential equations (1), (2) into their discrete-time equivalents. Due to accuracy and stability limitations, the maximum admissible discretization step for equation (1) is approximately 15 minutes of real time, while the time horizon is equal to 360 hours. The 15 minute time step would result in an LP problem with an unacceptable number of variables and constraints.

It is possible to overcome this problem by utilizing the superposition principle and the linearity of the equations.

Let $Q_{wi}(t)$ denote the water discharge at the control point (Fig.2). Because the system equations are linear the following decomposition is possible:

$$Q_{wi}(t) = Q_{wi}(t) + Q_{wi}^a(t) + Q_{wi}^b(t) + Q_{wi}^c(t) \qquad , \qquad (3)$$

where $Q_{wi}(t)$ is the solution of the system equations with $u_a(t) \equiv 0$,
$u_b(t) \equiv 0$, $u_c(t) \equiv 0$, nonzero initial conditions and
predicted $q_o(t)$,

$Q_{wi}^a(t)$ is the solution of the system equations with zero initial
conditions, $q_o(t) \equiv 0$, $u_b(t) \equiv 0$ and $u_c(t) \equiv 0$.

The other components of the formula can be defined in a similar way.

Making use of the following approximation

$$u_a(t) = \sum_{k=1}^{n} u_a(t_k)\phi_k(t) \qquad , \qquad (4)$$

where

$$\phi_k(t) = \begin{cases} 1 & \text{if } t \in |t_k, \ t_{k+1}) \\ 0 & \text{if } t \notin |t_k, \ t_{k+1}) \end{cases} \qquad ,$$

the solution is given by the formula

$$Q_{wi}^a(t) = \sum_{k=1}^{n} u_a(t_k)Q_{wik}^a(t) \qquad , \qquad (5)$$

where $Q_{wik}^a(t)$ is the solution of the system equations under the same conditions used to calculate $Q_{wi}^a$, but with $u_a(t) = \phi_k(t)$. We are interested only in the values of $Q_{wi}$ at discrete instants of time, and therefore the above formulas can be represented in matrix form:

$$\underline{Q}_{wi} = \underline{Q}_{wi} + A_q^i \underline{u}_a + B_q^i \underline{u}_b + C_q^i \underline{u}_c \quad , \tag{6}$$

where

$$\underline{u}_a = \{u_a(t_k)\}_{k=1}^n$$

$$\underline{u}_b = \{u_b(t_k)\}_{k=1}^n$$

$$\underline{u}_c = \{u_c(t_k)\}_{k=1}^n$$

$$\underline{Q}_{wi} = \{Q_{wi}(t_k)\}_{k=1}^n \quad .$$

The matrices $A_q^i$, $B_q^i$, $C_q^i$ can be derived from the above formulas. In practice the simulation program is used to calculate the elements of the matrices in (6); this can be done off-line because the parameters of the system remain constant during the interaction process. The same principle can be used for discretizing the reservoir equations (2):

$$\underline{x}_i = A_x^i \underline{q}_i - B_x^i \underline{u}_i \tag{7}$$

where $\underline{x}_i = \{x_i(t_k)\}_{k=1}^n \quad .$

Equations (6) constitute the objective rows; equations (7) with the additional constraints

$$\underline{x}_{i\ min} \leq \underline{x}_i < \underline{x}_{i\ max} \tag{8}$$

$$\underline{u}_{i\ min} \leq \underline{u}_i < \underline{u}_{i\ max} \tag{9}$$

constitute the set of LP constraints.

In practical applications the trajectories were calculated at 10 time points; the resulting LP matrix therefore consists of 60 columns, 30 objective rows and 60 bounds. The small size of the problem and the low density of the matrix made it possible to solve the problem using a microcomputer comparable with the IBM-PC.

The structure of the DIDASS-based flood control system is presented in Fig. 3.

The system was demonstrated during experimental sessions at the conference on Plural Rationality and Interactive Decision Making; selected numerical results are presented later in this volume.

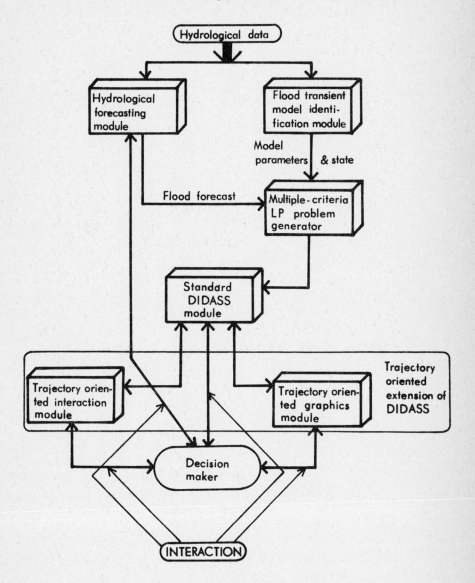

Fig. 3. Outline of the DIDASS-based flood control system

## 5. CONCLUSIONS

The methodology presented in this paper can also be applied to other systems governed by partial or ordinary differential equations. The only restriction is that these equalities should be linear. A specialized matrix generator for solving such problems is currently being implemented.

Experience has shown that graphical presentation of the results is necessary for successful application of the DIDASS methodology to dynamic problems. The resolution obtained using a standard terminal is not good enough, and we are therefore looking into the possibility of using a microcomputer with high-resolution color graphics as a working station for solving dynamic DIDASS problems. Work on the development of such a working station is currently in progress.

This work was done jointly by the International Institute for Applied Systems Analysis in Laxenburg, Austria, and the Institute of Automatic Control, Technical University of Warsaw, Poland.

## REFERENCES

1.  J.A. Cunge, F.M. Holy and A. Vervey. *Practical Aspects of Computational River Hydraulics*. Pitman Advanced Publishing Program, 1980.
2.  M. Grauer, A. Lewandowski and A. Wierzbicki. DIDASS - Theory, implementation and experiences. In M. Grauer and A. Wierzbicki, eds., *Interactive Decision Making*. Proceedings of an International Workshop on Interactive Decision Analysis and Interpretative Computer Intelligence, Lecture Notes in Economics and Mathematical Systems, Vol. 229, Springer-Verlag, 1984.
3.  M. Grauer, A. Lewandowski and L. Schrattenholzer. The generation of efficient energy supply strategies using multiple-criteria optimization. Proceedings of the 6th European Meeting on Cybernetics and Systems Research, Austrian Society for Cybernetic Studies, Vienna, Austria, 1982.
4.  T. Kręglewski and A. Lewandowski. MM-Minos - an integrated interactive decision support system. CP-83-63, International Institute for Applied Systems Analysis, Laxenburg, Austria, 1983.
5.  A. Lewandowski. A program package for linear multiple criteria reference point optimization. WP-82-80, International Institute for Applied Systems Analysis, Laxenburg, Austria, 1982.

# DECISION SUPPORT BASED ON THE SKELETON METHOD –
# THE HG PACKAGE

H. Górecki[1], G. Dobrowolski[2], T. Ryś[2], M. Więcek[1] and M. Żebrowski[2]
[1] *Institute for Control and Systems Engineering, Academy of Mining and Metallurgy, Cracow, Poland*
[2] *Systems Research Department of the Institute for Control and Systems Engineering and of the Institute for Industrial Chemistry, Cracow, Poland*

INTRODUCTION

Decision analysis in the area of multiobjective resource allocation calls for decision support based on specially devised software. Such is the case presented here. The necessary condition for development of such software is a thorough identification of decision environment so that the following is assured:

- software is tailored to fulfil the demand of a decision process,
- a user obtains clearly defined decision analysis support and is conscious of its advantage and limitations (the prime goal of this paper is to illustrate it).

Consider the following elements involved in the decision process:
- a model of the system to which resources are to be allocated,
- estimates of the availability of the resources,
- a decision maker, who tries to attain a satisfactory concordance between the first two elements.

It is assumed that for the moment the model is an adequate representation of reality. Meanwhile information about resources and expectations is a mixture obtained from various sources (like forecasts, experts' evaluations etc.) and therefore charged with uncertainty.

A step-wise process conducted by the decision maker should lead towards attaining the concordance. A single step of this process consists in validation of the resource estimates with respect to the model through solving a multiobjective optimization problem (MOP) followed by an appropriate analysis of results. Such a decision process was applied to the development analysis in the chemical industry and was presented in [ 1, 2 ]. These papers also contain methodological remarks about the arrangement of the whole decision process.

Let us, for the sake of simplicity, describe the above process with the help of a commonly understandable example. There are two critical resources in the process of implementation of a new technology: investment and completion time, which constitute a two-dimensional objective space (see Fig. 1). Now we ask experts (or a decision maker) how they estimate these two objectives. There cannot be an exact answer. This means that they cannot locate the desired point in the objective space. Instead of that it is natural to get lower and upper approximations of the resources in question. Lower approximation on investment may result from feasibility studies while the upper one may represent the decision maker's investment ability or willingness. In the case of time, the lower limit may result from identification of market competition (the sooner the better) while the upper one may represent an estimate of completion time. The above example shows that all we can expect as a representation of the resources availability in the objective space is a rectangle with uncertain boundaries. Although preferences of the decision maker are expressed, of course, by the choice of objectives and constraints in the model, it is necessary to formulate an achievement function which can differ solutions located inside the rectangle named an admissible demanded set (ADS) (see Fig. 1).

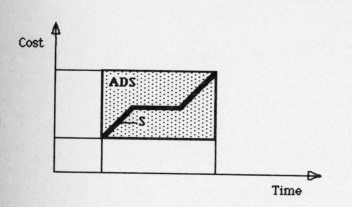

Fig. 1.   Admissible Demanded Set (ADS)
          and Skeleton Set (S).

The paper presents a software tool for supporting the decision maker in a situation as exemplified. The package is based on the so-called Skeleton Method introduced by Górecki [3] and then developed by Dobrowolski et al. [1]. The current version of the package deals with linear models. An extension to nonlinear problem has been investigated in [6] and the resulting procedures are to be embedded in a forthcoming implementation.

# THE CORE OF THE METHOD

This section contains only this information about the Skeleton Method which is important for the implementation of the HG-package.

## Definition 1.

The MOP under consideration is as follows * :

$$\min \; Fx$$
$$x \in X^o$$
$$X^o \; = \; \left\{ x \in R^n : Ax \leqslant b \right\} \tag{1}$$

where:

$b \in R^m$ ,

A - real valued $m \times n$ matrix,

F - real valued $k \times n$ matrix.

## Definition 2.

The (optimal) compromise set in the Pareto sense for the problem (1) is denoted by $Q$ .

## Definition 3.

A set $D \subset R^k$ (a rectangular parallelepiped) constructed as a Cartesian product of closed intervals as follows:

$$D \; = \; \mathop{X}\limits_{i=1}^{k} \; \left[ l_i^o \, , \, u_i^o \right] \tag{2}$$

where:

$l_i^o$, $u_i^o$, $i = 1, \ldots, k$ , are the coordinates of the points $l^o$ , $u^o$ respectively,

will be called an admissible demanded set (ADS).

$l^o$ , $u^o$ express lower and upper estimates of the availability of resources, which are represented by the objectives in problem (1).

## Definition 4.

The Skeleton $S_D$ of the set $D$ is the set of points in $D$ which

(i) belong to the set $E$ of locally equidistant points

$$E \; = \; \left\{ s \in D : \; \exists \, p,q \in \partial D, \; p \neq q : \; \| s - p \| \; = \; \| s - q \| \; = \right.$$

$$= \; \min_{z \in \partial D} \; \| s - z \|$$

where $\| \cdot \|$ is the Euclidean norm in $R^k$ ; $\partial D$ is the boundary of $D$ ;

(ii) form a broken line joining the edge points $l^o$ , $u^o$ .

---------------

* In the case of maximization of one of the objectives, the usual trick - sign inversion can be applied to satisfy the notation of this section.

<u>Construction of the skeleton $S_D$.</u> The skeleton consists of  2k-1  segments and in order to construct it,  2k-2  breaking points have to be computed.

1. Let us assign:

$$d_i = \frac{u_i^o - l_i^o}{2} ; \quad i = 1,\ldots,k$$

2. Let us reorder the set of  $d_i$ ,  i = 1,...,k  so that a new index  j  increases along with increasing values of  $d_j$ ,  j = 1,...,k.

3. Starting from  $l^o$,  $u^o$  the following equations allow for consequent computation of pairs of opposite breaking points.

$$
\left.
\begin{aligned}
l_i^{j+1} &= l_i^j + d_{j+1}\\
u_i^{j+1} &= u_i^j - d_{j+1}
\end{aligned}
\right\}
\qquad \text{for } i > j , \ j = 0,\ldots,k\text{-}2
$$

$$
\left.
\begin{aligned}
l_i^{j+1} &= l_i^j\\
u_i^{j+1} &= u_i^j
\end{aligned}
\right\}
\qquad \text{for } i \leqslant j
$$

$$(3)$$

The method of constructing the skeleton explains its interesting geometrical feature (see Fig. 2). Computation of a consequent pair of points, using eq. (3) , may be interpreted as a reduction of dimension of the set  D  together with its skeleton  $S_D$ . Then a reduced set is also a rectangular parallelepiped which has its skeleton being an internal part of the skeleton  $S_D$ . Consequently, also a parallel projection of the sets  D  and  $S_D$  on any axes plane gives a rectangle and a skeleton, satisfying construction as above.

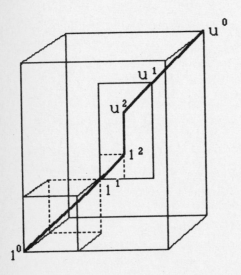

Fig. 2. The skeleton in three-dimensional
         objective space.

## Definition 5.

A concept of optimality: a point $x_o$ is called optimal in the sense of the Skeleton Method if:

1. $x_o \in X^o$ is Pareto optimal;

2. $x_o$ lies on the skeleton $S_D$ or locates as close as possible to $S_D$ in the sense of scalarizing function as follows:

$$f(w) = \min_{} \rho \min_i w_i ; \sum_{i=1}^{k} w_i - \varepsilon \sum_{i=1}^{k} w_i \qquad (4)$$

where:

$$w_i = (Fx)_i - s_i ; \quad i = 1,\ldots,k \text{ and } s \in S_D ;$$
$$\rho \geq k \text{ and } \varepsilon \geq 0 \text{ are parameters.}$$

The scalarizing function (4) was proposed by Wierzbicki [5]. A geometrical interpretation of the optimality concept is rather obvious. There are possible four mutual locations of the skeleton set $S_D$ and the point $x_o$ belonging to the optimal compromise set $Q$ :

1. $x_o$ is an intersection point of $Q$ and $S_D$ and is a desired solution;

2. There is no intersection between $Q$ and $S_D$ and

   (a) $x_o$ lies in $D$ - $x_o$ as an edge point of $Q$ is a desired solution;

   (b) $x_o$ lies "under" $D$ in the objective space and is an unattainable solution;

   (c) $x_o$ lies "above" $D$ and is a surplus solution.

Due to features of the scalarizing function and a fact that the set $Q$ is a weak-convex, plane-wise surface, a case when $x_o$ lies at the edge of $Q$ may be recognized by examination of values of $w_i$ , $i = 1,\ldots,k$ in eq. (4).


AN APPLICATION TO DECISION ANALYSIS PROCESS

The intention of this section is to locate the method in the context of a decision analysis process and to show what are its properties and implications. A more extended discussion of this subject goes beyond the scope of this paper and will be done separately.

We shall illustrate it with a case when ADS is attainable and for the sake of simplicity the problem discussed below is two-dimensional.

Let us start with the following remarks and observations referring to the Skeleton Method.

1. The Skeleton Method opens a possibility to search for a solution of
   the multiobjective allocation problem in the situation when resources are established as objectives and their availability is given by
   lower and upper estimates. Due to  uncertainty of the estimates the
   method introduces a safety principle based on the skeleton property
   of being equidistant from ADS boundary. The safety principle enables
   also to scalarize the multiobjective problem and to find an unique
   solution to it.
2. The safety principle implies that risk of taking the assumed estimates into consideration is equivalent with regard to the lower as
   well as the upper estimate.
3. The safety principle and consequently the assumed estimates constitute a subjective factor in the Skeleton Method. Another formulation
   of the safety principle may be of course considered but is not implemented  in the HG-package.
4. ADS is in form of a rectangle * with its skeleton located either
   horizontally or vertically (the case of ADS being a square is a
   neutral one).
5. We consider decision problems of resource allocation where the objectives represent either input or output or a combination of input
   and output resources. Therefore we can practically distinguish three
   types of the problems:
   (i)   Substitution analysis of the input resources;
   (ii)  Substitution analysis of the output resources;
   (iii) Efficiency analysis (output vs. input or vice versa).
   It naturally follows that the above cases represent optimization
   problems: (min, min), (max, max) and (max, min) respectively. The
   illustrative example used in the introduction belongs to the first
   type of problems since it discusses possible substitution of time
   and investment.

For further investigation let us focus our attention on the case of efficiency analysis. It may be done with the help of Fig. 3. This figure
shows that a solution obtained according to the safety principle (point
2) is different to a solution found as far as natural preference is
concerned  (point 1).  This natural preference is expressed in terms
of  unit per unit  of measurement of the resources in question.  The

----------------

* In the multidimensional case ADS would be a rectangular
  parallelepiped.

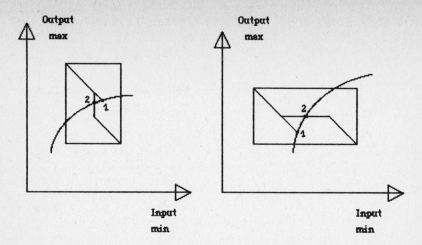

Fig. 3. Influence of the safety principle: 1 - solution according
to natural preference; 2 - solution according to the safety
principle.

safety principle introduces a specific kind of preference and moreover
not the same for a vertical and horizontal location of the skeleton. In
the case of a vertical position we can see that the solution (point 2)
on the vertical section of the skeleton, in comparison with the solution
at point 1, is burdened with preference to the input resource since it
is displaced in a direction favouring minimization. On the contrary, in
the case of the horizontal skeleton preference is given to the output
resource. The remaining sections of the skeleton are neutral with respect to the problem of preference. The safety principle sustains natural preference in the case of locating a solution within these sections.

We can therefore formulate the following remarks and observations in the
course of the decision analysis supported by the Skeleton Method.
1. Estimates of the resources (for the given units of measurement) are
   responsible for the size and the resulting vertical or horizontal position of ADS which introduces through the safety principle a specific kind of preference.
2. The preferred resource is the one which is extremalised in a direction perpendicular to the non-neutral section of the skeleton.
3. Proportions of the estimates of resources and the resulting location
   and shape of the skeleton imply a direction and the extent to which
   preference of the resources will be introduced.

4. Proportions of the estimates bring information about sensitivity of the analysed decision problem with respect to the efficiency ratio and scale of operation [*].

5. In the case when a solution could not be located on the skeleton the nearest point to it would be chosen according to the safety princi- ple. Therefore all the above considerations remain valid.

The above analysis can easily be extended to the remaining two cases referring to the input and output substitution analysis. The interpre- tation in terms of the resources will be obviously different.

All the above considerations can be generalized to the multidimensional case though preference generated by the safety principle becomes more complicated then. This extension together with discussion of methodolo- gical indications for the decision analysis will be done in a separate paper.

The essential point in the course of the decision analysis is that the decision maker should be fully aware of properties of any method he in- tends to use as an aid in a decision process. The considerations pre- sented in this section exemplify the properties and implications of the Skeleton Method.

THE SOLVING ALGORITHM

The algorithm searches for an optimal solution in the sense of defini- tion 5. and consists in solving a sequence of the MOP's (see eq. (1)) scalarized by the function as in eq. (4). Each of the MOP's uses a dif- ferent so-called reference point (described by 's' in eq. (4)), which is the consequent breaking point of the skeleton. The choice of a breaking point is carried out in the course of iteration equation (3). Each time, signs and values of $w_i$ , $i = 1,...,k$ in eq. (4) are checked in order that the mutual position of the actual reference point and the optimal compromise set could be found out and finally the algorithm could be completed.

1. $j = 0$ (index j corresponds to that in eq. (3))
2. Generating the scalarized MOP with $s = 1^j$
3. Simplex algorithm.
4. If $w_i \leq 0$ then go to 5. else stop "1".

----------------

[*] The former is the ratio of output/input, the latter is expressed by magnitude of output. A dual situation may also occur when input is more critical for a decision process.

5. Generating the scalarized MOP with $s = u^j$.
6. Simplex algorithm.
7. If $w_i > 0$ then go to 8. else stop "2".
8. $j = j + 1$
9. Calculation of $l^j$, $u^j$ .
10. While $j \leqslant 2$ then
    modification of the scalarizing function through fixing $w^{j-1}$
    to zero in order to avoid driving out the solution of a sub-
    space of $R^k$ , which corresponds to the currently reduced
    skeleton.
11. go to 1.

Remarks:
1. Such "jumping" choice of the breaking points brings about that a solution obtained in each step of the algorithm is a Pareto-optimal one.
2. For $j = 0$ stop "1" and stop "2" are in effect when an unattainable
   solution or a surplus one is found respectively. For $j > 1$ we have
   a desired solution.
3. In the case of any stop of the algorithm it is possible to make out
   the situation when a solution lies at the edge of the optimal compromise set. It occurs when non-fixed $w_i$ (in step 10.) are not
   equal to each other.


SOFTWARE IMPLEMENTATION


The method of solving the MOP problems described in the preceding section has been implemented as an interactive computer package named HG-
package. The package contains three main modules: Input Manager, Output
Manager and Solver (see Fig. 4). The first two are responsible for communication with a user, the third realizes the algorithm described in
the preceding section with MINOS [4] used as an LP-procedure.


Files used by the HG-package contain (see Fig. 4):
  MPS file - (input) the model under consideration written in
               MPS [4] format. All possible objectives are described
               here in a form of rows of any type. RHS values of these rows
               (if exist) are ignored.
  DICTIONARY file - (input) a cross-reference map between MPS codes and
               a real life description of the model.

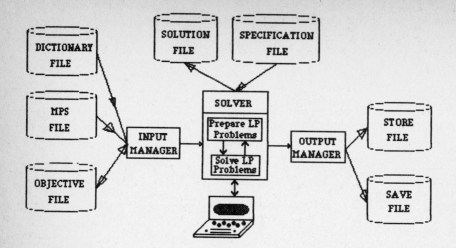

Fig. 4. Functional Structure of the HG-package.

OBJECTIVE file - (input´output) information necessary for a definition
of a current scalarized MOP. There are parameters for the
scalarizing function, MPS codes of objectives with respective directions (min or max) of optimization, ranges of
ADS, and names of RHS and BOUNDS vectors. The file may be
supplied by the user or may be established as well with
the help of Input Manager.

SPECIFICATION file - (input) all necessary parameters for MINOS [4].

SAVE file - (ouput) solutions of the scalarized MOP in a real life description. Each time the user requires to save the current
solution, it is appended to the file.

STORE file - (output) information about the mutual location between
ADS and a solution. It is stored automatically for each
realized MOP.

SOLUTION file - (output) a solution in MPS (MINOS) form which may be
used for an advance analysis.


A session with the HG-package.

A session with the HG-package starts from Input Manager. At this moment
the user has the following possibilities:

- printing all possible objectives. This information is taken from
  DICTIONARY file;
- formulation of the current MOP, it is: choosing a set of objectives,
  rhs vector, bound vector in MPS model and ADS data. If OBJECTIVE
  file exists the above operations may be omitted;

- updating the current set of objectives, it is: changing the set of objectives, updating the ADS data, adding a new objective and deleting an existing one;
- saving an actual set of objectives in OBJECTIVE file.

All possibilities of Input and Output Manager are controlled by a simple command language. If it is necessary, a manual can be printed by a special help command. When the user is sure that the problem is properly formulated, he can quit Input Manager and start Solver.

MPS file is then reformulated according to the currently considered MOP and a resulting LP problem is solved by MINOS as many times as necessary.

When the solving procedure is completed Output Manager is called and the current MOP solution is displayed in the real life description. The following possibilities are then available:
- displaying the solution in the real life description form,
- displaying the solution in a simple graphical form. For each pair from the set of objectives a location of the skeleton of ADS and the optimal solution is displayed,
- saving the solution in SOLUTION file,
- return to Input Manager and preparation of a new experiment,
- termination of the run of the package.

The solution in a numerical as well as a graphical form is cyclically accessible as long as the user needs it.


CONCLUSIONS

The HG-package presented in this paper has been applied to the development analysis in the chemical industry especially to the problem of the comparative study of chemical technologies reported in [2]. Some aspects of the comparative study have been demonstrated at an experimental session and, consequently, will be described in the same volume.

Our experience gained with the above applications shows that the Skeleton Method has a practical value.

Implications of the subjectivity factor in the decision process using the HG-package have been discussed in order to assure a concordance between decision support and a decision maker.

A user's possibility of modelling another safety principle is taken
into account as forthcoming extension, although the significant concordance mentioned above might be weakened.

REFERENCES

1. Dobrowolski G., H. Górecki, J. Kopytowski, M. Żebrowski (1982), The
   Quest for a Concordance Between Technologies and Resources as a
   Multiobjective Decision Process, Multiobjective and Stochastic
   Optimization, pp. 463–475, CP-82-S12, IIASA, Laxenburg, Austria.
2. Dobrowolski G., J. Kopytowski, J. Wojtania, M. Żebrowski (1982/83),
   Alternative Routes from Fossil Resources to Chemical Feedstock, IIASA
   Research Report, IIASA, Laxenburg, Austria (in printing).
3. Górecki H. (1981), Problem of Choice of an Optimal Solution in a
   Multicriterion Space, Proceedings of the VIII triennial World IFAC
   Congress, pp. 106–110, Kyoto, Japan.
4. Murtagh B.A., M. A. Saunders (1980), MINOS/Augmented, Technical Re-
   port SOL-80-14, System Optimization Laboratory, Stanford Univ., USA.
5. Wierzbicki A. (1980), A Mathematical Basis for Satisficing Decision
   Making, WP-80-90, IIASA Laxenburg, Austria.
6. Więcek M. (1983), Polyoptimization in Linear and Nonlinear Problems,
   PH.D. Thesis, Institute for Control and Systems Engineering of the
   Academy of Mining and Metallurgy, Cracow, Poland (in Polish).

# A PRINCIPLE FOR SOLVING QUALITATIVE MULTIPLE-CRITERIA PROBLEMS

Pekka J. Korhonen
*Helsinki School of Economics, Helsinki, Finland*

## 1. Introduction

In many practical applications, the final choice from among discrete alternatives is based on several criteria, which can be quantitative or qualitative. By the term quantitative we mean that the decision-maker is able to present his preferences over alternatives on some cardinal (interval or ratio) scale. If we call a criterion qualitative, we mean that the decision-maker can only express ordinal preferences by stating which of a pair of alternatives he prefers most. Very often the criteria are clustered in such a way that they have a natural hierarchical structure. In any case, we can assume that this kind of hierarchy can be constructed.

As a typical example, we can consider the problem of choosing a computer. We can think that we have found a hierarchical structure for criteria such that, at the lowest level of the hierarchy, we have several concrete criteria (e.g. Response time in interactive mode, Reliability, Disk units, Accounting aids etc.) , which have been refined from the more abstract criteria at the upper level (e.g. Global Performance, Hardware Performance etc.). The abstract criteria are too abstract for evaluation. Therefore the decision-maker needs help for aggregating evaluation information from the concrete criteria into the more abstract criteria. The solution of this problem has been considered more detailed in Roubens (1982) and Korhonen (1984).

Our aim is to develop an interactive approach, which aids a decision-maker to evaluate alternatives on any subset of criteria and to compose information from different evaluations. Initially, the decision-maker evaluates alternatives using the criteria at the basic level. For any criterion, he can give a cardinal scale to describe the strength of his preferencies or he can rank alternatives or he can only make pairwise comparisons between alternatives. Based on that information, we compute the "correlation matrix" to describe interdependencies between criteria. The correlation coefficient is defined for the qualitative criteria, too. The correlation matrix and the criteria hierarchy is the basic information used in aggregation. We aggregate criteria into the next upper level using the modified version of our interactive visual approach (see, Korhonen and Laakso (1984)). As a result, we obtain the correlation matrix between the criteria of the next level and the strength of the preference matrix for each criterion. The strength of the preference matrix describes how strongly the decision-maker prefers one alternative to another on each criterion. We continue until only one criterion is left. Using the strength of the preference matrix for that criterion, we produce the final ranking for alternatives using the model of Bowman and Colantoni (1973). In addition, the strength of the preference matrix can be given as a graph, where the directed edges describe the directions of preferences and the weights of the edges refer to the strengths of preferences.

Several approaches have been developed for solving discrete multiple criteria decision problems: The traditional multiattribute utility theory, (see, e.g. Keeney and Raiffa (1976) and Farquhar (1983)), the analytic hierarchy process (see, e.g Saaty (1980)), the outranking method (see, e.g. Roubens (1982) and Roy (1973)), interactive compromise programming methods (see e.g. Korhonen, Wallenius and Zionts (1984), Zionts (1981)), fuzzy-sets theory (see, e.g. Yager (1981)) and some others (see, e.g. Hinloopen, Nijkamp and Rietveld (1983)). However, most of them have been developed, primarily, to deal with the problems of a small set of quantitative (or ordinal) criteria.

A nice exception is an analytic hierarchy process developed by Saaty (1980). That method is designed to operate on qualitative information, which is transformed into a quantitative form. However, if the number of criteria increases to a quite large extent, the method requires quite a few pairwise comparisons. The analytic hierarchy process is a useful aid in the problems, where we have to find a cardinal scale for all basic criteria.

This paper is in five sections. In the introduction, we outlined the problem and our approach. In section 2, we develop the basic model and in section 3 we extend our model for qualitative criteria. In section 4, we describe our approach and conclusions are presented in section 5.

## 2. Development of the Basic Model

Let us first introduce notation to concisely describe our problem structure. We have n deterministic alternatives $A_j$, $j=1,2,...,n$ and the hierarchy of criteria such that every criterion $C_i^k$, $i=1,2,...,p_k$, at each hierarchy level k, $k=0,1,...,K$ - except at the lowest (basic) level 0 - has been decomposed into a set of criteria at the level k-1: $C_i^k = (C_{m+1}^{k-1}, C_{m+2}^{k-1}, ..., C_{r_i(k)}^{k-1})$, $i=1,2,...,p_k$, $m = r_{i-1}(k)$, when i > 1 and $r_0(k) = 0$. Thus $r_{p_k}(k) = p_{k-1}$. Each criterion is associated with one and only one criterion at the upper level. In this section, we assume that all criteria $C_i^0$, $i=1,2,...,p_0$, are quantitative at the basic level. In the next section we will generalize considerations.

In the sequel, for simplicity, we will use notation C to refer a criterion and notation $C = (C_1, C_2, ..., C_p)$ to refer to its decomposition into p criteria if it is not necessary to specify the level or the index of the criterion. We try to improve readability by avoiding the unnecessary use of indices.

We can suppose that the decision-maker evaluates alternatives using his internal value functions $v_C$ specified for each criterion C, separately. We do not assume the functions $v_C$ to be explicitly known. They are only used in the following theoretical considerations. We suppose that the value functions are additive such that

$$v_C = \mathbf{v}_C{'}\mathbf{b}, \tag{2.1}$$

where $\mathbf{b} = (b_1, b_2, ..., b_p)'$ and $\mathbf{v}_C = (v_{C_1}, v_{C_2}, ..., v_{C_p})'$. Let $\mathbf{y}$ be a vector representing the values of function $v_C^2$ on alternatives $A_j$, $j=1,2,...,n$ and let $X = (\mathbf{x}_1, \mathbf{x}_2, ..., \mathbf{x}_p)$ be a matrix describing the values of functions $v_{C_i}$. Hence, we have $\mathbf{y} = X\mathbf{b}$. We assume that all value functions are to be maximized.

Because $\mathbf{y}$ is an aggregated scale representing all scales $\mathbf{x}_i$, it is natural to assume that $\mathbf{y}$ is so compatible as possible with all scales $\mathbf{x}_i$, $i=1,2,...,p$. To measure the compatibility we use the correlation coefficients $r(\mathbf{y}, \mathbf{x}_i)$, $i=1,2,...,p$. Conflicts between $\mathbf{x}$ variables lead to a multiple criteria formulation for determining $\mathbf{y}$:

$$\max \quad r(\mathbf{y}, \mathbf{x}_i) \ , \ i = 1, 2, \ldots, p$$

subject to $\hspace{8cm}$ (2.2)

$$\mathbf{y} = X\mathbf{b}$$

$\mathbf{b}$ is finite

Without loss of generality, we can assume that the means of $\mathbf{x}$ variables are 0 and $\mathbf{x}_i'\mathbf{x}_i = 1$. Hence, it follows that the mean of $\mathbf{y}$ is 0, too. Let R be the correlation matrix of X, $R = X'X$. If we scale $\mathbf{y}'\mathbf{y} = 1$, so $\mathbf{y}'\mathbf{y} = \mathbf{b}'X'X\mathbf{b} = \mathbf{b}'R\mathbf{b} = 1$. Moreover, $r(\mathbf{y}, \mathbf{x}_i) = \mathbf{y}'\mathbf{x}_i = \mathbf{b}'X'\mathbf{x}_i = \Sigma\, b_j r_{ji}$, where $r_{ji} = r(\mathbf{x}_j, \mathbf{x}_i)$. Thus, we can formulate problem (2.2) for finding the most preferred weights $\mathbf{b}$ as follows:

$$\max \quad \mathbf{u} = R\mathbf{b}$$

subject to $\hspace{8cm}$ (2.3)

$$\mathbf{b}'R\mathbf{b} = 1$$

The vector $\mathbf{u}$, representing the correlations, is an objective vector to be maximized. The vector maximum problem (2.3) has no unique solution. Any nondominated (efficient, Pareto-optimal) solution $\mathbf{u} = R\mathbf{b}$ is an acceptable and reasonable solution for the problem. In this paper, we define the efficient solutions as follows:

**Definition** 1. Solution $\mathbf{u} = R\mathbf{b}$ is efficient (nondominated) iff there is no other feasible solution $\mathbf{u}^* = R\mathbf{b}^* \neq \mathbf{u}$ such that $\mathbf{u}^* \geq \mathbf{u}$.

If $\mathbf{u}$ is dominated by $\mathbf{u}^*$, we denote $\mathbf{u}^* > \mathbf{u}$.

**Lemma** 1. If $\mathbf{x}'A^2\mathbf{x} > 0$ for a p-vector $\mathbf{x}$ and a (pxp) positive semi-definite matrix A, then also $\mathbf{x}'A\mathbf{x} > 0$.

**Proof.** By the spectral decomposition theorem A can be written as

$$A = GLG',$$

where $L = \text{diag}(l_i)$ is a diagonal matrix of eigenvalues of A, and G is an orthogonal matrix whose columns are standardized eigenvectors. Since

$$A^2 = (GLG')^2 = GLG'GLG' = GL^2G',$$

we see that $\mathbf{x}'A^2\mathbf{x} = \mathbf{y}'L^2\mathbf{y} = \Sigma_i l_i^2 y_i^2 > 0$, where $\mathbf{y} = G'\mathbf{x}$. Because A is positive semi-definite, then $l_i \geq 0$ and thus $l_i^2 > 0$ if and only if $l_i > 0$. Hence it follows that $\Sigma_i l_i^2 y_i^2 > 0$ implies $\Sigma_i l_i y_i^2 > 0$. Q.E.D.

**Lemma** 2. (Farkas´ theorem) If A is a (mxn) matrix and **d** is a n-vector, then the statement

$$\mathbf{d}'\mathbf{x} \leq 0 \text{ for all } \mathbf{x} \text{ such that } A\mathbf{x} \leq 0$$

is equivalent to the statement that there exists $\mathbf{v} \geq 0$ such that

$$\mathbf{d} = A'\mathbf{v}.$$

**Proof.** (see e.g. Zoutendijk (1976)).

**Theorem** 1. The solution $\mathbf{u} = R\mathbf{b}$ of the problem (2.3) is nondominated iff $\mathbf{u} \in C = \{\mathbf{u} \mid \mathbf{u} = R\mathbf{b}, \ \mathbf{b} \geq 0\}$.

**Proof.** We first prove sufficiency. Let $\mathbf{u} = R\mathbf{b}$ be an arbitrary solution, $\mathbf{b}'R\mathbf{b} = 1$ and $\mathbf{b} \geq 0$ and let us assume that the problem (2.3) has a solution $\mathbf{u} + \Delta\mathbf{u}$ dominating $\mathbf{u}$, i.e. $\mathbf{u} + \Delta\mathbf{u} > \mathbf{u}$. Thus $\Delta\mathbf{u} \geq 0$ and having at least one strictly positive element. Hence it follows that $\Delta\mathbf{u}'\Delta\mathbf{u} > 0$. Moreover, we denote $\Delta\mathbf{u} = R\Delta\mathbf{b}$. Then

$$(\mathbf{b} + \Delta\mathbf{b})'R(\mathbf{b} + \Delta\mathbf{b}) = \mathbf{b}'R\mathbf{b} + \mathbf{b}'R\Delta\mathbf{b} + \Delta\mathbf{b}'R\mathbf{b} + \Delta\mathbf{b}'R\Delta\mathbf{b}$$
$$= 1 + 2\mathbf{b}'R\Delta\mathbf{b} + \Delta\mathbf{b}'R\Delta\mathbf{b} = 1 + 2\mathbf{b}'\Delta\mathbf{u} + \Delta\mathbf{b}'R\Delta\mathbf{b} > 1,$$

because $\Delta\mathbf{u}'\Delta\mathbf{u} = \Delta\mathbf{b}'R^2\Delta\mathbf{b} > 0$ implies $\Delta\mathbf{b}'R\Delta\mathbf{b} > 0$ by Lemma 1 and the term $\mathbf{b}'\Delta\mathbf{u} \geq 0$, because $\mathbf{b} \geq 0$ and $\Delta\mathbf{u} \geq 0$ by assumption. Hence, it follows that we cannot find a solution $\mathbf{u} + \Delta\mathbf{u}$ dominating $\mathbf{u}$. Because $\mathbf{u}$ was an arbitrary solution, $\mathbf{u} = R\mathbf{b}$ is a nondominated solution.

To prove necessity, we show that $\mathbf{u} = R\mathbf{b}$ is dominated if $\mathbf{u} \notin C$. We apply Farkas´ theorem (Lemma 2) and denote $\mathbf{d} = \mathbf{u}$ and $A = R$. If $\mathbf{u} \notin C = \{\mathbf{u} \mid \mathbf{u} = R\mathbf{b}, \ \mathbf{b} \geq 0\}$, then there exists $\mathbf{x}$ such that $\mathbf{u}'\mathbf{x} > 0$ and $R\mathbf{x} \leq 0$. $R\mathbf{x} < 0$, because $\mathbf{u}'\mathbf{x} = \mathbf{b}'R\mathbf{x} > 0$. By choosing $\Delta\mathbf{b} = -\mathbf{x}$, we can see that $\mathbf{u}'\Delta\mathbf{b} < 0$ and $R\Delta\mathbf{b} > 0$ and

$$(\mathbf{b} + t\Delta\mathbf{b})'R(\mathbf{b} + t\Delta\mathbf{b}) = \mathbf{b}'R\mathbf{b} + 2t\mathbf{b}'R\Delta\mathbf{b} + t^2\Delta\mathbf{b}'R\Delta\mathbf{b} = 1,$$

when

$$t = 0 \text{ or } t = -2\mathbf{b}'R\Delta\mathbf{b}/\Delta\mathbf{b}'R\Delta\mathbf{b} > 0.$$

Hence it follows that we can find the solution $\mathbf{u} + \Delta\mathbf{u} = R(\mathbf{b} + t\Delta\mathbf{b})$, $\Delta\mathbf{u} = tR\Delta\mathbf{b} > 0$, of the problem (2.3) which dominates $\mathbf{u}$, $(\mathbf{u} + \Delta\mathbf{u}) > \mathbf{u}$. It means that $\mathbf{u} = R\mathbf{b}$ is not a nondominated solution. Q.E.D.

**Remark** 1. All reasonable aggregated scales can be found by using nonnegative weights.

**Remark** 2. If R is non-singular, a solution is always dominated, if any of weights is negative. In this case **b**, $b=R^{-1}u$, is uniquely determined.

The problem formulation (2.3) gives a general framework to find an aggregated scale at any level. The variable **y** has the same properties as variables $x_i$ have, and therefore different **y** variables $y_j$, j=1,2, ..., $p^y$, can be aggregated in a similar way into a new variable **z** by solving the problem (2.3), where now R is replaced by the correlation matrix $R^y$, $R^y = Y'Y$, Y = ( $y_1$, $y_2$, ..., $y_p$) . The correlation matrix $R^y = (r_{ij}^y)$ can be presented by means of the correlations between **x** variables as follows:

$$r_{ij}^y = y_i'y_j = b_i'X_i'X_jb_j = b_i'R_{ij}b_j \qquad (2.4)$$

where $y_i = X_ib_i$ and $R_{ij}$ is the correlation matrix of $X_i$ and $X_j$.

Generally, the correlation matrix $R^m$ at level m can be introduced from the correlation matrix $R^o$ at level 0 as follows:

$$R^m = B^{m'}R^{m-1}B^m = ... = B^{m'}...B^{1'}R^oB^1...B^m, \qquad (2.5)$$

where a $p_{k-1}$ x $p_k$ matrix $B^k$, k=1,2,...,m, is defined such that

$$B^k = \begin{bmatrix} b_1^k & 0 ... & 0 \\ 0 & b_2^k ... & 0 \\ & ... & \\ 0 & 0 ... & 0 \\ 0 & 0 ... & b_{p_k}^k \end{bmatrix} \qquad (2.6)$$

The column vector $b_i^k$ refer to criteria $C_i^{k-1}$ , i = $r_{i-1}(k)+1$, $r_{i-1}(k)+2$, ..., $r_i(k)$, at level k-1 to be aggregated into criterion $C_i^k$ at level k. We shall denote a $p_o$ x $p_m$ - matrix $B^1B^2...B^m$ by $D^m$, and thus we can see that $D^m$ aggregates the criteria at the basic level into the criteria at level m.

## 3. Model for Qualitative Criteria

In this section we allow some criteria to be qualitative. We assume that the decision-maker is able to make at least pairwise comparisons on all criteria of the basic level. For describing pairwise comparisons, we define an n x n - matrix Z(C) to represent pairwise orderings of the alternatives specified on criterion C:

$$z_{ij}(C) = \begin{cases} 1, & \text{if } A_i(C) > A_j(C) \\ 0, & \text{if } A_i(C) = A_j(C) \\ -1, & \text{if } A_i(C) < A_j(C) \end{cases} \qquad (3.1)$$

$$z_{ii}(C) = 0$$

Notation $A_i(C) > A_j(C)$ means that $A_i$ is ranked higher than $A_j$ on criterion C. Matrix Z(C) is known as an ordering matrix for criterion C. It does not necessarily define a ranking for alternatives.

If it is possible for the decision-maker to find a cardinal scale for criteria, that information it is possible to take into account in the approach. In case of cardinal information we define Z(C) matrices as follows instead of (3.1):

$$z_{ij}(C) = x_i(C) - x_j(C), \quad i,j=1,2,\ldots,n, \qquad (3.2)$$

where $x_i(C)$ refer to the numerical value of the criterion C on alternative $A_j$. As in section 2, we denote by $x_i$ the values of the criterion $C_i$ and $X = (x_1, x_2, \ldots, x_p)$. Now we define the correlation matrix $R^0$ of criteria $C_i^0, i=1,2, \ldots, p_0$, by formula:

$$r_{ij}^0 = \Sigma z_{hm}(C_i^0) \, z_{hm}(C_j^0) \,/(s(C_i^0)s(C_j^0)), \text{ for all } i,j \quad (3.3)$$

where

$$s^2(C_i^0) = \Sigma z^2_{hm}(C_i^0) \quad, i= 1,2, \ldots, p_0.$$

We can show that definition (3.3) leads to the Pearson's product-moment correlation coefficient in case of quantitative criteria.

**Theorem** 2. Let us suppose $C_i$ and $C_j$ are two criteria, which can be evaluated on the cardinal scales $x_i$ and $x_j$. Then the correlation, calculated by formula (3.3), is the Pearson's product-moment correlation of variables $x_i$ and $x_j$.

**Proof.** For the terms $\Sigma\Sigma z_{hm}(C_i)z_{hm}(C_j)$ and $s^2(C_i)$ in formula (3.3) we can introduce the following expressions:

$$\Sigma \ \Sigma \ z_{hm}(C_i)z_{hm}(C_j) = \Sigma \ \Sigma \ (x_{hi} - x_{mi})(x_{hj} - x_{mj})$$

$$= 2(n \ \Sigma \ x_{hi}x_{hj} - (\Sigma \ x_{hi})(\Sigma \ x_{hj}))$$

and

$$s^2(C_i) = \Sigma \ \Sigma \ (x_{hi} - x_{mi})^2 = 2(n \ \Sigma \ x_h^2 - (\Sigma \ x_h)^2).$$

Now we can see that the first term is the cross-product of the variables $x_i$ and $x_j$ multiplied by 2n and the second term is the variance of the variable $x_i$ multiplied by 2n. By assigning the terms to formula (3.3), we get the result immediately. Q.E.D.

**Remark** 3. If the decision-maker can rank alternatives on each criterion and we define matrices Z(C) as in (3.2), where the values of vectors $x$ are ordinal numbers, it leads us to the use of Spearman's rank correlations, because Pearson's correlation coefficient calculated using ordinal numbers is Spearman's rank correlation coefficient.

If the ranking information is presented as in (3.1), so the correlation coefficient $r_{ij}^o$ computed by formula (3.3) is Kendall's rank correlation (cf., e.g. Siegel (1956)).

We denote

$$Q(C_i^o) = Z(C_i^o)/s(C_i^o) \tag{3.4}$$

and generally we define

$$Q(C) = \Sigma_i b_i Q(C_i). \tag{3.5}$$

Because $\Sigma \ q^2{}_{hm}(C_i^o) = 1$, i=1,2, ..., $q_o$, so we can see that

$$r_{ij}^o = \Sigma \ q_{hm}(C_i^o) \ q_{hm}(C_j^o) \tag{3.6}$$

The matrices Q(C) can be interpreted as the strength of preferences. The elements $q_{ij}(C)$ of Q(C) describe how strongly the decision-maker prefers $A_i$ to $A_j$ on criterion C. If $q_{ij}(C) < 0$, so $A_j$ is preferred to $A_i$.

Let C be the highest-level criterion. We determine the final ranking such that it is as compatible as possible with the preference strength matrix Q(C). Let U (by Bowman and Colantoni (1973)) be an n x n - matrix representing any complete, asymmetric pairwise ordering of alternatives (see, also Michaud (1983))

$$u_{ij} = \begin{cases} 1, \text{ if } A_i > A_j , i = j \\ \\ 0, \text{ if } A_i < A_j \end{cases} \qquad (3.7)$$

$$u_{ii} = \qquad 1/2$$

Bowman and Colantoni have proved that matrix U defines a ranking if and only if U is a solution to

$$u_{ij} \qquad\qquad = 0,1 , i \neq j \qquad\qquad (3.8a)$$

$$u_{ij} + u_{ji} \qquad\qquad = 1, \text{for all } i,j = 1,2, \ldots, n \qquad (3.8b)$$

$$u_{hi} + u_{ij} + u_{jh} \quad \leq \quad 2, \text{ for all } i,j,h = 1,2, \ldots, n \quad (3.8c)$$

$$u_{ii} \qquad\qquad = 1/2, \text{ for all } i=1,\ldots,n. \qquad (3.8d)$$

Now we can define the most preferred ranking as a solution to the problem

$$\text{max} \qquad f = \Sigma \, u_{hm}(C) q_{hm}(C) \qquad\qquad (3.9)$$

subject to constraints (3.8a-d).

As a solution to (3.9), we find the ranking maximizing the sum of the strength of preferences, which are consistent with the ranking, i.e. $q_{hm}(C)$ is included in the sum, if $A_h$ is not ranked lower than $A_m$.

Bowman and Colantoni's model (3.9) is also rational for quantitative criteria, i.e. matrices Z(C) are defined by formula (3.2).

**Theorem** 3. Let us assume that criterion $C^k$ is aggregated from the criteria $C_i^0$, $i=1,2,\ldots,p$ using weights $\mathbf{d} = B^1 B^2 \ldots B^k$ and let X = ( $\mathbf{x}_1, \mathbf{x}_2, \ldots, \mathbf{x}_p$) presents the values of criteria $C_i^0$ on alternatives. If we have defined

$$z_{hm}(C_i) = x_{hi} - x_{mi},$$

so the solution U of the model (3.9) ranks the alternatives according to the values of the vector $\mathbf{y} = X\mathbf{d}$.

**Proof.** Without loss of generality, we can assume that the means of $\mathbf{x}$ variables are 0 and $\mathbf{x}_i'\mathbf{x}_i = 1$, $i=1,2,\ldots,p$. Hence we get

$$q_{hm}(C_i^0) = z_{hm}(C_i^0)/s(C_i^0) = (x_{hi} - x_{mi})/(2n) \text{ and}$$

$$q_{hm}(C^k) = \sum_i d_i q_{hm}(C_i^0) = \sum_i d_i(x_{hi} - x_{mi})/(2n) = (y_h - y_m)/(2n).$$

The objective function of the model (3.9) can now be given in form:

$$f = \sum u_{hm} q_{hm} = \sum u_{hm}(y_h - y_m)/(2n).$$

In neglecting constraint (3.9c), it is obvious that f will be maximized, if we choose $u_{hm} = 1$, when $y_h \geq y_m$ and $u_{hm} = 0$, when $y_h < y_m$. Now we can see that u defines a ranking for alternatives and thus also constraint (3.9c) is fulfilled. Moreover, the alternatives are ranked according to the values of **y**. Q.E.D.

**Remark** 4. In the case of quantitative criteria, the aggregated scale for $C^k$ can be found by computing the row (column) sums of matrix $Q(C^k)$. That can also be done if we have operated on an ordinal scale like a cardinal scale.

In some problems it may be more convenient to consider only the preference matrix $Q(C)$, instead of ranking. For example Roy´s outranking method (1973) is a suitable approach for dealing with matrix $Q(C)$. However, a graph presentation for $Q(C)$ is a practical way of presenting to the decision-maker the information of the strengths of preferences and not necessarily dependant on Roy´s method.

### 3. An Approach

We now present the approach in a step-by-step manner followed by comments and detailed explanations after steps. In this section we assume that R is non-singular.

**Step** 1. Ask the decision-maker to compare alternatives on criteria $C_i^0$, i=1, 2, ..., $p_0$. The results of comparisons are presented on either cardinal or ordinal scales when it is possible. In the other case, ask the decision-maker to make pairwise comparisons between alternatives. Build up matrices $Z(C_i^0)$ and $Q_i^0$ and compute the correlation matrix $R^0$ between criteria $C_i^0$ as presented in (3.3).

**Step** 2. Set k=k+1 and solve the problem (2.3) for each criterion $C_i^k$, i=1, 2, ..., $p_k$ for finding the weight vectors $b_i^k$. Using these weights, compute the preference strength matrices $Q_i^k$ as presented in (3.5).

**Step** 3. If $p_k > 1$, compute the correlation matrix $R^k$ according to formula (2.5) and return to step 2. In the other case, present the final preference strength matrix $Q(C^K)$ multiplied by constant t as a directed graph, where the directed edges describe the directions of preferences and the weights of edges are the strength of preferences. The constant t can chosen such that the largest strength of preferences is 1. Solve the final ranking using the model (3.9).

In step 2, we suggest the use of the following interactive procedure for finding the weight vectors $b_i^k$ for each criterion i. The procedure is the modified version of our visual interactive approach to solving the multiple criteria problem (see, Korhonen and Laakso (1984)). We intersperse comments between steps.

## The modified visual interactive procedure

**Step** 1. Solve $b = e'/(e'Re)^{1/2}$, where $e = (1,1,...,1)'$ and compute $u = Rb$.

Thus we will find an efficient solution.

**Step** 2. Present u to the decision maker and ask which correlations he would, primarily, like to increase. Let us I, $I \subset \{1,2,...,p\}$, be an index set referring to those correlations. Construct vector $\Delta u$ such that $\Delta u_i = 1$, if $i \in I$ and $\Delta u_i = 0$, if $i \notin I$.

We use the vector $\Delta u$ as a reference direction vector. If you so wish, the strength of preferences can be taken into account in $\Delta u$, too.

**Step** 3. Compute $(u + \Delta u)'R^{-1}(u + \Delta u) = s^2$ and construct

$$\Delta u^* = (u + \Delta u)/s - u = (u(1-s) + \Delta u)/s.$$

Now the vector $u + \Delta u^*$ is the solution of the model (2.3) ($\Delta b^* = R^{-1}\Delta u^*$), because

$$(u + \Delta u^*)'R^{-1}(u + \Delta u^*) = 1 = (b + \Delta b^*)'R(b + \Delta b^*).$$

**Step** 4. Denote $s^2(t) = (u + t\Delta u^*)'R^{-1}(u + t\Delta u^*)$ and solve the problem:

$$\max_{t} \quad b + t\Delta b^* = (u + t\Delta u^*)'R^{-1} \geq 0.$$

Denote the maximum value by $t_{max}$.

The value $t_{max}$ tells us to what extent it is possible to go along the curve $(u + t\Delta u^*)/s(t)$, $s^2(t) = (u + t\Delta u^*)'R^{-1}(u + t\Delta u^*)$, from the current position $u$ until the solution is no longer efficient.

**Step** 5. Present to the decision-maker the nondominated curve

$$(u + t\Delta u^*)/s(t), \quad t:0 \rightarrow \quad t_{max},$$

where

$$s^2(t) = (u+t\Delta u^*)'R^{-1}(u+t\Delta u^*) \quad = 1+2t(t-1)u'R^{-1}\Delta u^*$$
$$= 1+2t(t-1)((1+u'R^{-1}\Delta u)/s-1),$$

in the graphical mode using the graphical display as described in Korhonen and Laakso (1984). Ask him to choose the most preferred solution and denote the corresponding value of t by $t_0$. Set $u = (u + t_0\Delta u^*)/s(t_0)$ and return to step 2, if $t_0 > t$. If $t_0 = t$, ask the decision-maker if he is willing to consider other directions. If the answer is "no", stop; otherwise return to step 2.

If the decision-maker prefers the solution with value $t_{max}$, we can continue from this position by setting the corresponding $\Delta b_i = 0$ and computing a new $\Delta u$ for transformed $\Delta b$.

Using the above procedure we find the weight vectors $B^k = (b_1^k, b_2^k, \ldots, b_{p_k}^k)$ and can calculate the matrices $Q_i^k$, $i=1,2,\ldots,p_k$. In step 3 we compute the correlation matrix $R^k$ by $R^k = B^{k\prime}R^{k-1}B^k$, if $p_k > 1$. If $p_k = 1$, we have achieved the top level, and we can find the final ranking to alternatives by solving the model (3.9).

In some problems it may be more convenient to consider only the preference matrix Q(C), instead of ranking. For example Roy´s outranking method (1973) is a suitable approach for dealing with matrix Q(C). However, a graph presentation for Q(C) is a practical way of presenting to the decision-maker the information of the strengths of preferences and not necessarily dependant on Roy´s method.

## 5. Conclusion

In this paper we have described a method, which helps the decision-maker to find the most preferred ranking for alternatives, which are evaluated on several qualitative or quantitative criteria with a hierarchical structure. We assumed that the decision-maker is able to make at least pairwise comparisons between alternatives on each criterion. That information was used for computing the intercorrelations between criteria, which is the basic information for aggregation.

The interactive method helps to aggregate information from the criteria of the basic level step by step until we reach the criterion of the highest level. As a result, we find the matrix of the most preferred preference strength matrix, which is used to find the final ranking by means of the model of Bowman and Colantoni.

The aggregation procedure is easy to implement on a microcomputer and it is efficient. In the contrary, the solving of the model of Bowman and Colantoni requires the capacity of a big computer even for quite a small problem. However, a fairly good approximation for finding the final ranking, and which is exact for quantitative criteria, is to determine it by means of the row sums of the most preferred preference strength matrix.

## References

**Bowman, V. and C. Colantoni** (1973), "Majority Rule under Transitivity Constraints", <u>Management Science</u>, Vol. 19, No. 9, pp. 1029-1041.

**Dyer, J. and R. Sarin** (1979), "Group Preference Aggregation Rules Based on Strength of Preference," <u>Management Science</u>, Vol. 25, No. 9, pp. 822-832.

**Farquhar, P.** (1983), "Research Directions in Multiattribute Utility Analysis," in Hansen, P. (ed.): <u>Essays and Surveys on Multiple Criteria Decision Making</u>, Springer-Verlag, pp. 63-85.

**Hinloopen, E., P. Nijkamp and P. Rietveld** (1983),"The Regime Method: A New Multicriteria Technique," in Hansen, P. (ed.): Essays and Surveys on Multiple Criteria Decision Making, Springer-Verlag, pp. 146-155.

**Keeney, R. and H. Raiffa** (1976), Decisions with Multiple Objectives, Wiley.

**Kendall, M.** (1962), Rank Correlation Methods, 3rd. ed., Hafner, New York.

**Korhonen, P. and M. Soismaa** (1981), "An Interactive Multiple Criteria Approach to Ranking Alternatives," Journal of Operational Research Society, Vol. 32, pp. 577-585.

**Korhonen, P., J. Wallenius and S. Zionts** (1984), "Solving the Discrete Multiple Criteria Problem Using Convex Cones", Forthcoming in Management Science.

**Korhonen, P. and J. Laakso** (1984), "A Visual Interactive Method for Solving the Multiple Criteria Problem," Forthcoming in European Journal of Operational Research.

**Korhonen, P.** (1984), "A Hierarchical Interactive Method for Ranking Alternatives with Multiple Qualitative Criteria," Forthcoming in European Journal of Operational Research.

**Michaud, P.** (1983), "Opinions Aggregation," in Janssen, J., J.-F. Marcotorchino and J.-M. Proth (eds.): New Trends in Data Analysis and Applications, North-Holland.

**Roubens, M.** (1982), "Preference Relations on Actions and Criteria in Multicriteria Decision Making," European Journal of Operational Research, Vol. 10, pp. 51-55.

**Roy, B.** (1973), "How Outranking Relation Helps Multicriteria Decision Making," in Cochran, J. and M. Zeleny (eds.): Multiple Criteria Decision Making, University of South Carolina Press, Columbia, SC, pp. 179-201.

**Saaty, T.** (1980), The Analytic Hierarchy Process, McGraw-Hill.

**Siegel, S.** (1956), Nonparametric Statistics for the Behavioral Sciences, McGraw-Hill, New York.

**Yager, R.** (1981), "A New Methodology for Ordinal Multiobjective Decisions Based on Fuzzy Sets," Decision Sciences, Vol. 12.

Zionts, S. (1981), "A Multiple Criteria Method for Choosing Among Discrete Alternatives," European Journal of Operational Research, Vol. 7, pp. 143-147.

Zoutendijk, G. (1976), Mathematical Programming Methods, North-Holland Publishing Company.

# A DECISION SUPPORT SYSTEM FOR PLANNING AND CONTROLLING AGRICULTURAL PRODUCTION WITH A DECENTRALIZED MANAGEMENT STRUCTURE

Marek Makowski and Janusz Sosnowski

*Systems Research Institute, Polish Academy of Sciences, Warsaw, Poland*

## 1. INTRODUCTION

This paper presents some work done by the authors as part of a project aimed at the construction of a model of Polish agriculture [1]. The project has been undertaken by an interdisciplinary team composed of researchers from the Systems Research Institute, the Institute of Agricultural Economy, the Institute for Rural and Agricultural Development, in close cooperation with the State Planning Commission and the Ministry of Agriculture. The project represents a joint case study performed with the cooperation of the Food and Agriculture Program and the System and Decision Sciences Program of the International Institute for Applied Systems Analysis. Due to limitations on the size of the paper, only a brief outline is presented here. Details of the research may be found in [1],[2],[3].

## 2. BACKGROUND AND STRUCTURE OF THE PROBLEM

The institutional and technical context described below is crucial for understanding the problem.

Poland has a centrally planned economy. Therefore basic decisions (for example, on the annual socioeconomic plan, setting prices, interest rates, taxes, control of foreign trade) are made by central authorities forming the *decision center* (the Sejm (Parliament), Government, State Planning Commission, Ministry of Agriculture, the central committees of political parties and the main administrative institutions).

Polish agriculture has a diversified structure. It is composed of about 3 million units (farms) which are independent in their economic activity and self-managed. Over 70% of agricultural land is privately owned. Under the new economic system cooperative and state farms also enjoy independence in management.

The problem of direct versus indirect control of economic activities in a centrally planned economy within the context of Polish Agriculture is discussed in [1] and [4]. In current practice, profit-oriented motives are used as the basic instrument for controlling agricultural production. The decision center is able to control both the production pattern and use of inputs more efficiently by setting prices and, if necessary, quotas than by any administrative measures (e.g. setting production targets).

Keeping in mind the context summarized above, we used the following approach to construct a decision support system for planning and control of agricultural production:

1.  Producers are divided into 5 groups, each one (called a sector) being composed of producers with similar technological and behavioral characteristics. It is assumed that producers behave in a rational way, i.e. given the prices of all products and inputs, the technological constraints, and available inputs, the producers are assumed to choose a production plan for each sector which would maximize their own goal function. An LP model has been constructed and verified for each sector (see Sec. 3).

2.  The agricultural production model (APM) is composed of sectoral models with appropriate linking conditions (see Sec. 4). The APM may be used by a decision center to assess the overall agricultural potential. In other words, it is possible, for assumed resources (inputs) and recognized overall goals, to determine a desired (and feasible) pattern and level of production and use of inputs for each sector.

3.  Having decided on an overall plan, it is necessary to determine the economic instruments (mainly prices) that would enable parametric control of agricultural producers (see Sec. 5). The set of prices should ensure that while maximizing his own income each producer would choose a production pattern consistent with overall plan adopted by the decision center.

3.  MODELS OF SECTORAL PRODUCTION

Keeping in mind the assumptions discussed in the previous section, we construct sectoral production models in the following form:

For each sector i (i = 1,2,..5) find an activity level (production pattern and use of production inputs) $x_i \in R^n$ such that the producer's income is maximized:

$$c \cdot x_i \rightarrow max \qquad (1)$$

$$A_i x_i \leq b_i \qquad (2)$$

$$l_i \leq x_i \leq h_i \qquad (3)$$

where:  c  - given vector of prices for products and inputs,

$A_i$ - matrix of fixed coefficients for technical constraints,

$b_i$ - vector of available local inputs and resources (land, labour, etc).

Lower (if non-zero) and upper bounds for some activities may correspond to the behavioral characteristics of the producers.  Lower bounds might be used for production targets for selected products, if required. Upper bounds may also reflect limits on available resources or quotas (see Sec. 5).

Sectoral models form the basis for constructing a set of admissible solutions for agricultural output as a whole.  Therefore a lot of effort has been put into the construction and verification of those models by an interdisciplinary team.

## 4.  THE AGRICULTURAL PRODUCTION PLANNING MODEL

Let us start by defining the admissible solution set for overall agricultural production.  The set is defined by sectoral technical constraints together with linking constraints and may be written as:

$$A_i x_i \leq b_i \qquad i = 1,2,..5 \qquad (4)$$

$$\sum_{i=1}^{5} B_i x_i \leq d \qquad (5)$$

where constraints (5) correspond to limitations on the availability of production inputs for agriculture as a whole (the latter are defined by vector d, whereas the matrices $B_i$ are composed of elements which are equal to one or to zero).  Appropriate constraints (3) are also included.

The structure of the admissible set for 3 sectors is illustrated in Figure 1.

Problems in agriculture are a specific feature of the current situation in Poland because of the imbalance between the supply of agricultural products and the demand for these goods.  Food consumption accounts for nearly 60% of the consumers' income.  The shortfall in the means of production (especially machinery and equipment, pesticides and concentrated feeds) stands in the way of increased agricultural production.  Therefore, and due to the institutional context described in Sec. 2, it is hardly possible to define a single objective that could be used for the selection of a feasible solution for overall agricultural planning.  Usually it is necessary to deal with several objectives, such as level of production of certain goods (others may be aggregated), level of use of selected inputs, balance of foreign trade

in competitive agricultural products, and agricultural incomes.  The
set of criteria chosen (and its precise definition) depends on the
user of the model and on the particular purpose to which the model is
being put.  Therefore a flexible software structure is necessary to
allow easy definition of the criteria set and easy modification of the
constraints set (selected variables may be either constrained or fixed
in different runs).

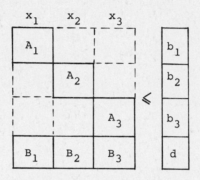

Figure 1.  The structure of constraints for the overall problem.


The multicriteria nature of the problem makes it necessary to
choose an appropriate methodology.  After examination of all possible
approaches the reference point (aspiration level) approach proposed by
A. Wierzbicki (see [5]) has been adopted.

The aspiration level approach is now widely known, and therefore
only a brief description will be given here.  Let vector q

$$q = \sum_{i=1}^{5} Q_i x_i \tag{6}$$

be a set of criteria (matrix $Q_i$ contains fixed weight coefficients).
A decision center selects an initial aspiration level $\bar{q}$ (which may be
attainable or non-attainable) and may attach weight coefficients to
each criterion (weights not defined are assumed to be equal to one).
With the help of an achievement function (see [7]) the problem is con-
verted into the equivalent LP problem.  The resulting solution is the
non-dominated (Pareto-optimal) point, in criteria space, which is
nearest (in the sense of a norm corresponding to a given achievement
function) to $\bar{q}$ if $\bar{q}$ is nonattainable (i.e. if the aspiration level is
too high) or is furthest from $\bar{q}$ if the aspiration level is too low.
The corresponding decisions are computed at the same time.  Having

obtained a solution, the decision center may change an aspiration level and/or the weights attached to some criteria and repeat the procedure until an acceptable solution is found.

## 5. CONTROLLING SECTORAL PRODUCTION

The problem can be formulated as follows:
Having decided on an overall plan for agriculture, find instruments that make it possible to meet the following requirements:

1. The optimal sectoral plans (see Sec. 3) are consistent with the overall plan.

2. Prices (the same for all sectors) are the main instruments used to control sectoral planning.

3. Prices should fulfill additional constraints (resulting from the requirement that the level of sectoral income be within certain bounds, or to reflect some desired consistency within the price system, etc).

4. If there are no prices which fulfill requirements 1 through 3, it is permissible to introduce a quota for products. If a quota is established, a fixed price is paid for a commodity only if the quantity sold does not exceed the quota. If there is a production surplus, a lower price may be paid. Constraints on inputs can also be introduced if necessary or used instead of quotas. However, the objective is to introduce as few quotas and/or limits as possible and - additionally - there should be almost no reason for the violation of any such quotas or limits.

Let us first examine a situation in which a set of prices that fulfill requirements 1 through 3 exists. Assume that $\hat{x}_i$, i = 1,2,...,5, is a solution of the APM and $\hat{A}_i$ are submatrices of $A_i$ composed of rows that were active in the solution considered. The conditions for optimality in $\hat{x}_i$ for sectoral problems can be formulated as follows:

$$c - \hat{A}_i^T \lambda_i - u_i = 0 \qquad i = 1,...,5 \qquad (7)$$

where:  c  - is a vector of prices (positive components are for pro-
           ducts, negative for inputs, zero for non-marketable com-
           modities),

       $\lambda_i$ - is a vector of Lagrange multipliers for active constraints
           in the i-th sector,

       $u_i$ - is a vector of Lagrange multipliers for upper or lower
           bounds; therefore

$$u_i^j \leqslant 0 \qquad \text{if} \qquad \hat{x}_i^j = 1_i^j$$

$$u_i^j = 0 \qquad \text{if} \qquad 1_i^j < \hat{x}_i^j < h_i^j \qquad\qquad (*)$$

$$u_i^j \geqslant 0 \qquad \text{if} \qquad \hat{x}_i^j = h_i^j$$

where j designates a particular product or input and T means matrix transposition.

According to requirement number 3, additional constraints on prices may be formulated, for example:

$$\underline{r}_i \leqslant c\hat{x}_i \leqslant \bar{r}_i \qquad\qquad (**)$$

$$\underline{\underline{c}} \leqslant c \leqslant \bar{\bar{c}}$$

where $\underline{r}_i$ and $\bar{r}_i$ are lower and upper bounds on income in sector i, and $\underline{\underline{c}}$ and $\bar{\bar{c}}$ are lower and upper bounds on prices. It is assumed that (**) is feasible.

If the system of conditions (7), (*), (**) has a solution, it is usually non-unique. Therefore the following problem A can be formulated:

$$\min \sum_{j=1}^{n} \frac{w1}{c_j} |c_j - \bar{c}_j| \qquad\qquad (8)$$

subject to (7), (*), (**), where $\bar{c}$ is a vector of reference (desired) prices. If problem A is feasible the set of prices that fulfill requirements 1 through 3 exists and can be determined.

It may happen that problem A is infeasible. To illustrate a possible situation let us consider an example with two sectors and two commodities. Let the optimal solution of an overall plan (see Fig. 2) be $\hat{x}_1$ and $\hat{x}_2$ for sectors 1 and 2, respectively, and E1, E2, D1, D2 be active constraints.

A price vector has to be a linear combination of gradients of active constraints for each sector. Obviously no such price vector would be the same for both sectors. More detailed discussion of this problem may be found in [2] or in [3].

If the problem A is infeasible one may formulate a partially perturbed problem B as follows:

$$\min \left( \sum_{j=1}^{n} \frac{w1}{c_j} |c_j - \bar{c}_j| + w2 \sum_{i=1}^{5} \sum_{j=1}^{n} v_i^j \right) \qquad\qquad (9)$$

subject to

$$c - \hat{A}_i^T \lambda_i - u_i - v_i = 0 \qquad i = 1,\ldots,5 \qquad (10)$$
$$v_i \geqslant 0$$

and (\*), (\*\*).

The non-zero (if any) components of vectors $v_i$ correspond to products for which quotas are allowed and to inputs for which limits are permitted (the concept of quotas has been proposed by A.P. Wierzbicki [8]). One may also add conditions for quota shadow prices (see [2]). If the problem B is feasible a set of prices can be determined. Note that $v_i^j > 0$ implies the introduction of a constraint on commodity j in sector i of the type $x_i^j \leqslant \hat{x}_i^j$ (where $\hat{x}_i^j$ is a component of the solution of the overall plan), i.e. introduction of either a quota or a limit (depending on whether the variable is a product or an input).

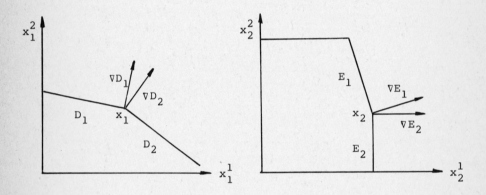

Figure 2.  A case for which a common set of prices does not exist.

Should the problem B be infeasible (which may be caused by "tight" conditions (\*\*)) the following perturbed <u>problem C</u> may be formulated:

$$\min \left( \sum_{j=1}^{n} \frac{w1}{c_j} \, |c_j - \overline{c}_j| + \sum_{i=1}^{5} \sum_{j=1}^{n} (w2 \cdot v_i^j + w3 |t_i^j|) \right) \qquad (11)$$

subject to

$$c - \hat{A}_i^T \lambda_i - u_i - v_i - t_i = 0 \qquad (12)$$

$$v_i \geqslant 0$$

and (\*), (\*\*).

It is easy to see that problem C is always feasible. However, its solution does not satisfy requirement number 1. If the values of vectors $t_i$ are small one may expect that the solutions of the sectoral problems would not differ much from those of the chosen overall plan. Therefore the sectoral problems have to be solved and the solutions examined to check whether the differences are acceptable. If the resulting sectoral solutions are not acceptable either some conditions on the prices have to be slackened or another overall plan should be examined.

The weight coefficients w1, w2 and w3 reflect the preferences of the decision center. Usually w3 has the biggest value because the consistency of sectoral and overall plans is generally of greatest importance. If it is preferred to have the price structure "closer" to the desired structure, at the expense of introducing more quotas or limits, then w1 should be greater than w2. In the opposite situation the relation should be reversed.

## 6. THE STRUCTURE OF THE DECISION SUPPORT SYSTEM

The decision support system is composed of a system of programs implemented on a UNIVAC 1100 at the Computation Centre of the State Planning Commission in Warsaw. The software may be used in different ways in order to meet the specific needs of particular users (see [9]).

The typical mode of operation of the decision support system is presented in Figure 3.

One starts with sectoral models, which are generated using a database according to the current requirements of the decision center. Then a set of requirements and sectoral models are used to generate a multiobjective planning problem covering the whole agricultural system. This problem is solved several times (for different assumptions concerning aspiration levels, constraints, etc.) until an acceptable solution is found. Then the next set of decisions on reference prices, quota conditions, etc.) is used to generate the price problem, which is also solved several times until an acceptable solution is found. It may then be necessary to re-examine sectoral problems if Problem C is being considered (see Sec. 5).

At each stage of computation, reports containing information necessary for the evaluation of a solution by the decision maker are produced. Programs that enable easy generation of new scenarios have also been developed.

The software allows efficient analysis of the problems described in this paper. However, for the time being at least, it is not a fully "automatic" system, and therefore it is necessary to contact one of the designers of the model for information on some parts of the computations.

304

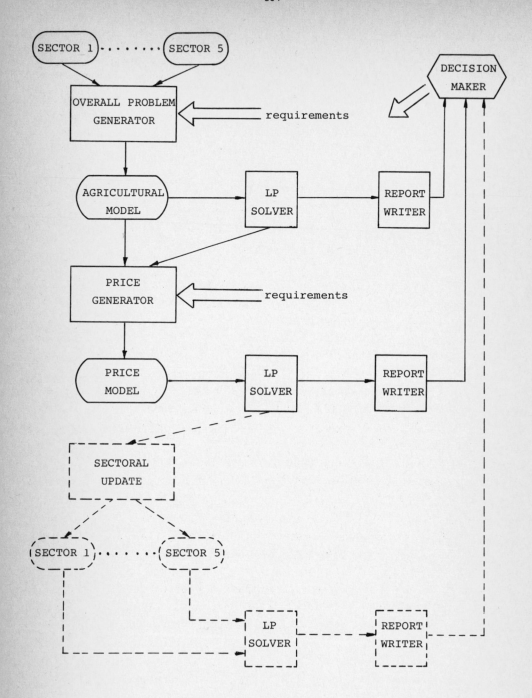

Figure 3. Structure of the decision support system.

ACKNOWLEDGEMENTS

   The authors thank Prof. A.P. Wierzbicki and Prof. Kirit S. Parikh
who have supported the research both by helpful discussions and by
arranging cooperation with IIASA.  Thanks are also due to Dr. L. Podkaminer for formulating the problem and for many fruitful discussions.
Dr. A. Lewandowski's help with regard to multiobjective software is
gratefully acknowledged.

REFERENCES

[1]  Polish Agriculture Model.  PAM-1, IIASA, forthcoming.

[2]  M. Makowski and J. Sosnowski.  Coordination of sectoral production
     planning using prices and quotas (a case study for the Polish
     agriculture model).  CP-81-38, IIASA, 1981.

[3]  M. Makowski and J. Sosnowski.  Planning and controlling agricult-
     ural production in a centrally planned economy with a decentra-
     lized decision structure.  Research Report, forthcoming.

[4]  L. Podkaminer.  Efficient use of prices and quantity constraints
     for control and coordination of linear sectoral production models.
     WP-81-110, IIASA, 1981.

[5]  A.P. Wierzbicki.  A methodological guide to multiobjective opti-
     mization.  WP-79-122, IIASA, 1979.

[6]  H. Nikaido.  Convex Structures and Economic Theory.  Academic
     Press, 1968.

[7]  A. Lewandowski.  A program package for linear multiple criteria
     reference point optimization, short user manual.  WP-82-80, IIASA,
     1982.

[8]  A.P. Wierzbicki.  Private communication, 1980.

[9]  M. Makowski and J. Sosnowski.  Implementation of an algorithm for
     scaling matrices and other programs useful in linear programming.
     CP-81-37, IIASA, 1981.

# V.  EXPERIMENTAL SESSIONS

# INTRODUCTION

When planning the meeting the organizers (who are also the volume editors) tried to include experimental sessions in the program to provide the opportunity for on-line testing of software for interactive decision support. Although there were some technical problems to overcome, the participants had access to one mini- and several microcomputers during the meeting.

This gave the participants the chance to assess the usefulness of the decision-support software presented at the meeting. To our knowledge, this is the first time that on-line demonstrations and experimental testing of approaches and applications have taken place at a meeting on interactive decision analysis. However, the continuing improvement in the performance and portability of microcomputers suggests that this type of presentation and verification of new ideas will become more common in the future.

In his contribution, Udink ten Cate discusses the determination of the optimal temperature for the growth of an early cucumber crop in a greenhouse. The multicriteria problem here is to weigh the economic gains of an early crop against the extra costs of heating the greenhouse. A nonlinear mathematical model of the complex relation between the temperature regime and the earliness of the crop is developed. The process of decision analysis is then demonstrated using the nonlinear version of the DIDASS package.

In his paper *DISCRET - a package for multicriteria optimization and decision problems with discrete alternatives*, Majchrzak presents a series of interactive sessions. The package selects nondominated alternatives and helps the decision maker to choose his final solution.

Lewandowski, Rogowski and Kręglewski present numerical experiments based on the trajectory-oriented extension of DIDASS (see Section IV); the example considered is a flood control problem.

The use of the HG package described in Section IV is demonstrated by Żebrowski, Dobrowolski and Ryś.

Support for another type of decision problem is provided by Kruś. He presents a method for two-person games and demonstrates how it may be applied to a regional planning problem. The interactive system generates a sequence of Nash equilibria for modified achievement functions which approximate the utilities of the players.

In his contribution *Two empirical tests with approaches to multiple-criteria decision making*, Bischoff questions underlying assumptions concerning

the decision maker's ability to provide information regarding his preferences, and the preference structure as a whole.  He describes the
experimental set-up for this work, which is still in progress.

Not included in the Proceedings are three other experimental
sessions, which we will describe briefly for the sake of completeness.

Manfred Strubegger demonstrated the use of the integrated programming package described in Section IV by analyzing a problem of
competing energy technologies.  The criteria were economic, energy
and "environmental" efficiency.

When developing long-term regional water policies it is necessary
to reconcile conflicting interests in regions with open-cast mining.
The most important interest groups in such areas are those responsible
for mining, the municipal and industrial water suppliers, agricultur-
alists and environmentalists.  Stefan Kaden presented a software
package based on the nonlinear version of DIDASS for dealing with this
type of multicriteria problem.

Finally, Ferenc Toth demonstrated the usefulness of operational
games as a method of improving communication between modelers and
decision makers.

M. Grauer

# ON THE DETERMINATION OF THE OPTIMAL TEMPERATURE FOR THE GROWTH OF AN EARLY CUCUMBER CROP IN A GREENHOUSE

Alexander Udink ten Cate
*International Institute for Applied Systems Analysis, Laxenburg, Austria*

ABSTRACT

A means of determining the optimal temperature for cultivation of a cucumber crop in a greenhouse is presented. The optimal temperature is derived from a comparison with a standard temperature regime and is selected on the basis of two criteria: (1) expected income from an early crop and (2) heating costs.

The nonlinear problem is solved using the reference point approach as implemented in the DIDASS/N software package.

## 1. INTRODUCTION

The main purpose of greenhouses is to provide a beneficial environment for crop growth. In the colder parts of the world, this means that greenhouses must be heated in winter, requiring an energy input which is equivalent to roughly 25% of the total capital costs of protected cultivation. This makes energy a significant cost factor and there has been much research on ways of using fuel more economically. Crop growth and development is closely related to the temperature of the greenhouse air, and traditional research in horticulture focuses on temperature patterns which are in some way "optimal" for production under average conditions, notably the average local weather conditions. These so-called "blueprints" for the greenhouse air temperature are available for a wide variety of crops in various regions. However, at a time of rapidly changing energy costs, the validity of such blueprints is questionable. More recently, research has been reported in which a relation between temperature and yield is used explicitly in an optimization procedure.

The relation between temperature and crop growth is extremely complex, and therefore a simplified relation between the temperature regime and the earliness of the crop is adopted. Earliness (or delay) is the difference between the time when the first fruits grown under some particular conditions can be marketed and the time of marketing of the first fruits grown under a standard or blueprint temperature regime. Because the prices are higher when the first fruits enter the market after the winter, earliness/delay has a significant effect on the economic results. The typical optimization problem in this area would try to weigh the economic gains of an early crop against the extra costs of heating the greenhouse. Note that the objective is not energy conservation as such, but rather the more economical use of fuel.

An example of the above approach is the drawing of thermal screen in a greenhouse when it is still light, in order to conserve energy. The savings are compared with the delay in production (Seginer and Albright, 1980). Another possibility is to make on-line calculations of the desired temperature by weighing the earliness of a cucumber crop against the heating costs (Challa et al., 1980) using an earliness model such as that developed by Challa and Van de Vooren (1980). Here the optimization problem is formulated using a single criterion. Because of the uncertainties associated with the parameters of the models used, however, a more appropriate approach would be based on the theory of multiple-criteria decision making. This paper reports on such a study using the interactive reference point approach (Wierzbicki, 1981) as implemented in the DIDASS/N software package (Grauer and Kaden, 1984).

## 2. PROBLEM FORMULATION

In general the effect of the temperature of greenhouse air on crop growth and subsequent yield is difficult to assess. The relation between short-term phenomena (processes with time constants up to one day) and long-term processes in particular is plagued with severe methodological difficulties (Udink ten Cate and Challa, 1983). However, with a cucumber crop the problem can be simplified by considering the period from planting until harvesting. The temperature maintained throughout this period affects the earliness of the yield, while the rate of production itself is not affected (Van de Vooren et al., 1978).

A relation can be established between earliness and temperature, with photosynthetically active radiation (light) as an external variable (Challa and Van de Vooren, 1980). Assume that the onset of flowering depends on the stage of development of the plant (expressed in terms of the total number of leaves per plant) and that the time between flowering and harvesting of the first fruits is constant. The rate of development can then be expressed as:

$$\dot{d}(\theta,\phi'';t) = 0.33[1-\exp\,(5.59-0.4\bar{\theta})(6-\exp\,(1.704-6.39\cdot10^{-3}\bar{\phi}''_p))]\qquad(1)$$

where

$\dot{d}(\cdot)$ - rate of development (leaves.day$^{-1}$)

$\bar{\theta}(\cdot)$ - average temperature in the crop canopy over the daylight period ($^\circ$C)

$\bar{\phi}''_p(\cdot)$ - average photosynthetically active radiation over the daylight period (W.m$^{-2}$) .

The averages depend on the number of hours of daylight (typically 8 hrs in winter); consequently $\bar{\phi}''_p$ may also be expressed in [J.day$^{-1}$] . Note that the unit of time is the day. (The night period (16 hrs) is not taken into account in eqn. (1).)

The effect of the optimal temperature $\theta_o$ is compared with that of the standard (blueprint) temperature $\theta_b$ and leads to a difference in development rate

$$\Delta\dot{d}(t) \triangleq \dot{d}(\theta_o;t) - \dot{d}(\theta_b;t) .\qquad(2)$$

Flowering of the (cucumber) crop occurs when $d_c$ leaves are formed. For the standard crop this happens at time $t_c$ , so that $d(\theta_b;t_c) = d_c$ . For the optimal crop at development stage $d(\theta_o;t)$ the earliness $\Delta t_c$ due to the difference in development $\Delta d(t_c) = d(\theta_o;t_c) - d(\theta_b;t_c)$ can be found. Making a linear approximation

$$d(\theta_o;t_c-\Delta t_c) = d(\theta_o;t_c) - \dot{d}(\theta_o;t_c)\,\Delta t_c\qquad(3a)$$

leads to

$$\Delta t_c = \frac{\Delta d(t_c)}{\dot{d}(\theta_o;t_c)} .\qquad(3b)$$

The fact that the time between flowering and production is not dependent on the temperature implies that $\Delta t_p = \Delta t_c$ . Furthermore, $\Delta d(t_c) = \int_{t=0}^{t_c} \dot{\Delta d} \; dt$ .

The standard crop and the optimal crop are terminated at the same time. Particularly with an exponentially decaying auction price, the increased earliness of the crop gives rise to the additional profit

$$\Delta p = y(t_p) \; p_f(t_p) \; \Delta t_p \tag{4}$$

where $p_f(\cdot)$ - price of fruits $(Dfl. \; kg^{-1})$
$\quad\quad y(\cdot)$ - production rate per unit of ground area $(kg.m^{-2}.day^{-1})$
$\quad\quad t_p$ - onset of production phase (day)
$\quad\quad \Delta p$ - additional profit per unit of ground area $(Dfl.m^{-2})$ .

On a daily basis, the effect of the difference in development is

$$\dot{\Delta p}(t) = y(t_p) \; p_f(t_p) \; \frac{\dot{\Delta d}(t)}{\dot{d}(\theta_o; t_c)} \tag{5}$$

where $\dot{\Delta d}(t)$ follows from eqn. (2) . The energy consumption rate and the corresponding costs are estimated using

$$\dot{c}(\theta; t) = KCP_g(\bar{\theta} - \bar{\theta}_a) - Q(\bar{\phi}'') \tag{6}$$

where $\dot{c}(\cdot)$ - cost of energy consumed per unit of ground area per day
$\quad\quad\quad (Dfl.m^{-2}.day^{-1})$
$\quad\quad K$ - heat loss coefficient per unit of ground area $(W.m^{-2}.K^{-1})$
$\quad\quad \bar{\theta}$ - average air temperature inside the greenhouse during the daylight period $(^{\circ}C)$
$\quad\quad \bar{\theta}_a$ - average air temperature outside the greenhouse during the daylight period $(^{\circ}C)$
$\quad\quad C$ - conversion factor from Watts to $m^3$ gas.day$^{-1}$ $(m^3.day^{-1}.W^{-1})$
$\quad\quad\quad$ for a period of 8 hours
$\quad\quad P_g$ - price of gas $(Dfl.m^{-3})$
$\quad\quad Q(\cdot)$ - effect of external heat sources.

Note that in the night period it is assumed that $\theta_o = \theta_b$ . The daily difference in energy costs between the optimal temperature regime and the standard temperature regime is obtained from eqn. (6) as

$$\Delta\dot{c}(t) \stackrel{\wedge}{=} \dot{c}(\theta_o;t) - \dot{c}(\theta_b;t) = KCP_g(\bar{\theta}_o - \bar{\theta}_b) \ . \tag{7}$$

The gains expressed in eqn. (5) have to be weighed against the costs given by eqn. (7). Because some of the parameters, especially $y(t_p)$ and $p_f(t_p)$ in eqn. (5), are uncertain, the problem is expressed as a multiple-criteria decision problem based on two objective functions

$$\text{max } \Delta\dot{p}(t) \text{ from eqn. (5)}$$
$$\tag{8}$$
$$\text{min } \Delta\dot{c}(t) \text{ from eqn. (7)} \ ,$$

where an *expected* average (over the daylight period) of the photosynthetically active radiation $\bar{\phi}_p''$ is used in eqns. (1) and (2). The decision strategy is not to deviate too much from the standard (blueprint) temperature.


3.   IMPLEMENTATION

The nonlinear problem described by eqn. (8) was implemented with DIDASS/N (Grauer and Kaden, 1984), using the parameters given in Table 1 (Challa et al., 1980).

The value of the parameter K given in Table 1 is dependent on the average wind velocity over the daylight period. Parameter C is based on a boiler-to-greenhouse efficiency of 72% and a combustion value of 35.7 MJ per normal $m^3$ of natural gas.


Table 1.  Parameter values.

| Parameter | Value | Parameter | Value |
|-----------|-------|-----------|-------|
| $y(t_p)$ | 0.195 $kg.m^{-2}.day^{-1}$ | K | $9.26 + 0.79 \cdot \bar{v}_{wind}$ $W.m^{-2}.K^{-1}$ |
| $p_f(t_p)$ | 1.50 $Dfl.kg^{-1}$ | C | 0.0011 $m^3.day^{-1}.W^{-1}$ |
| $\dot{d}(\theta_o;t_c)$ | 0.7 $leaves.day^{-1}$ | $P_g$ | 0.40 $Dfl.m^{-3}$ |

The objective functions of eqn. (8) have to be modified in order to comply with DIDASS/N requirements. Therefore, the original problem is reformulated as follows:

$$\max \begin{cases} \dot{\Delta p}(A;t) + 1 = obj1 \quad \text{(max. earnings due to earliness of crop)} \\ \\ -\dot{\Delta c}(A;t) + 1 = obj2. \text{(max. heating savings)} \end{cases} \tag{9}$$

$$15 < \theta_o < 35 .$$

The ground area $A = 10 \text{ m}^2$ is introduced to scale the objective. The value +1 is added in order to have positive objective functions, as required by DIDASS/N. The bounds on $\theta_o$ follow from the horticultural requirements. Using the reference point approach, it is necessary to identify an optimal value for $\theta_o$ based on daily expectations of the photosynthetically active radiation and wind velocity. The photosynthetically active radiation $\bar{\phi}_p''$ was estimated at 25% of the total external radiation (assuming 50% transmission through the greenhouse and 50% photosynthetically active radiation).

Table 2. Values of parameters[a] in typical weather situations.

| $\bar{\phi}_p''$ | $\bar{v}_{wind}$ | Description |
|---|---|---|
| 10-20 | 1 | Dark December day |
| 40-60 | 3 | Alternating periods of cloud and sun . |
| 80-100 | 4 | Bright February day |

[a] The ranges of these parameters are 10-100 for radiation intensity and 1-5 for wind velocity. A standard temperature ($\bar{\theta}_b$) of 20°C was assumed.

Several values of expected radiation are typically considered in making a decision (Table 2). The strategy is not to deviate too much from the standard regime. In the optimization procedure, a situation with $\bar{\theta}_o = \bar{\theta}_b$ corresponds to obj1=1 , obj2=1 .

The differences in income due to use of the optimal regime rather than the standard regime are of the order of 0.01 Dfl·m$^{-2}$. For an average commercial holding of 10,000 m$^2$ , a gain of 0.01 Dfl.m$^{-2}$ represents a total gain of Dfl 100. Table 3 presents some typical results.

Table 3.  Typical results with expected $\bar{\phi}_p''$ in the range 80-100. $\bar{\theta}_b = 20$ and $\bar{v}_{wind} = 1$ were assumed.

|  | obj1 | obj2 | $\bar{\theta}_o$ | Remarks |
|---|---|---|---|---|
| $\bar{\phi}_p'' = 100$ | 1.25 | 0.88 | 22.6 | Net gain = 0.013 Dfl.m$^{-2}$ |
| $\bar{\phi}_p'' = 80$ | 1.17 | 0.92 | 21.7 | Net gain = 0.009 Dfl.m$^{-2}$ |
| Reference point | 1.20 | 0.90 | | |

## 4. CONCLUSIONS

The optimal cultivation strategy for an early cucumber crop is studied as a multiple-criteria decision problem.  The objectives are maximization of extra income due to the earliness of the crop and minimization of extra heating costs relative to a standard or "blueprint" regime.  The decision variable is the temperature of the air inside the greenhouse.  Parameters considered in the decision include the standard (blueprint) temperature, the expected average photosynthetically active radiation over the daylight period, and the wind velocity.  The night period (no radiation) is not taken into account - here the standard temperature is employed in both cases.

The decision is made by comparing the trade-off between the two objectives, with the additional aim of not deviating too much from the standard temperature.  This last requirement makes it necessary to use a multiple-criteria formulation.  The results demonstrate that the multiple-criteria approach is a feasible way of studying such problems. Since the particular problem considered here is relatively small and uses only a single decision variable, however, a decision based on graphical representation of the objectives could also be envisaged in this case.  This would reduce the computational effort considerably.

REFERENCES

Challa, H. and J. van de Vooren (1980).  A strategy for climate control in greenhouses in early winter production. *Acta Horticulturae* 106: 159-164.

Challa, H., J.C. Bakker, G.P.A. Bot, A.J. Udink ten Cate, and J. van de Vooren (1980). Economical optimization of energy consumption in an early cucumber crop. *Acta Horticulturae* 118: 191-199.

Grauer, M. and S. Kaden (1984). A nonlinear dynamic interactive decision analysis and support system (DIDASS/N). Users' Guide. Working Paper WP-84-23, International Institute for Applied Systems Analysis, Laxenburg, Austria.

Seginer, I. and L.D. Albright (1980). Rational operation of greenhouse thermal curtains. *Trans. ASAE* 23(5): 1240-1245.

Udink ten Cate, A.J. and H. Challa (1983). On optimal computer control of the crop growth system. *Acta Horticulturae* 148.

Vooren, J. van de, P.J.A.L. de Lint, and H. Challa (1978). Influence of varying night temperature on a cucumber crop. *Acta Horticulturae* 87: 249-255.

Wierzbicki, A.P. (1981). A mathematical basis for satisficing decision making. In J.V. Morse (Ed.), *Organizations: Multiple Agents with Multiple Criteria*. Springer, Berlin, p. 465-485.

# DISCRET – A PACKAGE FOR MULTICRITERIA OPTIMIZATION AND DECISION PROBLEMS WITH DISCRETE ALTERNATIVES

Janusz Majchrzak

*Systems Research Institute, Polish Academy of Sciences, Warsaw, Poland*

## 1. INTRODUCTION

DISCRET has been developed to deal with multicriteria optimization and decision making problems with a finite number of discrete alternatives. The following problem structure is assumed:

(i)    All feasible alternatives (decisions) are explicitly listed in the set $X^0 = \{x_1, x_2, \ldots, x_n\}$.

(ii)   All of the decision maker's (DM) criteria are known. Both ordinal and cardinal criteria are permitted. Let $f(x) = (f^1(x), f^2(x), \ldots, f^m(x))$ be the criteria vector.

(iii)  For each alternative the criteria are evaluated and their values listed in the set $Q = \{f(x_1), f(x_2), \ldots, f(x_n)\}$.

The aim of the DM is to optimize his criteria simultaneously. The DISCRET package selects the nondominated (Pareto-optimal) alternatives and helps the DM in choosing his final solution. It is assumed that the DM works with the computer in an interactive way and gathers experience related to the problem as well as to his preferences during the session. He is expected to have only a very basic knowledge about multicriteria optimization theory and problems. No underlying utility function is assumed, but any of the DM's scalarizing functions may be adopted during the session, if they are included in the criteria vector f. At any stage of the decision making process an arbitrary subset of criteria may be used by the DM to express his current preferences.

A preliminary version of the package was created in the Systems Research Institute, Polish Academy of Sciences, Warsaw [1]. This paper concentrates on the version being developed in cooperation with IIASA. Only the utilities already implemented are described. An example of an interactive session is presented.

## 2. APPROACH AND IMPLEMENTATION

To start the session with DISCRET the user (DM) has to supply the file containing the set Q of criteria values for all alternatives and (optionally) the file containing the set $X^0$ of alternatives. These files, called the data and additional data file respectively, may be created by special problem generators or some other computational processes. To define the problem two specification files have to be created.

The command ysagen asks for the problem identifier, total number of criteria, number of alternatives (elements) and the dimensions of additional data or number of records in the case of non-numeric data. The command ysbgen enables the user to indicate for each criterion whether it should be minimized, maximized or ignored and to specify the criterion value tolerance. If for two alternatives the difference in criterion values is lower than the value of the criterion tolerance parameter, then the criteria values are assumed to be equal.

After the problem generation and specification phase the user may obtain information about the ranges of criteria values (yranges command) and he may put lower and/or upper bounds on the values of some of the criteria (ybounds command).

The command ysolve runs the discrete multicriteria optimization problem solver. The method chosen [2] (which is of the complete enumeration type) selects the set N of nondominated solutions from the set Q in the case of criteria value tolerances equal or close to zero. In the case when the tolerances have values equal to significant fractions of the related criteria value ranges, the solver returns a representative subset of the set N called its representation R(N). The idea of selecting a representation R from the set N is illustrated in Figure 1.

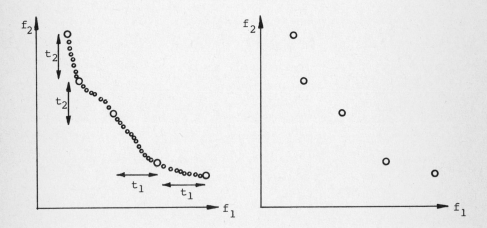

Figure 1. Representation R of set N.

321

If proper values are chosen for the tolerances, the representation R contains a small number of elements but still gives a good impression of the shape of set N.

The DM may use the command ysort to sort set R according to increasing/decreasing values of a chosen criterion in order to provide a better analysis of the set.

The command ypick selects those elements of set $X^0$ which relate to the elements of set R.

During the interactive session the commands briefly presented above may be used in any order, including command repetition. This feature of DISCRET transforms its very simple command structure into an efficient decision support system. By setting appropriate bounds the DM may change his region of interest, then by analysis of the representation R he learns about the shape of the set N in this region and the criteria tradeoffs. In the next step he may define his region of interest more precisely or scan the set N further. By proper bounds setting the DM may also adopt the equality/inequality method, switching, for example, into the analysis of two-criteria subproblems.

The ability to change the criteria under consideration allows the DM to use a lexicographic or group-lexicographic approach. He may also use scalarizing functions such as goal functions or utility functions or any other additional criterion at any stage of the decision making process.

It is worth mentioning that the package offers the possibility to return immediately to any of the previous stages of the session at any time.

## 3. AN EXAMPLE OF AN INTERACTIVE SESSION

We shall take a simple location decision problem adopted from [3] as an illustrative example. A firm is evaluating 6 potential production plant location sites in 4 different states to serve 4 distribution centers. Up to 3 facilities are to be opened. Their sizes are bounded by state production limits based on environmental quality standards. A lower bound on facility production size and a production increment step are introduced for technological reasons. For budgetary reasons the cost of constructing new facilities is limited. Command ygen generates the problem.

```
++++++++++++++++++++++++++++++++++++++++++++++++++++++++++++++++
                    +++ ygen +++
++++++++++++++++++++++++++++++++++++++++++++++++++++++++++++++++
+++ ygen +++ type identificator of the problem;
```

```
                    (up to five digits; example :<54321>)  i dpr=6666
+++ ygen +++ available criteria :
            1 - total unsatisfied demand
            2 - favored customer center demand satisfaction
            3 - total cost
            4 - averadge life quality score
            5 - fixed cost for opened locations
            6 - transportation cost
            7 - production cost
            8 - unsaled production
+++ type chosen criteria (example :<3,1,4,>)
:1,2,3,
+++ ygen +++ chosen criteria (remember their new numbers !):
            1 - total unsatisfied demand
            2 - favored customer center demand satisfaction
            3 - total cost


+++ ygen +++ for problem identificated by   i dpr=6666
                number of generated variants   nall=1486
                number of feasible variants    nfea= 640
                number of locations schemes    nloc=  35


*** ypspa file ***
----- text -------- name number
problem identific. idpr 6666
number of criteria    mm    3
number of elements    nn   640
additional data dim. nx    6
add. data records no nr     4
+++++++++++++++++++++++++++++++++++++++++++++++++++++++++++++++++++++
                    +++ end of ygen +++
+++++++++++++++++++++++++++++++++++++++++++++++++++++++++++++++++++++


% ysbgen.go
+++++++++++++++++++++++++++++++++++++++++++++++++++++++++++++++++++++
                    +++ begin ysbgen +++
+++++++++++++++++++++++++++++++++++++++++++++++++++++++++++++++++++++
+++ ysbgen +++ problem identific. idpr=6666, numb of criteria mm=3 +++
+++ ysbgen +++ default yispb file display: +++
 *** yispb file *** idpr=6666 , mm= 3   ***
 crit.num min/max tolerance *** min/max=-1 żmin ; =+1 -max ; =0 -not import.
     1        1    0.100e-09
     2        1    0.100e-09
     3        1    0.100e-09
+++ do you want to change someting ? type <y> or <n> : n
+++ ysbgen +++ your final version of yispb file ,

 *** yispb file *** idpr=6666 , mm= 3   ***
 crit.num min/max tolerance *** min/max=-1 -min ; =+1 -max ; =0 -not import.
     1        1    0.100e-09
     2        1    0.100e-09
     3        1    0.100e-09
+++++++++++++++++++++++++++++++++++++++++++++++++++++++++++++++++++++
                    +++ end of ysbgen +++
+++++++++++++++++++++++++++++++++++++++++++++++++++++++++++++++++++++
% yranges.go
+++++++++++++++++++++++++++++++++++++++++++++++++++++++++++++++++++++
                    +++ begin yranges +++
+++++++++++++++++++++++++++++++++++++++++++++++++++++++++++++++++++++
+++ yranges +++ criteria values ranges : +++

 *** ycran file *** id=6666 , m= 3 , nn=  640 ***
```

```
crit.num    lower value     upper value     difference
   1        0.272502e+03    0.105838e+04    0.785878e+03
   2        0.300000e+03    0.120000e+04    0.100000e+03
   3        0.136924e+07    0.207347e+07    0.704230e+06
++++++++++++++++++++++++++++++++++++++++++++++++++++++++++++++++++
                    +++ end of yranges +++
++++++++++++++++++++++++++++++++++++++++++++++++++++++++++++++++++
% ysbgen.go
++++++++++++++++++++++++++++++++++++++++++++++++++++++++++++++++++
                    +++ begin ysbgen +++
++++++++++++++++++++++++++++++++++++++++++++++++++++++++++++++++++
+++ ysbgen +++ problem identific. idpr=6666 , numb of criteria mm= 3 +++
+++ ysbgen +++ default yispb file display: +++
 *** yispb file *** idpr=6666 , m= 3 ***

 crit.num min/max tolerance *** min/max=-1 ; =+1 -max ; =0 -not import
    1       1    0.100e-09
    2       1    0.100e-09
    3       1    0.100e-09
+++ do you want to change someting ? type <y> or <n> : y

+++ ysbgen +++ now you can change the yispb file (record by record)
+++ type three numbers <integer,integer,real> standing for :
    (1)criterion number
    (2)min/max indicator : <-1>-min, <+1>-max, <0>-not important,
    (3)tolerance .
+++ example : <2, -1, 12.3>  +++ for termination hit <cr> (new line)  +++
 : 1, -1, .1e3,
 *** yispb file *** idpr=6666 , mm= 3 ***
 crit.num min/max tolerance *** min/max=-1 -min ; =+1 -max ; =0 -not import.
    1      -1    0.100e+03
    2       1    0.100e-09
    3       1    0.100e-09
(...)
+++ ysbgen +++ your final version of yispb file ,
 *** yispb file *** idpr=6666 , mm= 3 ***
 crit.num min/max tolerance *** min/max=-1 -min ; =+1 -max ; =0 -not import.
    1      -1    0.100e+03
    2       1    0.100e+03
    3      -1    0.100e+06
++++++++++++++++++++++++++++++++++++++++++++++++++++++++++++++++++
                    +++ end of ysbgen +++
++++++++++++++++++++++++++++++++++++++++++++++++++++++++++++++++++
% ybounds.go
++++++++++++++++++++++++++++++++++++++++++++++++++++++++++++++++++
                    +++ begin ybounds +++
++++++++++++++++++++++++++++++++++++++++++++++++++++++++++++++++++
+++ ybounds +++ this is the default ycbnd file : +++

 *** ybnds file *** idpr=6666 , m= 3 , nn=  640 ***
 crit. num    lower bound     upper bound     range
    1        0.272502e+03    0.105838e+04    0.785878e+03
    2        0.300000e+03    0.120000e+04    0.900000e+03
    3        0.136924e+07    0.207347e+07    0.704230e+06

+++ ybounds +++ now you can change the ybnds file (record by record)  +++
    type three numbers <integer, real,real> standing for:
    (1) criterion number ,
    (2) lower bound of the given criterion ,
    (3) upper bound of the given criterion .
+++ example : <2,-12.5,1.05> (to terminate type : <cr> or <new line>) +++
 :
```

```
++++ ybounds +++ this was the final version of the ybnds file +++
+++ ybounds +++ 640  ot of  640  alternatives satisfy the bounds

+++ ybounds +++ the following two files were generated :
*** yispa file *** file format : (a24,i5) ***
------ text ------- name number
problem identific. idpr 6666
number of criteria    mm    3
number of elements    nn   640
additional data dim   nx    6
add.data records no.  nr    4

*** ybnds file *** idpr=6666 , mm= 3 , nn=  640 ***
crit.num    lower bound    upper bound    range
    1       0.272502e+03   0.105838e+04   0.785878e+03
    2       0.300000e+03   0.120000e+04   0.900000e+03
    3       0.136924e+07   0.207347e+07   0.704230e+06
+++++++++++++++++++++++++++++++++++++++++++++++++++++++++++++++++++++
                    +++ end of ybounds +++
+++++++++++++++++++++++++++++++++++++++++++++++++++++++++++++++++++++

% ysolve.go
+++++++++++++++++++++++++++++++++++++++++++++++++++++++++++++++++++++
                    +++ begin ysolve +++
+++++++++++++++++++++++++++++++++++++++++++++++++++++++++++++++++++++
+++ ysolve +++ solution has been found !!!

*** yospa file ***
------ text ------- name value
problem identific. idpr 6666
number of criteria    mm    3
nond. points number   nnon  7
additional data dim.  nx    6
add. data records no   nr    4
input data points     nall 640
scalar comparisions ncmp 0.325e+04
expected comp numb.   ecmp 0.134e+05
+++ hit  <cr> (<new line>)  to continue

*** yoinf file *** idpr=6666 , mm= 3 ***
crit.no.    best value    worse value    difference
    1       0.272502e+03  0.908380e+03   0.635878e+03
    2       0.120000e+04  0.300000e+03   0.900000e+03
    3       0.136924e+07  0.207347e+07   0.704230e+06
+++++++++++++++++++++++++++++++++++++++++++++++++++++++++++++++++++++
                    +++ end of ysolve +++
+++++++++++++++++++++++++++++++++++++++++++++++++++++++++++++++++++++
```

REFERENCES

1. J. Majchrzak, "Package DISCRET", Technical Report MPD-11/83, Systems Research Institute, Polish Academy of Sciences, Warsaw (1980).

2. J. Majchrzak, "On relations between continuous and discrete multi-criteria optimization problems", Lecture Notes in Control and Information Sciences, Vol. 22, pp. 473-481, 1980.

3. S.M. Lee, G.I. Green and C.S. Kim, "A multiple criteria model for the location-allocation problem", Comput. & Op. Res., Vol. 8, pp. 1-8.

# APPLICATION OF DIDASS METHODOLOGY TO A FLOOD CONTROL PROBLEM – NUMERICAL EXPERIMENTS

A. Lewandowski, T. Rogowski and T. Kręglewski
*Institute of Automatic Control, Technical University of Warsaw, Warsaw, Poland*

## 1. INTRODUCTION

This paper presents selected numerical results obtained during an experimental session at the Conference on Plural Rationality and Interactive Decision Processes. The description of the problem is given earlier in this volume.

## 2. DESCRIPTION OF THE EXPERIMENT

It is rather difficult to present the whole experiment - 20-30 iterations are necessary to obtain satisfactory results.

It was observed that the main difficulty in using the algorithm was connected with the large amount of information which has to be processed by the decision maker - he has to work with 3 reference trajectories in parallel (Fig. 1).

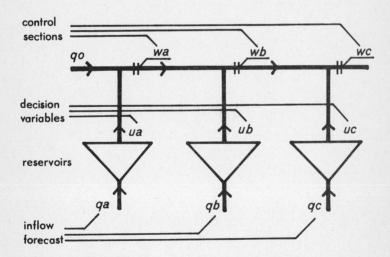

Fig. 1. Structure of the network

In order to simplify this task it was necessary to organize the interaction process properly.

The following procedure was established empirically:
- convert the downstream trajectories, i.e. (wb and wc) into free trajectories;
- set zero reference trajectory for wa and run DIDASS. This trajectory is evidently not attainable, and therefore the procedure minimizes the maximum distance between the trajectory and zero. In other words, it tries to minimize the flood peak for this control section;
- calculate the utopia trajectory for wa, exact or approximate;
- on the basis of available information, modify the reference trajectory in order to find the correct shape of wa;
- change wb from a free into an objective trajectory;
- perform the same steps as for wa, but watching wb;
- when the wb trajectory is satisfactory check wa again. If necessary correct wa;
- if wa was corrected, check wb. This loop must be performed until both trajectories are satisfactory. Experience shows that the interaction between wa and wb is not very strong, i.e. changing wb does not significantly affect wa. Usually 2-3 steps are necessary to find the compromise solution;
- convert the wc trajectory from free to objective and repeat the procedure listed above, considering only wc and correcting wa and wb if necessary. Terminate this procedure when all trajectories are satisfactory.

The procedure presented above seems to be rather complicated, but it would be difficult to solve a more complex problem without some structuring. This kind of structuring was quite evident in this case - the decision maker should move in the direction of water flow - this determines the direction in which decisions have a strong influence on the resulting trajectory. It is evident that if we are interested in controlling the wa trajectory, the wb and wc decision variables are not of interest (Fig. 1).

The situation is more complicated when the interaction is bilateral. Some research must be done on the methodology of such problems.

Due to lack of space we are able to present only selected results - Figs. 2,3,4. These represent an intermediate step in the decision process - the wa trajectory has been correctly tuned, and the decision maker is manipulating the wb reference trajectory.

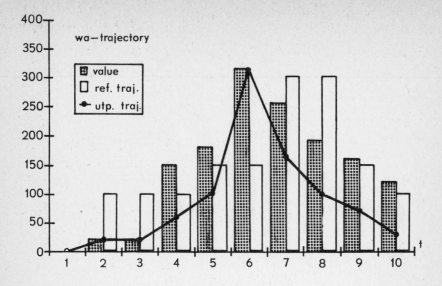

Fig. 2.  Trajectory wa - reference trajectory, utopia
trajectory and corresponding solution

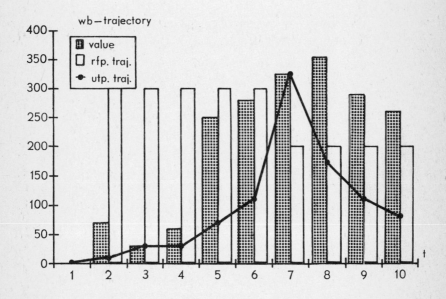

Fig. 3.  Trajectory wb - reference trajectory, utopia
trajectory and corresponding solution

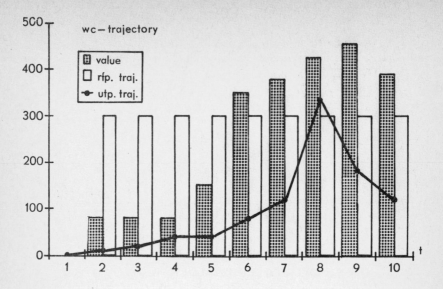

Fig. 4.   Trajectory wc - reference trajectory, utopia
trajectory and corresponding solution

## 3.   CONCLUSIONS

It follows from the experiments that:
- a proper structuring scheme is necessary to solve a complex decision problem;
- relatively long training is necessary to learn about the problem;
- flexible interaction and proper presentation of the results are extremely important in ensuring efficient DIDASS - decision maker interaction;
- strong feedback between the decision maker and the creators of decision support tools is necessary - without such feedback it would be difficult if not impossible to generate new tools or improve existing ones.

## REFERENCES

[1]  A. Lewandowski, T. Rogowski and T. Kręglewski.  A trajectory-oriented extension of DIDASS and its applications, this volume.

# AN EXPERIMENTAL SESSION WITH THE HG PACKAGE

M. Zebrowski, G. Dobrowolski and T. Ryś
*Systems Research Department of the Institute for Control and Systems Engineering
and of the Institute for Industrial Chemistry, Cracow, Poland*

## INTRODUCTION

The aim of the experimental session reported here is twofold. First,
to give an empirical evidence of applicability of the Decision Analysis
Aid based on the Skeleton Method. Second, to enable discussion on the
proposed approach and its confrontation with various experience represented by participants of the conference.

The method and its implementation is described in the paper "Decision
Support Based on the Skeleton Method - the HG-Package" by H. Górecki
et al. (published in this volume).  It is assumed that the reader is
familiar with this paper and therefore all specific terms already
introduced there will not be explained.

We shall give a brief introduction to the real case of decision analysis
which has been used as an example for the experimental session.

## AN EXAMPLE OF DECISION ANALYSIS  -  THE CASE OF METHANOL

The aim of the presentation was to show an application of the HG-package as a decision analysis support. Two aspects of such an analysis are
possible from the decision maker's point of view:
1. To check whether estimates and expectations (expressed in terms of
   ADS) are appropriate for an object described by a model.
2. To find a solution (in the sense of the safety principle in the allocation problem) which is in agreement with the estimates and expectations.

In the first case three basic results may occur [1,2]:
  (i)   The estimates are in agreement with the data represented by the
        model and a feasible solution can be obtained;
 (ii)   ADS cannot be attained;
(iii)   A result can be better than the estimates.
The second case corresponds to one of the examples presented at the experimental session.

For illustrative purposes we have used a real life example of the comparative study of methanol. The comparative analysis of technology is
one of the stages which are to be performed in the evaluation of development programs [1].  Besides, the methanol study has been reported
in an extensive form as a part of a research report [2].

We have chosen this example for several reasons:  it is a real, practical case of decision analysis, and up to now only results of the
analysis have been presented but not the use of decision support which
the HG-package is.  This paper and ["Decision Support ..." by H.Górecki
et al., this volume] are complementary with [1,2] and, therefore, full
information referring to the real case, results of the analysis, theory
of decision support and its implementation is available.

Seven various technologies of methanol production constitute the object
under investigation represented by a linear model of PDA-type [1].
Each technology is characterized by its ability to transform certain
resources into others. There are raw materials, products and by-products, waste products, and other resources required for the construction
and utilization of the technology. The analysis of various technological possibilities under different resource estimates may be performed
with the help of the HG-package and the above model by multifarious
validation of the assumed estimates or expectations expressed by them.
This constitutes in fact an auxiliary problem of the comparative study.
Such a single problem is presented in this paper.

The resources of main concern, i.e. investment, efficiency and energy
consumption were chosen as objectives in the multiobjective problem.
For given estimates of these resources and under the safety principle
we obtained an optimal solution which was in agreement with the estimates and pointed at an appropriate technological alternative of the
comparative study. As it turned out, the estimates were attainable but

the safety principle was maintained only to such an extent that the technologies, subject   to given conditions, could be engaged in their physical activity. This means that there was no feasible utilization of any choice of the proposed technologies, which is faithful to the principle. In our example the alternative consists of two methanol technologies consuming natural gas and a mixture of natural gas and carbide gas. Additionally, the solution contains amounts of all resources involved in the processing.


USER'S DIALOGUE WITH HG-PACKAGE

In this section we describe the printout given in the appendix which contains a hard-copy of the user's dialogue with the HG-package. We present only some possibilities of the package in order to give a simple and short sample of the package run.

The first part of the printout contains the dialogue with Input Manager. After the package banner has emerged, we can observe an effect of three control commands. Each of these commands starts with an asterisk. After the first command *p (print) has been entered, the set of possible objectives referring to the model under investigation is displayed in a tableau form. Columns of this table contain consequently: a sequence number, MPS code, a real life description of the code and, finally, a measure unit.
The next command *l (list) is entered to display the set of current objectives selected from the set of possible objectives displayed above. We can observe that three objectives have been picked out. One of them is maximized and the other two are minimized.
The  skeleton data (lower and upper estimates) are also printed. The values of these estimates are expressed in the units already displayed, i.e.,

     sprwn   -  efficiency in monetary units,
     nkldd   -  investment in monetary units,
     enrgg   -  energy consumption in tons of coal equivalent.
The "eps" and "rho" are parameters for the scalarizing function.
All these data have been prepared in a previous package run and saved on OBJECTIVE file.


The last command *q  (quit) finishes Input Manager work and starts Solver. When a solution is found, Output Manager becomes active and the

solution is printed in a short form. We can see that in the presented
case the desired solution has been obtained at the boundary of the
optimal compromise set.

The next section of the printout presents the solution in a simple graphical form. This has been induced by  v  (video) command.

The last part of the printout contains the real life description of the
solution.

The package run is terminated by  "no"  command.


CONCLUSIONS

The HG-package proved to be applicable, understandable and easy to handle for a user not familiar with theoretical background and computers
in general. The user, however, should be well instructed in properties
of this tool and aware of the meaning of the safety principle.

The HG-package was implemented as a part of research done by System
Research Dep. for the Programming of the Development of the Chemical
Industry in Poland. It was partly developed in cooperation with the
SDS Program at IIASA.


REFERENCES

1.  Dobrowolski G., H. Górecki, J. Kopytowski, M. Żebrowski (1982).
    The Quest for Concordance Between Technologies and Resources as a
    Multiobjective Decision Process. Multiobjective and Stochastic Op-
    timization, pp. 463-475. CP-82-S12, IIASA, Laxenburg, Austria.
2.  Dobrowolski G., J. Kopytowski, J. Wojtania, M. Żebrowski (1984).
    Alternative Routes from Fossil Resources to Chemical Feedstocks.
    IIASA Research Report, IIASA, Laxenburg, Austria.
3.  Górecki H. (1981). Problem of Choice of an Optimal Solution in a
    Multicriterion Space, Proceedings of the VIII triennial World IFAC
    Congress, pp. 106-110, Kyoto, Japan.

APPENDIX

An Example of User's Dialogue with HG-package

```
        O    O    0000
        O    O  O     O
    000000   O
        O    O  O  000
        O    O  O     O
        O    O    0000
```

+++ HELLO
+   enter cmd
*p
no. obcode    comment.......................... dim...
=== ========  ============================== ======
  1 sprwn     efficiency                       m.u.
  2 enrgg     energy consumption               t.c.e.
  3 nkldd     investment                       m.u.
  4 ztdnn     labour                           men
  5 gazzm     natural gas                      thou.Nm3
  6 wegil     coal                             tons
  7 cpzos     heavy residue                    tons
  8 benzn     benzine                          tons
  9 atmos     carbon bioxide                   thou.Nm3
 10 sciek     waste water                      m3
 11 popil     ash                              tons
 12 beton     concrete                         tons
 13 kstal     steel structure                  tons
 14 apart     equipment                        tons
 15 maszn     pumps and compressors            tons
 16 rurki     pipes                            tons
+ enter cmd
*l
no. obcode         ...lower....  ...upper.....
  1 sprwn     max   3000000.00    4000000.00
  2 nkldd     min   6000000.00    7000000.00
  3 enrgg     min     19000.00      25000.00
eps=    0.000100
rho=    3.000000
+ enter cmd
*q
+++ WAIT for results, please.
```

          D E S I R E D   S O L U T I O N
          ...............................

.....objectives.....          .....value.....
efficiency                    0.35429e+07
investment                    0.64571e+07
energy consumption            0.19752e+05
...at the boundary of compromise set.....
```

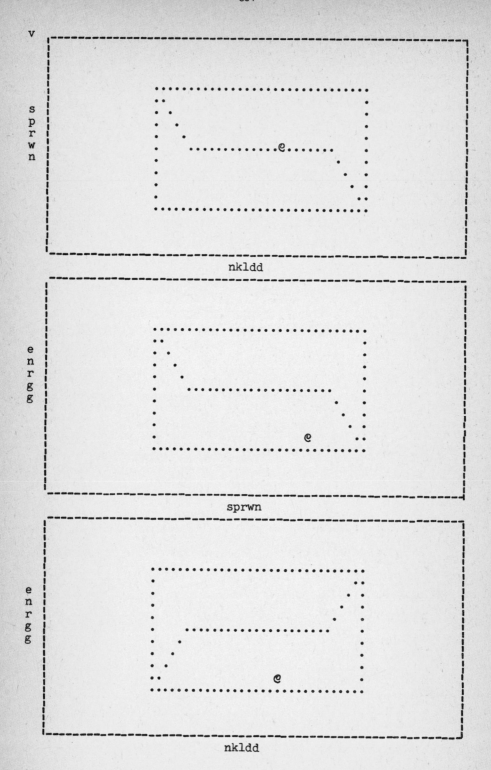

## G E N E R A L
. . . . . . . . . . . . . .

| | | |
|---|---:|---|
| efficiency | 3542937 | m.u. |
| energy consumption | 19751 | t.c.e. |
| investment | 6457062 | m.u. |
| labour | 133 | men |
| methanol total | 740000 | tons |
| methanol purchased | 109513 | tons |

## M E T H A N O L   P R O D U C E R S
. . . . . . . . . . . . . . . . . . . . . . . . . . . . . . . . . .

| | | |
|---|---:|---|
| natural and carbide gas unit | 130486 | tons |
| natural gas unit | 500000 | tons |

## R A W   M A T E R I A L S
. . . . . . . . . . . . . . . . . . . . . . . .

| | | |
|---|---:|---|
| natural gas | 575828 | thou.Nm3 |
| carbide gas | 29229 | thou.Nm3 |
| WMO catalyst | 18914 | kg |
| ZNO catalyst | 67746 | kg |
| reforming catalyst | 20806 | kg |
| synthesis catalyst | 126097 | kg |
| water | 6935354 | m3 |

## B Y - P R O D U C T S
. . . . . . . . . . . . . . . . . . . .

| | | |
|---|---:|---|
| higher alcohols | 4828 | tons |

## W A S T E   P R O D U C T S
. . . . . . . . . . . . . . . . . . . . . . . . . .

| | | |
|---|---:|---|
| waste water | 819205 | m3 |

## C O N S T R U C T I O N   D A T A
. . . . . . . . . . . . . . . . . . . . . . . . . . . . . .

| | | |
|---|---:|---|
| concrete | 29737 | tons |
| steel structure | 2200 | tons |
| equipment | 6948 | tons |
| pumps and compressors | 350 | tons |
| pipes | 2747 | tons |

```
n
+ restars -yes or no, repeat session - !, save - s
no
7%
```

# AN INTERACTIVE METHOD FOR DECISION SUPPORT IN A TWO-PERSON GAME WITH AN EXAMPLE FROM REGIONAL PLANNING

Lech Kruś

*Systems Research Institute, Polish Academy of Sciences, Warsaw, Poland*

## 1. INTRODUCTION

The basic idea of our interactive method was proposed by Wierzbicki (1982). The method was implemented and several modifications tested by Fortuna and Kruś (1983). A number of experiments based on this method have been carried out for a regional planning problem. This paper presents the results of one such experiment. A general outline of the method is also given.

## 2. THE METHOD

The method is designed for decision problems in which two players ($P_1$ and $P_2$) each try to maximize a pair of objectives. Let player 1 have objectives $Y_1, U_1$. The models describing the objectives are then

$$Y_1 = Y_1(x_1, x_2)$$

$$U_1 = U_1(x_1, x_2)$$

$$\text{subject to } x_1 \in \Omega_1 \quad ,$$

(1)

where $x_1$ is the control variable of player 1 and the set $\Omega_1$ is defined by constraints.

The objectives $Y_2, U_2$ of player 2 are described by the models

$$Y_2 = Y_2(x_1, x_2)$$

$$U_2 = U_2(x_1, x_2)$$

$$\text{subject to } x_2 \in \Omega_2 \quad ,$$

(2)

where $x_2$ is the control variable of player 2 and the set $\Omega_2$ is defined by constraints.

The decision problems of the players are interrelated, i.e., the decision of one player affects the outcome obtained by the other. In such two-person games the Nash equilibrium is typically considered as the status-quo point. The Pareto solutions of the individual players are then analyzed at this point.

The main purpose of implementing this method in the form of an interactive computerized system is to help the players (decision makers) to learn about the problem. It is assumed that there is no explicitly given utility function. Each player is however assumed to have his own ideas of the importance (utility) of each objective, and will use the system to identify the decisions (by selecting the best solutions) which maximize his own utility function. The selection is guided by aspiration levels established through a learning process. This choice provides information which is used to construct achievement functions approximating the player's utility function. The achievement functions are then used to calculate the Nash equilibrium point.

The method involves the following steps:

Step 0 Set the current iteration number i = 0.

Step 1 Choose an achievement function from the family of functions

$$s_1 = s_1(Y_1, U_1, \bar{Y}_1^i, \bar{U}_1^i) \quad ,$$

$$s_2 = s_2(Y_2, U_2, \bar{Y}_2^i, \bar{U}_2^i) \quad ,$$

where $\bar{Y}_1^i$, $\bar{Y}_2^i$; $\bar{U}_1^i$, $\bar{U}_2^i$ are the aspiration levels of players 1 and 2, respectively.

Step 2 Compute the Nash equilibrium for $s_1$ versus $s_2$, finding the objective vectors $Y_1^i$, $Y_2^i$, $U_1^i$, $U_2^i$ and the control variables $x_1^i$, $x_2^i$. Present the Nash equilibrium to the players.

Step 3a Ask player 1 to modify his aspiration level $\bar{Y}_1^i$, $\bar{U}_1^i$.

Step 3b Calculate the Pareto point in the space of objectives $Y_1$, $U_1$ by maximizing $s_1$ for the modified aspiration level. Go to step 3a and repeat steps 3a,b five times.

Step 3c Present the sample Pareto solutions to the player and ask him to select the one he likes best.
Go to step 3a and repeat the steps 3a-c five times.

Step 4 Repeat the sequence of steps 3a-c for player 2 modifying his aspiration levels $\bar{Y}_2^i$, $\bar{U}_2^i$.

Step 5 Take aspiration levels $\bar{Y}_1^{i+1}$, $\bar{U}_1^{i+1}$, $\bar{Y}_2^{i+1}$, $\bar{U}_2^{i+1}$ on the basis of the solutions selected by the players. Let i = i+1.
Go to step 1.

The procedure is linearly convergent if the influence of the other player is sufficiently small and if the players' actions are consequently such as to maximize their own utility function. Under these assumptions the achievement functions approximate the players' utility functions with increasing accuracy as the sequence of iterations proceeds, and the Nash equilibrium calculated for the achievement functions converges to the Nash equilibrium of the players' utilities.

This procedure has been implemented as an interactive computer system, in which the players can work at remote terminals.

Details of the method and the interactive system can be found in Fortuna and Kruś (1983).

## 3.   A REGIONAL PLANNING PROBLEM AND EXPERIMENTAL RESULTS

The following illustrative example is based on a regional planning problem which arose during the course of the Noteć Project. The Noteć Project (see Albegov et al., 1981) dealt mainly with the development of a water system designed to increase agricultural production in the Noteć region of Poland. Detailed linear optimization models describing the development of the water system and its effect on agricultural production were constructed to carry out benefit analysis. To evaluate the agricultural labor force properly it is necessary to take into account the rural-urban migration, which is relatively high in this region. This high migration rate is due to disparities in the standard of living between rural and urban areas. For this reason it was necessary to construct a Regional Development Model (see Kruś, 1981; Kulikowski, 1981) describing in an aggregate way the production and consumption levels in the rural and urban parts of the region. This model is designed to allow regional planners to analyze these production and consumption processes while taking into account the effects of migration. These analyses can take the form of a game between the planners responsible for development of the rural and urban parts of the region. Each planner (player) is assumed to have a given budget $Z_i$ which he must allocate between production $z_i$ and aggregate consumption (public services) $z_{i+2}$ $i = 1,2$. Each tries to maximize two objectives: net production and level of consumption.

The net production

$$Y_i = Y_i(y_i, z_i) \qquad i = 1,2$$

is a function of the labor force $y_i$ and the financial input $z_i$.

The labor force depends on population processes and in particular on the migration rate m:

$$y_i = y_i(m) \quad .$$

The migration rate is taken to be the ratio of net migration to the
total population of the rural area.

The level of consumption (see Kulikowski, 1981) is defined as a
function of public services, of the wage fund and of migration factors
(in particular, the migration rate), and can be written as follows:

$$U_i = U_i(z_{i+2}, z_i, m) \quad .$$

The migrants' behavior is described by the econometric relation

$$m = f(U_1/U_2) \quad .$$

Thus migration links the two areas of the region and hence the two
parts of the problem.

Let us make the substitutions $x_1 = z_3$, $z_1 - x_1 = z_1$, $x_2 = z_4$,
$z_2 - x_2 = z_2$. The regional planning game can then be written in the
form (1,2). The objectives $Y_i$, $U_i$, $i = 1,2$ are calculated by software
within the regional development model. The data used below relate to
the Noteć region in 1978.

During the conference several runs of the system were performed
with different players. One of the runs is presented below, and selected results are given in Tables 1–3.

At each iteration the players, for a given Nash equilibrium, have
the opportunity to experiment and study the solutions lying in the
Pareto set. Each player can try five different modifications of the
aspiration (reference) levels, each time obtaining a different Pareto
solution. After experimenting the player is asked to indicate his preferred solution (see steps 3 and 4 of the method). Examples of such
results are presented in Tables 1 and 2. In his first two experiments,
player 1 tested the maximum and minimum values of the objectives, assuming the maximum aspiration level for one and the minimum level for
the other. In later experiments he tried to find the solution closest
to his preferences, and selected the 4th solution as the best. (The
player's responses are underlined in the tables.) Player 2 behaved in
a similar way. In his 4th experiment he tested the system by introducing (0.,0) as an aspiration level, finally selecting the 6th solution

as the best. The aspiration levels related to the selected solution
are incorporated into the achievement function at the next iteration
and a new Nash equilibrium is calculated. The whole procedure is then
repeated at the new equilibrium.

Table 1.  Results obtained on experimenting with aspiration levels
          (player 1)

---

                1 message from master is finished
    player   1   (rural economy)

                            the following results are obtained:
                                            reference values:
net production |mld zl|
   20.000        0.          39.600      20.000       0.          0.
consumption level |thd zl/cap|
   20.000       39.600        0.         25.000       0.          0.

                                    resulting objectives:
net production |mld zl|
   18.993       12.693       20.925      17.634       0.          0.
consumption level |thd zl/cap|
   20.207       39.798       14.200      24.433       0.          0.
you can change reference point -
    type  y  if you want to give the new values
    type  n  if no
n

 decide please, which solution is the best for you ?
    type 1,2,...,6 respectively
 4
message is sent to master

---

Table 2.  Results obtained on experimenting with aspiration levels
          (player 2)

---

                3 message from master is finished.
    player   2   (urban economy)

                            the following results are obtained:
                                            reference values:
net production |mld zl|
   40.000        0.          59.400       0.         55.000      45.000
consumption level |thd zl/cap|
   40.000       59.400        0.          0.         40.000      40.000

                                    resulting objectives:
net production |mld zl|
   41.405       35.625       49.258      41.405      49.258      42.855
consumption level |thd zl/cap|
   42.449       59.819       18.850      42.449      18.850      38.093
you can change reference point -
    type  y  if you want to give the new values
    type  n  if no
n

 decide please, which solution is the best for you ?
    type 1,2,...,6 respectively
 6
message is sent to master

---

Table 3.  Final solutions obtained in the experimental session.

player  1  (rural economy)

the following results are obtained:

resulting objectives:

net production |mld zl|

| 16.927 | 17.269 | 17.773 | 18.993 | 0. | 0. |

consumption level |thd zl/cap|

| 27.302 | 26.391 | 24.530 | 20.207 | 0. | 0. |

allocated expenditures:

in aggregated consumption |mld zl|

| 1.557 | 1.483 | 1.333 | 0.984 | 0. | 0. |

in production |mld zl|

| 4.443 | 4.517 | 4.667 | 5.016 | 0. | 0. |

related socio-economic quantities:

employment |thousand of empl.|

| 104.821 | 107.237 | 110.037 | 117.066 | 0. | 0. |

wage fund |mld zl|

| 5.713 | 5.844 | 5.997 | 6.380 | 0. | 0. |

migration rate

| 0.085 | 0.082 | 0.121 | 0.200 | 0. | 0. |

number of migrants |thousand|

| 33.596 | 32.460 | 47.865 | 79.269 | 0. | 0. |

migration cost |mln zl|

| 176.715 | 170.742 | 251.770 | 416.956 | 0. | 0. |

population dependent on migration |thousand|

| 362.404 | 363.540 | 348.135 | 316.731 | 0. | 0. |

iterations

| 4 | 3 | 2 | 1 | 0 | 0 |

player  2  (urban economy)

the following results are obtained:

resulting objectives:

net production |mld zl|

| 43.063 | 43.506 | 42.750 | 41.405 | 0. | 0. |

consumption level |thd zl/cap|

| 36.729 | 35.499 | 37.960 | 42.449 | 0. | 0. |

allocated expenditures:

in aggregated consumption |mld zl|

| 2.822 | 2.662 | 2.982 | 3.565 | 0. | 0. |

in production |mld zl|

| 9.178 | 9.338 | 9.018 | 8.435 | 0. | 0. |

related socio-economic quantities:

employment |thousand of empl.|

| 266.980 | 268.679 | 266.538 | 262.949 | 0. | 0. |

wage fund |mld zl|

| 16.660 | 16.766 | 16.632 | 16.408 | 0. | 0. |

migration rate

| 0.085 | 0.082 | 0.121 | 0.200 | 0. | 0. |

number of migrants |thousand|

| 33.596 | 32.460 | 47.865 | 79.269 | 0. | 0. |

migration cost |mln zl|

| 176.715 | 170.742 | 251.770 | 416.956 | 0. | 0. |

population dependent on migration |thousand|

| 654.596 | 653.460 | 668.865 | 700.269 | 0. | 0. |

iterations

| 4 | 3 | 2 | 1 | 0 | 0 |

The run that we shall consider only consists of four iterations: the final difference between the Nash solutions (shown in Table 3) were relatively small so that the system stopped the run at this point. The objectives and control variables as well as some socio-economic quantities are also given in Table 3. It is clear that the net production and consumption level were smaller in the rural areas than in the urban areas in 1978. This is the result of a smaller rural budget and the lower efficiency of agricultural production. In such conditions it seems reasonable for player 1 to try to keep consumption above the level taken as a minimum. In this way he also tried to decrease the rural-urban migration. On the other hand player 2, with a relatively high net production and consumption level, gave more emphasis to production. As a result of these strategies the migration rate declined from 0.2 at iteration 1 to 0.085 at iteration 4. The migration cost (including associated housing, services and transportation costs) decreased from 416 to 170 mln zl over the same iterations. The number of people employed and the wage fund are correlated to the production value.

## 4. FINAL REMARKS

The iterative system generates a sequence of Nash equilibria for modified achievement functions which approximate the utility functions of the players. At each Nash equilibrium the players test the Pareto sets by varying their aspiration levels and choose their preferred solutions. The convergence of the method can be proved theoretically; practical experiments showed the method to converge in several iterations.

## REFERENCES

Albegov, M., B. Issaev, R. Kulikowski and F. Snickars (Eds.) (1981). Regional Systems Analysis: Final Report on the Case Study for the Upper Noteć Region in Poland. Collaborative Paper, International Institute for Applied Systems Analysis, Laxenburg, Austria.

Fortuna, Z. and L. Kruś (1983). Simulation of an Interactive Method Supporting Collective Decision Making Using a Regional Development Model. In Grauer and Wierzbicki (1983).

Grauer, M. and A.P. Wierzbicki (Eds.) (1983). Interactive Decision Analysis. Lecture Notes in Economics and Mathematical Systems, Vol. 229, Springer-Verlag, Berlin, 1984.

Kruś, L. (1981). An Interactive Regional Development Model (IRDM).
    In Albegov et al. (1981).
Kulikowski, R. (1981). Modelling Methodology for the Noteć Case Study.
    In Albegov et al. (1981).
Wierzbicki, A.P. (1982). An Idea of the Interactive Method Supporting
    Collective Decisions. An informal description of the game system.
    International Institute for Applied Systems Analysis, Laxenburg,
    Austria (unpublished).

# TWO EMPIRICAL TESTS WITH APPROACHES TO MULTIPLE-CRITERIA DECISION MAKING

Eberhard Bischoff

*Department of Management Science and Statistics, University College of Swansea, Swansea, UK*

## 1. INTRODUCTION

Intensive research, especially over the last 10 to 15 years, into approaches to multiple criteria decision making has led to the development
of a large number of formal methods. There is, however, generally little
agreement - and often fierce dissent - among the proponents of different
techniques as to the relative merits of these procedures.

Many debates on this topic focus on what can 'reasonably' be assumed
about the decision maker's ability to provide information regarding his
preferences, and about the preference structure as such. The arguments
used are mostly backed up by only very scant empirical evidence which,
moreover, is often far from unambiguous.

Although several authors have pointed out the need for more empirical
research into the assumptions underlying different methods for multiple
criteria decision making, few such studies have emerged to date. In an
attempt to start to remedy this situation two sets of experiments were
set up to be conducted during the Workshop. Both experiments relied on
the availability of computing facilities which in the event, however,
could not be fully provided due to hardware problems, so that no more
than a handful of experiments were actually carried out. What follows,
therefore, is merely a brief description of the research questions considered and of the experimental set-up, which is included here at the
editors' request for the sake of completeness of the proceedings. It is
intended, however, to carry out a full set of these experiments in the
near future.

## 2. EXPERIMENT A

The purpose of the first experiment was to compare the performance of
three reference point procedures for exploring the set of alternatives.
Conceptually, all three techniques considered represent variants of the
approach suggested by Wierzbicki (1979).

A commonly used implementation of Wierzbicki's approach is the computer
package DIDASS (cf. Grauer (1983)), which in its most elementary form
employs the weighted Chebyshev norm as a measure of the distance of an

alternative from the reference point. More precisely, if the decision problem under consideration is a vector maximum problem of the form

$$\max f_1(x)$$
$$\ldots$$
$$\max f_r(x) \tag{1}$$
$$\text{s.t. } x \in A$$

the best alternative with respect to a given reference point $g = (g_1, g_2, \ldots g_r)$ and an associated weighting vector $w = (w_1, w_2, \ldots, w_r)$ is calculated as the solution of

$$\min \quad s(d_1, d_2, \ldots, d_r) = \max_{i=1,\ldots,r} d_i + \varepsilon \sum_{i=1}^{r} d_i$$
$$\text{s.t.} \quad f_i(x) + d_i/w_i = g_i, \quad i = 1, \ldots, r \tag{2}$$
$$x \in A$$

where $\varepsilon$ is a small positive constant. (The second term in the scalarizing function s merely serves to ensure that the solution obtained is non-dominated.)

Many alternatives to formulation (2) exist, of course, and the question arises naturally whether the use of one method, as opposed to another, has a significant influence on the number of iterations needed to produce a "good" solution, or on the user's ability to find reasonable solutions in a practically feasible number of iterations. Two alternatives to the above procedure were considered in the experiment. The first was to replace the Chebyshev norm by the $L_1$-norm, i.e. to use the sum of the weighted deviations from g instead of the maximum over the criteria involved. The second alternative examined was to define the weighting vector w in (2) internally on the basis of the reference point given, rather than asking for a separate input from the user. The formula employed was

$$w_i = (f_i^+ - f_i^-) / (f_i^+ + \alpha_i - g_i)$$ where $f_i^+$ and $f_i^-$ represent the maximum and minimum, respectively, of $f_i$ over the feasible region and $\alpha_i$ is a small positive constant. The rationale behind this definition is that it might be reasonable to assume that a user places a higher degree of importance on an attribute if he specifies an aspiration level which, in relative terms, is closer to the highest value achievable.

The experiment involved a choice between 250 alternatives, described by their values with respect to 5 attributes. The alternatives were generated in such a way that none was dominated by any of the others. Subjects were told that the aim was to select the best candidate for a certain job and that the attribute values, all defined on a scale from 0 to 100, could be interpreted as an assessment of the candidates against criteria such as relevant experience, leadership qualities, creativity, etc.. No definite meaning, however, was given to any one of the attributes.

In addition to being given some general background information about the hypothetical decision problem they were asked to tackle, subjects were informed that their final choice would be judged on the basis of an additively separable pay-off function with increasing pay-offs - but decreasing marginal pay-offs - in each argument. The precise function used was illustrated graphically. Moreover, the computer program employed in conducting the experiment enabled subjects to calculate the value of the pay-off function at the reference points used as well as at the intermediate solutions obtained.

At the start of the experiment the subjects had no information about the alternatives available, apart from being presented with a matrix showing the highest value attainable for each of the 5 attributes, together with the best alternatives (with respect to the pay-off function used) which would provide these values. Subjects received a detailed briefing, however, about the reference point procedure they were asked to use. Each subject used only one of the three procedures described above and subjects were given no information about the other two methods being tested.

This experimental set-up clearly allows the final as well as the intermediate solutions obtained by the subjects to be evaluated against an objective yardstick, the pay-off function used, and could thus throw at least some light on the question of how the three procedures tested compare with each other. However, as mentioned earlier, the limited number of actual experiments which could be carried out during the Workshop does not permit conclusions of any significance to be drawn.

## 3.  EXPERIMENT B

The second experiment was closely related to the first, but concerned a somewhat more fundamental question. Instead of comparing procedures where reference points are a primarily technical means of exploring the feasible region, it addresses the question of what type of metric is most appropriate for modelling a decision maker's preferences in a neighbourhood of a reference point which represents a set of actual aspiration levels. Put succinctly, the concrete question posed is whether the Chebyshev norm, the $L_1$-norm, or some weighted average of the two norms is a better measure of a decision maker's preferences with respect to deviations from his aspiration levels.

Subjects taking part in the experiment were asked to assume that they had won a car in a competition and that they could influence the model they would get by specifying their aspiration levels on 4 criteria: price, top speed, acceleration, and petrol consumption. For each criterion the range of feasible values was presented to the subjects and they were told that if the price of a particular model was below the price of the most expensive model they would receive the difference in the form of petrol vouchers.

Having been given some time to reflect about their aspiration levels, subjects were requested to type the values they had decided upon into a terminal which then displayed a series of questions about their preferences with respect to a set of feasible alternatives. Unknown to the subject, these alternatives were generated on the basis of the aspiration levels specified and structured so as to allow inferences to be made about the metric underlying his/her choices. Again, however, the very small sample of results obtained at the Workshop does not permit any specific conclusions to be drawn from the experiment.

## REFERENCES

Grauer, M. (1983). A Dynamic Interactive Decision Analysis and Support System (DIDASS) - User's Guide. Working Paper WP-83-60. International Institute for Applied Systems Analysis, Laxenburg, Austria.

Wierzbicki, A.P. (1979). The Use of Reference Objectives in Multi-objective Optimization - Theoretical Implications and Practical Experience. Working Paper WP-79-66. International Institute for Applied Systems Analysis, Laxenburg, Austria.

# INDEX OF KEYWORDS

# THE INTERNATIONAL INSTITUTE FOR APPLIED SYSTEMS ANALYSIS

is a nongovernmental research institution, bringing together scientists from around the world to work on problems of common concern. Situated in Laxenburg, Austria, IIASA was founded in October 1972 by the academies of science and equivalent organizations of twelve countries. Its founders gave IIASA a unique position outside national, disciplinary, and institutional boundaries so that it might take the broadest possible view in pursuing its objectives:

*To promote international cooperation* in solving problems arising from social, economic, technological, and environmental change

*To create a network of institutions* in the national member organization countries and elsewhere for joint scientific research

*To develop and formalize systems analysis* and the sciences contributing to it, and promote the use of analytical techniques needed to evaluate and address complex problems

*To inform policy advisors and decision makers* about the potential application of the Institute's work to such problems

The Institute now has national member organizations in the following countries:

**Austria**
The Austrian Academy of Sciences

**Bulgaria**
The National Committee for Applied Systems Analysis and Management

**Canada**
The Canadian Committee for IIASA

**Czechoslovakia**
The Committee for IIASA of the Czechoslovak Socialist Republic

**Finland**
The Finnish Committee for IIASA

**France**
The French Association for the Development of Systems Analysis

**German Democratic Republic**
The Academy of Sciences of the German Democratic Republic

**Federal Republic of Germany**
Association for the Advancement of IIASA

**Hungary**
The Hungarian Committee for Applied Systems Analysis

**Italy**
The National Research Council

**Japan**
The Japan Committee for IIASA

**Netherlands**
The Foundation IIASA–Netherlands

**Poland**
The Polish Academy of Sciences

**Sweden**
The Swedish Council for Planning and Coordination of Research

**Union of Soviet Socialist Republics**
The Academy of Sciences of the Union of Soviet Socialist Republics

**United States of America**
The American Academy of Arts and Sciences

THE INTERNATI

Vol. 157: Optimization and Operations Research. Proceedings 1977. Edited by R. Henn, B. Korte, and W. Oettli. VI, 270 pages. 1978.

Vol. 158: L. J. Cherene, Set Valued Dynamical Systems and Economic Flow. VIII, 83 pages. 1978.

Vol. 159: Some Aspects of the Foundations of General Equilibrium Theory: The Posthumous Papers of Peter J. Kalman. Edited by J. Green. VI, 167 pages. 1978.

Vol. 160: Integer Programming and Related Areas. A Classified Bibliography. Edited by D. Hausmann. XIV, 314 pages. 1978.

Vol. 161: M. J. Beckmann, Rank in Organizations. VIII, 164 pages. 1978.

Vol. 162: Recent Developments in Variable Structure Systems, Economics and Biology. Proceedings 1977. Edited by R. R. Mohler and A. Ruberti. VI, 326 pages. 1978.

Vol. 163: G. Fandel, Optimale Entscheidungen in Organisationen. VI, 143 Seiten. 1979.

Vol. 164: C. L. Hwang and A. S. M. Masud, Multiple Objective Decision Making – Methods and Applications. A State-of-the-Art Survey. XII, 351 pages. 1979.

Vol. 165: A. Maravall, Identification in Dynamic Shock-Error Models. VIII, 158 pages. 1979.

Vol. 166: R. Cuninghame-Green, Minimax Algebra. XI, 258 pages. 1979.

Vol. 167: M. Faber, Introduction to Modern Austrian Capital Theory. X, 196 pages. 1979.

Vol. 168: Convex Analysis and Mathematical Economics. Proceedings 1978. Edited by J. Kriens. V, 136 pages. 1979.

Vol. 169: A. Rapoport et al., Coalition Formation by Sophisticated Players. VII, 170 pages. 1979.

Vol. 170: A. E. Roth, Axiomatic Models of Bargaining. V, 121 pages. 1979.

Vol. 171: G. F. Newell, Approximate Behavior of Tandem Queues. XI, 410 pages. 1979.

Vol. 172: K. Neumann and U. Steinhardt, GERT Networks and the Time-Oriented Evaluation of Projects. 268 pages. 1979.

Vol. 173: S. Erlander, Optimal Spatial Interaction and the Gravity Model. VII, 107 pages. 1980.

Vol. 174: Extremal Methods and Systems Analysis. Edited by A. V. Fiacco and K. O. Kortanek. XI, 545 pages. 1980.

Vol. 175: S. K. Srinivasan and R. Subramanian, Probabilistic Analysis of Redundant Systems. VII, 356 pages. 1980.

Vol. 176: R. Färe, Laws of Diminishing Returns. VIII, 97 pages. 1980.

Vol. 177: Multiple Criteria Decision Making-Theory and Application. Proceedings, 1979. Edited by G. Fandel and T. Gal. XVI, 570 pages. 1980.

Vol. 178: M. N. Bhattacharyya, Comparison of Box-Jenkins and Bonn Monetary Model Prediction Performance. VII, 146 pages. 1980.

Vol. 179: Recent Results in Stochastic Programming. Proceedings, 1979. Edited by P. Kall and A. Prékopa. IX, 237 pages. 1980.

Vol. 180: J. F. Brotchie, J. W. Dickey and R. Sharpe, TOPAZ – General Planning Technique and its Applications at the Regional, Urban, and Facility Planning Levels. VII, 356 pages. 1980.

Vol. 181: H. D. Sherali and C. M. Shetty, Optimization with Disjunctive Constraints. VIII, 156 pages. 1980.

Vol. 182: J. Wolters, Stochastic Dynamic Properties of Linear Econometric Models. VIII, 154 pages. 1980.

Vol. 183: K. Schittkowski, Nonlinear Programming Codes. VIII, 242 pages. 1980.

Vol. 184: R. E. Burkard and U. Derigs, Assignment and Matching Problems: Solution Methods with FORTRAN-Programs. VIII, 148 pages. 1980.

Vol. 185: C. C. von Weizsäcker, Barriers to Entry. VI, 220 pages. 1980.

Vol. 186: Ch.-L. Hwang and K. Yoon, Multiple Attribute Decision Making – Methods and Applications. A State-of-the-Art-Survey. XI, 259 pages. 1981.

Vol. 187: W. Hock, K. Schittkowski, Test Examples for Nonlinear Programming Codes. V. 178 pages. 1981.

Vol. 188: D. Bös, Economic Theory of Public Enterprise. VII, 142 pages. 1981.

Vol. 189: A. P. Lüthi, Messung wirtschaftlicher Ungleichheit. IX, 287 pages. 1981.

Vol. 190: J. N. Morse, Organizations: Multiple Agents with Multiple Criteria. Proceedings, 1980. VI, 509 pages. 1981.

Vol. 191: H. R. Sneessens, Theory and Estimation of Macroeconomic Rationing Models. VII, 138 pages. 1981.

Vol. 192: H. J. Bierens: Robust Methods and Asymptotic Theory in Nonlinear Econometrics. IX, 198 pages. 1981.

Vol. 193: J. K. Sengupta, Optimal Decisions under Uncertainty. VII, 156 pages. 1981.

Vol. 194: R. W. Shephard, Cost and Production Functions. XI, 104 pages. 1981.

Vol. 195: H. W. Ursprung, Die elementare Katastrophentheorie. Eine Darstellung aus der Sicht der Ökonomie. VII, 332 pages. 1982.

Vol. 196: M. Nermuth, Information Structures in Economics. VIII, 236 pages. 1982.

Vol. 197: Integer Programming and Related Areas. A Classified Bibliography. 1978 – 1981. Edited by R. von Randow. XIV, 338 pages. 1982.

Vol. 198: P. Zweifel, Ein ökonomisches Modell des Arztverhaltens. XIX, 392 Seiten. 1982.

Vol. 199: Evaluating Mathematical Programming Techniques. Proceedings, 1981. Edited by J.M. Mulvey. XI, 379 pages. 1982.

Vol. 200: The Resource Sector in an Open Economy. Edited by H. Siebert. IX, 161 pages. 1984.

Vol. 201: P. M. C. de Boer, Price Effects in Input-Output-Relations: A Theoretical and Empirical Study for the Netherlands 1949–1967. X, 140 pages. 1982.

Vol. 202: U. Witt, J. Perske, SMS – A Program Package for Simulation and Gaming of Stochastic Market Processes and Learning Behavior. VII, 266 pages. 1982.

Vol. 203: Compilation of Input-Output Tables. Proceedings, 1981. Edited by J. V. Skolka. VII, 307 pages. 1982.

Vol. 204: K.C. Mosler, Entscheidungsregeln bei Risiko: Multivariate stochastische Dominanz. VII, 172 Seiten. 1982.

Vol. 205: R. Ramanathan, Introduction to the Theory of Economic Growth. IX, 347 pages. 1982.

Vol. 206: M.H. Karwan, V. Lotfi, J. Telgen, and S. Zionts, Redundancy in Mathematical Programming. VII, 286 pages. 1983.

Vol. 207: Y. Fujimori, Modern Analysis of Value Theory. X, 165 pages. 1982.

Vol. 208: Econometric Decision Models. Proceedings, 1981. Edited by J. Gruber. VI, 364 pages. 1983.

Vol. 209: Essays and Surveys on Multiple Criteria Decision Making. Proceedings, 1982. Edited by P. Hansen. VII, 441 pages. 1983.

Vol. 210: Technology, Organization and Economic Structure. Edited by R. Sato and M.J. Beckmann. VIII, 195 pages. 1983.

Vol. 211: P. van den Heuvel, The Stability of a Macroeconomic System with Quantity Constraints. VII, 169 pages. 1983.

Vol. 212: R. Sato and T. Nôno, Invariance Principles and the Structure of Technology. V, 94 pages. 1983.